PHILO'S INFLUENCE
ON VALENTINIAN TRADITION

STUDIA PHILONICA MONOGRAPHS

General Editor
Michael B. Cover

Number 10

PHILO'S INFLUENCE ON VALENTINIAN TRADITION

Risto Auvinen

SBL PRESS

Atlanta

Copyright © 2024 by Risto Auvinen

All rights reserved. No part of this work may be reproduced or transmitted in any form or by any means, electronic or mechanical, including photocopying and recording, or by means of any information storage or retrieval system, except as may be expressly permitted by the 1976 Copyright Act or in writing from the publisher. Requests for permission should be addressed in writing to the Rights and Permissions Office, SBL Press, 825 Houston Mill Road, Atlanta, GA 30329 USA.

Library of Congress Control Number: 2024939287

Contents

Preface ix
Abbreviations xi

1. Introduction 1
   1.1. The Aim of This Study 1
   1.2. The Valentinian Tradition and Sethian Gnosticism 4
   1.3. Philo of Alexandria and the Valentinian Tradition 11
   1.4. Methodological Considerations 18
   1.5. Outline of This Study 21

2. The Valentinian Source in Clement's *Excerpts of Theodotus* 25
   2.1. The Category of the Valentinian Literature and
        Philo's Corpus 25
   2.2. The Valentinian Source of *Excerpta ex Theodoto* 43.2–65 34
   2.3. Conclusions 43

3. The Foundations of Allegorical Interpretation in
   Philo and among the Valentinians 47
   3.1. The School of Philo and the Jewish Revolt in Egypt 48
   3.2. The Founding of the School of Valentinus 55
   3.3. Allegorical Readers of Alexandria 69
   3.4. Conclusions 87

4. Protology: The Creation of the Intelligible Cosmos 89
   4.1. Philo, Valentinian Teachers, and Transcendental Monotheism 90
   4.2. Outline of the Valentinian Myth 98
   4.3. The Origin of Valentinian Protology 102
   4.4. Philo, *Excerpta* C, and the Prologue of the Gospel of John 113
   4.5. Philo's Interpretation of Day One and Traditions of
        Cosmic Creation 121

	4.6. Conclusions	125
5.	The Wisdom of God and the Creation of Matter.............................127	
	5.1. The Philosophical Background of the Creation of Matter	128
	5.2. The Creation of Matter in the Writings of Philo	132
	5.3. The Creation of Matter in the Valentinian Sources	137
	5.4. Wisdom as Mother and Matter in Philo and Valentinian Sources	141
	5.5. The Separation of Matter	146
	5.6. Heaven as a Boundary in Philo and Valentinian Writings	162
	5.7. Conclusions	166
6.	The Creation of the First Human in Allegorical Exegesis.................169	
	6.1. The Philosophical Background to Valentinian Anthropology	169
	6.2. The Threefold Structure of the Human Soul in Valentinian Sources	176
	6.3. The Creation of Adam in Philo and Valentinian Sources	188
	6.4. Valentinus's Psalm *Harvest* and Its Intellectual Background	205
	6.5. Conclusions	216
7.	Cain, Abel, Seth, and Israel in Allegorical Exegesis..........................219	
	7.1. Philo's Platonic Anthropology	221
	7.2. The Embodiment of the Soul and the School for Controlling Passions	227
	7.3. The Division of Humankind in the Valentinian Myth and Philo	233
	7.4. Seth as a Symbol for the Virtuous Human	244
	7.5. The Patriarchs and Israel	249
	7.6. The Immortality of the Soul and the Practice of Dying	256
	7.7. The Eschatological Wedding Feast and Unification with the Angels	260
	7.8. Conclusions	272
8.	The Valentians and the Survival of Philo's Works: Summary and Conclusions..275	
	8.1. Traditions of Exegesis in Philo and Valentinians	275
	8.2. Valentinians as Heirs of Philo	280
	8.3. Valentinians and the Survival of Philo's Corpus	281

Bibliography	285
Ancient Sources Index	307
Modern Authors Index	323
Subject Index	327

Preface

Since the discovery of the Nag Hammadi Scriptures in 1945, numerous studies concerning Valentinianism have been published. The new Valentinian documents not only open fresh perspectives on the Valentinian theology but help us to critically evaluate the descriptions of the Valentinian teaching by the patristic authors. Although there have been numerous monographs and essay collections on Valentinianism and Alexandrian tradition more broadly, this book is the first monograph dedicated solely to the relationship between Philo of Alexandria and the Valentinian gnostic tradition. I hope that the new perspectives disclosed herein will prompt further investigations and extensions of the findings presented in this book.

The evidence collected in this study confirms that the Valentinians, or at least some of them, were familiar with Philo's writings before Clement of Alexandria gained access to them as head of the Catechetical School of Alexandria. It is possible that the Valentinian teachers belonged among the scholarly circles that were responsible for the preservation of his works in the years after Philo's death. This would mean that also some works of Philo circulated not only in Alexandria but also in Rome even before they arrived in the city via Caesarea in the third century.

The main target of this study is the Valentinian tradition. This means that my aim is not always to present the scholarly consensus on Philo's teachings but to ponder how the Valentinians may have read Philo's works and what they may have thought inspiring in them. Although the widely accepted opinion among modern scholars is that Philo was not a precursor for Gnosticism, some Valentinians may have thought that he was a model allegorical exegete. This may have been why they were convinced, along with other Alexandrian Christian Platonists, that they would find suitable material in Philo's works for their own philosophical exegesis of the Bible.

The investigation of a common philosophical background was a necessary starting point when comparing Philo and Valentinians. However, my aim was not to search for common philosophical ideas or themes but for exegetical parallels with Philo. The chronological focus of this study is on the formative years of the Valentinian tradition, that is, during the second half of the second century, which means that the primary Valentinian sources come from the patristic authors, that is, Clement of Alexandria and Irenaeus, who preserved Valentinian teachings.

I have written this book while also working as a full-time Lutheran parish priest, which created some challenges to my work. I want to thank my wife, Ursula, for her support and patience during this process. I am also extremely grateful to Professors Gregory E. Sterling and Ismo Dunderberg for their encouragement and support. Sterling gave me a five-point list for revisions, which helped to improve my work. Professor Dunderberg, the supervisor of my dissertation, read the final draft of my book, sparing me from some embarrassing mistakes. He also helped me with practical issues without which this book could not have been published. Dr. Sami Yli-Karjanmaa's clear and distinct ideas, as René Descartes would say, of Philo's exegesis also challenged me in a positive way and helped me to improve the argumentation of my writing. Finally, I want to thank Professor Michael B. Cover for his support and extremely valuable comments to my work. It is an honor to have my book published as a part of the Studia Philonica Monograph Series.

Abbreviations

1 En.	1 Enoch
1QS	Serek Hayaḥad *or* Rule of the Community
4Q417	4Q Instruction^c
AB	Anchor Bible
Abr.	Philo, *De Abrahamo*
Abst.	Porphyry, *De abstinentia*
ACW	Ancient Christian Writers
AEML	Arundell Esdaile Memorial Lecture
Aet.	Philo, *De aeternitate mundi*
Agr.	Philo, *De agricultura*
A.J.	Josephus, *Antiquitates judaicae*
AJEC	Ancient Judaism and Early Christianity
AJP	*American Journal of Philology*
ALGHJ	Arbeiten zur Literatur und Geschichte des hellenistischen Judentums
An.	Tertullian, *De anima*
An. procr.	Plutarch, *De animae procreatione in Timaeo*
ANF	*The Ante-Nicene Fathers.* Edited by Alexander Roberts and James Donaldson. 1885–1887. 10 vols. Repr., Peabody, MA: Hendrickson, 1994
Anim.	Philo, *De animalibus*
ANRW	*Aufstieg und Niedergang der romischen Welt: Geschichte und Kultur Roms im Spiegel der neueren Forschung.* Part 2, *Principat.* Edited by Hildegard
Ap. Jas.	NHC I 2 Secret Book of James
Ap. John	NHC II 1 Secret Book of John
Apoc. Mos.	Apocalypse of Moses
Bell. civ.	Appian, *Bella civilia*
BG	Berlin Gnostic Codex

BGU	*Aegyptische Urkunden aus den Königlichen Museen zu Berlin, Griechische Urkunden.* Berlin. Vol. 4, 1912
BICS	The Bulletin of the Institute of Classical Studies
B.J.	Josephus, *Bellum judaicum*
BJS	Brown Judaic Studies
BZNW	Beihefte zur Zeitschrift für die neutestamentliche Wissenschaft
ca.	circa
Cael.	Aristotle, *De caelo*
Carn. Chr.	Tertullian *De carne Christi*
CBQ	*Catholic Biblical Quarterly*
CBQMS	Catholic Biblical Quarterly Monograph Series
Cels.	Origen, *Contra Celsum*
Cher.	Philo, *De cherubim*
Civ.	Augustine, *De civitate Dei*
ClQ	*Classical Quarterly*
Comm. Ezech.	Jerome, *Commentariorum in Ezechielem libri XVI*
Comm. Jo.	Origen, *Commentarii in evangelium Joannis*
Conf.	Philo, *De confusione linguarum*
Congr.	Philo, *De congressu eruditionis gratia*
Contempl.	Philo, *De vita contemplativa*
CP	*Classical Philology*
Corp. herm.	Corpus hermeticum
De an.	Aristotle, *De anima*
Decal.	Philo, *De decalogo*
Det.	Philo, *Quod deterius potiori insidari soleat*
Deus	Philo, *Quod Deus sit immutabilis*
Dial.	Justin, *Dialogus cum Tryphone*
Ebr.	Philo *De ebrietate*
ECCA	Early Christianity in the Context of Antiquity
Elem.	Proclus, *Elementatio theologica*
Enn.	Plotinus, *Enneades*
Ep.	Plato, *Epistulae*; Seneca, *Epistulae morales*
Epin.	Pseudo-Plato, *Epinomis*
Epist.	Jerome, *Epistulae*
Epit.	Alcinous, *Epitome doctrinae platonicae* (*Didaskalikos*)
Eth. nic.	Aristotle, *Ethica nicomachea*
Euthyphr.	Plato, *Euthyphro*
Exc.	Clement of Alexandria, *Excerpta et Theodoto*

Abbreviations   xiii

FC	Fathers of the Church
FGNK	Forschungen zur Geschichte des neutestamentlichen Kanons
Flacc.	Philo, *In Flaccum*
Flor.	Ptolemy, *Epistula ad Floram*; Stobaeus, *Florilegium*
Fr. Matt.	Origen, *Fragmenta ex commentariis in evangelium Matthaei*
frag(s).	fragment(s)
Fug.	Philo, *De fuga et inventione*
FZPhTh	*Freiburger Zeitschrift für Philosophie und Theologie*
Gen. an.	Aristotle, *De generatione anamalium*
Gen. corr.	Aristotle, *De generatione et corruptione*
Gen. Socr.	Plutarch, *De genio Socratis*
Gig.	Philo, *De gigantibus*
GnosSt	*Gnostic Studies*
Gos. Phil.	NHC II 3 Gospel of Philip
Gos. Thom.	NHC II 2 Gospel of Thomas
Gos. Truth	NHC XII 2 Gospel of Truth
HABES	Heidelberger althistorische Beiträge und epigraphische Studien
Haer.	Irenaeus, *Adversus haereses*; Hippolytus, *Refutatio omnium haeresium (Philosophoumena)*
Her.	Philo, *Quis rerum divinarum heres sit*
Hist. eccl.	Eusebius, *Historia ecclesiastica*
Hist. rom.	Dio Cassius, *Historiae romanae*
HTR	*Harvard Theological Review*
In. Arist. Metaph.	Syrianus, *In Aristotelis Metaphysica commentaria*
In. Arist. Phys.	Simplicius, *In Aristotelis Physicorum*
In Plat. Tim.	Proclus, *In Platonis Timaeum commentaria*
Interp. Know.	NHC XI 1 Interpretation of Knowledge
Is. Os.	Plutarch, *De Iside et Osiride*
ISNS	International Society for Neoplatonic Studies
JAC	*Jahrbuch für Antike und Christentum*
JBL	*Journal of Biblical Literature*
JEA	*Journal of Egyptian Archaeology*
JHI	*Journal of History of Ideas*
JHPS	Journal of the History of Philosophy Series
JJS	*Journal of Jewish Studies*
JLCRS	Jordan Lectures in Comparative Religion Series

JSJ	*Journal for the Study of Judaism in the Persian, Hellenistic, and Roman Periods*
JTECL	Jewish Traditions in Early Christian Literature
JTS	*Journal of Theological Studies*
LCL	Loeb Classical Library
Leg.	Philo, *Legum allegoriae*: Plato, *Leges*
LXX	Septuagint
Math.	Sextus Empiricus, *Adversus mathematicos*
Metaph.	Aristotle, *Metaphysica*
MH	Museum Helveticum
Migr.	Philo, *De migratione Abrahami*
Mor.	Plutarch, *Moralia*
Mos.	Philo, *De vita Mosis*
Mot. an.	Aristotle, *De motu animalium*
Mut.	Philo, *De mutatione nominum*
NA[28]	*Novum Testamentum Graece*, Nestle-Aland, 28th ed.
Nat. Rulers	NHC II 4 Nature of the Rulers
NHC	Nag Hammadi Codices
NHMS	Nag Hammadi and Manichean Studies
NHS	Nag Hammadi Studies
NovT	*Novum Testamentum*
NPNF	Schaff, Philip, and Henry Wace, eds. *A Select Library of Nicene and Post-Nicene Fathers of the Christian Church*. 28 vols. in 2 series. 1886–1889.
NT	New Testament
NTOA	Novum Testamentum et Orbis Antiquus
NTS	*New Testament Studies*
Orig. World	NHC II 5 On the Origin of the World
Opif.	Philo, *De opificio mundi*
PACS	Philo of Alexandria Commentary Series
Paed.	Clement, *Paedagogus*
Pan.	Epiphanius, *Panarion* (*Adversus haereses*)
Parm.	Plato, *Parmenides*
PhA	Philosophia Antiqua
Phaed.	Plato, *Phaedo*
Phaedr.	Plato, *Phaedrus*
Phileb.	Plato, *Philebus*
Phys.	Aristotle, *Physica*
Plac.	Aëtius, *Placita*

Plant.	Philo, *De plantatione*
PLCL	Philo. Translated by F. H. Colson et al. 12 vols. LCL. Cambridge, MA: Harvard University Press, 1929–1962.
Pol.	Plato, *Politicus*
Post.	Philo, *De posteritate Caini*
P.Oxy.	Grenfell, Bernard P., et al., eds. *The Oxyrhynchus Papyri.* London: Egypt Exploration Fund, 1898–
Praem.	Philo, *De praemiis et poenis*
Praep. ev.	Eusebius, *Praeparatio evangelica*
Praescr.	Tertullian, *De praescriptione haereticorum*
Princ.	Origen, *De principiis* (*Peri archōn*)
Prob.	Philo, *Quod omnis probus liber sit*
Prot.	Plato, *Protagoras*
Prov.	Philo, *De providentia*
QE	Philo, *Quaestiones et solutiones in Exodum*
QG	Philo *Quaestiones et solutiones in Genesin*
Quaest. conv.	Plutarch, *Quaestionum convivialum libri IX*
Quis div.	Clement, *Quis dives salvetur*
Rab.	Rabbah
RAC	*Reallexikon fur Antike und Christentum*
Resp.	Plato, *Respublica*
RevScRel	*Revue des sciences religieuses*
ROT	Revised Oxford Translation
RSV	Revised Standard Version of the Bible
SAC	Studies in Antiquity and Christianity
Sacr.	Philo, *De sacrificiis Abelis et Caini*
SB	*Sammelbuch griechischer Urkunden aus Aegypten.* Vol. 3, Berlin and Leipzig 1926–1927. Vol. 5, Heidelberg and Wiesbaden 1934–1955.
SBL	Society of Biblical Literature
SBLDS	Society of Biblical Literature Dissertation Series
SBLTT	Society of Biblical Literature Texts and Translations
SC	Sources chrétiennes
SHR	Studies in the History of Religions
Sobr.	Philo, *De sobrietate*
Somn.	Philo, *De somniis*
Soph.	Plato, *Sophista*
Spec.	Philo, *De specialibus legibus*
SPhilo	*Studia Philonica*

SPhiloA	*Studia Philonica Annual*
SPhiloM	Studia Philonica Monograph Series
SRHB	Studies in the Reception History of the Bible
STAC	Studien und Texte zu Antike und Christentum
StPatr	Studia Patristica
Strom.	Clement of Alexandria, *Stromateis*
Theaet.	Plato, *Theaetetus*
Tim.	Plato, *Timaeus*
Top.	Aristotle, *Topica*
Tri. Trac.	NHC I 5 Tripartite Tractate
TS	Texts and Studies
TU	Texte und Untersuchungen zur Geschichte der altchristlichen Literatur
Tusc.	Cicero, *Tusculanae disputationes*
Util. cred.	Augustine, *De utilitate credendi*
Val.	Tertullian, *Adversus Valentinianos*
Val. Exp.	NHC XI 2 A Valentinian Exposition
VC	*Vigiliae Christianae*
VCS	Variorum Collected Studies
Virt.	Philo, *De virtutibus*
Vit. Plot.	Porphyry, *Vita Plotini*
WGRWSup	Writings from the Greco-Roman World Supplement Series
WUNT	Wissenschaftliche Untersuchungen zum Neuen Testament
ZAC	*Zeitschrift für Antikes Christentum*
ZNW	*Zeitschrift für die neutestamentliche Wissenschaft und die Kunde der alteren*

1
Introduction

1.1. The Aim of This Study

The aim of this study is to compare exegetical and philosophical traditions in the writings of Philo of Alexandria and in Valentinian sources. I will compare these writings systematically with Valentinian systems, which contain protological, cosmological, and anthropological dimensions. Under each thematic heading, I will demonstrate the affinities between Philonic and Valentinian theology. My main argument is that the theology of the Valentinian teachers drew on Philo and cannot be properly understood without recourse to the inventions in his allegorical exegesis of the Scriptures. Although the origin of Gnosticism is not the main concern of this study, comparison of the accounts of Valentinian beliefs with Philo's will shed new light on the topic of the origins and development of the ancient gnostic traditions as well as of the evolution of the school of Valentinus.

Philo (ca. 20 BCE–50 CE) was the most prolific author of Hellenistic Judaism—specifically in Alexandria. Philo's family belonged to the aristocracy, and he presumably inherited multiple citizenships from his father being a citizen of the Jewish *politeuma* of Alexandria, the Greek city of Alexandria, and Rome.[1] Although Philo received a standard Greek educa-

---

1. Unlike Philo and his family, the Jews of Alexandria did not commonly enjoy full Greek citizenship. They occupied an intermediate position between the Greek citizens and the native Egyptians. From the beginning of the Ptolemaic period, the two ethnic groups, the Jews and the Greeks, existed rather peacefully side by side, but hostilities began to emerge after the Roman annexation of Egypt. The Jews benefited from the annexation, and they preserved their autonomous status and religious privileges because Pompey and Julius Caesar received military aid from the Jews of Alexandria. Jewish privileges were engraved by Augustus on a marble slab, which was set up in the city. Under Roman protection, the Jews of Alexandria sought to improve their

tion and advanced training in rhetoric and philosophy, he was committed to observing Jewish ritual laws and religious festivals, vital markers of his ethnic and religious identity. Philo valued the achievements of Hellenistic culture, and his Judaism belonged to a well-ordered Roman society, where different cultures and religions lived side by side. Philo did not think that the Jews of Alexandria were exiled from a home country to which they would one day return; rather, he conceived of the Jewish dispersion as voluntary emigration and a part of God's plan for the education of whole of humankind.[2]

---

civic status, and it is possible that the pro-Roman sympathies of the Jews were one of the reasons for the anti-Jewish attacks by the Greeks. Philo's brother, Caius Julius Alexander, held the Greek municipal office of alabarch during the reign of Tiberius and Gaius, and he had close relations with both Agrippa I, the grandson of Herod the Great, and the Julio-Claudian dynasty in Rome. Josephus informs us that Alexander's fortune was enormous, and he donated nine gates in Jerusalem "overlaid with massive plates of silver and gold." Alexander had two sons. The younger son, Marcus Julius Alexander, was married to Berenice, the daughter of Agrippa I. The older son, Tiberius Julius Alexander, abandoned the Jewish religion altogether. He was procurator of Judea in 45 CE and prefect of Egypt under Nero. During the siege of Jerusalem in 70 CE, he commanded the Roman troops. Philo's younger brother, Lysimachus, appears in Philo's *De animalibus*, which describes a dialogue between two brothers. For the political situation of the Jews in Alexandria during the time of Philo, see Ray Barraclough, "Philo's Politics," *ANRW* 21.1:417–553; Daniel R. Schwartz, "Philo, His Family, and His Times," in *The Cambridge Companion to Philo*, ed. Adam Kamesar (Cambridge: Cambridge University Press, 2009), 9–32; E. Mary Smallwood, *Philonis Alexandrini legatio ad Gaium* (Leiden: Brill, 1961), 3–14; Alan Appelbaum, "A Fresh Look at Philo's Family," *SPhiloA* 30 (2018): 93–113. For background on the pogroms against Jews in Alexandria, see Pieter Willem van der Horst, *Philo's Flaccus: The First Pogrom*, PACS 2 (Atlanta: Society of Biblical Literature, 2005), 18–37.

2. In *Flacc.* 46, Philo writes: "For so populous are the Jews that no one country can hold them, and therefore they settle in very many of the most prosperous countries in Europe and Asia both in the islands and on the mainland, and while they hold the Holy City where stands the sacred Temple of the most high God to be their mother city [μητρόπολις], yet those which are theirs by inheritance from their fathers, grandfathers, and ancestors even farther back, are in each case accounted by them to be their fatherland [πατρίς] in which they were born and reared, while to some of them they have come at the time of their foundation as immigrants to the satisfaction of the founders." Translations of Philo's texts come from Francis H. Colson and George H. Whitaker, trans., *Philo in Ten Volumes (and Two Supplementary Volumes)*, 10 vols. and 2 supplements, LCL (Cambridge: Harvard University Press, 1959–1969), unless otherwise stated. See Paula Fredriksen, *Paul: The Pagan's Apostle* (New Haven: Yale University Press, 2017), 48–49.

Philo's social background might have directed him toward business and politics, but he played a remarkable role in politics only later in his life, as the leader of the Jewish delegation to Caligula in 38/39 CE. Philo's main interest otherwise lay in leading a philosophical life, and it is possible that he occasionally withdrew into solitude, spending time among the community of Jewish intellectuals living on the shores of Lake Mareotis. Jean Daniélou points out that Philo's intellectual activity was two-sided: "Part of his activity is directed to believing Jews. It has an esoteric character. It is carried on within the community. On the other hand, Philo's activity has an apologetic component. He is careful to present the Jewish faith to Greeks so as to make it acceptable."[3]

Originally, Philo was a commentator on Scripture. He was not, however, an isolated exegete, but one within a specific hermeneutic tradition. The social setting of Philo's school is not clear, but the most plausible suggestion is that Philo operated a private school, where he taught philosophically orientated spiritual exegesis.[4] The survival of Philo's works after his death and during the turbulent years of the Jewish revolt in 115–117 CE is still an enigma for modern scholarship. Clement of Alexandria is the first ancient author to quote Philo by name at the end of the second century, but the history of the preservation of Philo's works before Clement remains a mystery. The scholarly consensus is that Philo's works must have been rescued by Christian communities, but, as David Runia says, "We cannot know how the rescue operation was effectuated. That it took place is certain."[5]

Valentinus was a famous Christian teacher who was influential in the mid-second century in Alexandria and Rome. His teachings are preserved only in some fragments in patristic sources. We know that Valentinus wrote homilies, letters, and psalms, which were used in the communities of later Valentinian disciples (Tertullian, *Carn. Chr.* 17). The disciples of Valentinus continued the school tradition of Valentinus, which was vehemently attacked by Irenaeus in his multivolume work *Adversus haereses*,

---

3. Jean Daniélou, *Philo of Alexandria*, trans. James G. Colbert (Eugene, OR: Cascade Books, 2014), 11.

4. See Gregory Sterling, "Philo," in *The Eerdmans Dictionary of Early Judaism*, ed. John J. Collins and Daniel C. Harlow (Grand Rapids: Eerdmans, 2010), 1064–65. On Philo's school, see §3.1 below.

5. David Runia, *Philo in Early Christian Literature: A Survey*, JTECL 3 (Leiden: Brill, 1990), 135.

written in the last quarter of the second century. Irenaeus maintained that the school of Valentinus was a reformation of preceding gnostic tradition (*Haer.* 1.11.1), though the actual relationship between these traditions is a matter of modern scholarly dispute.⁶ The Valentinian teachers intended to intellectualize Christian teachings, elevating them to the level of Greco-Roman philosophy.⁷

Indeed, there are parallel allegorical interpretations and biblical themes in Philo's writings and the Valentinian ones. The consensus is that both Philo and Valentinus represent exegetical traditions that integrated the Middle Platonic worldview with an allegorical interpretation of the Scriptures. Despite the apparent thematic continuity of thought between Philo and the Valentinian sources, however, there is no scholarly consensus on whether Valentinian teachers had direct access to Philo's writings or played any role in their preservation.⁸

1.2. The Valentinian Tradition and Sethian Gnosticism

The definition of Gnosticism is highly disputed in modern scholarship. Since the international colloquium held in Messina, Italy, in 1966, no scholarly consensus has been reached regarding the essence and origin of Gnosticism.⁹ The study of the Nag Hammadi gnostic writings has shown

---

6. For a short introduction to the research history of the Valentinian tradition, see Christoph Markschies and Einar Thomassen, "Introduction," in *Valentinianism: New Studies*, ed. Markschies and Thomassen, NHMS 96 (Leiden: Brill, 2020), 1–5.

7. Peter Lampe argues that from the time of Nerva there was a positive change in the imperial attitude toward the philosophers. They were respected as teachers of ethical education and moral rules. Many pagan philosophers affected Christian self-understanding: Christianity was increasingly considered a philosophical school. Justin Martyr was an example of a Christian teacher in Rome who represented himself as a philosopher. Justin argued that the Christians worship God intellectually, and he saw Christianity as the restoration of original philosophy. See Lampe, *From Paul to Valentinus: Christians in Rome in the First Two Centuries*, trans. Michael Steinhauser (London: T&T Clark, 2003), 258–61, 272–75, 279–84.

8. See Runia, *Philo in Early Christian Literature*, 125–26.

9. At the Messina colloquium, it was proposed that the term *Gnosticism* should be used to designate specifically the group of systems of the second century CE described by the patristic authors. The Messina proposal maintains that Gnosticism is a system of thought that contains the idea of "the divine spark in man, deriving from the divine realm, fallen into this world of fate, birth, and death, and needing to be awakened by the divine counterpart of the self in order to be finally reintegrated." Gnostic cosmol-

that the narrow definition of the term *Gnosticism* as a second-century dualist and deterministic Christian heresy based on the myth of Sophia is not applicable to all the texts of the Nag Hammadi Library. It is also noted that the term *gnostic* does not appear as the self-designated name in the writings of the Nag Hammadi Library but exists separately as a group designation by second-century patristic authors. Therefore, there have been proposals that we should forgo using the term *Gnosticism*, because it is a dubious category based on the late second-century discourse of orthodoxy and heresy. As soon as we talk about Gnosticism, we decide to talk about something other and apart from original and pure Christianity—that is, something that is not a part of "our" religious and cultural tradition. Karen King points out that, in this way, "a rhetorical term has been confused with a historical entity."[10]

In his 1995 "Prolegomena to the Study of Ancient Gnosticism," Bentley Layton sets out to identify gnostic texts rather than the essence or origin of Gnosticism. Layton argues that the definition of the category of gnostic writings should be based on the direct testimonials of ancient authors. Layton's starting point is Irenaeus's summary of the gnostic teaching in *Haer.* 1.29–30, which parallels the Secret Book of John in the Nag Hammadi Library. In addition, Porphyry mentions two books found in the Nag Hammadi Library (Zostrianos and Allogenes the Stranger) as well as a third in the Book of Zoroaster, alluded to in the Secret Book of John, which were discussed in Plotinus's seminar in Rome between 262 and 270 CE. Layton proposes, on the grounds of the content of these books, that the bulk of gnostic writings can be expanded to all other writings that contain a similar kind of cosmography, philosophical creation myth, and cast of characters (e.g., the Nature of the Rulers, Three Forms of First Thought, Three Steles of Seth, and Marsanes). Hence, Layton coins the

---

ogy is based on the double movement of "devolution and reintegration." This world has its basis in a crisis within the divine realm. The term *gnosis* is broadly defined as "knowledge of the divine mysteries reserved for an elite." See Ugo Bianchi, ed., *Le origini dello gnosticismo: colloquio di Messina, 13–18 Aprile 1966*, SHR 12 (Leiden: Brill, 1967).

10. Karen King, *What Is Gnosticism?* (Cambridge: Harvard University Press, 2003), 2–3. Ismo Dunderberg maintains that the situation does not get any better if the terms *gnostic* or *hairesis* are replaced by other terms that are less loaded with theological meaning, such as *sect* or *splinter group*, as these terms are also based on the same discourse of orthodoxy and heresy. See also Dunderberg, *Beyond Gnosticism* (New York: Columbia University Press, 2008), 18–19.

term *classic gnostic* to signify what Hans-Martin Schenke and most other scholars called the Sethian gnostic system.[11] According to Birger Pearson, Sethian Gnosticism consists of the following elements: "a focus on Seth as a Savior figure and spiritual ancestor of the gnostic elect; a primal divine triad of an ineffable Father, a Mother called Barbelo, and a Son referred to as Autogenes; four emanated luminaries named Harmozel, Oroaiel, Daveithe, and Eleleth, and other superterrestrial beings related to them; a salvation history thought of as three descents of the Savior, or three critical periods marked by flood, fire, and final judgement; and rituals of baptism and ascent."[12]

Layton argues, however, that the Valentinians should be kept apart "as a distinct mutation or reformed offshoot" of these original gnostics. He assumes that some Sethian (or classic gnostic) texts may have influenced Valentinus's followers, but they elaborated on these gnostic traditions extensively. Layton's solution is adopted by David Dawson, who describes Valentinus as a reformer of the Sethian myth in the Secret Book of John and in the Nature of the Rulers.[13] Ismo Dunderberg also suggests that Valentinus may have adopted the creation myth of Adam from Sethian

---

11. Bentley Layton, "Prolegomena to the Study of Ancient Gnosticism," in *The Social World of the First Christians: Essays in Honor of Wayne A. Meeks*, ed. L. Michael White and O. Larry Yarbrough (Minneapolis: Fortress, 1995), 334–50. On Sethian Gnosticism, see Hans-Martin Schenke, "The Phenomenon and Significance of Gnostic Sethianism," in *Sethian Gnosticism*, vol. 2 of *The Rediscovery of Gnosticism: Proceedings of the International Conference on Gnosticism at Yale New Haven, Connecticut, March 28-31, 1978*, ed. Bentley Layton (Leiden: Brill, 1981), 588–616. Many scholars regard Layton's proposal for the definition of Gnosticism as too narrow because it basically excludes the Valentinian texts from the category of gnostic writings. Antti Marjanen has balanced Layton's proposal by offering a bipolar definition of Gnosticism, grouping ancient religious texts and thinkers in way that enables closer analysis and comparison. The two characteristics of a gnostic text or doctrine are, according to Marjanen's definition, (1) the notion of an evil or ignorant world creator(s) separate from the highest divinity, and (2) the presupposition that the human soul or spirit originates from a transcendental world and has the potential of returning there after a life in this world. See Marjanen, "Gnosticism," in *The Oxford Handbook of Early Christian Studies*, ed. Susan Ashbrook Harvey and David G. Hunter (Oxford: Oxford University Press, 2008), 203–20.

12. Birger A. Pearson, *Ancient Gnosticism: Traditions and Literature* (Minneapolis: Fortress, 2007), 60–61.

13. David Dawson, *Allegorical Readers and Cultural Revision in Ancient Alexandria* (Berkeley: University of California Press, 1992), 132–33.

sources but elaborated on these teachings in light of Hellenistic Jewish models, as attested in the Wisdom of Solomon.[14]

In his 1992 book *Valentinus Gnosticus?*, Christoph Markschies presents a novel argument on the debate: Valentinus's teachings were independent from mythological gnostic traditions, but his followers may have been representatives of the gnostic "mythological heresy." This would mean that there was a drastic chasm between the teachings of Valentinus and the beliefs of his disciples, the latter of which may have adopted gnostic influences from Sethian sources.

Markschies's solution, which draws a distinction between Valentinus's teaching and the systems of his followers, is not widely accepted. Although Valentinus's fragments do not contain any explicit reference to the fall and restoration of Sophia, there is nothing in them that would make Valentinus's teachings incompatible with the beliefs of his followers. It is likewise unlikely that Valentinus's followers would have distorted the teachings of the father of their school in such a radical manner. It is more likely that Valentinus also taught some kind of protological myth of Sophia, though its details may have differed from those of the preceding gnostic myth and the systems of later Valentinian theologians.[15]

Markschies's provocative argument has nevertheless left an important legacy for scholarship on Gnosticism. As Dunderberg points out, "Markschies carefully located Valentinus in the intellectual milieu of second-century Alexandria, colored by Platonism and Hellenistic Judaism."[16] King has subsequently proposed that the myth of Sophia's fall and restoration can be seen as "a logical result of the intertextual reading of Platonic cosmology, Genesis and Wisdom literature."[17] Pearson also suggests that the gnostic worldview is dependent on Platonism, though the Platonist

---

14. Dunderberg, *Beyond Gnosticism*, 51, 104. According to Dunderberg, however, there is no definitive evidence that Valentinus used the story of Adam's creation in the Secret Book of John, despite common motifs between the narratives.

15. Irenaeus describes in *Haer.* 1.11.1 a version of the Sophia myth that can be traced back to Valentinus himself. Tertullian also reports some kind of protological myth that Valentinus purportedly taught, though Tertullian's account of the myth differs from later Valentinian systems (see Tertullian, *Val.* 4.3).

16. Dunderberg, *Beyond Gnosticism*, 20. Dunderberg maintains that Markschies's view forms a solid basis for all subsequent study of Valentinus's theology, even though he does not agree in all cases with Markschies's radical view.

17. Karen King, *The Secret Revelation* (Cambridge: Harvard University Press, 2006), 221–24, 233.

elements have been reinterpreted in a non-Platonic direction in light of apocalyptically oriented Judaism. In particular, both Gnosticism and the Jewish apocalypses emphasize the revelation of secret knowledge from on high. While the latter focuses on the coming end of the visible cosmos and the beginning of a new world order, ruled by the saints, the former stresses merely the return of the individual soul to its divine origin.[18] Most recently, Dylan Burns argues that four Platonizing Sethian writings in the Nag Hammadi Library (Zostrianos, Allogenes, Marsanes, and Three Steles of Seth) should be read predominantly as Judeo-Christian apocalypses or Platonic ascent manuals through which a reader can gain visionary experiences and participate angelic liturgy.[19]

It is notable that we do not have any evidence of the Sophia myth outside Christian literature. This would mean that the intertextual reading of these sources was actualized within the Christian tradition, possibly in Alexandria, which was the main center of the movement.[20] Although the fall of heavenly Wisdom could be explained in light of Platonic archetypes, Sophia's redemption by the Savior is barely conceivable in isolation from Christian tradition.[21] It seems, then, that the gnostics inherited these views from Pauline and Johannine theology.

---

18. Pearson, *Ancient Gnosticism*, 15–19.

19. Dylan Burns, *Apocalypse of the Alien God: Platonism and the Exile of Sethian Gnosticism* (Philadelphia: University of Pennsylvania Press, 2014), 1–7.

20. For the Christian origin of the gnostic myth, see Simone Pétrement, *Separate God: The Christian Origin of Gnosticism*, trans. Carol Harrison (New York: HarperCollins, 1984), 212; Alastair H. B. Logan, *Gnostic Truth and Christian Heresy: A Study in the History of Gnosticism* (Edinburgh: T&T Clark, 1996), 19–23; Bentley Layton and David Brakke, trans., *The Gnostic Scriptures*, 2nd ed. (New Haven: Yale University Press, 2021), 20–21; Robert McL. Wilson, "Half a Century of Gnosisforschung—in Retrospect," in *Doctrinal Diversity: Varieties of Early Christianity*, vol. 4 of *Recent Studies in Early Christianity: A Collection of Scholarly Essays*, ed. Everett Ferguson (New York: Garland, 1999), 95–105; Edwin Yamauchi, "The Issue of Pre-Christian Gnosticism Reviewed in the Light of the Nag Hammadi Texts," in *The Nag Hammadi Library after Fifty Years*, ed. John Turner and Anne McGuire, NHMS 44 (Leiden: Brill, 1997), 72–88; David Brakke, *The Gnostics: Myth, Ritual and Diversity in Early Christianity* (Cambridge: Harvard University Press, 2010), 29–51.

21. Stead argues that the idea of the fallen heavenly Sophia, as the Universal Soul, may have its archetype in the Platonic notion of the fall of the individual soul before its incarnation. See Christoph G. Stead, "The Valentinian Myth of Sophia," *JTS* 20 (1969): 101. Although the fall of Sophia could have been derived from Platonic archetypes, the

It is also worth noting that there are a number of significantly different accounts of the gnostic Wisdom myth. Irenaeus informs us in *Haer.* 1.29–30 that, in addition to the Valentinian sources, an account of Sophia's fall and restoration forms the basis for the cosmological model in Ophite, Barbeloite, and Sethian accounts. In *Gnostic Truth and Christian Heresy*, Alastair Logan proposes that the Valentinian school of thought reformed the gnostic myth of Sophia, but the myth in question may have differed from its later "Sethianization."[22] Logan suggests that the intellectual basis of the gnostic myth lies in Platonic-Pythagorean theology, which was applied to the interpretation of Genesis and the prologue to John's Gospel by innovative Christian theologians. Logan summarizes his analysis of the origin of Gnosticism as follows:

> The world-view of these Gnostics is undoubtedly Platonic. It reflects the attempt to derive the Many from the One, and to explain the visible universe as the work of a lower god, the Demiurge, emanated from the transcendent One beyond being, in terms of the inexplicable self-revelation and unfolding of the supreme God as Father, Mother and Son ... but as the fundamental concept of the self-revelation of the divine triad suggests, it is essentially a Christian scheme. It reflects Christian ideas and ways of interpreting the Old Testament in the light of the message of Paul and John.[23]

In this study, the origin of the gnostic movement is located in mid-second-century Alexandria, which served as an urban milieu for innovative Christian theologians who incorporated Hellenistic Jewish exegetical patterns and neo-Pythagorean transcendental monism into their interpretation of Christianity. John Turner points out, however, "Gnosticism is not phenomenologically reduced to Platonism, nor is Platonism reduced to Gnosticism, but each tends to be treated as an index to a single way of construing the world and interpreting its received symbols and traditions, be they of mythical or of philosophical character."[24]

---

idea of the redemption of Sophia can hardly have been derived from Platonic tradition or the Hellenistic Jewish wisdom traditions.

22. Logan, *Gnostic Truth*, 19–23.
23. Logan, *Gnostic Truth*, 22.
24. John D. Turner, *Sethian Gnosticism and the Platonic Tradition* (Quebec: Presses de l'Université Laval, 2001), 26.

I suggest that we do not have any historical reason to doubt that there was a group of early Platonizing Christian teachers who were called gnostics by outsiders and who may have used that name as a term of self-designation as well. In fact, Clement of Alexandria did not hesitate to accept the name "gnostics" (γνωστικοί) for his own group of Christians (*Strom.* 5.1.1,5). The gnostics can be seen as nonprofessional Platonists whose Platonism may have been seen as rather peculiar by the professional philosophers.[25] Although some gnostic myths of Sophia may have antedated both Valentinian and Sethian versions, it cannot be ruled out that these traditions might have interacted with each other later on.[26]

With regard to this study, it is crucial to note that the gnostic theologians, whether Sethians or Valentinians, were dependent not only on Middle Platonic philosophy but also on Hellenistic Jewish exegetical traditions of the Scriptures, which may have included some works of Philo. However, the main task of this study is to compare allegorical and philosophical parallels between Valentinian sources and Philo. Therefore, any parallels with Sethian and other gnostic texts are discussed in passing, focusing only on those cases where the Philonic parallels explain any *differences* between Valentinian and Sethian theologians. In these cases, as will be shown below, the Valentinian exegetes downplayed gnostic *mythopoiēsis* and refined the distinctively gnostic motifs, such as the denigration of the God of the Old Testament and radical cosmological dualism, by integrating the cosmic myth more closely with the textual basis of the Bible.[27]

---

25. Bianchi states that, rather than "an acute Hellenization of Christianity," the gnostic movement can be regarded as "an acute Christianization of Hellenism" (*Le origini dello Gnosticismo*, 556–58). See also Arthur D. Nock, "Gnosticism," *HTR* 57 (1964): 266.

26. See Logan, *Gnostic Truth*, 48–49, 55–56. Antti Marjanen points out that the Sethian and Valentinian Sophia traditions have a common origin, "but there is no evidence indicating a clear priority of one tradition over the other. It is very possible that they represent two basically independent trajectories which may have had points of contacts." See Marjanen, "The Relationship between the Valentinian and Sethian Sophia Myth Revisited," in Markschies and Thomassen, *Valentinianism: New Studies*, 119–20.

27. A good example of the Valentinian reformation of the gnostic myth is the exegesis of the creation of the first human being, in which the purely gnostic motifs of the fear and jealousy of the creator angels fade away. In Valentinus's fragment, the angels do reflect some tenets of the preceding myth, but in the later Valentinian anthropol-

1.3. Philo of Alexandria and the Valentinian Tradition

In an article titled "Philo of Alexandria and Gnosticism," Robert McLean Wilson outlines trends of scholarship concerning Philo's relation to ancient Gnosticism: Philo is treated as either a part of the gnostic movement or as a precursor of the later gnostic *haireseis*. Wilson prefers the latter, arguing that Philo is not a gnostic in the strict sense of the term; his writings do contain some affinities with Gnosticism, even though the gnostic repudiation of the God of the Old Testament was totally alien to Philo. The radical dualism of the gnostic myth, which presupposes a rupture between the ideal world and the visible cosmos, is also incompatible with Philo's moderate Platonic dualism. Rather than speaking of Philo as a representative of the gnostic *hairesis*, then, it is more reasonable to examine *gnosis* in Philo's oeuvre.[28]

In his essay "Philo and Gnosticism," Pearson mainly adopts Wilson's view, concluding that, even though there are clearly some parallel themes in Philo and gnostic texts, Philo can be treated neither as a gnostic nor as representative of a proto-gnostic system.[29] Although Philo shared the Platonic view of drawing a sharp distinction between the world of Ideas and the visible cosmos, he did not neglect the blessedness of the whole creation. According to the gnostic system, on the other hand, the creator God was blind, ignorant, and evil, having created the world to deceive human beings. Pearson argues that it is impossible to derive such a hostile

---

ogy, the angels are not malevolent archons but rather cocreators and archetypes of the soul of Adam. For details, see §6.3.3 below. David Brakke points out that the differences between Valentinian and Sethian literature indicate different methods of reading and producing texts among these communities. The Valentinians can be placed in the group of early Christians who sought intellectual illumination through authoritative interpretation of the Bible. The Valentinians differed from the gnostic communities, who wrote revelatory literature attributed to persons of the mythological past. See Brakke, "Scriptural Practices in Early Christianity: Towards a New History of the New Testament Canon," in *Invention, Rewriting, Usurpation: Discursive Fights over Religious Traditions in Antiquity*, ed. David Brakke, Anders-Christian Jacobsen, and Jörg Ulrich, ECCA 11 (New York: Lang, 2012), 271–75.

28. Robert McL. Wilson, "Philo of Alexandria and Gnosticism," *Kairos* 14 (1972): 213–19; see also Birger Pearson "Philo, Gnosis, and the New Testament," in *The New Testament and Gnosis: Essays in Honor of Robert McL. Wilson*, ed. Alistair H. B. Logan and Alexander J. M. Wedderburn (Edinburgh: T&T Clark, 1983), 165–82.

29. Birger Pearson, "Philo and Gnosticism," *ANRW* 21.1:295–341.

worldview from the writings of Philo. Pearson does think, however, that some of Philo's antinomian Jewish opponents may have been predecessors of gnostic theologians, though these Jewish groups cannot be directly equated with the Ophite or Barbelo-gnostic groups mentioned by Irenaeus in *Haer.* 1.29–30.[30]

It is notable that neither Pearson nor Wilson draws a distinction between the systems in the Valentinian sources and those in the Sethian gnostic texts. The Valentinian tradition forms a more intriguing case because the Valentinian teachers significantly downplayed such gnostic motifs as distinguished other gnostic teachers from Philo. In his article "The Valentinian Myth of Sophia," Christopher Stead maintains that "one can reconstruct most of the presuppositions of Valentinus merely by rearranging Philo's mental furniture."[31] The main elements of the Valentinian myth of Sophia were, according to Stead, already "in the margins of Philo's writings." In a later article, "In Search of Valentinus, " Stead elaborated this thesis, reevaluating the alleged contradictions between the Valentinian and the second-century Platonic tradition to prove that the Valentinian myth can in fact be derived from Middle Platonic principles.[32] He locates the Valentinian theory of aeons in the Platonic tradition, according to which ideas are not only intelligible but intelligent.[33] Stead argues that Philo and Valentinus used the same Platonic themes in their biblical exegesis. Valentinus's description of the creation of Adam, for

---

30. For an example in scholarship of the equation of the extreme allegorists of Philo with the proto-gnostic groups, see Moriz Friedländer, *Der vorchristliche jüdische Gnosticismus* (Göttingen: Vandenhoeck & Ruprecht, 1989). Although the identification of Philo's antinomian opponents with some proto-gnostic groups is intriguing, we do not have decisive information to confirm this connection. Pearson writes, "Although much of the detail of Friedländer's argument is open to question, he has been vindicated in his basic contention, that Gnosticism is a pre-Christian phenomenon that developed on Jewish soil." See Birger Pearson, "Friedländer Revisited: Alexandrian Judaism and Gnostic Origins," *SPhilo* 2 (1973): 23–39.

31. Stead, "Valentinian Myth of Sophia."

32. Christopher. G. Stead, "In Search of Valentinus," in *School of Valentinus*, vol. 1 of *The Rediscovery of Gnosticism: Proceedings of the International Conference on Gnosticism at Yale New Haven, Connecticut, March 28–31, 1978*, ed. Bentley Layton (Leiden: Brill, 1980), 75–95.

33. In making this argument, Stead refers to Chaldean Oracles, frags. 37 and 81. He also mentions Xenocrates, who suggested that the ideas were numbers and desired unity, meaning that they were not only archetypes but also living beings.

1. Introduction

instance, is similar to Philo's exegesis of Gen 1:26 as indicating the plurality of the creators (*Opif.* 72) and evidencing the ideal human being that is associated with the Logos. Stead also finds parallels between Philo and the Valentinian threefold division of humankind in *Gig.* 60 (see also 12–15).[34]

Stead's proof of a thematic and intellectual continuity between the Valentinian tradition and Philo's writings led to further scholarly exploration of this lineage. Layton, for his part, supposes that Valentinus's Platonic attitude toward the Scriptures may have come to him through the study of Hellenistic Jewish interpretations of the Bible in the writings of Philo. He also suggests that the motif of the thoughts of God as the plants of paradise in the Valentinian Gospel of Truth (NHC I 36.35–37.2) possibly draws on the allegorical interpretation of Gen 2:8 by Philo in *QG* 1.6.[35] Dawson, in *Allegorical Readers in Alexandria*, places Valentinus in the same exegetical tradition as Philo, but he does not propose any direct historical relationship between them. Valentinus may have been influenced by a similar allegorical framework and intellectual milieu without knowing the exact works of Philo.[36] Francis Fallon also sees parallels in the categorization of the law of Moses in Philo's writings and Ptolemy's *Letter to Flora*, maintaining that Ptolemy's writing reflects the use of the hermeneutical traditions of Hellenistic diaspora Judaism, which were similar to those of Philo. However, we do not have firm evidence that Valentinus or Ptolemy would have drawn

---

34. The tripartite division of humankind in Philo was also noted by Hans Jonas in *The Gnostic Religion: The Message of the Alien God and Beginnings of Christianity*, 3rd ed. (Boston: Beacon, 2001), 212–14.

35. Layton and Brakke, *Gnostic Scriptures*, 275, 324. See also Gregory Sterling, "The School of Sacred Laws," *VC* 53 (1999): 162. Layton suggests that the author of the Gospel of Truth (NHC I 5) is Valentinus. Irenaeus mentions in *Haer.* 3.11.9 that the Valentinians read a certain book called *Evangelium Veritatis*. While the Gospel of Truth (NHC I 5) does not contain a title for the book, it does begin with the words, "The gospel of truth is a joy for those who have received from the Father of truth the grace of knowing him." Thomassen is of the opinion that the incipit can be read as a title, and it is unlikely that there would have been two independent gnostic works with the same name. See Einar Thomassen, *The Spiritual Seed: The Church of the "Valentinians,"* NHMS 60 (Leiden: Brill, 2006), 146–48. I suggest that this is only an assumption. It is highly unlikely that the Gospel of Truth is an authentic work by Valentinus. Actually, Irenaeus does not identify Valentinus explicitly as an author of the text but "Valentinians."

36. Dawson, *Allegorical Readers*, 145–82.

their teachings directly from the works of Philo.³⁷ Markschies, who draws a sharp distinction between Valentinus and the gnostic tradition, maintains that there is nothing in Valentinus's fragments that indicates direct contact with Philo's works. This does not mean, however, that the contacts with Philo's teachings were not possible—they were even probable. Moreover, Markschies proposes that Valentinus represented an intellectual intermediate stage between Philo and Clement of Alexandria.³⁸

Two remarkable studies have recently been published concerning the Valentinian tradition. Einar Thomassen's *The Spiritual Seed* came out in 2006, followed two years later by Dunderberg's *Beyond Gnosticism*. In his monograph, Thomassen presents a systematic analysis of the traditions of the Valentinian school, though his emphasis is mainly on the so-called Eastern branch of Valentinianism. Thomassen sees one possible parallel between Valentinus's psalm *Harvest* (Hippolytus, *Haer.* 6.37.7) and Philo's *Mos.* 2.121, concerning the "cosmic chain" of creation. Although Thomassen detects neo-Pythagorean influences in the Valentinian sources, he stresses the influence of the Jewish apocalyptic tradition on the Valentinian system of thought rather than of the Platonizing Jewish Wisdom theology attested in Philo's writings.³⁹

Dunderberg's approach, on the other hand, is a social-historical analysis of the Valentinian movement. He sees aspects in Valentinus's school that connect it with traditions of ancient philosophical schools and Hellenistic Jewish Wisdom theology. Dunderberg notes that Valentinus's view of immortality, quoted by Clement in *Strom.* 4.89.1–3, is closer to Philo's teachings than to early Christian views, which connected immortality to the expectation of Jesus's parousia and the resurrection of the dead.

---

37. Francis T. Fallon, "The Law in Philo and Ptolemy: A Note on the Letter to Flora," *VC* 30 (1976): 45–51.

38. Christoph Markschies, *Valentinus Gnosticus? Untersuchungen zur valentinianischen Gnosis mit einem Kommentar zu den Fragmenten Valentins*, WUNT 65 (Tübingen: Mohr Siebeck, 1992), 406–7. Markschies writes: "Von seinem Fragmenten her ist kein zwingender Rückschluß auf direkte Kontakte zu alexandrinischen Mittelplatonikern oder dem hellenistischen Judentum der Stadt möglich. Sie sind wohl wahrscheinlich" (327).

39. Thomassen, *Spiritual Seed*, 315–26, 481–82. Thomassen sees in some Valentinian documents, e.g., Tri. Trac. 118.14–28; Gos. Truth 20.6–24; Ap. Jas. 16.8–11, some notion of the manifestation of the saints and the union with angels at the end of days. A similar theme is attested in Jewish apocalyptic literature (see 1 En. 38.1; 1QS XI, 7–9).

Dunderberg also points out that some biblical allegories—for example, the allegory of Israel—in the Valentinian sources may go back to the Jewish archetypes attested in Philo's writings.[40]

In Philonic studies, the question of whether Valentinus or his followers knew Philo's works is discussed by Runia in *Philo of Alexandria in Christian Literature*. There, Runia argues that, despite the apparent thematic continuity of thought between the second-century Alexandrian Christian communities and Jewish communities of Philo's time, there is no clear evidence that Valentinus actually had access to Philo's writings. Runia remarks that the closest parallels with Philo before Clement of Alexandria can be found in the group of Platonizing Christians of Alexandria, who made use of Greek philosophical ideas in their attempt to understand the Christian message. An early Christian document, the Teachings of Silvanus, offers an enlightening example of common elements with Philo's thought, which can be categorized as follows:[41]

1. the conception of the transcendence of God, based on Platonic categories of thought;
2. the doctrine of personified Wisdom;
3. an anthropology based on Platonism but also showing Stoic features;
4. emphasis on the importance of virtue and the struggle against the passions, coupled with a decidedly negative attitude toward the body;
5. use of an allegorical method of interpreting Scripture.

However, Runia considers the Christian gnostics of Alexandria as a separate group from other Platonic Christians. Although the gnostics shared much in common with Philo and Hellenistic Judaism, Runia argues, they

---

40. Dunderberg, *Beyond Gnosticism*, 40–41; see also Ismo Dunderberg, "Gnostic Interpretations of Genesis," in *The Oxford Handbook of the Reception History of the Bible*, ed. Michael Lieb and Emma Mason (Oxford: Oxford University Press, 2011), 385–89.

41. Runia, *Philo in Early Christian Literature*, 126. For the results of Zandee's article concerning Philo and the Teachings of Silvanus, see Pearson, "Philo, Gnosis, and the New Testament"; see also Jan Zandee, "Les enseignements de Silvanos et Philon d'Alexandrie," in *Mélanges d'histoire des religions offerts á H. C. Puech* (Paris: Presses universitaires de France, 1974), 337–45.

"introduced a radical twist" that separated them sharply from Philonic thought: a deterministic soteriology and an anticosmic worldview. In addition, the possession of *gnosis* separated humans radically into the categories of the elect and the others, leading to division at the gatherings of ordinary Christians. For Philo, the freedom of choice was fundamental, and he also held a positive view of the cosmos, which was sustained by an all-pervasive Logos. This positive estimation of the cosmos differs greatly from the teachings of the gnostics, who regarded the world as a hostile place ruled by the malevolent heavenly archons.[42] Therefore, Runia suggests that it is rather unlikely that the gnostics would have found anything of exegetical value in Philo's works.

The findings of recent scholarship on gnostic currents show that the eclectic characteristic of the Valentinian communities did not differ from other philosophical schools, rabbinical schools, or the Hermetic tradition. Dunderberg points out that Irenaeus's information about the Valentinian myth reveals that the Valentinians were interested in discussing cosmological myths with outsiders in an attempt to convert them.[43] The goal of the Valentinian myth was to show the world in a new light and to change how the audience perceived the world and how they should behave accordingly.[44] Moreover, the view of Valentinian tradition as a deterministic and anticosmic religion is based on a biased reading of the Valentinian sources. Although Valentinian teachers saw the body and fleshly impulses as evil, as Philo and contemporary Platonists did, the attitude toward the heavenly powers in some Valentinian sources is rather positive, because they reflect the harmony of the aeons of the intelligible realm.

It is notable that all the elements that Runia takes in the Teachings of Silvanus as proofs of continuity with Philo's thoughts can also be found in various Valentinian sources. In addition, the Teachings of Silvanus contains a tripartite anthropology that parallels Valentinian teaching.

---

42. Runia, *Philo in Early Christian Literature*, 126.

43. Dunderberg, *Beyond Gnosticism*, 191–95. See also Pheme Perkins, "Valentinians and the Christian Canon," in Markschies and Thomassen, *Valentinianism: New Studies*, 380.

44. See Dunderberg, *Beyond Gnosticism*, 25. On the importance of ethical improvement in Valentinian teaching, see Philip L. Tite, "An Exploration of Valentinian Paraenesis: Rethinking Gnostic Ethics in the Interpretation of Knowledge (NHC XI 1)," *HTR* 97 (2004): 275–304; Minna Heimola, *Christian Identity in the Gospel of Philip* (Helsinki: Finnish Exegetical Society, 2011), 170–85.

Pearson suggests that the division of humankind in early Christian sources is based on an allegorical reading of Gen 2:7 that goes back to Hellenistic Jewish sources, which were "well known to Philo, if not in fact derived from him."[45]

It is an oversimplification, however, to suggest that the Valentinian cosmic myth can be derived almost exclusively from the writings of Philo. The parallels between Philo and Valentinian teachers may be marginal exegetical similarities, without any essential contribution to the origin of the Valentinian system or the Sophia myth itself. Moreover, the Valentinian tradition was not monolithic, such that the works of Philo may have been known only by the teachers of some Valentinian groups. While the positive reception of Philo's allegories in Valentinian works may indicate the dependency of Valentinians on Philo, their explicit rejection of his thinking may also indicate a connection to Philo's exegesis.

The Valentinian communities were not isolated from the other early Christian communities in Rome or Alexandria; they participated in the early Christian debate on the creation of the world, the law of Moses, the essence of the divine realm, and the correct interpretation of the canonical gospels. Ptolemy's *Letter to Flora*, which I discuss in chapter 2, must have enjoyed remarkable popularity among Christians because Epiphanius still had access to this text about two hundred years after Ptolemy composed it in Rome.[46] Thus, the difference between the Valentinians and other Alexandrian Platonists, such as Origen and Clement, was not as clear-cut as is commonly suggested on the grounds of the rhetorical slander by Irenaeus and other proto-orthodox authorities. In some cases, Clement and other Christian Platonists found certain Valentinian themes and interpretations valuable. They did collect excerpts from Valentinian sources not only to prove their heretical content but also to learn from them.[47] For instance, Origen cites Heracleon's commentary on John's Gospel in his own book, indicating that the exegetical innovations of Valentinian teachers were not only mocked but were rather

---

45. Birger A. Pearson, *Gnosticism, Judaism and Egyptian Christianity* (Minneapolis: Fortress, 1990), 177–81. See also Pearson, "The Teachings of Silvanus," in *The Nag Hammadi Scriptures*, ed. Marvin W. Meyer (New York: HarperCollins, 2007), 499–522. Pearson writes: "So it is not out of the question that the author was familiar with Gnostic writings, such as those of the Alexandrian teacher Valentinus."

46. See Dunderberg, *Beyond Gnosticism*, 77–79.

47. See Judith L. Kovacs, "Clement of Alexandria and Valentinian Exegesis in the Excerpts from Theodotus," StPatr 43 (2006): 187–200.

taken seriously.[48] It stands to reason, then, that Valentinus and his followers would also have had access to the same scholarly sources, including the works of Philo, as their theological rivals in Alexandria and Rome.

1.4. Methodological Considerations

In his article "Comparisons Compared: A Methodological Survey of Comparisons of Religion from 'A Magic Dwells' to 'A Magic Still Dwells,'" David M. Freidenreich outlines four types of approaches to the comparison of religion: "comparative focus on similarity," "comparative focus on difference," "comparative focus on genus-species relationship," and "the use of comparison to refocus." The methodological approach in this study is primarily a combination of the first and second approaches, examining both similarities and dissimilarities.[49]

Jonathan Z. Smith stresses that the similarities as well as the dissimilarities of religions are not objective facts but rather the results of the "mental operations" of the observer.[50] Smith points out that a comparatist is attracted to a particular datum "by a sense of its uniqueness," remembering having seen "something like it" before and seeking therefore an explanation for that resemblance or difference. That is, comparison is a subjective experience, one that can be linked to "an objective connection through some theory of influence, diffusion, borrowing, or the like." Smith thus ponders whether "comparison [is] an enterprise of magic or science? Thus far, comparison appears to be more a matter of memory than a project for inquiry; it is more impressionistic than methodical."[51]

---

48. See Judith L. Kovacs, "Echoes of Valentinian Exegesis in Clement of Alexandria and Origen: The Interpretation of 1 Cor 3.1-3," in *Origeniana Octava: Origen and the Alexandrian Tradition; Papers of the Eighth International Origen Congress, Pisa 27-31 August 2001*, ed. Lorenzo Perrone (Leuven: Leuven University Press, 2003), 1:317-29.

49. David M. Freidenreich, "Comparisons Compared: A Methodological Survey of Comparison of Religion from 'A Magic Dwells' to 'A Magic Still Dwells,'" in *Method and Theory in the Study of Religion* (Leiden: Brill, 2004), 80-101.

50. Jonathan Z. Smith, *Drudgery Divine: On the Comparison of Early Christianities and the Religions of Late Antiquity*, JLCRS 14 (London: School of Oriental and African Studies, University of London, 1990), 51-52. See also Niko Huttunen, *Paul and Epictetus on Law: A Comparison* (London: T&T Clark, 2009), 10-19.

51. Jonathan Z. Smith, "In Comparison a Magic Dwells," in *A Magic Still Dwells: Comparative Religion in the Postmodern Age*, ed. Kimberley C. Patton and Benjamin C. Ray (Berkeley: University of California Press, 2000), 23-41.

William E. Paden stresses the heuristic nature of the comparative enterprise in his article "Elements of New Comparativism."[52] He points out that the comparative study is heuristic because it provides instruments for further discovery. He says, "Just identifying patterns, therefore, is not the end matter but the starting point for investigation."

The subjective dimension in the process of comparison does not, however, mean that it cannot be done scientifically. Mental operations should be subordinated to conceptual self-control, meaning that the framework of comparison should be analytically controlled and the significant aspects of the phenomena in question selected in a theoretically plausible way.

Comparative scholarship not only *presents* the similarities between objects of comparison but seeks to *explain* why they are similar or the historical relationship between them. The emphasis of the historical survey can lead, however, to parallelomania, a tendency not only to exaggerate similarities but "to describe source and derivation as if implying literary connection flowing in an inevitable or predetermined direction."[53] I would suggest, however, that the opposite attitude, parallelophobia, would be as pernicious for comparative study. Such an attitude would entail exaggerating differences between texts to dismiss their mutual dependency altogether, as if all ancient texts and their traditions had been developed in isolation, without any historical dependency on each other. The methodological pattern of this study is based on the following premises.

1. The starting point for comparison is exegetical. The focus is not in the first place on common philosophical ideas or theological themes but on linguistic similarities or dissimilarities related to the interpretation of specific biblical texts or themes and the use of similar kinds of allegorical schemes. In most cases, comparison is made between interpretations of Genesis. Commonalities therebetween may also be related to a similar philosophical idea that forms the basis for the allegorical interpretation of the text, even if the text used for allegorical interpretation might be different. The crucial issue in drawing comparisons is determining how much context should be taken into account. As more context is taken into consideration, the similarity between objects of comparison inevitably diminishes. In hermeneutical studies, parallel interpretations are rarely absolutely identical, even in the writings of the same author, because the

---

52. Williman E. Paden, "Elements of New Comparativism," in Patton and Ray, *Magic Still Dwells*, 186.
53. See Samuel Sandmel, "Parallelomania," *JBL* 81 (1962): 1–13.

contexts of the interpretations may be different. As Freidenreich points out, comparative study is not interested in religious texts within absolutely similar contexts, because it is the contextual dissimilarity that makes the comparison interesting in the first place.[54]

2. The objects of comparison in this study are texts in the corpus of Philo's writings and specific Valentinian sources that contain similar kinds of interpretations of the Bible. It is of note that the degree of similarity between these interpretations does not necessarily define the form of dependency. An identifiable quotation can come from secondary source material, notebooks, or through oral transmission, without direct contact with the original text itself.[55] Indeed, in his study *Philo of Alexandria and Early Christianity*, Runia observes that most of the fourth-century references to Philo's texts in Christian literature were not adopted by reading Philo himself but from Christian authors such as Origen, Eusebius, and Ambrose, who incorporated quotations from Philo in their writings. On the other hand, a short reference or allusion that faintly resembles another text can be the result of a careless direct reading of the source or of the ancient scholarly technique of borrowing. The latter is especially apparent in the writing of Clement of Alexandria, which Annewies van den Hoek describes in her study *Clement of Alexandria and His Use of Philo in the "Stromateis"*:

> Characteristic of his technique is the abrupt way that material borrowed from Philo jumps into his text. These discontinuities give a strange flavor to his sentences and lead to illogical turns of thought. In these various ways, therefore, Philo's text is nearly always presented in a damaged and defective form. Repeatedly, confusion and disorder appear; words are shifted strangely, and sentences are chopped into cryptic fragments. The development of Clement's thought would be entirely incomprehensible in these sections if Philo's text were not at hand. This applies not only to the readers of today but must also have held true for his own contemporaries.[56]

These caveats should warn against drawing conclusions too easily concerning the form of dependency or historical relationship between ancient

---

54. Freidenreich, "Comparison Compared," 94–96.
55. Runia, *Philo in Early Christian Literature*, 35, 341.
56. Annewies van den Hoek, *Clement of Alexandria and His Use of Philo in the "Stromateis": An Early Christian Reshaping of a Jewish Model* (Leiden: Brill, 1988), 214–15.

texts solely on the grounds of the degree of literal similarity or dissimilarity. It is clear, however, that the degree of textual similarity correlates with the probability of dependency, though the exact form of the dependency may remain beyond any historical study.

3. The historical focus of this study is on to the formative years of Valentinian tradition, that is, on the latter half of the second century. The parallels with Philo in the Valentinian sources written during that time form an intriguing case of direct dependency on Philo, given the lack of any contemporary evidence for extensive borrowings from Philo in the early Christian literature that could have served as source material for Valentinian authors.

4. The historical relationship between objects of comparison is not the only concern of comparative study. The similarities between religions or their literary traditions may also function as a lens (see above on the fourth approach of comparison that Freidenreich outlines). This means that comparative analysis may produce data that can be used to refocus issues in question. Freidenreich defines this approach in the following way: "Much as a microscope offers new insights even into specimens that can be seen with the naked eye, the religious tradition being brought for the purpose of comparison serves to provide a new perspective on the tradition being examined, to raise new questions or offer a new possible way of understanding the target tradition."[57] In this study, the target tradition is the Valentinian tradition. The Valentinian sources are thus read and analyzed in the light of Philo, not vice versa. I will provide new perspectives on interpreting the Valentinian texts on the ground of parallels with Philo. Therefore, the aim of this study is not only to collect parallels between the Valentinian sources and Philo's works but to refocus the Valentinian tradition and to learn from the Philonic parallels. Differences between Philo and the Valentinians do not necessarily imply independence, as is usually presumed, but rather help us to understand how the Valentinian teachers read and modified Philo's interpretations.

1.5. Outline of This Study

Chapter 2 explores the sources of this study and definitions for the category of Valentinian literature. The terms *the school of Valentinus* or *the Valentin-*

---

57. See Freidenreich, "Comparisons Compared," 91.

ians do not appear in any of the Valentinian writings in the Nag Hammadi Library. Rather, the Valentinian group designation and the description of the Valentinian heresy come from the patristic sources. The finding of the Nag Hammadi writings in 1945 expanded our knowledge of early Christian traditions in general and Valentinianism in particular. However, the problem remains in deciding which writings in the Library of Nag Hammadi can be defined as Valentinian. Although the leaders of the nascent orthodoxy do not describe the teachings of the Valentinians objectively, we should be careful not to expand the category of the Valentinianism uncritically on the grounds of Nag Hammadi writings alone. Based on an extensive reading of the Valentinian sources, the closest exegetical and thematic parallels with Philo seem to come from the Valentinian source (*Exc.* 43.2–65) that is enclosed in the so-called eighth book of the *Stromateis* by Clement of Alexandria. This particular Valentinian teaching goes back to the Valentinian traditions in Alexandria and is connected to the teachings of the disciples of Ptolemy in Rome, which is described by Irenaeus in *Haer.* 1.1–7.

I begin chapter 3 by investigating the formation of the school of Valentinus and its social-historical contexts in early second-century Alexandria. The Jewish revolt and collapse of the Alexandrian Jewry created an urban social setting for the school of Valentinus and other gnostic *haireseis*. The allegorical method of interpretation connects these early second-century Christian Platonists in Alexandria to the hermeneutical heritage of the Hellenistic Judaism that includes the works of Philo. It is of note that both Philo and the Valentinians were proponents of multiple exegesis, meaning that the interpretation of a given text ought to be presented differently according to the intellectual level of their target audience. At the end of this chapter, I investigate two case studies (the firstborn in Exod 13:2–12 and the division of the law of Moses) that illustrate the multidimensionality of the exegetical tradition of Philo and Valentinians.

Chapter 4 presents a comparative analysis of the protological systems of Philo and the Valentinians. Both Philo and the Valentinians can be regarded as scriptural Middle Platonists who integrated biblical texts with neo-Pythagorean and Peripatetic metaphysics. I argue that the Valentinian protological model system described in Irenaeus, *Haer.* 1.1.1–3, was developed on the grounds of a Platonizing interpretation of the prologue of the Gospel of John attested in *Exc.* 6–7 and Irenaeus, *Haer.* 1.8.5. The Valentinian exegetes must have been aware that John 1:1–5 was written as a Platonizing description of the creation account in Genesis. John's prologue was therefore not chosen accidentally as a biblical basis for protological speculations in the Valentinian sources. Moreover, the Valentinian exegetes modified the structure of the prologue in a way that indicates that they also were familiar with exegetical patterns in Philo's *De opificio mundi* and the Allegorical Commentary.

In chapter 5, the focus of analysis shifts from the intelligible realm to the creation of the visible cosmos. First, I present a short philosophical introduction to the creation of matter in the Middle Platonic tradition, which formed the basis for speculations concerning the creation of matter both in Philo and in the Valentinian systems. While Philo can be associated with the school of Eudorus of Alexandria, the Valentinian view is closer to Moderatus of Gades. In the Valentinian accounts, Wisdom (or Sophia) has manifold intellectual links, which are related to the dyadic and monadic aspects of the divine world. I will argue that these views are found in a nascent stage in Philo's texts. Although Philo interpreted Gen 1:1 as denoting the intelligible cosmos, Valentinian exegetes saw it as a separation of psychic and hylic essences on the grounds of the ancient theory of *diakrisis*. A similar theory concerning the division of matter according to its physical characteristics into the four cosmic elements can be found in Philo. Notably, both Philo and the Valentinians interpreted Gen 1:3 as the manifestation of the everlasting light, which Valentinians associated with the manifestation of the psychic essence.

In chapter 6, I analyze the interpretations of the creation of humankind in Gen 1:26–27 and 2:7. Both Philo and the Valentinians were dependent on Middle Platonic anthropological theories, which formed the philosophical background for their allegorical interpretation. In the Allegorical Commentary, Philo's anthropological interpretations no longer describe the history of the first human beings; rather, Gen 1:26–27 and 2:7 are seen as universal realities about humankind, the structure of the soul, and ethics. I argue that Valentinian teachers were familiar with similar kinds of anthropological interpretations to that which Philo gives in this work, though they modify them in light of the myth of Sophia. At the end of this chapter, I investigate two anthropological fragments of Valentinus (the creation of Adam in *Strom.* 2.36.2–4 and the psalm *Harvest* in Hippolytus, *Haer.* 6.37.7).

The discussion in chapter 7 is an expansion of the anthropological issues handled in the previous chapter. The tripartite division of humankind is one of the main features of Valentinian anthropology. Although the names of the anthropological categories may have been derived from Paul, the division itself is closer to Philo's division of humankind on the grounds of an allegorical reading of Gen 1:26–27 and 2:7. The tripartite division of humankind forms also the basis for the allegory of Abel, Cain, and Seth, as well as the allegory of Israel as a spiritual human being who sees God, which parallel Philo's interpretations in the Allegorical Commentary. At the end of the chapter, I compare theories about the afterlife in Philo and the Valentinian sources. Valentinus maintained that the gift of immortality had been present in the world since the creation of Adam, although it must be activated through the practice of dying. Both the Valentinian teachers and Philo suggest that the ultimate telos of the human soul was assimilation with the intelligible cosmos, described as a translation of the soul into an angel.

Finally, in chapter 8, I offer some concluding remarks on the comparative analysis presented in chapters 4–7. I primarily address two questions. First, what kind of historical relationships can be derived from these parallels? Did Valentinian teachers know the works of Philo personally, or did they learn of these teachings indirectly, through notebooks or oral transmission? This historical conclusion also aims to provide some new insight into the question of the preservation of Philo's library after his death. Second, how can these parallels with Philo help modern scholars interpret the Valentinian texts? Do these parallels offer new insights or focal perspectives into Valentinian source material and the evolution of the gnostic school of thought in general?

Taking into account all the parallels with Philo in the Valentinian sources investigated in this study, I conclude that it is rather likely that there was a historical relationship between Philo's oeuvre and the Valentinian teachers. This study shows that Philo's influence on Valentinian exegesis may have come from various sources and through different groups of Valentinians, each with their own exegetical interests. These notions expand our knowledge not only concerning the preservation and circulation of Philo's texts in the latter part of the second century but also concerning the importance of the allegorical traditions of Hellenistic Judaism on Valentinus's school of thought and on Gnosticism in general.

2
The Valentinian Source in Clement's *Excerpts of Theodotus*

Before the finding of the Nag Hammadi scriptures in 1945, the teachings of the Valentinians were known only through the descriptions of their opponents. Research on the Valentinian writings of the Nag Hammadi Library has changed the situation remarkably. For the first time, the voice of the Valentinian communities could be heard directly through their own words. Dunderberg maintains that the Valentinian texts of the Nag Hammadi Library clearly show that the Valentinian teachers were not solely mythmakers, as they are portrayed in the patristic sources, but their texts contain moral exhortations for their followers as well.[1]

2.1. The Category of the Valentinian Literature and Philo's Corpus

The fourth-century Valentinian writings of the Nag Hammadi Library are commonly regarded as primary sources, compared with the patristic writings, which are considered secondary sources for understanding Valentinianism. It is assumed that the Valentinian writings in the Nag Hammadi Library offer an authentic description of the Valentinian belief systems, presenting an inside view into the religious phenomena under investigation. However, we cannot know for sure, for example, whether opinions similar to those expressed in Nag Hammadi texts such as the Gospel of Truth or the Gospel of Philip, which are commonly regarded as Valentinian, were ever held by Valentinus or his earliest followers, whose teachings are described in the patristic sources.[2]

---

1. Dunderberg, *Beyond Gnosticism*, 10.
2. For the dating of the Nag Hammadi texts, see page 33 below.

Given that the patristic sources are hostile sources, they likely do not describe the Valentinian teachings objectively. Irenaeus's rhetorical strategy was to erect a social boundary between normative beliefs and those of the Valentinians, marking the Valentinian tradition as a deviation from the true apostolic church.[3] However, simply correcting the bias in second-century patristic sources on the grounds of fourth-century documents remains problematic. First, writings of the Nag Hammadi Library are classified as Valentinian only insofar as one accepts the characteristics attested in the patristic sources. We have already formulated a definition of some form or another in the very act of choosing the writings we suspect of representing Valentinian teaching.[4] Second, the characteristics that distinguish the Valentinian writings of the Nag Hammadi Library from the patristic information may reflect more the particular social and theological context in which they were written than the difference between the belief systems of the second-century Valentinian teachers and those described by the patristic authors.[5]

In this study, I define the category of Valentinian writings on the grounds of a critical evaluation of the information attested in the patristic sources. Although they are hostile secondary sources, we can detect the rhetorical bias through a critical reading of the text. The rhetorical slander can be detected rather easily, and in some cases we have independent descriptions of the same Valentinian teaching, which can be used to evalu-

---

3. See Dunderberg, *Beyond Gnosticism*, 8–9.

4. It seems that we are confronted with Meno's classical paradox when trying to select Valentinian writings from among the Nag Hammadi codices. Plato explains that those who do not already know what virtue is will not know when they have found it (see *Meno* 80d). This dilemma was noted by Michel R. Desjardins, who argues that "the decision to call a work 'Valentinian' rests exclusively on finding similarities between its content and the patristic descriptions of that group." On the problem of defining the category of the Valentinian source material, see Desjardins, *Sin in Valentinianism*, SBLDS 108 (Atlanta: Scholars Press, 1990), 3–12.

5. In some cases, the rhetorical technique in the descriptions of the patristic authors is that of exaggeration. However, while Irenaeus mocked Valentinians and took their interpretations out of context, this does not mean that his intention was to distort everything he found in his Valentinian source material. For example, a comparison between the First Apocalypse of James (NHC V 4) and Irenaeus's description in *Haer.* 1.21.5 shows that a reader is able to gain a rather reliable conception of the Valentinian teaching in question on the grounds of Irenaeus's report. See Thomassen, *Spiritual Seed*, 406–10.

ate the reliability of the sources in question. There are also some accounts in the patristic sources that can be equated with the primary sources of the second-century Valentinian tradition. Epiphanius quotes in *Panarion* the Valentinian *Letter to Flora* in its entirety and the Valentinian Letter of Instruction. Although the quotations of Valentinus are only short fragments, we do not have any reason to suspect their authenticity.

The scholarly consensus classifies the following texts of the Nag Hammadi Library as Valentinian: Gospel of Truth (NHC I 3), Tripartite Tractate (NHC I 5), Treatise on the Resurrection (NHC I 4), Gospel of Philip (NHC II 3), First Revelation of James (NHC V 3), Interpretation of Knowledge (NHC XI 1), and Valentinian Exposition (NHC XI 2). In this study, the following documents are considered as spurious, even though some scholars incorporate them into their list of Valentinian writings: Second Revelation of James (NHC V 4), Letter of Peter to Philip (NHC VIII 2), Exegesis of the Soul (NHC II 6), Revelation of Paul (NHC V 2), Authoritative Discourse (NHC VI 3), and Prayer of the Apostle Paul (NHC I 1).[6]

---

6. For different catalogs of the Valentinian writings in the Nag Hammadi Library, see Dunderberg, *Beyond Gnosticism*, 10; Desjardins, *Sin in Valentinianism*, 6–7. Michael Kaler argues for the inclusion of the Revelation of Paul into the list of Valentinian writings. See Kaler, *Flora Tells a Story: The Apocalypse of Paul and Its Context* (Waterloo, ON: Wilfrid Laurier University Press, 2008). For a critical view, see Dylan M. Burns, "Is the Apocalypse of Paul a Valentinian Apocalypse? Pseudepigraphy and Group Definition in NHC V,2," in *Die Nag-Hammadi-Schriften in der Literatur- und Theologiegeschichte des frühen Christentums*, ed. Jens Schröter and Konrad Schwarz, STAC 106 (Tübingen: Mohr Siebeck, 2017), 97–112. The Authoritative Discourse is a good example of an ancient text containing many themes that recall Valentinian language, with words such as *fullness, bridegroom,* and bridal *chamber.* E.g., Philip Tite includes the Authoritative Discourse in the category of Valentinian writings. See Tite, *Valentinian Ethics and Paraenetic Discourse: Determining the Social Function of Moral Exhortation in Valentinian Christianity*, NHMS 67 (Leiden: Brill, 2006), 8–15. Although the Authoritative Discourse can be read in the light of Valentinian myth, these features do not motivate the main message of the text in a way that would make it Valentinian. Ulla Tervahauta is of the opinion that the author of the book may have known some Valentinian teachings, but she does not regard the text as Valentinian. See Tervahauta, *A Story of the Soul's Journey in the Nag Hammadi Library: A Study of the Authenticos Logos (NHC VI,3)*, NTOA 107 (Göttingen: Vandenhoeck & Ruprecht, 2015), 101–108. In addition to the Authoritative Discourse, the Teaching of Silvanus also contains similarities with Valentinian theology, as it may have been composed by an author who was familiar with Valentinianism. For my discussion on the Teachings of Silvanus, see §1.3 above.

The Valentinian sources in the patristic writings include (1) quotations of Valentinus or his followers and (2) summaries of the Valentinian teaching collected from various sources. Seven fragments of Valentinus belong to the first category. They are included in the works of Clement of Alexandria (*Strom.* 2.36.2-4, 114.3-6; 3.59.3; 4.89.1-3, 89.6-90.1; 6.52.3-53.1) and Hippolytus of Rome (*Haer.* 6.37.7).[7] Ptolemy's *Letter to Flora* is quoted in its entirety in Epiphanius's *Panarion* (33.3.1-33.7.10) as well as the Valentinian Letter of Instruction ("Lehrbrief").[8] *Excerpta ex Theodoto* by Clement of Alexandria in so-called book 8 of the *Stromateis* contains fragments of Theodotus and the teachings of some other unknown Valentinians.[9] In addition, Origen quotes the teachings of Heracleon in his commentary on John's Gospel (*Comm. Jo.* 1-13).

In the second category of sources, we have descriptions of the Valentinian system in Irenaeus's *Haer.* 1.1-8 and 11-20, Clement's *Exc.* 6-7 and 43.2-65 (so-called section C), Hippolytus's *Haer.* 6.29-36 and 41-42, Tertullian's *Adversus Valentinianos*, and Epiphanius's *Panarion*. Tertullian also comments on Valentinian teachings in *De anima* and *De resurrectione*. In addition, Adamantius's *Dialogue on the True Faith in God*, which is part of Methodius's fourth-century work *De libero arbitrio*, presents a fictious Valentinian disciple whose teachings concerning matter may go back to Valentinus himself.[10] There is also a fragment called *De sancta ecclesia* by fourth-century bishop Marcellus of Ancyra, who mentions Valentinus's

---

7. Markschies enumerates eleven fragments of Valentinus. In addition to the indisputable fragments mentioned above, he mentions fragments in Hippolytus, *Haer.* 6.42.2; 10.13.4; and fragments in Pseudo-Anthimus/Photius (Markshies, *Valentinus Gnosticus?*).

8. It is rather certain that the Valentinian Lehrbrief is not the work of Valentinus but written by some of his pupils. The majority of scholars place the work in mid-third century. Giuliano Chiapparini is of the opinion that the system in the Lehrbrief is related to one of the sources used by Irenaeus in his *Haer.* 1.1-7. This would mean that it could be dated to the second half of the second century. See Chiapparini, "Fragments of An Early 'Lost' Valentinianism," in Thomassen and Markschies, *Valentinianism: New Studies*, 122-42.

9. According to Casey, the following sections go back to Theodotus: *Exc.* 1.1-2; 2-3; 17.1; 21-24.1; 25-26; 28-30.1; 31-33.1, 3-4; 33-36.1; 37-41; 66-86. See Robert Casey, ed., *The Excerpta ex Theodoto of Clement of Alexandria* (London: Christophers, 1935), 5. Thomassen attributes to Theodotus only those passages where he is explicitly mentioned and passages in 1.1-2, 22.

10. See Dunderberg, *Beyond Gnosticism*, 67-72. Dunderberg maintains that this account has been notoriously overlooked in previous scholarship.

writing called *On the Three Natures*. We are unable to confirm, however, that Valentinus wrote a book with that name. Marcellus may have thought that the Valentinian Tripartite Tractate was written by Valentinus himself, and it is also possible that this particular Valentinian document was named *On the Three Natures*. Nevertheless, Marcellus's statement concerning Valentinus's invention of the three persons of the Godhead may be authentic: "Valentinus the heresiarch … was the first to invent three hypostases and three persons of Father, Son and Holy Spirit, and he is discovered to have filched this from Hermes and Plato."[11]

As Einar Thomassen points out, there has never been one authoritative version of the Valentinian myth; rather, individual teachers produced their own versions and innovations of it. Thus, we should not think that one particular system represents the standard version of the myth.[12] There are nevertheless certain criteria for classifying a text as Valentinian, which are as follows:

1. the protological system, which includes the genealogy of the intellectual aeons or other intellectual beings from the transcendent One;
2. the precosmic fall and salvation of Sophia as the origin of matter and a paradigm for the salvation of humankind;
3. the notion of the Demiurge as a lower creator God, who is used as an instrument in the creation of the visible cosmos;
4. the spiritual seed of Sophia as the highest part of the human soul;
5. the tripartite division of humankind into hylic, psychic, and pneumatic categories; and
6. the salvation as a unification of the soul with its angelic counterpart.

A text need not contain all these elements to be classified as Valentinian. In some cases, the information is fragmentary, containing only select allu-

---

11. Trans. Alistair H. B. Logan, "Marcellus of Ancyra (Pseudo-Anthimus), 'On the Holy Church': Text, Translation and Commentary," *JTS* 51 (2000): 81–112; see also Markschies, *Valentinus Gnosticus?*, 264–70.

12. Einar Thomassen, "The Relative Chronology of the Valentinian System," in Thomassen and Markschies, *Valentinianism: New Studies*, 17–18. Thomassen proposes that the Valentinian system, with some variations, can be constructed from the following accounts: Irenaeus, *Haer.* 1.1–7; Hippolytus, *Haer.* 6.29.2–36; Tripartite Tractate; A Valentinian Exposition (NHC XI 2), Irenaeus, *Haer.* 1.11.1; 1.14; Epiphanius, *Pan.* 31.5–6 ("Lehrbrief"); *Exc.* 43.2–65.

sions to the specifically Valentinian ideas. The evolution of the Valentinian school tradition should also be taken into account: the fragments of Valentinus do not contain the myth of Sophia, while some later documents, such as the Tripartite Tractate, began to merge with the metaphysics of nascent orthodoxy and Neoplatonic philosophy. In some cases, the identity of a text is unclear, as it could be a Valentinian text or may simply contain some influences from the Valentinian belief system without being a Valentinian text as such.

In this study, the teachings in the Valentinian writings are compared with the writings of Philo of Alexandria. Although Philo was an innovative interpreter, his writings also offer a window into the traditions of allegorical exegesis among the Jewish exegetes of Alexandria of the first century CE. The corpus of Philo's writings has been preserved to this day in various Greek manuscripts, sixth-century Armenian translations, and some texts extant only in Latin. The decisive point in the preservation and use of Philo's writings was in 233 CE, when Origen took the copies of the whole Philonic corpus with him and deposited them in the library of the episcopal school of Caesarea.[13] Eusebius provides a list of Philo's works in *Hist. eccl.* 2.18.1–9, mentioning many works that have since been lost. We can also assume that some work is missing when there is a significant lacuna in a series of Philo's allegorical commentaries. It has therefore been estimated that only two-thirds of Philo's works have been preserved to this day.[14]

---

13. Colin H. Roberts argues that Origen took the whole library of Philo's writings from Egypt to Palestine, and there seems to be a break between Origen's departure from Alexandria and the arrival of Philo's writings back to their Alexandrian hinterland after a decade. This view is supported by the papyrus codex found in Lower Egypt in 1889 (dated to the beginning of the fourth century), which, according to Cohn-Wendland, represents the Caesarean textual tradition in Alexandria. After Origen, the next Christian author in Alexandria to use Philo extensively and mention his name explicitly was Didymus the Blind, the leader of the catechetical school of Alexandria during the late fourth century. See Roberts, *Buried Books in Antiquity: Habent sua fata libelli*, AEML 1962 (London: Library Association, 1963), 11–15. According to Runia, the papyrus codex mentioned by Cohn-Wendland is a witness to the fact that Origen *did not take* all the copies of Philo with him to Palestine but rather that some of Philo's writings were circulating during the late third and early fourth century in Egypt. Runia locates Pseudo-Justin's *Cohortatio ad Graecos* in third-century Alexandria, which supports his theory that the writings of Philo remained in Alexandria, even though Origen took private copies of them to Egypt (*Philo in Early Christianity*, 184–89).

14. For an overview of Philo's writings, see Sterling, "Philo," 1065–67; James R. Royse, "The Works of Philo," in Kamesar, *Cambridge Companion to Philo*, 32–64. The

Philo's works are divided into three categories: the exegetical treatises, the apologetic treatises, and the philosophical treatises. In this study, comparison with the Valentinian writings is mainly done with Philo's exegetical writings, which can be divided into (1) the Allegorical Commentary (twenty-one treatises), (2) the *Questiones et Solutiones in Genesin et in Exodum* (six treatises), and (3) the Exposition of the Law (twelve treatises). In the Allegorical Commentary, which proceeds sequentially through Gen 2:1–41:24, Philo introduces philosophical topics into his discussion of biblical texts. Gregory Sterling points out that Philo seems to be confident that he does not have "to read Plato into Moses, but out of Moses."[15] However, careful attention must be paid to the different genres, the implied audience, and the chronology of Philo's writings. The books in the Allegorical Commentary are not directly connected to Philo's philosophical writings, and the *Questiones et Solutiones in Genesin et in Exodum* is not a direct continuation of the Exposition of the Law, which lacks the radical Platonic transcendentalism of the Allegorical Commentary.[16]

---

writings of Philo are preserved in the medieval and Byzantine manuscripts that are brought together in the critical edition of Philo's works in *Philonis Alexandrini opera quae supersunt*, ed. Leopold Cohn and Paul Wendland, 6 vols. (Berlin: de Gruyter, 1896–1915). The main early modern editions of Philo are *Editio princeps Turnebus* (1552), in Greek, and *Editio princeps Iustianianus* (1520) and *Sichardus* (1527), in Latin. Some of his texts are known only in sixth-century Armenian translations (*QG* 1–4; *QE* 1–2; *Prov.* 1–2; *De animalibus*; two fragments of *De Deo*; arithmological fragments). Some Greek quotations have been preserved by Eusebius (*Prov.* 2; *Hypothetica*). In addition, there are some other references and quotations in the exegetical catenae of patristic writings and Greek anthologies (e.g., the *Sacra parallela* of John of Damascus). Some books that are mentioned in the writings of Philo or by Eusebius are still missing from our present collection of Philo's works (e.g., *On Numbers*; *On Covenants*; *On Rewards*; and the *Lives of Isaac and Jacob*). On the textual transmission of Philo's works during Byzantine and medieval times, see Runia, *Philo in Early Christian Literature*, 16–31.

15. Sterling, "Philo," 1070–72. Eusebius mentions that Philo himself gave the title *Allegory of the Sacred Laws* to the distinct group of texts (*Hist. eccl.* 2.18.1).

16. Maren R. Niehoff, *Philo of Alexandria: An Intellectual Biography* (New Haven: Yale University Press, 2018), 14–22. Niehoff suggests that the Allegorical Commentary belongs to Philo's early Alexandrian period, whereas his treatises of the Exposition of the Law, together with his philosophical and apologetic writings, belong to Philo's later career, after his stay in Rome in 38/39 CE. Although the *Questiones et Solutiones in Genesin et in Exodum* was intended for beginning students, it is not clear whether it was written earlier than the Allegorical Commentary. Evidently, the Exposition of the Law was written for wider audience (both Jews and non-Jews) but

Based on an extensive reading of the Valentinian sources, the closest exegetical parallels with Philo of Alexandria seem to be found in Clement's *Exc.* 43.2–65. This section has many parallel themes and interpretations with Irenaeus's "great account" in *Haer.* 1.1–7.[17] *Excerpta ex Theodoto* 6–7 also contains a protological commentary on the prologue of the Gospel of John, which has a close parallel in Irenaeus, *Haer.* 1.8.5. Although this primitive protological account seems to represent an isolated Valentinian source, I suggest that it serves as the basis for the Valentinian model system described in Irenaeus, *Haer.* 1.1.1–3, and it also contains remarkable parallels with Philo's protological interpretations.

Although the starting point for comparison with Philo's writings in this study is the allegorical interpretations of Genesis in *Exc.* 43.2–65, I will expand my investigation to other Valentinian sources and to those Valentinian writings in the Nag Hammadi Library that are valuable for comparison purposes. In addition to Valentinus's fragments, the Tripartite Tractate is an important document because it is the only extant Valentinian primary source for the Valentinian belief system and protological myth in its entirety. Although the Tripartite Tractate represents a later phase of the Valentinian school tradition than *Exc.* 43.2–65, it may contain elements stemming from an earlier phase of Valentinian theology. In addition to the Tripartite Tractate, the Valentinian sections in the Gospel of Philip, as

---

it does not necessarily imply Roman context, as Niehoff suggests. For the chronology of Philo's works, see also Royse, "Works of Philo," 59–62.

17. In this study, the Greek text of Irenaeus's *Adversus haereses* comes from *Irénée de Lyon, Contre les heresies: livre I*, ed. Adelin Rousseau and Louis Doutreleau, SC 264 (Paris: Cerf, 1979), 2:18–137. I follow mainly the translation in Dominic J. Unger, trans., *St. Irenaeus of Lyons Against Heresies, Book One*, ed. Walter J. Burghardt, Thomas Comerford Lawler, and John J. Dillon, vol. 1, ACW 55 (New York: Newman, 1992), and Layton's translation in *Gnostic Scriptures*, 347–74. The Greek text and the translation of the *Excerpta ex Theodoto* is based on Geoffrey S. Smith, *Valentinian Christianity: Texts and Translations* (Berkeley: University of California Press, 2020), 91–170; Brakke's translation in *Gnostic Scriptures*, 506–29; and the translation in Casey, *Excerpta ex Theodoto*. The Greek text of Philo's works is based on Peder Borgen, Kåre Fuglseth, and Roald Skarsten, eds., *The Works of Philo: Greek Text with Morphology* (Bellingham, WA: Logos Library Systems, 2005). The Greek text of the Bible is based on NA[28] and Alfred Rahlfs, ed., *Septuaginta* (Stuttgart: Deutsche Bibelgeschellsaft, 2012). The English translations of the biblical texts, if not included in citations taken from the secondary literature, are from the RSV. The citations from Nag Hammadi Scriptures are from Marvin Meyer, ed., *The Nag Hammadi Scriptures* (New York: HarperCollins, 2007), unless otherwise stated.

well as the fragments of Heracleon's commentary on the Gospel of John, provide notable elements for comparison with Philo's works, especially concerning the basis for the allegorical method.

There are, however, some crucial methodological issues, which should be taken into account when using the aforesaid Valentinian source material in this study. As noted, the starting point of this study is exegetical. The focus is not on common philosophical ideas or theological themes but on exact textual or linguistic similarities or dissimilarities, which are based on a specific text of Genesis. In the Tripartite Tractate, only the short middle section (Tri. Trac. 105–107) contains biblical allusions, which may include parallels to Philo, but even these affinities are expressed in a rather general manner, as a part of a sophisticated philosophical myth, without explicit references to the biblical texts in question. The Gospel of Philip, in turn, contains direct references to Genesis, but it is unlikely that these passages belong to the Valentinian material of the book.

Second, the historical focus of this study is on the formative years of Valentinian tradition—that is, on the last half of the second century. According to recent research, the Nag Hammadi codices, including the Valentinian texts, can be located in the fourth-century monastic context of Upper Egypt.[18] It is far from certain that the hypothetical Greek originals of these writings can be situated earlier than the latter half of the third century. This means that the Valentinian documents of the Nag Hammadi Library represent rather late modifications of the Valentinian tradition, and some of them contain apparent influences of post-Nicaean theology.[19]

---

18. The most convincing theory of the origins of the Nag Hammadi codices is that they were produced in book-exchange networks in monasteries by monks who were interested in philosophically oriented Christian theology. This does not, however, rule out the urban milieu in which the texts were likely originally written. Dating of the Nag Hammadi codices ranges from the fourth century into the fifth and possibly even beyond. For the historical origin of the Nag Hammadi codices, see Hugo Lundhaug and Lance Jenott, *The Monastic Origins of the Nag Hammadi Codices*, STAC 97 (Tübingen: Mohr Siebeck, 2015), 1–11.

19. Hugo Lundhaug argues that the soteriology and Christology of the Gospel of Philip is in harmony with the theology of Cyril of Alexandria and reflects theological tendencies of the fourth and fifth centuries: "The one version of the Gospel of Philip that has come down to us, in Coptic in Nag Hammadi Codex II, should therefore no longer be used as evidence of 'Gnosticism,' or even of 'Valentinianism,' but should rather be understood as a highly poetic—and polemical—expression of Egyptian Christianity at the turn of the fifth century." See Lundhaug, "Begotten, Not Made, to

In the Tripartite Tractate, the influences from Origen are commonly recognized by scholars.[20] Therefore, it is likely that the thematic parallels with Philo may have also come through these theological influences. As Runia notes, most of the fourth-century references to Philo's texts in Christian literature were not adopted by reading Philo himself but from Christian authors such as Origen, who incorporated quotations from Philo into their writings. As noted, parallels with Philo in the Valentinian sources written during the latter part of the second century form a more interesting case concerning a direct dependency on Philo due to the lack of evidence of extensive borrowings from Philo in early Christian literature of the time that could have served as source material for Valentinian authors.

2.2. The Valentinian Source of *Excerpta ex Theodoto* 43.2–65

As noted above, the basis for the comparison with Philo in this study is section C (chapters 43.2–65) of the *Excerpts from Theodotus* by Clement of Alexandria, which is part of so-called book 8 of the *Stromateis*.[21] The

---

Arise in This Flesh: The Post-Nicene Soteriology of the Gospel of Philip," in *Beyond the Gnostic Gospels: Studies Building on the Work of Elaine Pagels*, ed. Eduard Iricinschi et al., STAC 82 (Tübingen: Mohr Siebeck, 2013), 235–71. In this study, the Gospel of Philip is considered a theological anthology deriving from different sources. It is not excluded, however, that at least some sections of the book could go back to the third-century Valentinian traditions. However, the view that the Gospel of Philip as a whole represents Valentinian theology is evidently flawed.

20. Paul Linjamaa claims that the Tripartite Tractate derives from a third-century Alexandrian context, from the milieu of Origen, Clement, and Didymus. See Linjamaa, *The Ethics of the Tripartite Tractate (NHC I, 5): A Study of Determinism and Early Christian Philosophy of Ethics*, NHMS 95 (Leiden: Brill, 2019), 18–38, 265–71. See also Alberto Camplani, "Per la cronologia dei testi valentiniani: il Trattato Tripartito e la crisi Ariana," *Cassiodorus* 1 (1995): 171–95; Jean-Daniel Dubois, "Le Traité Tripartite (Nag Hammadi I, 5) est-il antérieur à Origène?," in Perrone, *Origeniana Octava*, 303–16. Einar Thomassen maintains that the influences from Origen's thought in the Tripartite Tractate indicate that a date in the third century is the most probable. See Thomassen, *Le Traité Tripartite (NH I, 5)*, ed. Louis Painchaud and Einar Thomassen (Québec: Presses de l'Université Laval, 1989), 18–20; Thomassen, *Nag Hammadi Scriptures*, 57–61.

21. Sagnard divides Clement's *Excerpta* into four parts. Section A contains chapters 1–28, B chapters 29–42, C chapters 43.2–65, and D chapters 66–86. François Sagnard, ed. and trans., *Clément d'Alexandrie, Extraits e Théodote, texte grec,*

2. The Valentinian Source in Clement's *Excerpts of Theodotus*   35

closest exegetical parallels with Philo can be detected in this particular Valentinian source. The tentatively listed parallels are as follows:

- the creation of light in Gen 1:3 as the manifestation of the everlasting light (*Opif.* 31);
- the association of biblical Wisdom with precosmic matter (*Ebr.* 31);
- the use of ancient theory of *diakrisis* referring to the separation of precosmic matter (*Her.* 133);
- the creation of Adam's body in Gen 2:7 as a description of the earthly mind (*Leg.* 1.31–32);
- the distinction of Gen 1:26 and 1:27 as referring to the irrational and rational soul of the first human being (*Fug.* 71–72);
- the use of a "metaphysics of prepositions" in the description of the creation of the human soul (*Cher.* 125);
- the garment of skin in Gen 3:21 referring to the fleshly body (*QG* 1.53);
- the threefold division of humankind based on Gen 1:26–27; 2:7 (*Her.* 56–57, *Post.* 78–79);
- the allegory of Cain, Abel, and Seth (*Post.* 124, *Sacr.* 2–3); and
- the allegory of Israel as a spiritual human being who sees God in contrast with Ishmael (*Fug.* 208).

The similarities between Clement's *Exc.* 43.2–65 and Irenaeus's *Haer.* 1.1.–7 are commonly noted by scholars.[22] It is assumed that both accounts represent the so-called Italian school tradition of Valentinianism, which is distinguished from the Eastern school tradition.[23] Although there are evident similarities between Clement's and Irenaeus's accounts of Valen-

---

introduction, traduction et notes (Paris: Cerf, 1948), 28–29. Casey includes also ch. 42 in section C (= 42–65).

22. In addition to Sagnard (*Clément d'Alexandrie, Extraits De Théodote*) and Casey (*Excerpta ex Theodoto*), the connection between *Haer.* 1.1.1–7 and *Exc.* 43.2–65 is noted in following studies: Georg Heinrici, *Die valentinianische Gnosis und die Heilige Schrift* (Berlin: Wiegandt & Grieben, 1871); Paul Ruben, *Clementis Alexandrini Excerpta ex Theodoto* (Leipzig: Teubner, 1892); Otto Dibelius, "Studien zur Geschichte der Valentinianer: Die Excerpta ex Theodoto und Irenäus," *ZNW* (1908): 230–47; Werner Foerster, *Von Valentin zu Heracleon* (Giessen: Töpelmann, 1928); Gilles Quispel, "The Original Doctrine of Valentinus," *Gnostic Studies* 1 (1974): 27–36.

23. The definition of the two school is handled in chapter 3.

tinian theology, there are also some remarkable differences, which are not commonly noted in scholarship. I next present a detailed source-critical investigation of these texts, which forms the basis for my comparison of the texts with Philo's writings.

2.2.1. General Remarks

Clement's so-called book 8 of the *Stromateis* consists of an unfinished beginning, which investigates logical analysis, based on Plato and Aristotle.[24] The beginning of the book is followed by two sections. The title of the first is ἐκ τῶν Θεοδότου καὶ τῆς ἀνατολικῆς καλουμένης διδασκαλίας κατὰ τοὺς οὐαλεντίνου χρόνους ἐπιτομαί ("Excerpts from the Works of Theodotus and the So-Called Oriental Teachings, Contemporary with Valentinus"), and the second is named *Eclogae propheticae*. Even though the chronology of Clement's writings has been a subject of controversy, the consensus is that books 6–7 of the *Stromateis*, together with the unfinished book 8, were written and compiled after his departure from Alexandria at the beginning of the third century, possibly in Caesarea.[25]

It is of note that in the medieval manuscript of the eighth book of the *Stromateis* (Codex Pluteus 5.3), there is a decorated line before the beginning of the *Excerpta ex Theodoto* and *Eclogae propheticae*. A reader of the manuscript might thus think that the superscription "Stromateis 8" (στρωματεὺς ὄγδοος) at the beginning of the book would only cover the first section of the book, and the rest should be treated separately. However, Eusebius's follower Acacius quotes a passage from book 8 that was taken from the *Eclogae propheticae*. This indicates that the Caesarean library held a fourth-century manuscript of the eighth book of the *Stroma-*

---

24. There has been some doubt concerning the authenticity of book 8 because it lacks the name of the author. Christoph Markschies proposes that the assumption that Clement was the author of this text should be reexamined. See Markschies, "Valentinian Gnosticism: Toward Anatomy of the School," in Turner and McGuire, *Nag Hammadi Library after Fifty Years*, 401–38. It is noteworthy that the name of the author does not appear in book 6 or 7, which evidently bear all the marks of Clement as their author. See John Ferguson, *Clement of Alexandria* (New York: Twayne, 1974), 154–61; Ferguson, trans., *Stromateis: Books 1–3*, FC 85 (Washington, DC: Catholic University of America Press, 1991), 3–16.

25. Runia, *Philo in Early Christian Literature*, 144; see also Ferguson, *Clement of Alexandria*, 106–108. Runia's chronology of Clement's works is based on André Méhat, *Études sur les "Stromates" de Clement d'Alexandrie* (Paris: Le Seuil, 1966), 42–54.

teis, which included the fragmentary section as well, or at least the second part of it.²⁶

There have been various attempts to solve the aforementioned problems. According to the standard view, the fragmentary sections are considered Clement's private notes from different sources for his forthcoming book, which his pupils published after his death. Theodor Zahn revised this view and postulated the theory that the *Excerpta ex Theodoto* and *Eclogae propheticae* were excerpts made by somebody else based on Clement's completed book 8, and only the short philosophical introduction belongs to the original version of the book.²⁷ Pierre Nautin finds it implausible that Clement or his disciples would have purposely published Clement's private drafts. Instead, Nautin refers to the papyrus codex discovered in Tura (Egypt) in 1941, which contains the scribe's extracts from Origen's writings at the end of the manuscript. Nautin suggests that the author of book 8 of the *Stromateis* is not Clement but that the material was taken from the original eighth book of the *Stromateis* and the *Hypotyposeis* by the copyist of Clement's original works.²⁸

---

26. On questions concerning the riddle of the eighth book of the *Stromateis* and solutions proposed to them, see Matyáš Havrda, *The So-Called Eighth Stromateus by Clement of Alexandria: Early Christian Reception of Greek Scientific Methodology*, PhA 144 (Leiden: Brill, 2016), 1–24.

27. Theodor von Zahn, *Supplementum Clementinum*, FGNK 3 (Erlangen: Deichert, 1884), 119–21; see also Kovacs, "Clement of Alexandria and Valentinian Exegesis," 187–89.

28. Pierre Nautin, "La fin des Stroemates et les Hypotyposes de Clément d'Alexandrie," *VC* 30 (1976): 268–302. Nautin argues that there is no evidence that the unfinished private notes were published during Clement's time. In fact, keeping notebooks for written works was a common practice in antiquity. Plutarch and Galen composed *memoranda* (τὰ ὑπομνήματα), and Pliny the Younger described how his uncle, Pliny the Elder, made notes and excerpts from books that were read aloud to him. The purpose of a notebook, however, could vary. Private notebooks were made by authors before composing the final version of the book. Notes could also serve as memory aids for lectures, rituals, or magical practices. On some occasions, a notebook contains a description, suggesting that the notes were made from auditory instruction (ἀπὸ φωνῆς). There were also well-edited notebooks, which were used for pedagogical instruction or philosophical contemplation. Clement's *Stromateis* can be regarded as a well-edited notebook, which collects material from various sources. The term τὰ ὑπομνήματα ("memorials") appears in the full title of the books of the *Stromateis*: κατὰ τὴν ἀληθῆ φιλοσοφίαν γνωστικῶν ὑπομνάτων Στρωματεύς. See also Annewies van den Hoek, "Techniques of Quotation in Clement of Alexandria: A View of Ancient

It seems evident, at any rate, that Clement is not the author of the whole book 8 of the *Stromateis*. However, we do not have any reason to doubt that the material in the book does come from Clement. Whether the material is based on Clement's own drafts or excerpted from his finished works is not crucial to this study. As Matyáš Havrda concludes, "Between Clement and Eusebius someone must have decided that these texts together constituted the eighth book of the *Stromateis*. Presumably, when making this decision, he was not thinking of them as mere drafts, rather perhaps supposing that their disorderly character suited the genre of the work as a whole."[29]

It is almost certain that the title of the fragmentary section comes from the excerptor's pen and cannot be used as an unquestionable basis to draw conclusions concerning the date and location of the material in book 8. Geographically, the title indicates that the Valentinian teachings preserved in the *Excerpta ex Theodoto* come from the East—that is, from Syria or Palestine—though the chronological information is clearly misleading.[30] Evidently, some of the source material, especially the passages in 43.2–65, go back to Alexandria, but the geographical location of Theodotus and other Valentinians mentioned by Clement remains uncertain. It seems, then, that the fourth-century excerptor who chose the title of Clement's fragment was not necessarily familiar with the material he was working with.

Clement's excerpts from Theodotus contains a loose collection of teachings that are picked up from various sources. Despite the apparent literal discontinuity of the book, there is a block of Valentinian teaching that forms a distinct unit compared with the other parts of the text. Primarily, the so-called section C of *Excerpta ex Theodoto* (43.2–65) stands

---

Literary Working Methods," *VC* 50 (1996): 238 n. 18. The Gospel of Philip, in the Nag Hammadi Library, can also be defined as a notebook that may have been used for ritual practices. See Martha Turner, *The Gospel of Philip: The Sources and Coherence of an Early Christian Collection*, NHMS 38 (Leiden: Brill, 1996).

29. Havrda, *So-Called Eighth Stromateus*, 23–24.

30. Judith Kovacs is of the opinion that the "oriental school" (τῆς ἀνατολικῆς καλουμένης διδασκαλίας) refers to the area centered in Alexandria ("Clement of Alexandria," 187). Also, Layton locates Theodotus and the Eastern school mostly in Alexandria (*Gnostic Scriptures*, 332–33). In my opinion, however, it is unlikely that a fourth-century excerptor in the Caesarean library would have located Alexandria in the East.

out from the other parts of the text in its literary style and content in the following ways:

1. The group names "hylics" (ὑλικοί), "psychics" (ψυχικοί), and "pneumatics" (πνευματικοί) are only used in 43.2–65, whereas the group designations "the called" (ἡ κλῆσις), "the elect" (ἡ ἐκλογή), "the dispersed seed" (τὸ διαφέρον σπέρμα), and the speculation concerning "the name" (τὸ ὄνομα) are used in other parts of the excerpts.
2. The incoherent and fragmentary structure of *Excerpta ex Theodoto* changes in 43.2–65 to a coherent narrative, proceeding from protology and cosmology to anthropological, soteriological, and eschatological dimensions of the Valentinian myth.
3. Notably missing are Clement's usual critical comments or citation formulas, such as "Theodotus says" (ὥς φησιν ὁ Θεόδοτος), "he says" (φησί) "they say" (φασί), "according to the Valentinians" (κατὰ τοὺς Οὐαλεντινιανούς), "the Valentinians say" (οἱ Οὐαλεντινιανοί λέγουσιν), or "followers of Valentinus say" (οἱ ἀπὸ Οὐαλεντίνου λέγουσιν), which frequently appear in other parts of the text before and after this section.

It is also notable that *Exc.* 43.2–65 interrupts the discussion of the incarnation of the dispersed seed in 41.1–4, which is continued in section 66 with an allegorical interpretation of the words of Jesus in the Gospel of the Egyptians concerning the birth of the previously reckoned seed. The reader could thus easily jump straight from chapter 41 to 66 without perusing *Exc.* 43.2–65. Moreover, if *Exc.* 43.2–65 is left out from Clement's book, it would make more sense to see it as a private notebook, where Clement discusses and comments on the teachings of Theodotus and other Valentinian groups and presents his own teachings. It seems, then, that *Exc.* 43.2–65 forms an independent Valentinian block in the middle of Clement's notes, which is not part of his private notes from the Valentinian source material but represents an independent summary or even an extant copy of the primary source text itself. It is possible that the collection of Clement's excerpts from Theodotus existed originally without *Exc.* 43.2–65, which was only later included in the text of the unfinished book 8, when the whole material was brought together in fourth-century Caesarea. Heretofore, I refer to whole section *Exc.* 43.2–65 as *Excerpta* C.

2.2.2. The Relationship between *Excerpta* C and Irenaeus, *Haer.* 1.1–7

It is evident that Irenaeus's account of Valentinian theology in *Haer.* 1.1–7 was compiled from various Valentinian sources.[31] At the beginning of the work, he claims that he "came across the commentaries of, as they claim, the disciples of Valentinus." Irenaeus calls these people "the disciples of Ptolemy, an offshoot of the Valentinian School" (*Haer.* 1.*praef.*). Parallels between *Haer.* 1.1–7 (or, more precisely, 1.4.5–7) and *Excerpta* C vary from exact word-to-word similarities to more general parallel ideas concerning the Valentinian myth. A synopsis of *Excerpta* C and *Haer.* 1.1–7 is presented at the end of this chapter (see fig. 2.1). The parallel sections of these accounts are indicated in bold. It is notable that Irenaeus's account follows the same thematic sequence as *Excerpta* C but differs whenever he deviated from the chronology of events in *Excerpta* C.

The Valentinian account in *Excerpta* C begins abruptly with a description of the generation of the Savior as an "angel of the Pleroma" and of his descent to suffering Sophia.[32] There are, however, terminological similarities, which indicates that the protological narrative in *Excerpta* C did not differ remarkably from that presented in *Haer.* 1.1–3. It is told in *Exc.* 44.1 that Sophia recognized the Light, who had deserted her, which parallels Sophia's abandonment by the Christ in *Haer.* 1.4.1. In *Exc.* 63.1, the realm of Sophia below the Pleroma, that is, the Fullness, is called the Ogdoad, which is also a technical term in the pleromatology of *Haer.* 1.1–3.

Despite many parallel themes and ideas between *Excerpta* C and *Haer.* 1–7, there are also some crucial differences:

1. Sophia is not called "Achamoth" in *Excerpta* C, as in Irenaeus's account (*Haer.* 1.4.1). Both versions seem to represent, however, a system with "two Sophias."[33]

---

31. See Dunderberg, *Beyond Gnosticism*, 197–201. Thomassen points out that Irenaeus may have also used earlier heresiological works, especially Justin's *Syntagma*, which is now lost. The use of preceding heresiological sources can be assumed especially in *Haer.* 1.11–12, 23–27. See Thomassen, *Spiritual Seed*, 19.

32. According to Casey, section C begins already in *Exc.* 42. The quotation formula φησί appears, however, in *Exc.* 43.1, which means that it may belong to teaching that goes back to Theodotus (see Casey, *Excerpta ex Theodoto*, 22–25). I follow Sagnard, who draws the line of division for section C at *Exc.* 43.2 (*Extraits de Théodote*, 30–31).

33. It is commonly noted that there are two versions of the Sophia myth in Ire-

2. *Excerpta* C does not mention the psychic essence as an outcome of Sophia's conversion. Although *Excerpta* C mentions the psychic essence (e.g., *Exc.* 47.3), there is no explanation of its precosmic origin, as there is in *Haer.* 1.4.1.
3. In *Excerpta* C, the Demiurge is created by Sophia as an image of the Father of All (*Exc.* 47.2–3), but Irenaeus maintains that the Demiurge is an image of the Only Begotten Son (*Haer.* 1.5.1).
4. In *Excerpta* C, the angels are mediators of the seeds but not their archetypes (*Exc.* 53.3). In Irenaeus's account, the seeds of Sophia are created as images of the angels of the Savior (*Haer.* 1.4.5).
5. In *Excerpta* C, the seed is inserted directly into Adam's soul by Sophia (*Exc.* 53.2), whereas in Irenaeus's account Sophia inserts the seed into the Demiurge. Thus, it is the breath of the Demiurge that mediates the spiritual seed to Adam (*Haer.* 1.5.6).
6. Irenaeus's account lacks *all* the biblical evidence taken from Gen 1:1–3 that is mentioned in *Excerpta* C (*Exc.* 47.1–48.1)

---

naeus's book, which are called version A (*Haer.* 1.2.2) and version B (*Haer.* 1.2.3). Version B is also described in Hippolytus's *Haer.* 30.6–9. The main difference between these versions concerns the reason for Sophia's pernicious action. In version A, Sophia wants to comprehend the greatness of the Father, whereas in version B Sophia tries to imitate the Father by making a creation of her own. The difference between these versions is also related to another question: whether the Father of All produces the aeons together with his female consort or whether he is solitary and produces the Pleroma by himself. The outcome of Sophia's action is also different: in version A, it is the personified "intention" or "desire" of Sophia who is expelled from the Pleroma and transformed into the lower Sophia figure, called Achamoth, whereas in version B it is the formless offspring of Sophia who is cast out from the divine realm. The Valentinian myths of Sophia can also be divided into two groups based on the destiny of Sophia herself. There are systems that consist of one Sophia and systems with two Sophia figures. In the former systems, it is Sophia herself who is excluded from the Pleroma and there produces her Son—i.e., Christ. Eventually, the Son of Sophia abandons his mother and ascends to the Pleroma as an adopted Son of the aeons. This view is attested in the Tripartite Tractate; the Valentinian Exposition; *Exc.* 32.3–33.2; *Haer.* 1.11.1. In the latter version, with two Sophias, it is the amorphous offspring of Sophia or her Intention that is expelled from the Pleroma, not Sophia herself. This means that Sophia is split into higher and lower Sophias, which is described in *Haer.* 1.2.2; Hippolytus, *Haer.* 30.6–9; *Exc.* 43.2–65. Thus, versions A and B, described above, are subcategories of the system with two Sophias. See Stead, "Valentinian Myth," 77–78, 84–85; Thomassen, *Spiritual Seed*, 248–61; Dunderberg, *Beyond Gnosticism*, 98–99. For the chronological order and different Christologies of these systems, see Thomassen, "Relative Chronology," 18–25.

7. Sophia is not explicitly identified with biblical Wisdom in Irenaeus's account, as in *Excerpta* C (*Exc.* 47.1)

Thomassen suggests that the apparent differences between *Excerpta* C and *Haer.* 1.1–7 indicate that they are more likely to be based on two independent reworkings of the same Valentinian source, rather than a common source.[34] It seems, however, that at least in some cases, the modifications to the source material were made by Irenaeus himself, detaching some passages from their logical context. For example, the teachings concerning the incarnation and the suffering of the Savior were inserted into the polemical discussion in *Haer.* 1.1.6, which contains material from different sources. Also, the idea of the threefold division of humanity represented by Cain, Abel, and Seth is not handled in the anthropological context, as it is in *Excerpta* C, but at the end of the account of Valentinian theology, in *Haer.* 1.7.5. Moreover, it is unlikely that any Valentinian author would have reworked the source material by deleting all biblical prooftexts related to the allegory of Gen 1:1–3 mentioned in *Excerpta* C. The most credible solution is that it was Irenaeus himself who omitted these biblical references to combine these teachings with material from other sources.

The reworking of the of the original Valentinian source becomes evident in a comparison of *Exc.* 46.1–2 and *Haer.*1.4.5, which describe the separation of the emotions of Sophia and the creation of precosmic matter by the Savior. The parallel terms in these accounts are indicated with a single underline, and the thesis concerning the origin of the psychic essence (missing in *Excerpta* C) is double underlined.

> Πρῶτον οὖν ἐξ ἀσωμάτου πάθους καὶ συμβεβηκότος εἰς ἀσώματον ἔτι τὴν ὕλην αὐτὰ μετήντλησεν καὶ μετέβαλεν· εἶθ' οὕτως εἰς συγκρίματα καὶ σώματα· (ἀθρόως γὰρ οὐσίαν ποιῆσαι τὰ πάθη οὐκ ἐνῆν)· καὶ τοῖς σώμασι κατὰ φύσιν ἐπιτηδειότητα ἐνεποίησεν. Πρῶτος μὲν οὖν Δημιουργὸς ὁ Σωτὴρ γίνεται καθολικός. (*Exc.* 46.1–2)

> ἀλλ' ἀποκρίναντα χωρὶς συγχέαι καὶ πῆξαι, καὶ ἐξ ἀσωμάτου πάθους εἰς ἀσώματον [τὴν] ὕλην μεταβαλεῖν αὐτά· εἶθ' οὕτως ἐπιτηδειότητα καὶ φύσιν ἐμπεποιηκέναι αὐτοῖς, ὥστε εἰς συγκρίματα καὶ σώματα ἐλθεῖν, πρὸς τὸ γενέσθαι δύο οὐσίας, τὴν φαύλην ἐκ τῶν παθῶν, τήν τε ἐκ τῆς

---

34. See Thomassen, *Spiritual Seed*, 62, 82.

ἐπιστροφῆς ἐμπαθῆ· καὶ διὰ τοῦτο δυνάμει τὸν Σωτῆρα δεδημιουργηκέναι φάσκουσι (Irenaeus, *Haer.* 1.4.5)

Although there are minor terminological differences between these passages, the main teaching is the same: the Savior healed the emotions of Sophia by transforming them into unstructured matter. The common terms and the structure of the passage are close enough to argue that Irenaeus's sources were dependent on the teaching attested in *Excerpta* C. Irenaeus's account does, however, contain the theory about the origin of the psychic essence that is based on Sophia's "will to turn back" (ἐπιστροφῆς ἐμπαθῆ), which is lacking in *Excerpta* C. It is unlikely that Irenaeus himself invented the theory of the origin of the psychic essence, which he integrates into the text as part of his description of the Valentinian teaching (see also *Haer.* 1.4.1; 5.1). Although the two essences and the separation of the psychic essence of the hylic matter are also mentioned in *Excerpta* C (see *Exc.* 47.1–3), the psychic essence is not associated with Sophia's will to turn back but is simply presupposed as a luminous essence out of which the Demiurge, Christ, and the angels were made. The most probable explanation for this discrepancy is that the theory of the origin of psychic essence was a later elaboration made by Ptolemy's disciples in Rome.

2.3. Conclusions

According to scholarly consensus, *Exc.* 43.2–65 (= *Excerpta* C) forms a distinct unit in Clement's *Excerpta ex Theodoto*. It stands out from the other parts of the text in its literary style and content. It is also notable that this block of Valentinian teaching does not contain any of Clement's source-critical markers or his comments on Valentinian teaching, which can be noticed elsewhere in the book. We have good reason to believe, therefore, that *Excerpta* C is not simply Clement's paraphrasing of the Valentinian myth, but it is likely a copy of the primary source itself. Presumably, a later redactor of Clement's unfinished book 8 of the *Stromateis* included the text in the middle of Clement's fragments from Theodotus. Thus, *Excerpta* C may contain the oldest-surviving exposition of Valentinian myth and may even predate the account of Valentinian theology that Irenaeus gives in *Haer.* 1.1–7, given that Irenaeus was evidently familiar with a more elaborated version of the same Valentinian source, which goes back to the disciples of Ptolemy in Rome, circa 180 CE. Figure 2.1 illustrates the relation of these sources.

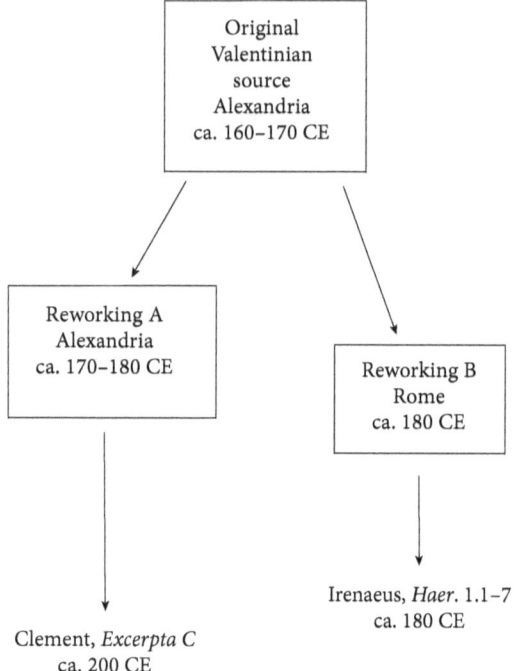

Fig. 2.1. Traditions behind Irenaeus's and Clement's Accounts

Although the title of the *Excerpta ex Theodoto* refers to the Eastern origin of the source material, it is likely that the teachings attested in *Excerpta* C go back to the Valentinian traditions of Alexandria. The other material in Clement's excerpts represents the Eastern school tradition, which Clement possibly became acquainted with during his stay in Palestine or Syria, where he may have met Theodotus and some other Valentinian teachers. Unfortunately, we do not have enough information to confirm the identity of the author of the teachings described in *Excerpta* C. That the disciples of Ptolemy preserved and elaborated the same teachings indicates that it was influential also for the Valentinians in Rome.

Although *Excerpta* C and the parallel sections in Irenaeus, *Haer.* 1.1–7, contain the closest exegetical parallels with Philo, these are not the only Valentinian sources containing similarities with Philo's biblical interpretations. In the next chapter, I will show that Ptolemy's *Letter to Flora* contains a theory concerning the division of the Mosaic law and allegorical interpretations of its cultic commandments that can be found in Philo's writings in the Exposition of the Law. It seems that, as a moderate allegorist, Ptolemy was not interested in speculative interpretations of the transcendental realm, like his disciples were. We can conclude, however, that the Valentinian texts that contain the closest parallels with Philo go back in one way or another to Ptolemy and his disciples in Rome, who continued earlier the Valentinian traditions in Alexandria presented in *Excerpta* C (parallel sections of the Valentinian myth bolded below).

Irenaeus, *Adversus haereses* 1.1–7

1.1–3	The formation of the Pleroma
2.1–6	The fall of Sophia and the generation of Christ and the Holy Spirit
3.1–5	Scriptural speculations by the Valentinians
3.6	Polemical passage
4.1–2	The passions of Achamoth
4.3–4	Polemical passages
4.5	**The descent of the Savior and the creation of matter**
5.1–3	**The Demiurge and his role in creation**
5.4	**The cosmic elements created by the Demiurge**
5.5	**The creation of Adam**
5.6	**The implantation of the spiritual seed by Achamoth**
6.1–4	Polemical passage concerning the soteriology of Valentinians
7.1	**Eschatology**
7.2	**Christology: the psychic Christ and the incarnation, baptism, and suffering of the Savior**
7.3–4	The prophetic revelation in the Scriptures according to the Valentinians
7.5	**The threefold division of humans, allegorized by Cain, Abel, and Seth**

Excerpta C (= 43.2–65)

(The protological section is missing.)

43.2–46	**The descent of the Savior and the creation of matter**
47	**The Demiurge and his role in creation; the formation of the psychic Christ**
48–49	**The cosmic elements created by the Demiurge;** the allegory of Gen 1:1–3
50–53.1	**The creation of Adam;** the allegory of the separation of the sexes

53.2–5	The implantation of the spiritual seed by Sophia
54–57	The threefold division of humanity; allegory of Cain, Abel, and Seth; allegory of Israel
58–61.2	The incarnation and psychic body of the Savior
61.3–62	The passion and the resurrection of the Savior
63	Eschatology and the heavenly wedding feast

3
The Foundations of Allegorical Interpretation in Philo and among the Valentinians

In this chapter, I locate the formation of the school of Valentinus in its religious-historical context, in the aftermath of the Jewish revolt in 115–117 CE in Alexandria. Valentinus was influential in mid-second-century Alexandria, where he founded his school. In *Haer.* 1.11.1, Irenaeus reports that Valentinus adopted the principles of his teachings from the so-called gnostic school of thought (γνωστικὴ αἵρεσις). He complains that "a multitude of Gnostics have sprung up and shot out of the ground like mushrooms" and that their teachings deviated from the rule of faith of the apostolic church (*Haer.* 1.29.1 [Unger]).[1] In this study, I will argue that the Valentinian teachers reformed and refined preceding gnostic traditions in light of the Hellenistic Jewish allegories attested in the works of Philo. The Valentinian allegorical interpretation differed from the Sethian gnostic *mythopoiēsis* in that it was based more closely on biblical texts, which they gave a philosophically articulated meaning. As Pearson points out, the Sethian gnostic myth, on the other hand, was "constructed with an attitude of absolute sovereignty over the biblical text, to the point of explicitly refuting it."[2] Philo and the Valentinian teachers were also proponents of multiple exegesis, meaning that the text in question ought to be presented differently depending on the audience. It seems that in an initial stage of the school, the study groups around Valentinian teachers were comparable with the schools of popular philosophers; the Valentinian school later became more like a church movement, with specific cultic observances.

---

1. For Irenaeus's defense of the faith of the apostolic teaching, see *Haer.* 1.10.1–3.
2. Pearson, "Philo and Gnosticism," 338.

3.1. The School of Philo and the Jewish Revolt in Egypt

The famous library and the museum in Alexandria offered an inspiring atmosphere for scholarship and science. In the second century BCE, Aristophanes of Byzantium produced the first critical edition of Plato's works, and Aristarchus of Samothrace (216–144 BCE), head of the Alexandrian library, wrote text-critical and philological commentaries on the Homeric epic. First-century Alexandria provided an urban setting for the revival of Pythagoreanism and the formation of various Middle Platonic school traditions. These intellectual influences also shaped the mindset of Philo as a commentator of the Bible.[3]

The social setting of Philo's scholarly activity, on the other hand, is less than clear. There are elements in Philo's writings that connect Philo's presentation of the philosophy of Moses with Greek notions of *hairesis* in the sense of philosophical persuasion. In some cases, however, Philo seems to evaluate philosophical *haireseis* negatively. In *Mos.* 1.21–29, Philo describes how Moses differed from the quarrelling "sectarians" (αἱρεσιομάχοι), who put forward conflicting philosophical assumptions, whereas Moses taught the truth. Although Philo calls himself in *Det.* 86 a "disciple" (γνώριμος) of Moses and speaks about Moses as a founder of a philosophical way of life, he seems to see Moses as the founder of a nation, a "commonwealth" (πολιτεία), rather than a leader of a philosophical school (see *Spec.* 1.59–63).[4] In addition, Philo was convinced that the philosophical doctrine of Moses superseded teachings presented in other philosophical schools and their doctrinal divisions. The school of Moses was not only a philosophical *hairesis* but something better, because the law of Moses was the truest reflection of the Logos and an exact representation of the natural law (see *Opif.* 1–3).[5]

It is notable that Philo never uses the terms σχολή or διατριβή to refer to his "school." However, in *Opif.* 128, he does use the verb σχολάζειν to denote philosophical investigations during the Sabbath (see also *Decal.* 98). In *Mos.* 2.211–216, Philo says that the order for the Sabbath

---

3. See Niehoff, *Philo of Alexandria*, 26–27, 182–83.

4. It is also possible that Philo used terminological expressions related to the *hairesis* model for apologetic reasons, to gain a wider audience for his writings. For Philo's use of the *hairesis* model, see David Runia, "Philo of Alexandria and the Greek *Hairesis*-Model," *VC* 53 (1999): 117–47.

5. See David Winston, "Philo's Ethical Theory," *ANRW* 21.1:381–88.

rest is based on the "laws of nature" (θεσμοί φύσεως) and uses the term διδασκαλεῖον in the sense of a school of wisdom, where the Scriptures are studied on the seventh day.[6] Although the most natural context for Philo's teaching would have been the synagogue, it is difficult to imagine how Philo's rather complicated allegorical teachings could have functioned in that kind of public context.[7] Thus, the most probable social setting for Philo would have been a private school in his own home or a personally owned structure for advanced students capable of extended philosophical expositions of the Bible. Philo's writings can be seen as a part of a pedagogical curriculum for students of biblical philosophy: the *Quaestiones et Solutiones in Genesin et in Exodum* for beginners, the Allegorical Commentary for advanced students, and the Exposition of the Law for a wider audience, both Jews and non-Jews, who had taken "a journey to a better home, from idle fables to the clear vision of truth" (*Spec.* 1.49).[8]

---

6. In *Spec.* 1.345, Philo calls the followers of Moses "scholars and disciples" (φοιτηταὶ καὶ γνώριμοι; see Sterling, "School of Sacred Laws," 154–58).

7. For an argument that the synagogue was the setting of Philo's school, see R. Alan Culpepper, *The Johannine School*, SBLDS 26 (Missoula, MT: Scholars Press, 1975), 212–14; Harry Wolfson, *Philo: Foundations of Religious Philosophy in Judaism, Christianity, and Islam* (Cambridge: Harvard University Press, 1948), 1:79. Erwin Goodenough argues that Judaism in Alexandria had been organized long before Philo as a mystery cult. See Goodenough, *By Light, Light: The Mystic Gospel of Hellenistic Judaism* (New Haven: Yale University Press, 1935), 1–10. Kåre Fuglseth suggests that Philo's school was not a sect or cult but an institution that functioned within the Jewish *politeuma*. See Fuglseth, *Johannine Sectarianism in Perspective: A Sociological, Historical and Comparative Analysis of Temple and Social Relationships in the Gospel of John, Philo and Qumran*, NovTSup 119 (Leiden: Brill, 2005), 363–64.

8. See Sterling, "School of Sacred Laws," 160–64; Gregory Sterling, "The School of Moses in Alexandria: An Attempt to Reconstruct the School of Philo," in *Second Temple Jewish "Paideia" in Context*, ed. Jason Zurawski and Gabriele Boccaccini, BZNW 228 (Berlin: de Gruyter, 2017), 141–66; Sterling, "Philo's School: The Social Setting of Ancient Commentaries," in *Sophisten in Hellenismus und Kaiserzeit: Orte, Methoden und Personen der Bildungvermittlung*, ed. Beatrice Wyss, Rainer Hirsch-Luipold, and Solmeng-Jonas Hirschi, STAC 101 (Tübingen: Mohr Siebeck, 2017), 123–42. Maren Niehoff argues that Philo's role as the head of the Jewish embassy to Rome in 38 CE had a remarkable impact on his scholarly activity. In Rome, Philo acted as a Jewish diplomat who tried to convince his Greek opponents that the Mosaic law introduced a philosophical way of life sharing in the ethical principles of the Greco-Roman world. Niehoff argues that unlike the highly esoteric and transcendental writings in the Allegorical Commentary, the texts Philo composed following his visit to Rome in 38–41

For Philo, the ideal social setting for the study of the law of Moses was the esoteric community of the Therapeutae, who lived on the shores of Lake Mareotis.⁹ In *Contempl.* 28–30, Philo describes sages who are totally devoted to "spiritual exercise" (ἄσκησις)—that is, "philosophizing" (φιλοσοφεῖν) and interpreting allegorically the ancestral "philosophy" (φιλοσοφία) of the Scriptures. The community used "memorials" (μνημεῖα), or allegorical notebooks, that had been written by the founders of their "school of thought" (αἵρεσις). The Therapeutae considered the law of Moses to be a living organism. While the literal meaning parallels the body, the spiritual meaning of the text is its soul:

> The exposition of the sacred scriptures treats the inner meaning conveyed in allegory. For to these people the whole law book seems to resemble a living creature with the literal ordinances for its body and for its soul the invisible mind laid up in its wording. It is in this mind especially that the rational soul begins to contemplate the things akin to itself and looking through the words as through a mirror beholds the marvellous beauties of the concepts, unfolds and removes the symbolic coverings and brings forth the thoughts and sets them bare to the light of day for those who need but a little reminding to enable them to discern the inward and hidden through the outward and visible. (*Contempl.* 78)¹⁰

The philosophical allegorists received spiritual visions as they studied the written text. Philo condemned, however, the extreme allegorists, who abandoned the literal level altogether, being like "bodiless souls":

> There are some who, regarding laws in their literal sense in the light of symbols of matters belonging to the intellect, are extremely accurate [ἄγαν ἠκρίβωσαν] about the latter, while treating the former with easy-

---

CE were directed to the non-Jews interested in the Jewish way of life (see *Philo of Alexandria*, 160–64, 176).

9. Some modern scholars suggest that Philo's Therapeutae was purely fictious community, a utopian fantasy. See Troels Engberg-Pedersen, "Philo's *De Vita Contemplativa* as a Philosopher's Dream," *JSJ* 30 (1999): 40–64. Although Philo presented Therapeutae idealistically, there is no reason, in my opinion, to suggest that it was purely fictious.

10. David Winston points out that Philo must have been influenced by Plato's *Phaedr.* 264c, where Socrates says that "every discourse must be organized as a living being." See David Winston, *Philo of Alexandria: The Contemplative Life, The Giants, and Selections* (New York: Paulist Press, 1981), 321.

going neglect. Such people I for my part should blame for handling the matter in too easy and off-hand a manner: they ought to have given careful attention to both aims, to a more full and exact investigation of what is not seen and in what is seen to be stewards without reproach. As it is, as though they were living alone by themselves in a wilderness, or as though they had become disembodied souls [ἀσώματοι ψυχαὶ γεγονότες], and knew neither city nor village nor household nor any company of humans at all, overlooking all that many regard, they explore reality in its naked absoluteness. (*Migr.* 89–90, modified)

It is not easy to explicate the difference between Philo's allegorical method and the extremism of other allegorists. It seems that the allegorical radicals neglected any literal interpretation of the Bible, which was relevant for Jewish communal living. The biblical text, then, functioned solely as a tool for individual and spiritual revelation. Philo may have owed much to the allegorical inventions of pure allegorists, but this did not lead to a separation from Jewish religious observances and rejecting Jewish ethnic identity.

Although Philo's school can be seen as a part Greco-Roman philosophical milieu, his apologetic works (*In Flaccum* and *Legatio ad Gaium*) inform us about tensions among the Jewish and Greek population of Alexandria and the harsh anti-Jewish attitudes of Roman authorities. These tensions and the Jewish War in Palestine in 66–73 CE formed the religious and political background for the Jewish uprising in Egypt in 115–117 CE, which had a remarkable effect on the social and religious milieu of Alexandria.[11] During the revolt, the Jewish community of Alexandria was practically destroyed, and it was only toward the end of the third century

---

11. The events of the Jewish revolt in Egypt are documented in various sources. The most extensive report is attested by church historian Eusebius of Caesarea (*Hist. eccl.* 4.2.1–2). Dio Cassius (*Hist. rom.*, epitome of 68.32.1–2) and Appian of Alexandria (*Bell. civ.* 2.90.380 and frag. 19) also preserved some descriptions of the revolt. For scholarly descriptions of the revolt, see Josef Modrzejevski, *The Jews of Egypt from Rameses II to Emperor Hadrian* (Edinburgh: T&T Clark, 1995), 207–25; Viktor Tcherikover, "The Decline of the Jewish Diaspora in Egypt in the Roman Period," *JJS* 14 (1963): 1–32; Peder Borgen, "Judaism in Egypt," in *Early Christianity and Hellenistic Judaism*, ed. Borgen (Edinburgh: T&T Clark, 1996), 93–94; Carl B. Smith, *No Longer Jews: The Search for Gnostic Origins* (Peabody, MA: Hendrickson, 2004), 72–112; William Horbury, *Jewish War under Trajan and Hadrian* (Cambridge: Cambridge University Press, 2014), 209–22.

that the Jewish community began to recover.¹² The devastation to the city itself was also immense. Several papyri state that Hadrian had to launch a rebuilding program and reconstruct Alexandria, as it had been demolished by the Jews."¹³ Josef Modrzejevski summarizes the effects of the revolt on the Egyptian Jewry as follows:

> Under these conditions, the Jewish community in Egypt had practically no chance of recovery. The rare survivors, stunned by the harsh verdict of imperial justice, had become totally impoverished. Deprived of their homes and their lands, they could no longer form a nucleus for a possible reconstruction. The accounts of Roman provincial administration in Egypt throw a cold light on the tragic balance sheet of the revolt. In Alexandria and all the rest of the country, the days of Hellenized Jewry had come to an end.¹⁴

It is commonly assumed that after the revolt the traditions of Hellenistic Judaism continued in the gentile Christian communities of Alexandria.¹⁵

---

12. Christopher Haas, *Alexandria in Late Antiquity: Topography and Social Conflict* (Baltimore: Johns Hopkins University Press, 1997), 99–109. Nevertheless, it is possible that a small number of Jews were able to remain in the city. Thus, the revolt did not lead to the absolute extinction of the Jews. It is mentioned in a fifth-century Christian letter that the Jews "had inhabited the city from the time of Alexander of Macedon." See William Horbury, "Jewish Egypt in the Light of the Risings under Trajan," in *Israel in Egypt: The Land of Egypt as Concept and Reality for Jews in Antiquity and the Early Medieval Period*, ed. Alison Salvesen, Sarah Pearce, and Miriam Frenkel, AJEC 110 (Leiden: Brill, 2020), 347–66; Horbury, *Jewish War*, 228, 233–34, 270–73.

13. Hadrian's rebuilding program is attested in several papyri (P.Oxy. 7.1045; BGU 4.1084; SB 3.7239, 5.7561) and in the Syriac *Notitia urbis Alexandrinae*. There is also an inscription found in one of the bathhouses of Cyrene commemorating how the city was rebuilt after the *tumulto Iudaico*. It is possible that a quarter in Alexandria that was built after the revolt around a temple dedicated to an imperial cult (an inscription dated to 170 CE) can be located in the same place in northeast Alexandria where the Jews were supposed to have lived before the revolt. See Haas, *Alexandria in Late Antiquity*, 407–8n32; Alon Gedaliah, *The Jews in Their Land in the Talmudic Age: 70–640 C.E.* (Cambridge: Harvard University Press, 1989), 382–404.

14. Modrzejevski, *Jews of Egypt*, 222. Several papyri evidence the confiscation of the land and property owned by the Jews according to the Roman law of *confiscatio bonorum* (214–22).

15. Roeloef van den Broek, "Juden und Christen in Alexandrien im 2. und 3. Jahrhundert," in *Juden und Christen in der Antike*, ed. Jacobus van Amersfoort and

3. Allegorical Interpretation in Philo and among the Valentinians 53

The repression of Alexandrian Jewry also formed an arena for innovative early Christian intellectuals, who had learned the skill of theologizing and allegorizing of the sacred Scriptures from their Jewish forerunners.[16] It is also rather likely that Philo's library had ended up in the hands of Christian students of Philo already before the revolt.[17]

Although we lack exact information concerning the earliest phases of Alexandrian Christianity, it seems that, at the beginning of the second century, the theology of Paul and the Gospel of John was combined with Platonizing Judaism and Middle Platonic metaphysics, paving the way for a predominantly gnostic type of Christianity.[18] It is an oversimplification,

---

Johannes van Oort (Kampen: Kok, 1990), 108–11. See also King, *Secret Revelation*, 9–17.

16. On the relationship between the Jewish revolt and the origin of Gnosticism, see Smith, *No Longer Jews*, 244–52. Smith argues that Judaism, Christianity, and Platonism—in that order—were all needed for the generation of Gnosticism. Smith argues that the crucial point for the birth of Gnosticism was the disappointment of the Jews after their messianic expectations had failed. It is unlikely, in my opinion, that the disappointment of the Jews would have been the big bang of gnostic thought. The first gnostics were educated—and, quite likely, privileged—Christian Platonists who learned the skill of theology from the Hellenistic Jewish Platonists.

17. I will handle this issue more thoroughly in the conclusion of my work.

18. The consensus is that the traditions of early Christianity were brought to Alexandria by the Jewish missionaries from Jerusalem before the Pauline mission reached the region. In Acts 11, some of the first missionaries traveled to Phoenicia, Cyprus, and Antioch, spreading the gospel among the Jews and Greek-speaking gentiles. The Apollos episode in Acts 18:24–27 indicates that the earliest form of Christianity in Alexandria was not wholly compatible with the Pauline theology. Apollos, who was probably educated in his hometown in Alexandria, knew initially only about the way of the Lord, being taught more fully in Ephesus by the Pauline missionaries. See Charles Wilfred Griggs, *Early Egyptian Christianity: From Its Origins to 451 CE* (Leiden: Brill, 1990), 16–17. Eusebius reports that the ascetic community of the Therapeutae mentioned by Philo consisted of proto-orthodox Christian monks converted by the apostle Mark. Although this information is evidently not authentic, it may contain some information about the earliest Christian communities in Alexandria, who lived a contemplative life similar to that of the Jewish philosophers mentioned by Philo in *De vita contemplativa*. See Eusebius, *Hist. eccl.* 2.16, 24; 3.14, 21; 5.9; Robert Grant, "Theological Education in Alexandria," in *The Roots of Egyptian Christianity*, ed. Birger A. Pearson and James E. Goehring, SAC (Philadelphia: Fortress, 1986), 180. It is possible that some of the literary traditions of the earliest non-Pauline communities were preserved in such documents as the Gospel of the Hebrews, the Gospel of the Egyptians, and the Gospel of Thomas. See Helmut Koester, *History and Literature of*

however, to suppose that the development of second-century Christianity in Alexandria was solely gnostic in character.[19] The Epistle of Barnabas, which can be located in second-century Alexandria, continued the Jewish apocalyptic tendencies and reflects the existence of other Christian groups—not only Platonizing gnostics but ascetically oriented Christians as well.[20] Although Barnabas's letter contains harsh anti-Jewish polemics, it is notable that the author was thoroughly acquainted with Hellenistic Jewish exegetical traditions and their method of allegorizing.[21] Hence, Alexandrian Christianity was not purely gnostic but was rather attested a great variety of Jewish and Jewish Christian traditions that continued to be practiced by the gentile Christian communities of Alexandria.[22]

It is assumed, however, that gnostic Christians dominated the intellectual life in Alexandria after the revolt in 115–117 CE. The gnostic traditions spread from Alexandria also to other regions of the empire, which led to harsh attacks from the prominent teachers of the nascent orthodoxy. Irenaeus wrote his multivolume book attacking gnostic heresies, but the main target of his criticism was the school of Valentinus. Irenaeus's book also circulated in Alexandria, which implies that the heresy hunting of the nascent orthodoxy was not restricted merely to Rome but spread to Alexandria as well.[23] At the end of the second century, the Catechetical School was founded in Alexandria, and Demetrius was nominated bishop

---

Early Christianity, vol. 2 of *Introduction to the New Testament* (New York: de Gruyter, 2000), 228–29; Griggs, *Early Egyptian Christianity*, 29–32).

19. Walter Bauer assumed that the earliest Christianity in Egypt was "gnostic" in character and was formed in opposition to the nascent orthodoxy. See Bauer, *Orthodoxy and Heresy in Earliest Christianity*, trans. and ed. Robert A. Kraft and Gerhard Krodel (Philadelphia: Fortress, 1971), 44–60. Evidently Bauer's view exaggerates the influence of the gnostic tradition on second-century Alexandrian Christianity.

20. For the date and place of Barnabas's letter, see Runia, *Philo in Early Christian Literature*, 90–91.

21. Runia, *Philo in Early Christian Literature*, 90–93; see also Koester, *History and Literature*, 280–82.

22. See Birger Pearson, "Earliest Christianity in Egypt: Further Observations," in *The World of Early Egyptian Christianity: Language, Literature, and Social Context; Essays in Honor of David W. Johnson*, ed. James E. Goehring and Janet A. Timbie (Washington, DC: Catholic University of America Press, 2007), 120–21.

23. P.Oxy. 405 (dated ca. 200 CE, Egypt) contains a part of the Greek text of Irenaeus's *Adversus Haereses*. Colin H. Roberts considers this to be "evidence of the immediate circulation of Irenaeus' attack on Gnosticism among the Egyptian churches and yet another witness to the close relationship subsisting between the Church of

of Alexandria, helping to centralize church organization in Egypt and suppress the preceding gnostic school traditions.

3.2. The Founding of the School of Valentinus

Valentinus may have been born around 100–110 CE. His birthplace is based on the rumors heard by Epiphanius, according to which Valentinus was born in the Egyptian Delta, at Phrebonis. Valentinus received a Greek education in the metropolis of Alexandria (*Pan.* 31.2.2–3), where he may also have converted to Christianity. Clement of Alexandria tells us that Valentinus was a pupil of a Christian teacher called Theudas, who had himself been the disciple (γνώριμος) of Paul (*Strom.* 7.106.4). Although the historicity of Theudas is questionable, it is possible that he came to Alexandria from Corinth or Ephesus, where he became familiar with Pauline Christianity. In the Valentinian sources, the apostle Paul represents a sort of supersage, similar to Moses in Philo's writings: Paul is simply called "the Apostle," or the apostle working "in the fashion as the Paraclete" (ἐν τύπῳ δὲ Παρακλήτου; see, e.g., *Exc.* 22.1, 23.3–4). Valentinians considered Paul as a chosen instrument for the Holy Spirit, and his mission was related to the mythological drama in the supra-cosmic realm. As Jesus had been sent from the Pleroma to help the fallen Sophia, so was Paul the advocate for Sophia's offspring in the world. This was thought to explain the reference in Col 1:24, according to which Paul must fill up "the remainder of Christ's suffering."[24]

Irenaeus reports that Valentinus came to Rome during the time of Bishop Hyginus, and he remained in the city until the time of Anictetus (*Haer.* 3.4.3). Tertullian situates Valentinus's stay in Rome during the reign of Antonius Pius (*Praescr.* 30.2).[25] Thomassen concludes that the activity of Valentinus in Rome falls between the years 140 and 160 CE and

---

Alexandria and the West." See Roberts, "Early Christianity in Egypt: Three Notes," *JEA* 40 (1954): 94; Griggs, *Early Egyptian Christianity*, 33.

24. See Ismo Dunderberg, "Paul and the Valentinian Morality," in Markschies and Thomassen, *Valentinianism: New Studies*, 438–41. Paul's mythological role is attested in the Revelation of Paul (NHC V 2) and the Prayer of the Apostle Paul (NHC I 1), but it is not absolutely clear whether these writings of the Nag Hammadi codices can be considered purely Valentinian.

25. Thomassen, *Spritual Seed*, 417–18. See also Ismo Dunderberg, "The Valentinian Teachers in Rome," in *Christians as a Religious Minority in a Multicultural City*, ed. Jürgen Zangenberg and Michael Labahn (London: T&T Clark, 2004), 157–59.

that he must have already been in Rome when Justin mentioned Valentinians in his list of heresies (see *Dial.* 35.6).[26] Epiphanius reports in *Pan.* 7.1-2 that Valentinus preached first in Alexandria before coming to Rome, which would mean that he founded his school in Alexandria not long after the end of the Jewish revolt. It is rather likely that Valentinus also knew Basilides, who was another Christian philosopher in Alexandria before Valentinus's activity.[27]

Valentinus acquired gifted disciples in Rome, whose teachings are reported by the patristic authors.[28] One of the most prominent of the Valentinian teachers was Ptolemy, who represented the so-called Italian school of Valentinianism (Hippolytus, *Haer.* 6.35.6). Irenaeus became acquainted with the teachings of Ptolemy's disciples in Rome, which formed the basis for his description of the Valentinian model system (*Haer.* 1.praef.1-7). Another famous Valentinian was Heracleon, but, contrary to Hippolytus's report, he can more likely be located in Alexandria, since Origen knew of his commentary on the Gospel of John during his career in Alexandria. It is

---

26. Thomassen points out that Justin's reaction was not based on the authority of ecclesiastical officials but more likely stemmed from his personal opinion, as there was not yet any centralized church organization in Rome during the time of Valentinus's activity. See Einar Thomassen, "Orthodoxy and Heresy in Second-Century Rome," *HTR* 97 (2004): 241-56; Dunderberg, "Valentinian Teachers in Rome," 168-69; Thomassen, *Spiritual Seed*, 421.

27. Brakke and Layton, *Gnostic Scriptures*, 607-9. Basilides's system is attested in Irenaeus, *Haer.* 1.24.3-7. Fragments of Basilides's teaching are also found in the writings of Clement of Alexandria and Origen.

28. The Valentinian movement expanded quite rapidly to the eastern part of the empire and to western Gaul, where Irenaeus had his first contacts with some Valentinian teachers. Tertullian mentions Axionicus as a follower of Valentinus and places him in Antioch (*Val.* 4:3; see also Hippolytus, *Haer.* 6.35.7). In the list of heresies of Ephrem Syrus (22.2), the "Quqites" are chronologically placed after the Valentinians, which means that the Valentinians had reached Syria by the end of the second century. Jacob of Edessa also says that the Quqites proceeded from the Valentinians. In some Syrian sources, Valentinus is considered the spiritual father of Bardesanes (ca. 154-223 CE). The influence of Valentinus on Bardesanes is also mentioned by Eusebius (*Hist. eccl.* 6.30:3), who claims that Bardesanes began as a Valentinian but later condemned the Valentinians. There is only one existing work of Bardesanes, which, however, contains nothing distinctly Valentinian, as Thomassen points out (*Spiritual Seed*, 503). It is plausible that the Valentinian movement had reached the eastern part of Syria by the beginning of the third century. See Han J. W. Drijvers, "Quq and the Quqites," in *East of Antioch: Studies in Early Syriac Christianity*, ed. Drijvers (London: Variorum Reprints, 1984), 108-11.

3. Allegorical Interpretation in Philo and among the Valentinians 57

possible, however, that, at some point Heracleon also taught in Rome, or at least he was known as a prominent Valentinian teacher among the Roman Valentinians.²⁹ Alexandria remained a dominant center of the Valentinian school, even though the school expanded to the eastern and western parts of the Roman Empire. Most fragments of Valentinus's teachings are preserved in the writings of Clement of Alexandria. It is also possible that Valentinus went back to his home city after he left Rome.³⁰

3.2.1. The Social Setting of the School of Valentinus

Irenaeus mentions in *Haer.* 1.11.1 that Valentinus approved of the principles of the "gnostic heresy" (γνωστικὴ αἵρεσις) and founded his own school (διδασκαλεῖον). It is not clear, however, whether the term *gnostic* was ever used as a designation of a school of thought by the disciples of Valentinus themselves or whether it was used as a pejorative by the church fathers and professional philosophers to designate the group of Christian Platonists. The term *hairesis*, however, had had a long history as an unstigmatized designation for a philosophical school of thought.

John Glucker argues in his study *Antiochus and the Late Academy* that, from the second century BCE onward, the term αἵρεσις referred to philosophical schools of thought or persuasion. The technical terms for institutionalized philosophical schools were σχολή, διατριβή, or διδασκαλεῖον, whereas the term αἵρεσις denoted a school of thought in a more abstract and general manner. The difference between αἵρεσις and

---

29. See Dunderberg, "Valentinian Teachers in Rome," 158–59, 163. Thomassen locates Heracleon in Rome. See Einar Thomassen, "Heracleon," in *Legacy of John: Second-Century Reception of the Fourth Gospel*, NovTSup 132 (Leiden: Brill, 2010), 174. One of Origen's patrons, Ambrose, a former Valentinian gnostic in Alexandria, may have recommended Heracleon's commentaries to Origen. Eusebius says in *Hist. eccl.* 6.14.10 that Origen made a short visit to Rome during the papacy of Zephyrinus. It is thus possible that Origen got to know Heracleon's writings during his stay in Rome. See Thomassen, *Spiritual Seed*, 495; Ansgar Wucherpfennig, *Heracleon Philologus: Gnostische Johannesexegese im zweiten Jahrhundert*, WUNT 142 (Tübingen: Mohr Siebeck, 2001), 370.

30. See Dunderberg, "Valentinian Teachers in Rome," 160. Epiphanius reports that Valentinus finally left Rome, traveled to Cyprus, and there went mad (*Pan.* 31.7.2). Although this information lacks historical reliability, it is not far-fetched to think that Valentinus left Rome at some point in his career and possibly returned to his home country.

σχολή is thus that αἵρεσις designates philosophical *opinions* or doctrines held by some group of people, whereas σχολή is a locally institutionalized philosophical *association* with an identifiable membership.³¹ Neoplatonic philosopher Elias wrote in his commentary on Aristotle's *Categoriae* that αἵρεσις is "the opinion of educated men, agreeing among themselves and disagreeing with others."³² For example, the four great Hellenistic schools (Platonic, Peripatetic, Stoic, and Epicurean) represented *haireseis*, and there were many sub-*haireseis* in these schools of thought that originated from divisions in opinion.

Runia lists some characteristics of Greco-Roman *haireseis*. First, there was in each *hairesis* a "father of the school" (πατὴρ τοῦ λόγου). Second, the *haireseis* had a body of distinctive "doctrines" (δόγματα) attributed to their founder. Third, *haireseis* were concentrated on conducting creative exegeses of their founder's writings. Fourth, each *hairesis* had its "succession" (διαδοχή) of teachers, whose authority went back to the beginning of the movement. Fifth, the membership in each *hairesis* was based on loyalty or

---

31. John Glucker, *Antiochus and the Late Academy* (Göttingen: Vandenhoeck & Ruprecht, 1978), 174–92, esp. 181–82. In addition to the classical philosophical *haireseis*, the term *hairesis* was also related to other ancient associations as well—e.g., to the ancient medical schools. The institutionalization of the Alexandrian medical *hairesis* of Herophilus happened some 250 years after the founding of the *hairesis*, when it started then to be called διδασκαλεῖον. See Heinrich von Staden, "Hairesis and Heresy: The Case of the *haireseis iatrikai*," in *Self-Definition in the Greco-Roman World*, vol. 3 of *Jewish and Christian Self-Definition*, ed. Ben E. Myer and Ed P. Sanders (London: SCM, 1982), 76–100. Layton has argued that the term *hairesis* "primarily denotes a *member* of a distinct social group or professional school of thought, not a kind of doctrine.... Their literary artifacts can be called Gnostic only in a secondary way, by reference to the name of the ancient group" ("Prolegomena to the Study of Ancient Gnosticism," 334–50). In fact, according to Glucker's analysis, the situation is just the opposite: the term *hairesis* denotes, in the first place, a doctrine or a doctrinal identity, not a socially identifiable group of people, and only secondarily designates group identity. In the context of the second-century intellectual milieu, the term *hairesis* is always understood as a designation for a certain opinion, without any qualification of group identity. This means that a person might have been called as a representative of the Platonic *hairesis* without being a member of any Platonic school.

32. Cited in Glucker, *Antiochus*, 181. Glucker suggests that the definition of *hairesis* presented by Elias goes back to Proclus. Philo of Alexandria defines the practitioners of *haireseis* in a strikingly similar manner in a fragment of *Quaestiones in Exodum*: "Here is clear proof, namely the disagreements and discords and doctrinal difference of the practitioners of each *hairesis* who refute each other and are refuted in turn" (trans. Runia, "Philo of Alexandria and the Greek *Hairesis*-Model," 126).

3. Allegorical Interpretation in Philo and among the Valentinians

affiliation. That is, membership in a *hairesis* involved a publicly recognized commitment to a particular school of thought.[33]

The Greek *hairesis*-model was also adopted to describe the Hellenistic Jewish traditions. Josephus describes the Pharisees, the Sadducees, and the Essenes as representing the three "philosophies" (φιλοσοφίαι) of Judaism. He compares the Pharisees with the Stoics and the Essenes with the Pythagoreans. The Jewish group led by Judas the Galilean was not, according to Josephus, a *hairesis* in any real sense, because Judas was not a philosopher but a sophist who started a *hairesis* of his own. Although Josephus says that he had himself joined the Pharisees, this does not necessarily mean that he joined the institutionalized group of the Pharisees but rather that he may have shared certain Pharisaic doctrines (*B.J.* 2.119–162; *A.J.* 13.171–173; 18.11–22; *Vita* 12).[34] It is likely that Josephus used the Greek *hairesis* model for apologetic reasons, to make the Jewish traditions more familiar to his Roman audience.

In New Testament writings, the word *hairesis* is used both as a neutral designation of an opinion and pejoratively as a synonym for a false belief. Luke mentions the *haireseis* of the Nazarenes, Sadducees, and Pharisees as three belief systems or sects within Judaism (see Acts 5:17; 15:5; 24:5, 14; 28:22). In Acts 25:5, Paul testifies that as a Pharisee he has lived "according to strictest persuasion" (κατὰ τὴν ἀκριβεστάτην αἵρεσιν) of Judaism (see Acts 26:5; also Phil 3:5–6). In Paul's letter to the Corinthians, the term *hairesis* refers dismissively to a divergent opinion—namely, there must be different "opinions" within the Christian congregation, since the faithfulness of believers is tested by them (1 Cor 11:19).[35] Although Paul did not restrict the meaning of the term *hairesis* solely to false teaching, in the Pastoral Epistles *hairesis* is used pejoratively as group designation for "false teachers" (ψευδοδιδάσκαλοι) or "erroneous human beings" (αἱρετικοὶ ἄνθρωποι; see 2 Pet 2:1, Titus 3:10).

According to Glucker's analysis, the shift from the *hairesis* model to the school model meant a shift from the level of abstract opinions to that of an institutionalized and localized school setting. While "gnostic *hairesis*" referred to a philosophical school of thought, a distinct gnostic school represented a socially identifiable group of members. Clement of Alexan-

---

33. Runia, "Philo of Alexandria and the Greek *Hairesis*-Model," 119–20.
34. See Glucker, *Antiochus*, 184.
35. In Gal 5:20, *hairesis* is mentioned in the list of the works of the flesh in the sense of a sect.

dria reports that Heracleon, a student of Valentinus himself, came from "Valentinus's school" (Οὐαλεντίνου σχολή, *Strom.* 4.71.1). Hippolytus mentions those who are "from the school of Valentinus" (ἀπο τῆς Οὐαλεντίνου σχολῆς) and reports that there were two schools (διδασκαλίαι) among the Valentinians (*Haer.* 6.42.2; 6.35.5). Tertullian mentions the "two Valentinian schools" (*scholae*) in an analogy with the philosophical schools of Plato and Epicurus (*Val.* 11.2; 33.1). Irenaeus claims to have met some people who regarded themselves as disciples of Valentinus: ὡς αὐτοὶ λέγουσιν Οὐαλεντίνου μαθητῶν (*Haer.* 1.praef.2) who can be identified with the "disciples around Ptolemy": οἱ δὲ περὶ τὸν Πτολεμαῖον ἐμπειρότεροι (1.21.1).[36]

Although *hairesis* can designate various kinds of ancient associations, according to patristic writings, the Valentinian-gnostic *hairesis* was seen predominantly as a philosophical persuasion. Irenaeus accuses the Valentinians of deriving the theory of the emanations of Pleroma from Pythagoras (*Haer.* 1.1.1). Hippolytus claims that Valentinian gnostics were disciples of Pythagoras and Plato (*Haer.* 6.24.1). Tertullian argues that the best way to refute Valentinian teachers was to refute Plato, who was their teacher (*An.* 22). It is notable that Neoplatonic teachers also condemned the gnostics for deviating from authentic Platonism. Plotinus maintains in *Enn.* 2.9 that these teachers had built up a "school of thought of their own" (ἡ ἰδία αἵρεσις) from Greek philosophy and Plato. Porphyry argues in *Vit. Plot.* 16 that the gnostics were inauthentic Platonists who had parted ways "from the ancient philosophical tradition" (ἐκ τῆς παλαιᾶς φιλοσοφίας). Origen declares in *Cels.* 5.61 that some Christians called themselves gnostics in a manner similar to how the Epicureans called themselves philosophers.

There has been some doubt about the authenticity of the information attested in the patristic sources that the gnostic *hairesis* can be compared with a philosophical persuasion. Barbara Aland points out that the role of philosophy in gnostic schools was rather artificial. She maintains that the gnostic *hairesis* was not philosophy, not even corrupted philosophy, but "a religion of revelation and redemption."[37] Thomassen also argues

---

36. Thomassen, *Spiritual Seed*, 17–22. Markschies points out that, since Aristotle and Theophrastus, the word μαθητής had been used in Greek literature (albeit not exclusively) to refer to students of philosophers or to members of the same philosophical school of thought ("Valentinian Gnosticism," 420, 404).

37. Barbara Aland, "Gnosis und Philosophie," in *Proceedings of the International Colloquium on Gnosticism, Stockholm, August 20-25, 1973*, ed. Geo Widengren (Stockholm: Almqvist & Wiksell, 1977), 34–73.

3. Allegorical Interpretation in Philo and among the Valentinians 61

that the school of Valentinus was not a school comparable to the philosophical schools but a representative of the Christian *ecclesia*. According to Thomassen, "the vision of a salvation process that unfolds in time and history does not derive from Greek philosophy, but from the heritage of Judeo-Christian soteriology." Thomassen maintains that "school terminology" belongs to the same rhetorical toolbox of heresiologists as "*hairesis* terminology."[38]

I suggest, however, that the main bases of the Valentinian system of thought did not solely come from early Christian beliefs but from transcendental Platonism, which was integrated with Johannine and Pauline theology. In fact, the Valentinian gnostic myth became conceivable only as a part of a Platonic-Pythagorean worldview. The main thesis of the myth of Sophia was to explain how the world of multiplicity came out of the unity and how one can be rescued from the realm of matter through the consciousness of one's heavenly origin. It is also notable that gnostics were rejected not only by some early Christian teachers but also by teachers of the philosophical schools. Gnosticism caused conflict not only within early Christian communities but among the philosophical schools as well. Thus, the gnostic movement was not merely part of an inner-Christian debate.

In this study, the school of Valentinus is compared with a Greco-Roman philosophical "school of thought" (αἵρεσις). Valentinus founded a "school" (διδασκαλεῖον) whose "succession" (διαδοχή) allegedly went via Theudas back to Paul, who was the "founding figure" (πατὴρ τοῦ λόγου) of the school of thought. There were distinctive "doctrines" (δόγματα), such as the theory of the structure of the intelligible world, the tripartite division of humankind, and the therapy of emotions, which made Valentinianism discernible from the other philosophical schools and congregations of the nascent orthodoxy as well. Valentinus's disciples also continued to elaborate the teachings of their intellectual father. The psalms and homilies composed by Valentinus were used in the worship of the Valentinian communities (see Tertullian, *Carn. Chr.* 17.1).

The social theory of religious groups employed by Rodney Stark and William Bainbridge can help to describe the social setting of the Valentinian school of thought.[39] According to this model, religious communities

---

38. Thomassen, *Spiritual Seed*, 5, 315, 491–92.
39. William Bainbridge, *The Sociology of Religious Movements* (New York: Routledge, 1997); Rodney Stark and William Bainbridge, *The Future of Religion: Secularization, Revival and Cult Formation* (Berkeley: University of California Press, 1985).

can be defined as cult movements or sect movements that have deviated from their parent body—that is, the mother religion. While a sect splinters from the parent body to reestablish the old, authentic, and purified religion, a cult is the beginning of a new religion, based on a new revelation or new insight that changes the original tradition. Sects and cults also differ from the parent body in creating tension around the values of society. While sects and cults exhibit higher degrees of tension regarding the values and mores of the social environment, the parent body exhibits low tension, with common mores, or might even represent the sociocultural environment in toto.[40]

The rhetorical strategy of the patristic teachers was then to demonstrate that the Valentinian movement was a cult that had deviated from its parent body—that is, the church. The Valentinian innovations broke from the apostolic faith through innovations and fables derived from Greco-Roman philosophy and myths. The problem is, however, that, during the second century, a doctrinally centralized church that could have served as a parent body for the school of Valentinus or any other Christian group did not yet exist. There was no authorized church from which the school of Valentinus could have splintered. This means that the teachers of the nascent orthodoxy not only created the heretic but the church as well.[41]

I suggest, then, that the school of Valentinus cannot be seen as a deviation from the church but an independent group of Christians, who intend to revitalize especially the theology of the apostle Paul and the Gospel of John in the light of transcendental Platonic philosophy. It is evident, however, that the social context for the Valentinian teachers was the Christian *ecclesia*. Although many Valentinians may have been noneducated members of the local congregations, as Irenaeus claimed, their teachers

---

40. Fuglseth, *Johannine Sectarianism in Perspective*, 51–57.

41. Denise Kimber Buell argues that Clement presents his version of Christian truth rhetorically by using terms such as *procreation, lactation, paternity, maternity*, and *sexual difference*. Buell stresses that it is crucial to interpret Clement's writings as arguments *for a particular vision of Christian identity*, not articulations of already-determined doctrinal position. See Buell, *Making Christians: Clement of Alexandria and the Rhetoric of Legitimacy* (Princeton: Princeton University Press, 1999), 10–14, 180–84. Thomassen points out that during the activity of Valentinus in Rome, the Christian communities in the city were independent of one another. There existed no centrally directed body of Christians which could have had authority over other Christians until the monarchic episcopacy began to be recognized toward the end of the second century (see Thomassen, *Spiritual Seed*, 420–21).

were a fairly rich and privileged elite who provided their students with guidance toward the right way of life as non-Christian philosophers did.[42] John Dillon locates the Valentinian school of thought within the "Platonic underworld," together with the Chaldean Oracles and the Hermetic tradition.[43] Layton likewise proposes that "the Valentinian movement had the character of a philosophical school or network of schools rather than a distinct religious sect."[44] In a similar vein, Markschies argues that the school of Valentinus is comparable with the ancient philosophical schools.

It is not clear, however, whether the Valentinian teachers were more like popular or professional philosophers. Markschies refers to the study made by Johannes Hahn, according to which the phenomenon of forming a school was not restricted to professional philosophical schools only. Popular philosophers such as the Platonist Maximus of Tyre, who taught in Rome during the time of Valentinus, also offered regular lectures, while students took notes and engaged in discussions. Questions about what life one ought to live played an important role in these settings. Markschies states that the difference between popular and professional philosophers lay mainly in the degree of formal-logical argumentation in the philosophical curriculum.[45]

It seems, then, that the Valentinian teachers can be compared with Greco-Roman popular philosophers who had both a neo-Pythagorean and Christian orientation. Although some theologically well-written Valentinian documents, such as Ptolemy's the *Letter to Flora* or Valentinus's psalm *Harvest*, bear all the marks of philosophical competence, the colorful myth of Sophia does not belong to the same level of philosophical sophistication, though it may have had, as Markschies states, its own philosophical quality and charm in the Valentinian *paideia*.[46] The philosophical myths were used rather commonly to illustrate intellectual doctrines. Mark Edwards summarizes the attraction of the philosophical myths as follows:

---

42. See Lampe, *From Paul to Valentinus*, 292–315, esp. 299–313.

43. John Dillon, *The Middle Platonists 80 B.C. to A.D. 220* (New York: Cornell University Press, 1996), 384–89. The phrase "Platonic underworld" may have a misleadingly dismissive tone.

44. Brakke and Layton, *Gnostic Scriptures*, 331.

45. Johannes Hahn, *Der Philosoph und die Gesellschatft: Selbstverständis, öffentliches Auftreten und populäre Erwartungen in der hohen Kaiserzeit*, HABES 7 (Stuttgart: Steiner, 1987).

46. Markschies, "Valentinian Gnosticism," 436–38. The relationship between *mythos* and *logos* is mentioned already in Plato, *Prot.* 320c.

"If the impatient reader has been deceived by the obliquity of the teaching, he has failed to meet the test of a true disciple; all adepts of the mysteries are aware that what is senseless or abhorrent to the vulgar may first excite, then edify and finally illuminate the initiated mind."[47]

3.2.2. Valentinian Tradition and Rituals: Early Christian Theurgy versus *religio mentis*

In the first three centuries CE, Platonism increasingly began to attain the characteristics of a religion. The realms of philosophical schools and religious cults began to merge, though this development reached its peak with the writings of late Neoplatonic teachers.[48] Gregory Shaw points out, however, that attitudes toward rituals varied in the Platonic tradition. There was a tendency to combine *theologia* with *theurgia* and place rituals at the center of philosophical *paideia*. Plato himself was claimed to have participated in the Egyptian or Chaldean mysteries, and his writings were sometimes regarded as a *propaideia* to these deeper mysteries.[49] There were also some other Platonists who completely rejected ritual practices. In *Abst.* 2.49.2, Porphyry advises the philosopher to forgo ritual activities, because the philosopher is the savior of himself. The rituals may serve merely as *propaideia* for philosophical wisdom.

Shaw maintains that the different attitudes toward rituals were based on a more fundamental difference concerning the degree of the descent of the soul in the body. Those Platonists who valued rituals maintained that the soul had been fully incarnated into the body. The material elements of rituals provided the necessary tools for the liberation of the soul from the body. Those who rejected rituals, on the other hand, were

---

47. See Mark Edwards, "Pauline Platonism: The Myth of Valentinus," in *Christians, Gnostics and Philosophers in Late Antiquity*, VCS (London: Routledge, 2012), 208.

48. John Turner, "The Curious Philosophical World of Later Religious Gnosticism: The Symbiosis of Late Antique Philosophy and Religion," in *Religion and Philosophy in the Platonic and Neoplatonic Traditions: From Antiquity to the Early Medieval Period*, ed. Kevin Corrigan and John Turner (Sankt Augustin: Academia, 2012), 180–81.

49. Plato taught that the deeper mysteries cannot be achieved through written documents (*Ep.* 7.341c–d). Some Platonists took Plato's various references to the Oriental or Egyptian mysteries (*Pol.* 290c–e; *Tim.* 21; *Phaedr.* 275b; *Leg.* 819b; *Phileb.* 18b) as references to these deeper mysteries which are necessary for the illumination of the mind.

3. Allegorical Interpretation in Philo and among the Valentinians 65

of the opinion that the highest part of the soul did not become incarnate, but only its image did so. Therefore, its perfection was not dependent on rituals; rather, the undescended soul served as a savior of the individual soul.[50]

It is rather likely that the division among the Platonists about the role of rituals and the degree of the soul's incarnation can explain different attitudes toward Christian rituals by Valentinian teachers. Hippolytus maintains that the division between the Eastern and the Italian branches of Valentinianism reflects different views concerning the body of the Savior (*Haer.* 35.5–7). The representatives of the Italian school taught that the Savior did not have a physical body but a psychic body, into which the Spirit, that is, the Logos of Sophia, descended during his baptism. Some other teachers of the Eastern school, such as Axionicus and Ardesianes, suggested that the Savior had the Spirit since his birth. The Tripartite Tractate and related Eastern texts, for example the teachings of Theodotus in Clement's *Excerpta ex Theodoto*, represent the view that the spiritual Savior adopted a real body without any mediating psychic essence.[51] I suggest, however, that, behind the christological division a more essential disagreement concerning the degree of the incarnation of the soul may have existed. The Italian school taught that the spiritual seed of Sophia, which was inserted into the soul of the first human being, did not incarnate in the flesh but only in the psychic soul. The Eastern view, on the other hand, maintained that the spiritual seed incarnated absolutely in fleshly existence, being like a formless aborted fetus (*Exc.* 68). This division of opinions had an impact on the degree of the incarnation of the Savior and

---

50. Gregory Shaw, *The Theurgy of the Soul: The Neoplatonism of Iamblichus* (University Park: Pennsylvania State University Press 1995), 1–17; Garth Fowden, *The Egyptian Hermes: A Historical Approach to the Late Pagan Mind* (Princeton: Princeton University Press, 1993), 142–53. See also Birger Pearson, "Gnostic Ritual and Iamblichus' Treatise on the Mysteries of Egypt," in *Gnosticism and Christianity in Roman and Coptic Egypt* (New York: T&T Clark, 2004), 224–48.

51. Thomassen, *Spiritual Seed*, 39–50. Thomassen points out that Hippolytus does not actually describe the difference between Eastern and Western schools, only an internal debate within the Western school, concerning the moment when the spiritual and psychic parts of the Savior came together. This would imply that we cannot use Hippolytus's description as a proof for the *reason* of the school division within Valentinianism. In addition, Hippolytus may have exaggerated the differences within the Italian school. In *Excerpta* C, the Savior had the spiritual element since his birth, but during his baptism he got a special gift, *donum superadditum* (see *Exc.* 61).

the role of rituals as well. If the spiritual seed was incarnated fully in the flesh, this meant that the Savior must also have adopted the same bodily existence to be able to save them. As a result, the Eastern view held a more positive view toward rituals, because it posited that the soul was trapped in the body and that it could not be released without material sacraments. In the Italian school, such rituals were seen merely as a *propaideia* for the deeper mysteries, which were given through intellectual enlightenment. These differences might help to explain why the Eastern Valentinian tradition began to change from a school movement to a church movement with unique cultic observances.[52] It seems that the Eastern view was influenced by the incarnational theology according to which the Savior adopted a real human body.

The ritual practices of the Valentinian School are also discussed in Irenaeus's testimonies concerning the prophetical society of the Marcosians (*Haer.* 1.13–22; see also Hippolytus, *Haer.* 6.41). The Marcosians made a distinction between the psychic aspect of Jesus's baptism (ascending to the water) and his spiritual redemption (descending of the Spirit), which they called ἀπολύτρωσις. The former mediated the forgiveness of sins, whereas the latter represented a conjugal union, a sort of spiritual marriage, with the powers of the Pleroma. There were also some teachers in the sect of Marcus who abandoned ritual practices altogether. The spiritual seed did not have any participation in material creation, and therefore its reception and formation could not be channeled through ritual practices. Rituals were only images of spiritual reality and were thus trivial, functioning merely as signs of spiritual reality and *propaideia* for the transformation of the self through knowledge.[53]

---

52. See Dunderberg, *Beyond Gnosticism*, 3. Dunderberg points out that the terminology that Irenaeus uses for his opponents implies that there were two branches in ancient Valentinianism, one tending toward a separate cult movement and one tending toward a school movement. In my opinion, this development actualized later when the Valentinian tradition began to merge with third-century nascent orthodoxy. The Tripartite Tractate and the Valentinian blocks of the Gospel of Philip represent Valentinianism as a cult movement. It became a cultic splinter group from the orthodox Christian parent body, which they intended to reform. This was not, however, the situation almost a century earlier, when Valentinus and his first followers began their career.

53. In addition to the conventional Christian rituals (viz., baptism, anointment, the Eucharist), the Valentinians may have had a distinct ritual (e.g., the use of water, oil, and invocations) as a sign of conjugal union with the spiritual reality and redemption.

The Valentinian Exposition, one of the Valentinian writings of the Nag Hammadi Library, differs from the Marcosian community in the attitude expressed therein toward baptism. It contains five liturgical readings (one on anointing, two on baptism, and one on the Eucharist) as a kind of appendix to the main document. On Baptism B 41.21 and 42.39 refer to the "first baptism," which has been interpreted in light of Irenaeus's testimony concerning the distinction between ordinary church practice and the second spiritual rite of redemption.[54] Thomassen maintains, however, that there is nothing incomplete or psychic about the first baptism mentioned in that document. According to this tradition, the bridal chamber was not a separate rite apart from baptism and anointment but referred to the invisible nature of baptism itself.[55] Antti Marjanen also suggests that the first baptism mentioned in the liturgical readings of the Valentinian Exposition transforms the status of the participant from a material existence to a spiritual one. Therefore, this particular document has a very optimistic view concerning the transformative power of baptism, which differs from the critical view attested in Irenaeus, *Haer.* 1.21.[56]

It is not contrary to reason to think that the different attitudes among Valentinian teachers might have been the outcome of different anthropological views in the Middle Platonic tradition. The Valentinian writings of the Nag Hammadi Library mainly represent the view that saw the transformative power of cultic rituals. In these texts, the early Christian rituals are converted into Platonic theurgy and function as a means to spiritual redemption. The Valentinian tradition that is preserved in the accounts of the patristic authors mainly belongs to the

---

It is possible that the ritual of redemption was a mortuary rite. On the evidence of a Valentinian deathbed ritual, see H. Gregory Snyder, "The Discovery and Interpretation of the Flavia Sophe Inscription: New Results," *VC* 68 (2014): 1–59; Dunderberg, *Beyond Gnosticism*, 113–17. Thomassen suggests that the deathbed ritual was not a distinct ritual of redemption but a sort of baptismal *anamnesis* for the dying person (*Spiritual Seed*, 350–53).

54. See John D. Turner, "Ritual in Gnosticism," in Turner and Majercik, *Gnosticism and Later Platonism*, 97–102; Desjardins, *Sin in Valentinianism*, 95–96; Elaine Pagels, "A Valentinian Interpretation of Baptism and Eucharist—and Its Critique of 'Orthodox' Sacramental Theology and Practice," *HTR* 65 (1972): 157.

55. Thomassen, *Spiritual Seed*, 355, 357–76.

56. Antti Marjanen, "A Salvific Act of Transformation or a Symbol of Defilement," in *Gnosticism, Platonism and the Late Ancient World*, ed. Kevin Corrigan and Tuomas Rasimus, NHMS 82 (Leiden: Brill, 2013), 245–50.

Italian tradition (esp. Irenaeus, *Haer.* 1.1–7 and *Excerpta* C). According to this tradition, the spiritual part of the human soul was not held captive in the flesh but only within the psychic soul, which means that material rituals were not essential to the process of the transformation of the self but were seen merely as *propaideia* for a deeper illumination of the mind. However, in both Valentinian traditions, Eastern and Western, the Christian rituals were seen in the light of the Valentinian protological myth, combined with a curious Platonic insight. Therefore, Irenaeus complains that the Valentinians speak the same language as other members of the church, but they think differently (see *Haer.* 1.*praef*; 3.15.2; 4.33.3).

This study will show that the Valentinian sources, which contain the closest parallels with Philo, mainly belong to the Italian branch of Valentinianism. The closest parallel with this kind of tradition is the *religio mentis* of the philosophical Hermetica. Garth Fowden describes how the charismatic teachers of the Hermetic school of thought were surrounded by disciples who sought philosophical understanding of the divine realm and longed for personal illumination through the study of religious texts, instruction, question and answer, prayer, the singing of hymns, and the enjoyment of other sorts of close fellowship between master and pupil. The ritual practices were *propaideia* for intellectual enlightenment, which was achieved through education and *gnosis*.[57] The Canon Muratori, which is perhaps the oldest early Christian list of canonical texts among the Roman congregation at the end of the second century, mentions *a liber psalmorum* by Valentinus, which is explicitly excluded from the canonical texts.[58] This would mean that Valentinus's psalms were used in worship at Valentinian gatherings, which recalls the role of singing in the community of

---

57. Fowden, *Egyptian Hermes*, 95–115.

58. See Einar Thomassen, "Going to Church with the Valentinians," in *Practicing Gnosis: Ritual, Magic, Theurgy and Liturgy in Nag Hammadi, Manichean and Other Ancient Literature: Essays in Honor of Birger A. Pearson*, ed. April D. DeConick, Gregory Shaw, and John D. Turner, NHMS 85 (Leiden: Brill, 2013), 185–88. The dating of the Muratorian Canon is problematic. Albert Sundberg places the document in the fourth century. See Sundberg, "Canon Muratori: A Fourth-Century List," *HTR* 66 (1973): 1–41. Most recently, Clare Rothschild considers it to be a late antique forgery. See Rothschild, "The Muratorian Fragment as Roman Fake," *NovT* 60 (2018): 55–82. Christophe Guignard argues that second-century dating "remains the most likely and economical one." See Guignard, "The Muratorian Fragment as a Late Antique Fake? An Answer to C. K. Rothschild," *RevScRel* 93 (2018): 73–90.

the Jewish philosophers and their nocturnal choral practices described by Philo in *Contempl.* 83–89.

3.3. Allegorical Readers of Alexandria

It became common in the Middle Platonic tradition to assume that philosophy was concealed by gods in symbolical poetry and religious revelations, which could only be grasped by allegorical exegesis. During the second century BCE, the first literary commentaries on the Homeric epic were written by the Alexandrian scholars at the museum. They paved the way for purely philosophical explanations of the inconsistencies, contradictions, and gaps in the texts. Maren Niehoff points out, "Alexandrian Jews were familiar with this type of scholarship, and some applied it to their Scriptures."[59] The allegorical method was discussed in rhetorical textbooks by the Hellenistic philosophers, an allegory having been defined as "to mean something other than one says." Famous rhetorician Quintilian maintained that "continuous metaphor makes an allegory, which was related to the personification of abstract qualities."[60]

The origin of the allegorical exegesis of Greco-Roman myths was not in Plato but in Aristotle, who says that the lover of myths is the lover of wisdom, for myth is composed of wonder, and the experience of wonder is the root of philosophy.[61] Aristotle also maintains that the ancient myths are basically metaphysical—that is, they contain hidden philosophical

---

59. Niehoff, *Philo of Alexandria*, 182–83.

60. Frances M. Young, *Biblical Exegesis and the Formation of Christian Culture* (Cambridge: Cambridge University Press, 1997), 176–77. The continuous metaphor means that once the metaphor is defined, it can be also applied to new situations where the same term is mentioned, although the context of the term is changed. For example, the Valentinians interpreted the term *pleroma* as referring to the entirety of the aeons in all cases where the term was used in the New Testament. See, e.g., John 1:16: ἐκ τοῦ πληρώματος αὐτοῦ ἡμεῖς πάντες ἐλάβομεν καὶ χάριν ἀντὶ χάριτος ("From his *fullness* have we all received, grace upon grace"), and Col 2:9–11: ἐν αὐτῷ κατοικεῖ πᾶν τὸ πλήρωμα τῆς θεότητος σωματικῶς, καὶ ἐστὲ ἐν αὐτῷ πεπληρωμένοι ("For in him the whole *fullness* of deity dwells bodily, and you have come to *fullness* of life in him"). In all these instances, the term *pleroma* is seen as referring to the eternal realm of the aeons.

61. Luc Brisson, *How Philosophers Saved Myths: Allegorical Interpretation and Classical Mythology*, trans. Catherine Tihanyi (Chicago: University of Chicago Press, 2008), 44.

truths (*Metaph.* 12.1074b.1–14). Aristotle regards the figure of Zeus as a symbol of the Prime Mover, who challenged all the other gods. Zeus hung down from heaven a golden chain, which gods would grab onto and pull their way, but only Zeus was able to pull them up to him. Thus, the metaphysical doctrine of the Prime Mover was hidden in the myth.[62] The Stoics were also famous for their allegorical readings of Homer and Hesiod. They argued that the ancient poets had unknowingly written down the wisdom of an earlier stage of history, which could be revealed in the text through the allegorical method.[63]

3.3.1. Philo and the Allegorical Method

The writings of Philo are a testimony to the Hellenistic Jewish allegorical tradition, which intended to integrate philosophy with the Scriptures. Philo maintains that the Scriptures had a twofold meaning: an obvious meaning and a symbolical meaning (see *Leg.* 2.13–14; *Deus* 133). In *De vita contemplativa*, Philo exemplifies his view concerning the hidden nature of the Scriptures: "They read the Holy Scriptures and seek wisdom from their ancestral philosophy by taking it as an allegory, since they think that the words of the literal text are symbols of something whose hidden nature is revealed by studying the underlying meaning" (*Contempl.* 28). The underlying level of the text Philo calls allegory (ἀλληγορία), declaring that it is "obscure to the many" (*Abr.* 200). A symbolical meaning of the

---

62. Brisson, *How Philosophers Saved Myths*, 53–54.
63. For the Stoic views, see George R. Boys-Jones, "The Stoics' Two Types of Allegory," in *Metaphor, Allegory, and the Classical Tradition: Ancient Thought and Modern Revisions*, ed. Boys-Jones (Oxford: Oxford University Press, 2003), 189–216. The Stoics were not the only allegorical interpreters of the Greek myths. Some Platonists saw in Homer's writings allegories and symbols for intellectual search. The adventures of Odysseus, for example, could be seen as descriptions of the soul's journey to its true homeland in heaven. In *Quaest. Conv.* 9.14.6, Plutarch's teacher M. Annius Ammonius discusses how to interpret the encounter between Odysseus and the sirens, noting that the music of the sirens attracts the soul upward after its death. See A. Long, "Allegory in Philo and Etymology in Stoicism: A Plea for Drawing Distinctions," *SPhiloA* 9 (1997): 198–200, 207–10; Thomas Tobin, *The Creation of Man: Philo and the History of Interpretation*, CBQMS 14 (Washington, DC: Catholic Biblical Association of America, 1983), 150–51; Wolfson, *Philo* 1:132–33; Winston, *Philo of Alexandria*, 4–7; James Drummond, *Philo Judaeus; or, the Jewish-Alexandrian Philosophy in Its Development and Completion* (London: Williams and Norgate, 1888), 1:120–25.

Scriptures is clear only to "those who can contemplate bodiless and naked facts" (*Abr.* 236). It is "dear to humans with their eyes opened" (*Plant.* 36). For Philo, only those who are qualified by preliminary training and succeeded in mastering their passions can be trained in the method of allegorical interpretation.[64]

As noted, the degree of allegorizing varies between different texts in Philo's corpus. In the *Quaestiones et Solutiones*, the web of intertextual associations typical of the Allegorical Commentary is lacking. In the Exposition of the Law, Philo stresses the historicity of the biblical narratives and the importance of the role of Israel as a unique nation among nations.[65] Philo was thus a proponent of multiple exegesis, meaning that a text ought to be handled at different levels depending on the reader's spiritual capability or the context of the text. In some cases, however, allegorical interpretation was obligatory. For Philo, literal interpretations of anthropomorphic descriptions of God would have been blasphemous. Moreover, passages that were irrational, such as planting the paradise or the creation of Eve from Adam's rib, had to be interpreted allegorically. The allegorical method also served an apologetic function especially in Philo's works, addressed to a wider audience. The Jewish people were not to be ashamed of their cultural and religious heritage, because allegorical method revealed the highest level of human wisdom hidden in the Scriptures, which exceeded even the Greek philosophical tradition.[66]

---

64. See Wolfson, *Philo*, 1:115–38.

65. Maren Niehoff suggests that in the *Quaestiones et Solutiones* Philo intended to downplay the textual problems and variations of interpretations mentioned in the Allegorical Commentary to stress the plain truth of the biblical text. See Niehoff, *Philo of Alexandria*, 195–98.

66. David Runia, "Philo, Alexandrian and Jew," in *Exegesis and Philosophy: Studies on Philo of Alexandria* (Aldershot: Variorum, 1990), 4–5; Dawson, *Allegorical Readers*, 73–129. The Letter of Aristeas can be dated to the beginning of the second century BCE; it contains the high priest Eleazer's ethical interpretation of the Jewish dietary laws. Eusebius cites two fragments of Aristobulus, who uses the allegorical method of interpretation to avoid the anthropomorphic descriptions of God: the hands of God denote God's power. It is assumed that the goal of the allegorical method used by these authors was apologetic. On the one hand, Jewish allegorists intended to show that the best parts of Greek intellectual and moral values could also be found in the Scriptures. On the other hand, the aim was to build a bridge to Greco-Roman society and its cultural and political values. See Ellen Birnbaum, "Allegorical Interpretation and Jewish Identity among Alexandrian Jewish Writers," in *Neotestamentica et Philonica: Studies in Honor of Peder Borgen*, ed. David E. Aune,

It is clear that Philo was not a solitary interpreter of the Scriptures; he was working within the exegetical tradition, and he frequently refers to other Jewish allegorical readers of the Bible and criticizes their views. In *Conf.* 1–5, Philo criticizes some "impious scoffers" inspired by Homeric scholarship at the museum for comparing Gen 11:1–9 to a passage in Homer's *Odyssey*.[67] Kåre Fuglseth divides the allegorical readers of Alexandria referred to by Philo into three subgroups:[68]

1. The extreme allegorists, whom Philo dislikes, because they seem to have neglected the prescriptions of the law.
2. Moderate or nonmystical allegorists, who do not follow Philo's path and are more bound to the literal meaning of the text.
3. Mystical allegorists, described in *De vita contemplativa*, who are models for Philo's own allegorical reading.

It is notable that Philo's allegorical exegesis differed from the approach of the Hellenistic philosophers. Especially in the Allegorical Commentary, Philo assumes that Moses wrote *intentionally* in allegorical language. The allegorical level is not artificially added by the interpreter of the text, but rather the original message is hidden in symbols, numbers, and etymologies. Thus, the biblical text itself is originally an allegorical presentation of the reality of the world.

Dawson points out that Philo's allegorical method is based on the theory of the corruption of language.[69] God confused the languages to pre-

---

Torrey Seland, and Jarl Henning Ulrichsen (Leiden: Brill, 2003), 307–29. Roberto Radice points out that the use of allegorical method was not mere speculation, but its goal was to reveal philosophical truths, which will lead to a correct way of living. See Radice, "Philo's Theology and Theory of Creation," in Kamesar, *Cambridge Companion to Philo*, 125–26.

67. Niehoff, *Philo of Alexandria*, 184.
68. Fuglseth, *Johannine Sectarianism*, 94. For Philo's "quarrelsome colleagues," see Maren Niehoff, "Homeric Scholarship and Bible Exegesis in Ancient Alexandria: Evidence from Philo's 'Quarrelsome' Colleagues," *ClQ* 57 (2007): 166–82. For Alexandrian literalists, see Montgomery J. Shroyer, "Alexandrian Jewish Literalists," *JBL* 55 (1936): 261–84.
69. Dawson, *Allegorical Readers*, 92; see also Daniel Boyarin, "Origen as a Theorist of Allegory: Alexandrian Contexts," in *The Cambridge Companion to Allegory*, ed. Rita Copeland and Peter T. Struck (Cambridge: Cambridge University Press, 2010), 39–54.

vent wickedness from reaching its goal as humankind endeavored to build the Tower of Babel. As a result, language lost its capacity to mediate real meaning. Philo explains the confusion of languages at Babel as follows:

> This is our explanation, but those who merely follow the outward and obvious think that we have at this point a reference to the origin of the Greek and barbarian languages. I would not censure such persons, for perhaps the truth is with them also. Still I would exhort them not to halt there, but to press on to allegorical interpretation and to recognize that the letter is to the oracle but as a shadow to the substance and that the higher values therein revealed are what really and truly exist. Indeed, the lawgiver himself gives openings for this kind of treatment to those whose understanding is not blinded as he certainly does in the case now under discussion when he calls what was then taking place a "confusion." (*Conf.* 190)

Philo stresses that God not only divided the language into "Greek and barbarian languages," as is commonly suggested, but he confused languages semantically. In *Conf.* 191–193, Philo draws a distinction between "confusion" (σύγχυσις) and "separation" (διάκρισις). God not only separated languages but confused their semantic apparatus. This means that the confusion concerns all human languages, which are like shadows of the bodily appearances. At a literal level, language contains "prodigies and marvels, one serpent emitting a human voice and using quibbling arguments to an utterly guileless character and cheating a woman with seductive plausibility," but for those who interpret words according to allegory, "all that is mythical is removed out of our way, and the real sense becomes as clear as daylight" (*Agr.* 96–97). Yet, when Moses wrote out the law, he had to use fallen language, and it had to be decrypted through the allegorical method to mediate real meanings. For this purpose, Moses left clues and invitations that pointed to the vision of the intelligible realm beyond the written text. Philo and other allegorists were able to find these clues in the peculiarities of words, etymologies, numerical codes, phraseology, grammar, and syntax.[70] Through the allegorical method, then, God's voice could be seen once again through the Scriptures:

---

70. Burton L. Mack, "Moses on the Mountain Top: A Philonic View," in *The School of Moses: Studies in Philo and Hellenistic Religion in Memory of Horst R. Moehring*, ed. John Peter Kenney, BJS 304 (Atlanta: Scholars Press, 1995), 16–28.

> For what life is better than a contemplative life, or more appropriate to a rational being? For this reason, whereas the voice of mortal beings is judged by hearing, the sacred oracles intimate that the words of God are seen as light is seen; for we are told that "all the people saw the Voice," not that they heard it; for what was happening was not an impact of air made by the organs of mouth and tongue, but virtue shining with intense brilliance, wholly resembling a fountain of reason, and this is also indicated elsewhere on this wise: "You have seen that I have spoken to you out of Heaven," not "you heard," for the same cause as before. (*Migr.* 47)

For Philo, allegorical interpretation was not solely an isolated program to find proofs for philosophical opinions but was also an instrument for spiritual ascent. In *Contempl.* 78, the deeper meaning of the word is conveyed in allegory, which means that the allegorists are able to "see the invisible through the visible" (τὰ ἀφανῆ διὰ τῶν φανερῶν θεωρεῖν).[71] The ascension of Moses can be understood as paradigmatic, because a properly initiated allegorist would be able to reach the same noetic vision. Moses ascended "in thick clouds" to the spiritual realm, where bodily eyesight was useless, and "he saw with the soul's eye the immaterial forms of the material objects about to be made" (*Mos.* 2.74; see also *QE* 2.52).

3.3.2. Valentinian Allegorists as Heirs of Philo

The Valentinian allegorists belonged to a similar hermeneutical tradition to Philo and other Alexandrian Jewish allegorists. The theme of language as a tool for confusion and deception is also found in the Valentinian Gospel of Philip (NHC II 3):

> The names of worldly things are utterly deceptive, for they turn the heart from what is real to what is unreal. Whoever hears the word "God" thinks not of what is real but rather of what is unreal. So also with the words "father," "son," holy spirit," "life," "light," "resurrection," "church," and all the rest, people do not think of what is real but of what is unreal, [though] the words refer to what is real. The words [that are] heard belong to his world. [Do not be] deceived. If words belonged to the eternal realm, they would never be pronounced in this world, nor would

---

71. See Scott D. Mackie, "Seeing God in Philo of Alexandria: Means, Methods, and Mysticism," *JSJ* 43 (2012): 162–68; see also *Spec.* 3.1–6.

3. Allegorical Interpretation in Philo and among the Valentinians 75

they designate worldly things. They would refer to what is in the eternal realm. (Gos. Phil. 53.23–54.5)

Gospel of Philip 54.13–31 then goes on to explain how the archons corrupted language so that it became a method of deception:

> Truth brought forth names in the world for us, and no one can refer to truth without names. Truth is one and many, for our sakes, to teach us about the one, in love, through the many. The rulers wanted to fool people, since they saw that people have a kinship with what is truly good. They took the names of the good and assigned them to what is not good, to fool people with names and link the names to what is not good. So, as if they are doing people a favor, they take names from what is not good and transfer them to the good, in their way of thinking. For they wished to take free people and enslave them forever. (Gos. Phil. 54.13–31)

It is stated in Gos. Phil. 67.9–27 that truth did not come into the world naked but in "symbols and images," because the world could not receive truth any other way. The Valentinian innovation was to use the allegorical method not only with the Jewish Scriptures but also with the early Christian texts, which means that also Jesus's biography described in the gospels reflects the realities of the eternal realm.

Irenaeus presents a number of Valentinian interpretations of the gospels, which reveals their allegorical technique. The thirty years of no public ministry by Jesus is taken to refer to the thirty aeons of the Pleroma (Matt 20:1–16); the twelve-year-old Jesus in the temple and the twelve apostles, the twelve aeons (Luke 2:42; 6:13); the hemorrhaging woman healed by the Savior (Mark 5:24b–34), the suffering of Sophia; and the raising of the synagogue ruler's twelve-year-old daughter (Luke 8:41), the healing of Achamoth by the Savior. Simeon, who takes Christ in his arms, is understood as a type of Demiurge, whereas Anna, who has lived seven years without her husband, represents Achamoth, who must wait in the intermediate place until she is restored to her proper consort (Luke 2:25–40; see *Haer.* 1.3.1–5; 8.1–5).

The fragments of Heracleon's commentary on John's Gospel preserved by Origen provide another example of Valentinian allegorical exegesis (Origen, *Comm. Jo.* 1–13). Heracleon pays attention to the choice of words in their contexts and analyzes their semantic connotations. Heracleon allegorizes the characters and objects of the Gospel of John as types of mythological figures or ideas. In commenting on John 1:23, he explains that the self-description of John the Baptist as the voice crying in the wilderness refers to the relationship between the Baptist and the Savior: John is the "voice," whereas the Savior is the "logos."[72] In John 1:26–27, John the Baptist refers to the Demiurge, and the sandals of the Savior are his body. When Jesus "went down" to Capernaum, this signifies the descent of the Savior into the material realm (John 2:12), while his ascent to Jerusalem is going to the "psychic place" (2:13–16). The cleansing of the temple by the Savior is a symbol of the cleansing of the soul inhabited by demons (2:13–22). It is of note, however, that Heracleon does not refer to Sophia's fall or pleromatic realities except in a rather general way, which does not necessitate distinctively Valentinian assumptions.[73]

The allegorical method used by the Valentinian teachers was vehemently criticized by Irenaeus, who accused them of subverting "Scriptures according to their own intention" to "arrive at their contrived exegeses," whereas truthful interpretation ought to follow a "clear and open sense of Scripture" and build interpretation on "clear and unambiguous parts" (see *Haer.* 1.3.6; 1.9.1; 2.27.1–4). Irenaeus echoes aforesaid Philo's criticism toward extreme allegorists. He accuses Valentinians of acting like philosophers who incorporated their views into the poems of Homer so that the "ignorant [might] imagine that Homer actually composed the verses bearing upon that hypothesis" (*Haer.* 1.9.4 [Roberts and Rambaut, *ANF* 1]). Despite Irenaeus's harsh criticism, allegorical interpretation was not absent from the writings of patristic authors, nor from those of Irenaeus himself.[74] When some of the early Christian writings, especially the gos-

---

72. Heracleon also distinguishes John from other prophets of lower rank, who are only "echoes." It is of note that the logos-voice-echo tripartition is not derived from the Valentinian precosmic myth but is a literary commonplace (see Wucherpfenning, *Heracleon*, 224–28).

73. See Thomassen "Heracleon," 179–85.

74. Irenaeus interpreted not only the Hebrew Scriptures but also the New Testament allegorically. A good example is the parable of the lost sheep (Matt 18:12–14). In *Haer.* 3.18–23, the shepherd is the Christ who descended into hell to save the lost generations before Christ's advent, whereas in *Haer.* 5.9–12 the shepherd symbolizes bishops and presbyters. Origen maintains in *Princ.* 4.11–13 that the threefold nature of the Scriptures is based on allegorical reading of Prov 22:20–21: "We find some such rule as this laid down by Solomon in the Proverbs concerning the divine doctrines written therein: 'Do thou portray them threefold ($\tau\rho\iota\sigma\sigma\tilde{\omega}\varsigma$) in counsel and knowledge, that thou mayest answer words of truth to those who question thee.'" Trans. George W. Butterworth, *Origen: On First Principles* (Notre Dame, IN: Ave Maria,

pels, became normative, it was natural that they could be interpreted in the same allegorical fashion as the Hebrew Scriptures.[75]

The problem with the Valentinian teachers was not the allegorical method as such but the philosophical myth that formed their basis for interpretation. Origen and Clement criticized Valentinian teachers for deriving allegorical interpretations from the philosophical myth without any connection to historical context.[76] Strikingly, Origen faced almost the same criticism from the Antiochian bishop Eustathius, who criticized Alexandrian allegorists for neglecting history and paying too much attention to names and terms instead of deeds. It would seem that the criticism that Irenaeus leveled against the Valentinian teachers was repeated by the leaders of the church of Antioch against Alexandrian allegorists, such as Origen and Clement, who were likewise accused of breaking the coherence of the texts and twisting its original intention.[77] The teachers of Antioch

---

2013). Origen defends the use of allegorical method, comparing it to human beings. Just as human beings are divided into body, soul, and spirit, so do the Scriptures yield three meanings: literal (σωματικόν), moral (ψυχικόν), and spiritual (πνευματικόν), which are related to one's capacity for understanding. Also, Jerome defends allegorical understanding of the Scriptures, which has historical, moral, and intellectual/spiritual meaning (see *Epist.* 120.12; *Comm. Ezech.* 5.16.30–31). In a similar vein, Augustine says in *Util. cred.* 3.5 that the Jewish Scriptures were "handed down fourfold to them who desire to know it, according to history, according to aetiology, according to analogy and according to allegory" (trans. C. L. Cornish, *NPNF* 2/3). For a summary of the allegorical method of the church fathers, see Harry Wolfson, *Faith, Trinity, Incarnation*, vol. 1 of *The Philosophy of the Church Fathers* (Cambridge: Harvard University Press, 1956), 43–72.

75. Richard P. C. Hanson, *Allegory and Event: A Study of the Sources and Significance of Origen's Interpretation of the Scripture* (Richmond, VA: John Knox, 1959), 125–26. See also David W. Jorgensen, "Valentinian Influence on Irenaeus: Early Allegorization of the New Testament," in Thomassen and Markschies, *Valentinianism: New Studies*, 400–413. Jorgenssen argues that the influence of the Valentinian exegetes on Irenaeus is not commonly recognized in scholarship.

76. Elaine Pagels, *The Johannine Gospel in Gnostic Exegesis: Heracleon's Commentary on John* (New York: Abingdon, 1973), 20–35; Hanson, *Allegory and Event*, 144–49.

77. The rivalry between Antioch and Alexandria concerning biblical exegesis can be understood, respectively, as a rivalry between rhetorical (*to historikon*) and philosophical (*to methodikon*) schools. The Alexandrian exegetes emphasized philosophical education and the linguistic aspects of the text (e.g., etymologies, tropes, styles), whereas the school of Antioch stressed more the context of the texts (e.g., history, context). This does not mean that the Antiochian exegetes did not explore allegories at all but that the historical and typological interpretations were primary. Nor

and Irenaeus stressed that the text must be read as a literary unit, which forms an "iconic" starting point even for its hidden intention. Instead, the allegorical approach was based on the "inspiring Spirit," which could only enlighten readers so that they could reach the deeper spiritual meaning of the text. Thus, the difference between Origen and the Valentinian exegetes was not so much about method of reading but the content of the Spirit that revealed the hidden meaning of the text.[78]

At first glance, it would seem that Philo and the Valentinian exegetes introduced allegorical interpretations into the text artificially. There were, however, some signs in the texts that were taken to serve as indicators for the opportunity to ascend from the literal level to the level where the spiritual vision could be reached. In *Plant.* 26, Philo calls these textual details starting points or "stimuli" (ἀφορμαί) for the use of allegory, which is "dear to men with their eyes opened." These textual clues can be of various sorts. Some are etymological (*Det.* 15–17), some are based on factual errors in the literal text (*Somn.* 2.246), and others are based on absurd details in

---

did Origen and Clement, for their part, neglect the historical meaning altogether, but instead they considered the allegorical meaning to be more valuable. The difference between allegory and typology, however, is less than clear. In both cases, the texts say something that cannot be derived solely from the context of the text. The typological interpretation used by Antiochean exegetes also admits that the texts contain a hidden spiritual intention (*scopus*). The difference between the allegorical and the typological approach, then, seems to have been the method through which the intention of the text was achieved. The allegorists stressed more the "inspiring Spirit" than the literal context of the text. On the traditions of early Christian exegesis, see Alan J. Hauser and Duane F. Watson, "Introduction and Overview," in *The Ancient Period*, vol. 1 of *A History of Biblical Interpretation*, ed. Hauser and Watson (Grand Rapids: Eerdmans, 2003), 37–43; Frances M. Young, "Alexandrian and Antiochene Exegesis," in Hauser and Watson, *History of Biblical Interpretation*, 341–51.

78. Although the Valentinians had a sense of belonging to an elite association with a philosophical awareness, they used the same early Christian sources—the gospels and Paul's letters—as the other second-century Christians. The Valentinian Ptolemy says in his *Letter to Flora* that "we shall draw the proofs of what we say from the words of our Savior, or through these alone are we led without stumbling to the comprehension of that which is." Thus, the reading practices of the Valentinian communities did not differ substantially from the other early Christian communities. As Pheme Perkins points out, rather than a congregation with a closed list of canonical texts, the Valentinian groups formed a complex network of reading clubs where inspiring texts were freely analyzed, interpreted, discussed, and copied ("Valentinians and the Christian Canon," 373–84).

the text (*Agr.* 130–131). Also, repetitions of the same word or narrative are invitations for allegorical interpretation. As certain terms, names, or themes are given an allegorical meaning, they function as new invitations to interpret other texts allegorically where these terms appear.

Before entering into a detailed comparison of the allegories of Philo and the Valentinians, I will investigate two case studies that illustrate the multidimensionality of the hermeneutical method used by these teachers. Whereas the first example illustrates an extreme case, the latter case serves as an example of a moderate allegorical reading of the text.

3.3.3. Allegorical Interpretation of Exod 13:2–12 in Philo and Irenaeus

The first example is related to the allegorical interpretation of Exod 13:2–12, which describes the law concerning sanctifying firstlings. The double use of words with the same meaning (πρωτότοκος and πρωτογενές) in these sentences serves as an invitation for allegorists to postulate a theory of the twofold opening of the womb. I will present first the Valentinian interpretation of the text that is included in the protological myth of Sophia in Irenaeus, *Haer.* 1.3.4: "Moreover, they assert that Savior, who derives from all, is the All. This is proved by the following passage: Every male who opens the womb (Exod 13:12); for he, being the All, opened the womb of Intention of the Aeon who suffered passion when she was cast out of the Pleroma. He also calls this second Ogdoad, of which we shall speak a little later" (Unger, modified). It is clear that Irenaeus's quotation of this Valentinian myth is an allusion to the sanctification of the firstborn mentioned in Exod 13:12. "Consecrate to me every firstborn [πρωτότοκος] male. The first offspring [πρωτογενές] of every womb among the Israelites belongs to me, whether human or animal." However, the lemma (πᾶν ἄρρεν διανοῖγον μήτραν) is a direct quotation from Luke 2:23, describing how Jesus was brought into the temple according to Mosaic law—namely, every firstborn boy that "opens his mother's womb" should be dedicated to God.

In the Valentinian interpretation, the sanctification of the firstborn and opening the womb of the mother are projected into the spiritual realm as part of a protological myth. First, the Savior is identified with "all males," because he was the male offspring of the "all" (i.e., the Pleroma). Second, the Savior does not open the womb of Sophia from "inside" through his birth but opens the womb of the suffering Sophia from the outside by healing her emotions through knowledge to make Sophia capable of procreating spiritual offspring as her firstborn (*Haer.* 1.4.5).

Strikingly, Philo gives a similar allegorical reading of Exod 13:2 in *Her.* 117–119, though the context of interpretation is different. Philo's allegory is part of the preceding discussion in *Her.* 105–110, in which he criticizes those who maintain that the human mental and sense faculties are not attributed to God. Philo says that this kind of view represents a selfish attitude toward God's gifts because God's immaterial power fundamentally energizes all the activities of mind, speech, and sense perceptions. Philo finds support for his view in an allegorical reading of Exod 13:1–2:

> And elsewhere he says "The Lord spoke unto Moses saying 'sanctify to me every first born [πρωτόγονος], first in generation [πρωτογενές] opening every womb among the sons of Israel from human beings to animals. It is to Me.'" Thus, it is admitted here also that the first in time and value are God's possessions and especially the first in generation. For since genus in every case is indestructible, to the indestructible God will it be justly assigned. And that is true too of one who opens the womb of all from man, that is reason and speech, to beast, that is sense and body. For he that opens the womb of each of these, of mind, to mental apprehensions, of speech, to the activities of the voice, of the senses, to receive the pictures presented to it by objects, of the body, to the movements and postures proper to it, is the invisible, seminal artificer, the divine Logos, which will be fitly dedicated to its Father. (*Her.* 117–119, modified)

Philo plays attention to the words πρωτότοκος and πρωτογενές in Exod 13:2. In some other passages, Philo suggests that the term *firstborn* (πρωτογενές) is the name of the Logos (i.e., in *Conf.* 146). Therefore, the meaning of πρωτογενές can be shifted to a new context, and the biblical passage in question can be read as referring to two distinct beings—that is, the one who is brought forth from the womb (πρωτότοκος) and the one who opens the womb for them (πρωτογενές). The term *firstborn* (πρωτότοκος) is associated with reason and speech, which are brought forth when the Logos (πρωτογενές) opens the human mind like a womb. Therefore, the human mental activities should be attributed to God, because their cause, the Logos, is the real firstborn dedicated to Father.

Although the context of the allegory in Exod 13:2 in Philo's text differs from *Haer.* 1.3.4, the logic in interpreting the passages is strikingly similar: it is not only the firstborn (πρωτότοκος) who opens the womb from the inside through birth, but there is another being dedicated to the Father as his firstborn (πρωτογενές) that opens the womb from the outside. In Philo, the womb represents the mind, speech, or the body; the offspring, the activities of these faculties (understanding, voice, sense perception, and bodily motions); and the one that opens the womb, the Logos dedicated to the Father. In the Valentinian allegory, the emotions of Sophia are referred to as the womb, the offspring represents Sophia's spiritual seed, and the one who opens her womb through knowledge represents the Savior, being the All—that is, the perfect fruit of the Pleroma. Despite the apparent differences in the context of allegorical interpretation, the Valentinian reading of the text evidently requires an allegorical double reading of Exod 13:12 similar to that of Philo in *Her.* 117–119.

3.3.4. A Moderate Allegorical Teaching in Ptolemy's *Letter to Flora*

The second example of Valentinian allegorical exegesis, in Ptolemy's *Letter to Flora*, represents the moderate approach. As the example demonstrates, the protological myth was not always the starting point for Valentinian exegesis. The *Letter to Flora* is preserved as a whole in Greek in Epiphanius's *Panarion* (33.3–7). The letter is didactic, and it is composed stylistically according to the pattern of Greco-Roman public speeches.[79] The argumentative technique of the letter follows the philosophical method of διαίρεσις, "division," according to which the subject matter is divided into categories, and specific differences between terms are made explicit.

Ptolemy's letter is addressed to Flora, who is addressed as "my honorable sister." It is possible that the epistle is not a real private letter but is comparable to the philosophical letters written by Epicurus or Porphyry.[80] It is thus possible that Flora is a fictitious recipient of the letter, which intends to simulate a real situation in which someone who does not yet belong to the inner circle of the Valentinian community would be in need of further instruction to "prove worthy of the apostolic tradition."[81]

---

79. See Dunderberg, *Beyond Gnosticism*, 79–80.

80. See Christoph Markschies, "New Research on Ptolemaeus Gnosticus," *ZAC* 4 (2000): 228–33.

81. There have been attempts to connect the author of the letter to the incident mentioned by Justin in his *Second Apology*. There, Justin recalls a Christian teacher in Rome called Ptolemy whose female disciple converted to Christianity and left her husband on account of his debauchery. Justin mentions that this Ptolemy was arrested and eventually executed for being a Christian under the prefect Urbinus (144–160 CE). Although it cannot be said with certainty whether the Ptolemy of Justin's *Apology* is identical with the Valentinian Ptolemy, it is interesting that the *Letter to Flora* handles the question of the permission to divorce under certain conditions and the ethics

The consensus is that the intellectual background of Ptolemy's letter was the Marcionite schism in Rome in the middle of the second century.[82] Ptolemy intends to solve one main problem, which was related to the two erroneous opinions of the origin of the Mosaic law. On the one hand, Ptolemy's opponents were ordinary Christians, who suggested that Moses's law came from the highest God. On the other hand, some radical Marcionites thought that the law of Moses came from the devil.[83] Ptolemy represents a sophisticated middle way between these extremes. He argues that the law of Moses came not from the perfect God or the devil but from God of the Hebrew Bible, who, though not perfect, is just.

Ptolemy found evidence for his argument in John's Gospel. He explains that "all things" (τὰ πάντα) in John 1:3 refers to *the creation of the visible cosmos* by the Demiurge, who is just and hates evil:

> For our Savior declared that a house or city divided against itself will not be able to stand [Matt 12:25]. And, further, the apostle states that the craftmanship of the world is his, and that "all things were made through him, and without him was not anything made" [John 1:10–11], thus anticipating these liars' flimsy wisdom. And the craftmanship is that of a

---

of revenge, issues that are also present in Justin's story about Ptolemy and his female disciple (see Dunderberg, *Beyond Gnosticism*, 90–92). Tuomas Rasimus is rather confident that the Ptolemy mentioned by Justin can be identified with the author of the *Letter to Flora*; Thomassen is, however, skeptical on the matter. See Rasimus, "Ptolemaeus and the Valentinian Exegesis of John's Prologue," in *The Legacy of John: Second-Century Reception of the Fourth Gospel*, ed. Rasimus, NovTSup 132 (Leiden: Brill, 2010), 154–55; Thomassen, *Spiritual Seed*, 494. I suggest that we do not have enough information to identify the Ptolemy in Justin's *Apology* with the Valentinian Ptolemy who wrote the *Letter to Flora*. Jesus's prohibition of divorce was central to Marcion's argumentation, and the topic of the letter may therefore have been part of anti-Marcionite polemics rather than the personal circumstances of the suggested recipient of the letter (see Markschies, "New Research," 248).

82. Perkins is skeptical of the Marcionite influences on Ptolemy's letter ("Valentinians," 381–84). Ptolemy may have corrected gnostic exegesis and the harsh distinction between the Demiurge and God of Jesus without participating in the particular anti-Marcionite discussion. Certainly it is possible, but unlikely.

83. Rasimus notes that Marcion himself never identified the Jewish God with the devil. Marcion's disciple Apelles considered the lawgiver to be the devil, though the good God is taken to be the one who created the world. Dunderberg remarks that Ptolemy's view in the debate is actually rather close to the moderate Marcionite position (see Rasimus, "Ptolemaeus and the Valentinian Exegesis," 147; Dunderberg, *Beyond Gnosticism*, 87–90).

god who is just and hates evil, not a pernicious one as believed by these thoughtless people, who take no account of the craftsman's forethought and so are blind not only in the eye of the soul but even in the eyes of the body. (*Flor.* 33.3.5–6)[84]

Evidently, the demiurgic agent in this passage is the Savior, who entered into the world on his own (John 1:11), and the just God—that is, the Demiurge—is a separate agent through whom all things in the world were made (John 1:3).[85] Ptolemy thus says that the apostle "took away in advance the baseless wisdom of the false accusers, and shows that the creation is not due to a God who brings corruption but to the one who is just and hates evil."

It is notable that Ptolemy seems to give a significantly different interpretation of John's prologue in the *Letter to Flora* than in the protological commentary attributed to him in *Haer.* 1.8.5, in which "all things" (John 1:3) refers to the creation of the *intelligible cosmos* by the Logos. Irenaeus criticizes the latter view, arguing that "all things" must refer to the creation of the visible cosmos by the Logos, because it is stated in the Gospel of John that the Savior came to his own world, "but according to Marcion and those like him, neither was the world made by him nor did he come to his own things, but to those of another" (Roberts and Rambaut, *ANF* 1).

It is unlikely, however, that Ptolemy is the author of the protological interpretation in *Haer.* 1.8.5. The ascription of the text ("et Ptolemaeus quidem ita") exists only in the Latin translation of Irenaeus's work but is missing in Epiphanius's Greek text. Markschies argues that the ascription in the Latin texts is an error. Therefore, Ptolemy's *Letter to Flora*, which does not contain any cosmological myth, is the only reliable source for a reconstruction of Ptolemy's own teaching. Dunderberg agrees with Markschies and is doubtful whether the commentary on John's prologue

---

84. Trans. Brakke and Layton, *Gnostic Scriptures*, 440.
85. Thomassen, *Spiritual Seed*, 122–23; Rasimus, "Ptolemaeus and the Valentinian Exegesis," 149–50. Ptolemy's view can also be found in some other Valentinian sources (e.g., *Exc.* 45.3): the Savior is the "first creator," who delegated the final task of creation to Sophia and the Demiurge, who finally shaped the psychic heaven and material earth out of precosmic matter (Gen 1:1). It is notable that Heracleon also interpreted "all things" in John 1:3 to be a reference to "the cosmos and its contents" (Origen, *Comm. Jo.* 2.14.100–103, frag. 1 Vö; see Thomassen, "Heracleon," 177–78; Pagels, *Johannine Gospel*, 23–35).

comes from Ptolemy.[86] It should also be noted that Clement presents in *Exc.* 6–7 a parallel version of the same protological commentary without any mention of Ptolemy's name. Moreover, Clement's source material goes back to Alexandria, whereas Ptolemy can be located in Rome. Thus, it is rather likely that the original author of the commentary on John's prologue in *Haer.* 1.8.5 is not Ptolemy but some unknown Valentinian teacher in Alexandria.

It is of note that both Irenaeus and Ptolemy used a common anti-Marcionite argumentation, which circulated among Christian teachers in Rome. Ptolemy's view differed, however, from Irenaeus in that, in addition to the Savior, who was the principal creative agent, there was another agent, the just Demiurge, through whom the Savior created the world. From Ptolemy's point of view, Irenaeus represented the other extreme view, according to which the creation, as well as the Mosaic law, came from a perfect God. Ptolemy, however, used practically the same method as Irenaeus to reject the notion of some radical opponents that the devil created the cosmos.[87]

Ptolemy's *Letter to Flora* can be regarded as an introductory teaching that is said to be followed by a more elaborated teaching about the first principles and the origin of the cosmos, which would then explain "how different natures evolved from the Father of All." Dunderberg notes correctly that we cannot be sure whether the cosmological myth Ptolemy had in mind was identical with what we now find in *Haer.* 1.1.1–3.[88] It seems that Valentinian exegesis was not in all cases as radical or otherworldly as Irenaeus tried to depict it but was instead multidimensional. That is, there may be different levels of interpretation for the same biblical texts, the level of interpretation depending on the intellectual level of the audience and the context in which the texts were read and studied. On that point, Valentinian exegesis parallels Philo, who is also a proponent of multiple exegesis.

---

86. See Dunderberg, *Beyond Gnosticism*, 197–99. Thomassen and Rasimus suggest that the ascription is authentic and that the author of the protological commentary attested in *Haer.* 1.8.5 is Ptolemy. Rasimus points out that that Epiphanius follows Hippolytus rather than Irenaeus in identifying various heresies. Hippolytus maintains in his *Syntagma* and *Refutatio* that a variant of the model system goes back to Valentinus, not Ptolemy. This would explain why Epiphanius dropped the ascription from his text (see Thomassen, *Spiritual Seed*, 20–22, 263–68; Rasimus, "Ptolemaeus and the Valentinian Exegesis," 165–66).

87. See Rasimus, "Ptolemaeus and the Valentinian Exegesis," 149–54.

88. See Dunderberg, *Beyond Gnosticism*, 79.

3. Allegorical Interpretation in Philo and among the Valentinians

There are also allegorical teachings in the *Letter to Flora* that parallel Philo's teachings concerning the division of Mosaic law and his spiritual interpretations of its cultic observances. Ptolemy divides the Mosaic law into three parts. First is the law of God, which comes from the Demiurge but is imperfect; second, the commandments, which contain human additions by Moses or the elders; third is the law interwoven with injustice (i.e., *lex talionis*), which was abolished absolutely by the Savior as being incompatible with his own nature.

Ptolemy shows that the Ten Commandments represents the pure law, which contains both "commands" (προστάξεις) and "prohibitions" (ἀπαγορεύσεις). This is the law that was made perfect by the Savior. The cultic law (offerings, circumcision, the Sabbath, fasting, Passover, the Feast of Unleavened Bread, and the like) is the "typical and symbolic" (τυπικὸν καὶ συμβολικόν), which "the Savior changed from the perceptible, visible level to the spiritual, invisible one" (ὃ μετέθηκεν ὁ σωτὴρ ἀπὸ αἰσθητοῦ καὶ φαινομένου ἐπὶ τὸ πνευματικὸν καὶ ἀόρατον; *Flor.* 33.5.1–6.6).[89]

Philo divides in *Praem.* 1–3 the historical from the legislative parts of the law. In addition to the creation of the world, the historical part contains the history of the families as well as the punishments of and rewards for wicked and virtuous human beings. In *Mos.* 2.46, the legislative part—that is, the Ten Commandments and particular laws—is divided into "commandments" (προστάξεις) and "prohibitions" (ἀπαγορεύσεις).[90] It seems that Ptolemy was familiar with a categorization of the Mosaic law similar to that used by Philo in *Mos.* 2.46.[91]

Philo also makes in *Decal.* 175–176 critical comments on the delivery of the law. While the Ten Commandments were dictated directly by God, the particular laws came through Moses, whom God filled with the Spirit to become capable of interpreting his will. However, Philo regards the whole law as perfect, regardless of the means through which it was

---

89. Trans. Brakke and Layton, *Gnostic Scriptures*, 442; see Fallon, "Law in Philo and Ptolemy," 46–47.

90. Philo's view concerning the division of the law is not consistent. In *Mos.* 2.45–48, the creation of the world is included in the historical part of the law, whereas in *Praem.* 1–3, Philo sees creation as distinct from history and legislation. Moreover, in *Abr.* 2–5, the lives of the noble humans described by Moses serve as archetypes for the general and particular laws. They were "living and rational laws," who accepted "that nature itself was—as in truth it is—the eldest of statutes."

91. Fallon, "Law in Philo and Ptolemy," 49.

distributed to humankind. There are only some problems in the execution of the penalties of the law. For Philo, it is intolerable that a good God could himself have been responsible for the execution of penalties for breaking the law of God. Therefore, God delegates the punishments to his subordinate punitive powers or angels (see *Conf.* 180; *Fug.* 66). Ptolemy's criticism of the law is harsher than Philo's. It is not only the execution of the death penalty but the law of retaliation itself that is mixed with evil and must be rejected altogether.

In addition to the theory concerning the division of the law, Ptolemy presents in his letter allegorical interpretations of the cultic commandments "according to the image of the spiritual level." Animal sacrifices are not allowed. Rather, Christians should offer only spiritual sacrifices such as praise, fellowship, and beneficence. In the same manner, circumcision does not mean a fleshly, outward ritual but a circumcision of the heart. Likewise, the real meaning of the Sabbath and fasting is about spiritual rest and abstention from evil deeds.[92]

The symbolic interpretation of the law of Moses is attested in various Jewish and early Christian sources (see, e.g., Epistle of Barnabas). Circumcision as a symbol for spiritual improvement and the excision of pleasures was a commonplace in Hellenistic Jewish teaching.[93] In *Spec.* 1.8–10, Philo mentions this interpretation, and Paul also draws a distinction between the external sign and the spiritual significance of the covenant (see Rom 2:29). Likewise, Philo mentions in *Mos.* 2.108 the metaphor of sacrifice as the "piety of the soul who loves God" and "the thanksgiving of the sages," which parallels Paul, who teaches that piety is the real sacrifice of the believer (see Rom 12:1–2). It is likely, then, that Ptolemy's source for these allegories was not Philo but Paul.

There are, however, allegories of cultic law in Ptolemy's letter that have exact parallels not in the New Testament but in Philo. Paul does not mention, for instance, the spiritual interpretation of the Sabbath as avoiding evil deeds, as Ptolemy does, nor does he allegorize the Jewish dietary laws (see *Flor.* 33.5.12–14). These ideas are rather found in Philo, who says that the Sabbath is not only the day of philosophizing and contemplation

---

92. See Dunderberg, *Beyond Gnosticism*, 83.

93. Abraham's circumcision as a symbol of the excision of pleasures is mentioned also in the Gos. Phil. 82.26–29: "When Abraham [was able] to see what he was to see, [he] circumcised the flesh of the foreskin, thus teaching us that it is necessary to destroy the flesh."

of the creation but also the day for repentance and ethical improvement (see *Mos.* 2.215; *Decal.* 98). In addition, fasting is not solely abstinence or avoidance of certain foods but a symbol of the fight against bodily passions together with the holy prayers, "in which they are wont to ask that their old sins may be forgiven and new blessings gained and enjoyed" (*Mos.* 2.24). In addition to the division of the Mosaic law, Ptolemy's spiritual interpretations of the Mosaic law bring his hermeneutics rather close to the interpretations that are found in the writings of Philo, especially in the *De vita Mosis*.

3.4. Conclusions

The origin of the Valentinian tradition can be traced back to the years after the Jewish revolt in Alexandria, during the first half of the second century CE. The religious and intellectual milieu of Alexandria served as an urban setting for the birth of various gnostic school traditions, which continued the traditions of philosophical Judaism. The school of Valentinus can be compared with a philosophical school movement, which intended to revise especially the theology of the Gospel of John and the apostle Paul in the light of teachings derived from Platonism. The Valentinian teachers endeavored to intellectualize Christianity in a similar manner to how Philo endeavored to intellectualize Judaism in order to make it more compatible with the Greco-Roman society.

The attitude of the Valentinians toward Christian cultic observances was twofold. On the one hand, the Christian rituals were seen merely as *propaideia* for the deeper mysteries, without any transformative power. On the other, the sacraments were converted into Platonic theurgy and were construed as the means to gain spiritual redemption from the bondage of the flesh. It is not unreasonable, then, to think that the different views concerning the rituals were related to more profound anthropological disagreements among Platonists concerning the degree of the incarnation of the soul.

The Valentinian teachers adopted the method of allegorical interpretation of the Bible from their Jewish forerunners. The allegorical method was also used by the Hellenistic philosophers as a hermeneutical tool to interpret Greco-Roman myths and poetry. Philo and the Valentinians differed from them in assuming that the allegorical level of meaning was not something to be artificially added to the text but rather that the texts of the Scriptures were intentionally written allegorically. Therefore, they had to be decoded through the allegorical method to gain information on their true and everlasting meaning. In many cases, the Valentinian exegetes reformed the preceding gnostic *mythopoiēsis* by aligning the gnostic myth more closely with the actual biblical text and thus downplaying the distinctively gnostic motifs of the myth.

The two case studies handled at the end of this chapter demonstrate that the Valentinian exegesis was multidimensional. The degree of allegorical symbolism depended on the intellectual level of the intended audience and the context of interpretation, an approach that parallels Philo, who was also a proponent of this method of multiple exegesis. Although Irenaeus tried to create the impression that Valentinians were producing arbitrary readings of the scriptures, Valentinian exegesis was in fact based on a careful reading of the text, in search for clues and invitations for the use of the allegorical method. The allegorical meaning was thus not added arbitrarily to the text but followed certain methodological rules of interpretation.

Ptolemy's *Letter to Flora* proves that the author of the letter was familiar with the categorization of Mosaic law and the symbolical interpretations of Jewish cultic law that are also found in Philo's *De vita Mosis*. Although Valentinian theologians may have found especially Philo's transcendental exegesis in the Allegorical Commentary valuable for their own hermeneutical systems, this was not always the case. Ptolemy was not interested in speculative interpretations of the Bible, and he seems to represent a rather moderate allegorical approach, similar to Heracleon's, whose hermeneutical method set limits on extreme allegorical imagination.

4
Protology: The Creation of the Intelligible Cosmos

In this chapter, I investigate issues related to the conception of the creation of the eternal realm, the so-called intelligible cosmos (κόσμος νοητός), a term first mentioned by Philo. The Valentinian protological account becomes comprehensible in light of Middle Platonic philosophy, which intended to harmonize the Platonic two-world model with Aristotelian transcendent philosophy and Pythagorean first principles. Philo can be located in the initial stage of this same Platonic-Pythagorean tradition.[1] It seems, then, that in most cases a common Middle Platonic intellectual background can explain the parallels between Philo and Valentinians. I will show, however, that Valentinus and his followers found some of Philo's protological allegories inspiring for their own Platonizing exegesis of the Bible, especially concerning the prologue of the Gospel of John.

---

1. David Winston points out that the philosophical-mystical tradition of Plato was "the first intellectual love for Philo" (*Logos*, 13). In *Fug.* 82, Philo regards Plato as a fellow traveler in the pursuit of a vision of the truth (see Niehoff, *Philo of Alexandria*, 205–6). The question concerning Philo's philosophical orientation is a matter of scholarly debate in Philonic studies. David Winston, Gregory Sterling, and John Dillon are of the opinion that Philo can be regarded as a Middle Platonic philosopher. See Winston, *Philo of Alexandria*, 1–37; Dillon, *Middle Platonists*, 139–83; Sterling, "Platonizing Moses: Philo and Middle Platonism," *SPhiloA* 5 (1993): 99–103. David Runia maintains that Philo was not a Platonist in the sense that he would have belonged to any institutionalized Platonic school. Although Philo was familiar with Platonic doctrines, primacy was given to the actual text, which the commentator was obliged to follow wherever it led. Thus Philo was not a philosopher but an exegete. See Runia, *Philo of Alexandria*, 544; Runia, "The Rehabilitation of the Jackdaw: Philo of Alexandria and Ancient Philosophy," in *Greek and Roman Philosophy 100 BC–200 AD*, ed. Robert W. Sharples and Richard Sorabji, BICS 94 (London: Institute of Classical Studies, 2007), 2:491–95.

4.1. Philo, Valentinian Teachers, and Transcendental Monotheism

In his article "Eudorus of Alexandria and Early Imperial Platonism," Mauro Bonazzi describes the closure of the Academy and the Lyceum in the period between the first century BCE and the first century CE; Aristotle's school treatises were then put into circulation, and there was a revival of interest in Pythagorean pseudepigrapha. Aristotle's philosophy became a tool to discuss philosophical issues linked to interpreting Plato's writings.[2] It was Eudorus of Alexandria (ca. 30 BCE) who revised Plato's cosmological model in the *Timaeus* in light of Aristotle's metaphysics and neo-Pythagorean principles in a way that became standard among later Middle Platonic teachers. Bonazzi says, "Eudorus' doctrine appears as one of the first attempts to break with Stoic tradition, with the aim of promoting a turn (or return) to a transcendent principle."[3] The Pythagorean turn in Eudorus had a significant impact on the intellectual milieu, especially in Alexandria. During this development, some pseudo-Pythagorean works (e.g., Pseudo-Archytas and Pseudo-Timaeus's *On the Nature of the World*) were written in Eudorus's circle to emphasize the Pythagorean nature of the Old Academy.[4]

The discussion concerning Pythagorean protology started during the Old Academy. In the *Parmenides*, Plato takes up the problem of how the world of multiplicity can be derived from unity, which is beyond understanding (*Parm.* 141e–142a; see also *Phileb.* 26e–30e). The systematic development of the series of paired principles was also introduced by Plato's immediate successors (Speusippus and Xenocrates), but their views were still based on dualist philosophy. Eudorus, for the first time, articulated the idea of the transcendent One above the Monad and the Dyad, bringing these opposite principles together.[5]

---

2. Mauro Bonazzi, "Eudorus of Alexandria and Early Imperial Platonism," in Sharples and Sorabji, *Greek and Roman Philosophy*, 2:365–77. For Eudorus's transcendentalizing Platonism, see Michael Trapp, "Neopythagoreans," in Sharples and Sorabji, *Greek and Roman Philosophy*, 2:351–55.

3. Bonazzi, "Eudorus of Alexandria," 373; see also Turner, *Sethian Gnosticism*, 345–55.

4. See Riccardo Chiaradonna, "Platonist Approaches to Aristotle: From Antiochus of Ascalon to Eudorus of Alexandria," in *Aristotle, Plato and Pythagoreanism in the First Century BC*, ed. Malcolm Schofield (Cambridge: Cambridge University Press, 2013), 41–42; see also Niehoff, *Philo of Alexandria*, 202–6.

5. Eudorus's system is preserved in the sixth-century Neoplatonist Simplicius's *In Arist. phys.* 181.10–30. See Mauro Bonazzi, "Pythagoreanizing Aristotle: Eudorus and the Systematization of Platonism," in Schofield, *Aristotle, Plato and Pythagoreanism*,

4. Protology: The Creation of the Intelligible Cosmos 91

The most influential critic of Plato's *Timaeus* was Aristotle, whose supreme God was a transcendent and metacosmic intellect that did not engage in any practical activity in the physical cosmos. Rather than an efficient cause of the changes of the visible world, God was an unmoved mover, who moved everything through attraction (ὄρεξις), like a magnet (see Aristotle, *Metaph.* 12.1072b.1–30). Eudorus's innovation was to identify the Aristotelian prime mover with the Platonic idea of good, which became the "highest God" (ὁ ὑπεράνω θεός). At the same time, the supreme God was identified with the Pythagorean "one" (τὸ ἕν), and Ideas—which had, in Plato's cosmology, an independent existence—became the thoughts of God. As the Ideas externalized from God's mind, they became the Monad (ἡ μονάς), which was commonly associated with the rational aspect of Plato's World Soul. Besides the Monad was the Dyad (ἡ δυάς), which was also derived from the One to become the principle of matter and multiplicity. In Pseudo-Archytas's *Principles*, the first pair of principles (the Monad and the Dyad) are equated with Aristotelian form and matter, but there is a third principle above them, the highest God, which brings them together.[6]

In the various Middle Platonic systems, the discussion concerning the first principles is related to these basic ontological structures, the One, the Monad, and the Dyad, although the systems may differ in detail. In some systems, the demiurgic activity of the transcendent God is delegated to the Monad, which was divided or infected as it came in contact with

---

160–86; John Peter Kenney, "Ancient Apophatic Theology," in *Gnosticism and Later Platonism: Themes, Figures and Texts*, ed. John D. Turner and Ruth Majercik (Atlanta: Society of Biblical Literature, 2000), 260–64; John Peter Kenney, *Mystical Monotheism: A Study in Ancient Platonic Theology* (Hanover, NH: Brown University Press, 1991), 32–43; David Runia, *Philo of Alexandria and the Timaeus of Plato*, PhA 44 (Leiden: Brill, 1986), 46–55; Dillon, *Middle Platonists*, 114–39, esp. 128.

6. See Bonazzi, "Eurodorus of Alexandria," 376. The author of Pseudo-Archytas's *Principles* is not the early Pythagorean Archytas of Tarentum, though in antiquity Iamblichus, followed by others within the tradition, believed that Archytas had composed this text. Griffin points out that the local context for the ideas given in this treatise suggests that its author was writing in the middle of the first century BCE, possibly at the time of the Peripatetics Andronicus and Boethus and the Platonist Eudorus of Alexandria, each of whom wrote on Aristotle's *Categories* to challenge Stoic materialistic cosmology. See Michael Griffin, *Aristotle's "Categories" in the Early Roman Empire* (Oxford: Oxford University Press, 2015), 97–102.

preexistent matter.[7] In some other systems, the opposition of the first principles (the Monad and the Dyad) is stressed in a manner that led to a strict cosmological dualism.[8]

The Valentinian protology can be seen as a Christianized version of the neo-Pythagorean philosophy, which saw the intelligible cosmos as a combination of form (i.e., active, male) and matter (i.e., passive, female), above which was located the transcendent One, who possessed the characteristics of the Aristotelian self-thinking God. The Valentinian theology is in harmony with the description of the Middle Platonic doxographer Aëtius, who explains Plato's view about God in the following way:

> Socrates and Plato (say that the deity is) the One, the single-natured, the monadic, the true Being, the Good. All such names immediately refer to the Intellect. The deity, then, is an Intellect, (that is,) a separate Form; Of this (God) as Father and Maker the other intelligible divine beings (the so-called intelligible cosmos) are the descendants, and they are the models for the visible cosmos. In addition to these there are ethereal powers (these are incorporeal logoi), and powers that inhere both in air and in water, as well as the sense-perceptible descendants of the first god, sun, moon, stars, earth and the all-embracing heaven. (*Plac.* 1.7.22)[9]

---

7. In Numenius's system, the first Monad is absolute unity, but the second Monad is unstable, because he desires Matter, and divided, because he seized material things. On the system of Numenius, see Dillon, *Middle Platonists*, 367–68. In Numenius, the distinction between the first and second God is that the first God is at rest, while the second God is in intellectual outward motion. The intellectual life of the first God is directed toward himself, which generates an attraction toward himself and forms the order of the world. The intellectual motion of the second God is directed toward creation and matter. See John Dillon, "Numenius: Some Ontological Questions," in Sharples and Sorabji, *Greek and Roman Philosophy*, 2:397–402.

8. Plutarch was still working with dualistic systems in which the principle of the Dyad was associated with an evil world-soul. On the dualistic system in *De animae procreatione in Timaeo*, see Jan Opsomer, "Plutarch on the One and the Dyad," in Sharples and Sorabji, *Greek and Roman Philosophy*, 2:379–83.

9. Trans. Jaap Mansfeld and David Runia, eds., *Aëtiana V: An Edition of the Reconstructed Text of the Placita with a Commentary and a Collection of Related Texts*, PhA 153 (Leiden: Brill, 2020), 4:2077. See also David Runia, "The Beginnings of the End: Philo of Alexandria and Hellenistic Theology," in *Traditions of Theology: Studies in Hellenistic Theology, Its Background and Aftermath*, ed. Dorothea Frede and André Laks, PhA 89 (Leiden: Brill, 2002), 282.

These views can also be found in the writings of Philo, who may have been earlier than Aëtius.[10] Although it is unlikely that Philo would have been a member of any philosophical school, his allegorical commentaries on the Scriptures have all the hallmarks of the Middle Platonic tradition. Philo can thus be located within the earliest phase of the Platonic tradition that goes back to the circle of Eudorus of Alexandria. For Philo, Moses was a Platonic philosopher, one who encrypted neo-Pythagorean principles in numbers, etymologies, and symbols in the law.[11] In fact, Philo's cosmological or anthropological allegories only become comprehensible through the philosophical discussion of the Middle Platonic tradition. As Dillon points out:

> Certainly, God is in his heaven, and he is the creator of our world, but he did not create it according to a pattern laid up in his mind, which is co-extensive with his heaven. If we find such a concept in a Jewish thinker such as Philo, or later Christian theorists such as Clement or Origen, we reckon that it has been imported from somewhere else; and the same is the case if we come upon it in a document of Gnosticism, Christian or otherwise.[12]

In this study, Philo is located in the Platonic-Aristotelian tradition, which owes much to the Pythagorean revival among the philosophical circles

---

10. For the dating of Aëtius, see Mansfeld and Runia, *Aëtiana V*, 1:43–44.

11. Harry Wolfson hypothesizes that Philo was the founder of a religious philosophy that was adopted by the later Middle Platonists and Platonizing dogmatists of the nascent orthodoxy (*Philo*, 2:434–60). Although Wolfson's theory has gained little support, it goes without saying that Philo did not only repeat the doctrines of the contemporary philosophical schools but also created his own. Although the influence of Philo's philosophy remained mainly inside the Christian tradition, it is possible, even probable, that Numenius was familiar with Philo's works. In *Praeparatio evangelica*, for instance, Eusebius mentions the famous saying of Numenius: "What is Plato but Moses speaking in Attic Greek?" Evidently, then, Numenius must have been familiar with and used Jewish material (frag. 9 = Eusebius, *Praep. ev.* 9.8.1–2; 10a = Origen, *Cels.* 4.51). Gregory Sterling argues that Numenius may have altered standard Platonic vocabulary in frag. 13 (= Eusebius, *Praep. ev.* 11.18.13–14) in a way that parallels Philo's *Mut.* 11–14 (see also *Post.* 171). See Sterling, "The Theft of Philosophy: Philo of Alexandria and Numenius of Apamea," *SPhiloA* 27 (2015): 71–85.

12. John Dillon, "*Pleroma* and Noetic Cosmos: A Comparative Study," in *Neoplatonism and Gnosticism*, ed. Richard T. Wallis and Jay Bregman, ISNS 6 (Albany: State University of New York Press, 1992), 99.

of Alexandria.¹³ The three main topics discussed within these circles—namely, ideas, matter, and the role of the Demiurge—and presented in the quotation of Aëtius above were also fundamental in Philo's philosophical exegesis. The main principles of the Middle Platonic tradition relevant to Philo's writings are:

1. the unknowable and transcendent first principle, called the One, God, or the first Monad, who is also the Creator of All;
2. the use of the Pythagorean principles in conceptualizing the first principles of the cosmos;
3. the second Monad, which is derived from the first Monad and is identified with the Logos and associated with the Platonic world soul;
4. ideas as the thoughts of God, which are located in the second Monad (i.e., the Logos); and
5. the precosmic principle of matter (i.e., the Dyad), which is derived from the Logos.

In his exegetical treatises, Philo does not present philosophical teachings systematically, as the ancient doxographers did. Philosophical ideas are instead revealed from the Scriptures through spiritual exegesis. In his later career, Philo also wrote philosophical works in which he systematically discusses some fundamental philosophical questions, such as the eternity of the world or providence.¹⁴ Although Philo may have regarded himself mainly as an interpreter of the sacred Scriptures, his writings contains many of the theories that became dominant in first- and second-century Platonic tradition.¹⁵

---

13. Philo knew some works of the Pythagoreans by name (*Aet.* 12), and he also praised the excellence of the doctrines of the Pythagoreans (*Prob.* 2). Clement of Alexandria even called Philo "a Pythagorean" (*Strom.* 2.100.3).

14. Niehoff asserts that Philo's philosophical works as well as the Exposition of the Law "gravitate toward Stoic position, engage Roman discourses, and tend to avoid the radical Platonic transcendentalism of the Allegorical Commentary from his early Alexandrian period" (*Philo of Alexandria*, 19).

15. In an Armenian fragment of Philo (*Anim.* 7) that contains a discussion between Philo and his nephew Alexander, Philo says that he is not a teacher but an interpreter. This would mean that Philo was an interpreter of ancient philosophical teachings, but he did not regard himself as a teacher of a philosophical school, who initiated others (see Runia, "Philo of Alexandria and Ancient Philosophy," 493).

4. Protology: The Creation of the Intelligible Cosmos 95

In Philo's model community, Therapeutae, the object of worship is "the Self-existent who is better than the good, purer than the One and more primordial than the Monad" (*Contempl.* 2).[16] According to Philo's transcendental monism, God "resembles nothing among created things, but so completely transcends them, that even the swiftest understanding falls far short of apprehending Him and acknowledges its failure" (*Somn.* 1.184). Philo's theory concerning the origin of matter was influenced by teachings that supposedly went back to Eudorus of Alexandria.[17] In addition, the theory of ideas as God's thoughts and the externalization of God's thinking as his Logos (= Monad) is first found in Philo. It would be far-fetched to suppose, however, that this teaching originated in Philo.[18] The most credible explanation, rather, is that Philo adapted the conception of ideas as God's thought(s) from the Platonic circles of Alexandria, possibly from Eudorus, which he integrated into his Logos

---

16. Philo stresses that God is apprehensible to himself alone: "For this which is better than the good, more venerable than the monad, purer than the unit, cannot be discerned by anyone else; to God alone is it permitted to apprehend God" (*Praem.* 40).

17. Willy Theiler suggests that Philo drew his teachings from the commentary by Eudorus on Plato's *Timaeus*. See Theiler, "Philo von Alexandria und der hellenisierte *Timaeus*," in *Philomathes: Studies and Essays in the Humanities in Memory of Philip Merlan*, ed. Robert B. Palmer and Robert G. Hamerton-Kelly (The Hague: Nijhoff, 1971), 25–35.

18. According to Plato's *Timaeus*, the Ideas exist independently from the Demiurge and the Receptacle as the third *arche* of creation. It became common within the Middle Platonic tradition to locate the origin of the Ideas in the mind of God. There were, however, two phases to their generation: first, collectively in the mind of the transcendent One; second, as the objects of his thought. This sequence is attested in the *Placita* of Aëtius (1.3.20): Πλάτων ... τρεῖς ἀρχάς, τὸν θεὸν τὴν ἰδέαν· ὑφ' οὗ, ἐξ οὗ, πρὸς ὅ. ὁ δὲ θεὸς νοῦς ἐστι τοῦ κόσμου, ὕλη δὲ τὸ ὑποκείμενον πρῶτον γενέσει καὶ φθορᾷ, ἰδέα δὲ οὐσία ἀσώματος ἐν τοῖς νοήμασιν καὶ φαντασίαις τοῦ θεοῦ. See Roger Jones, "The Ideas as the Thoughts of God," *CP* 21 (1926): 321. Roberto Radice agrees with Wolfson in that Philo was the inventor of the notion that the Ideas are the thoughts of God. This view was adopted by the later Middle Platonists. See Radice, "Observations on the Theory of the Ideas as Thoughts of God in Philo of Alexandria," *SPhiloA* 3 (1991): 128. Actually, Varro (116–27 BCE) mentions the same concept in the allegory of Minerva springing from the head of Jupiter as the Ideas springing from the mind of God (Augustine, *Civ.* 7.28). Elsewhere, Varro identifies Jupiter with the God of the Jews and called him "Iao," which was the Greek form of Yahweh. See George H. van Kooten, *Paul's Anthropology in Context: The Image of God, Assimilation to God, and Tripartite Man in Ancient Judaism, Ancient Philosophy and Early Christianity*, WUNT 232 (Tübingen: Mohr Siebeck, 2008), 350–52; Dillon, "*Pleroma* and Noetic Cosmos," 101.

theology. Aristotle's conception of God as a self-thinking Nous may have influenced Philo's theory of God (see Aristotle, *Metaph.* 12.1074b.15–34, 1075a.3–5).[19] In Philo, however, God is not solely thinking of himself, as Aristotle's Prime Mover does. Rather, the object of his thinking is both God himself and his own "thoughts," νοήματα—that is, the Ideas. In the intelligible realm, God is identical with his thought, but at the moment he thinks of something distinct from himself, these thoughts—that is, the Ideas—are externalized from himself. Therefore, the ideas do not have an existence of their own but were created by God, who began to think about them. These objects of God's thoughts are the archetypes of the visible cosmos.[20] David Winston points out, "The Logos is not a second entity by the side of God acting on his behalf, nor is it an empty abstraction, but rather a vivid and living hypostatization of an essential aspect of the Deity, the face of God turned toward creation."[21] Thus, the ideas in Philo do not enjoy an independent existence, as in Plato, but are inseparable from God, whose thinking ("ideas") and acting ("powers") operate simultaneously. That is, Philo's God creates the world by thinking about it, and should he ever stop thinking, the whole world would collapse.

Philo conceived of Plato's ideas as not only patterns or representations but also "causes" (αἰτίαι) and "powers" (δυνάμεις). Philo wanted to show that this teaching was revealed to Moses: the glory that surrounds God consists of the powers of God, meaning the Ideas in their precreated stage. Although the powers are in their essence incomprehensible, they produce a sort of "impress" (ἐκμαγεῖον) to be contemplated by "the unsleep-

---

19. See Harry Wolfson, "Extradeical and Intradeical Interpretations of Platonic Ideas," *JHI* 22 (1961): 5; Jones, "Ideas as the Thoughts," 323–24.

20. It was rather difficult for Philo to find biblical proofs for the theory that the Logos of God is a pattern according to which the visible cosmos is created. Philo infers this idea from Gen 1:26–27, where the human being is said to have been created according to the image of God. This image of God was the Logos, and it served as the archetype for the creation of the first human being—or at least the rational part of his soul. In *Opif.* 25, Philo infers that, if the human soul is an image of the Logos, there is no reason to reject the view that the whole visible cosmos is also fashioned according to the Logos, which contained all the archetypical patterns of the visible world. See David Runia, *On the Creation of the Cosmos according to Moses: Introduction, Translation and Commentary*, PACS 1 (Leiden: Brill, 2001), 149–50.

21. See Winston, *Logos*, 49–50.

ing eyes of the mind" (*Spec.* 1.45–48).²² Thus, the intelligible world was framed through these powers, or ideas, and they play the additional role of structuring matter, because God cannot directly shape chaotic matter by himself (*Conf.* 171–173; *Spec.* 1.329). Commenting on the cherubim and the flaming sword in Gen 2:24, Philo explains in *Cher.* 27–28 that God's powers are divided into two categories, "goodness" (ἀγαθότης) and "sovereignty" (ἐξουσία), which are united through the Logos. Thus, the Ideas are not solely patterns of the visible world, but they signify qualities of God's essence.²³

In Philo's worldview, it is the Logos, not the powers, that forms the fundamental intelligible reality. In *Plant.* 9, Philo says that the whole world is interrelated through the Logos, which is a cosmic bond that holds all things together, and in *Cher.* 30 Philo states that the Logos is "fierce and burning heat, that moves with unswerving zeal, teaching thee to choose the good and eschew the evil."²⁴ It is acceptable to suggest, however, that the Logos and the powers are linked among themselves and form a single fabric in order to reconcile God's transcendence with his creative providence in the world and human mind.²⁵

---

22. See Wolfson, *Philo* 1:217–19. Notably, Plato also presents the conception of ideas as powers and causes in *Phaed.* 95e–100a; *Soph.* 247d–e.

23. Philo, *Cher.* 27–28: "The voice told me that while God is indeed one, His highest and chiefest powers [δυνάμεις] are two, even goodness [ἀγαθότης] and sovereignty [ἐξουσία]. Through His goodness He begat all that is, through His sovereignty He rules what He has begotten. And in the midst between the two there is a third which unites them, Reason [λόγος], for it is through reason that God is both ruler and good. Of these two potencies sovereignty and goodness the Cherubim are symbols, as the fiery sword is the symbol of reason." See David Winston, "Philo's Conception of the Divine Nature," in *Neoplatonism and Jewish Thought*, ed. Lenn E. Goodman (Albany: State University of New York Press, 1992), 21–23. God's ruling and creative powers can be equated with Plato's two principles, *peras* and *apeiron* (*Phileb.* 23C–31A). On Philo's understanding of the divine powers, see also Ellen Birnbaum and John Dillon, *Philo of Alexandria On the Life of Abraham: Introduction, Translation, and Commentary*, PACS 6 (Leiden: Brill, 2021), 270–72.

24. For the Logos as a cosmic bond, see Albert C. Geljon and David T. Runia, *Philo of Alexandria on Planting: Introduction, Translation and Commentary*, PACS 5 (Leiden: Brill, 2019), 91–94.

25. Radice, "Philo's Theology," 140–41. David Litwa argues that in Philo's "cosmology, divinity was not a quality of the uncreated God alone. It was shared by a hierarchy of beings existing on a broad scale." See Litwa, "The Deification of Moses in Philo of Alexandria," *SPhiloA* 26 (2014): 6–7.

4.2. Outline of the Valentinian Myth

It became rather common in first-century Middle Platonism to depict God in an apophatic manner, stressing the transcendence of God. Nothing could be used to define the transcendent One, because this would mean that there would be a more profound principle that could then determine the primal God.[26] Alcinous thus describes the first God as eternal, unspeakable, and perfect (see Alcinous, *Epit.* 10.164.30).[27] As noted above, Philo likewise claimed that God was unutterable, unknowable, and absolutely without physical qualities. One could know only the *existence* of God through his Logos and powers, but the *essence* of God remained incomprehensible. For that reason, Philo uses a method of deprivation, according to which God is dissociated from all predicates (see *Deus* 55–56).[28]

According to the Valentinian myth, the primal God is "invisible and unknowable, eternal and unbegotten who remained throughout innumerable cycles of ages in profound serenity and quiescence" (*Haer.* 1.1–2). In the Tripartite Tractate, the Father of All "is the one who has been born by no one, but who, on the contrary, has given birth to the All and has brought it into being." He is "also unchangeable in his eternal being, in that which he is, in that which makes him immutable and that which makes him great," and he does not have a partner as he creates, because this would imply a limitation. The eternal Father has no name that suits him, and his essence is not comprehensible (see Tri. Trac. 51.8–54.35). The primal God cannot be known except through his hypostasized Mind, who can only contemplate the Father's immeasurable greatness surpassing all definitions and limits of understanding (see *Haer.* 1.1.1).

Unfortunately, the Valentinian account of Clement in *Exc.* 43.2–65 (= *Excerpta* C), which forms the basic source text in this study, begins abruptly, without any description of the creation of the intelligible realm,

---

26. Kenney, "Ancient Apophatic Theology," 260–64. Although Aristotle did not claim that God's essence is unknowable, he maintained that God is incorporeal, simple, indivisible, and indefinable (see, e.g., *Phys.* 8.267b; *Metaph.* 12.1072a). See also Richard Norman, "Aristotle's Philosopher-God," in *Psychology and Aesthetics*, vol. 4 of *Articles on Aristotle*, ed. Jonathan Barnes, Malcolm Schofield, and Richard Sorabji (London: Duckworth, 1979), 92–102.

27. See Wolfson, *Philo*, 2:110–15.

28. The same method is attested in Alcinous, *Epit.* 10.165.15; and Clement of Alexandria, *Strom.* 5.71.2–3.

4. Protology: The Creation of the Intelligible Cosmos

that is, the Pleroma (or the Fullness). The first thing mentioned is the descent of the Savior to Sophia, who has been cast out from the Pleroma (*Exc.* 43.2). It is clear that *Excerpta* C presupposes some kind of preceding protological narrative, but we cannot know for sure whether such a protology would be similar to that of Ptolemy's disciples reported by Irenaeus in *Haer.* 1.1.1–3. Taking into account many thematic and terminological similarities, we do not have any reason to suppose that the protological accounts would have differed significantly from each other. I begin my investigation of Valentinian protology by presenting an outline of the myth in *Haer.* 1.1–4, which will be compared with the accounts in *Haer.* 1.8.5, 12.1; Hippolytus, *Haer.* 6.29.3–4; *Excerpta* C; and *Exc.* 6–7.

1. The ultimate transcendent deity Profundity (Βυθός), which is also called First Beginning and First Father (Προαρχή, Προπάτωρ), possesses Thought (Ἔννοια), which is also called Grace and Silence (Χάρις, Σιγή), which depicts the primal Deity as a self-thinking unity.[29]
2. The First Father duplicates himself by emitting the Beginning of all things as a seed in the womb of Silence, who becomes pregnant and gives birth to Mind. The Mind is also called the Only Begotten, Father, and the Beginning (Μονογενής, Πατήρ, Ἀρχή).
3. Mind (Νοῦς) is the *manifested* double of the Father, whereas Thought (Ἔννοια) is the *hidden* double of the Father. Mind is "like and equal to the one who projected him, and who alone comprehends the greatness of the Father." As a copy of the primal unity in duality, the Mind is joined to his pair called Truth (Ἀλήθεια). These four (Profundity, Silence, Mind, and Truth) comprise the principal Pythagorean Tetrad, which is the root of all things.
4. The Mind (i.e., the Only Begotten) and Truth produce Logos and Life (Λόγος, Ζωή), which in turn bring forth the conjugal pair

---

29. Ἔννοια is mentioned as a concept in the Stoic epistemological sequence *phantasia–katalepsis–ennoia*. Philo also uses the term ἔννοια to denote term *concept* (see, e.g., *Opif.* 36). In the Valentinian accounts, ἔννοια describes self-reflection of the Father, and in *Exc.* 7.1–4 ἐνθύμησις is used synonymously with ἔννοια denoting the Father's intention or plan to create intelligible beings (see note 38 below). *Enthumēsis*, which is translated in Latin as *intentio*, *excogitatio*, or *concupiscentia*, seems to contain an element of volition or passion. In *Val.* 9.4., Tertullian calls it *animatio* (see Unger, *Against Heresies*, 138 n. 11).

Human Being and Church (Ἄνθρωπος, Ἐκκλησία). Out of this first-begotten Ogdoad (Profundity, Mind, Logos, Human Being, and their female conjugal pairs) the whole Pleroma, that is, the Fullness, consisting of thirty aeons, is brought forth.[30]

5. The youngest of the aeons, Sophia, wants to know the greatness of the Father of All, but she is prevented from doing so by an aeon called Boundary (Ὅρος), who is produced by the Father as a guardian. His task is to prevent the aeons from knowing the Father. The Boundary keeps the unlimited female aspect of the intelligible world in control.[31] Passion for knowing the Father began already with Mind and Truth, but it spreads like an infec-

---

30. The ten aeons emitted by Logos and Life are Profound and Mingling, Ageless and Union, Self-Producing and Pleasure, Immobile and Blending, and Only Begotten and Happiness. The twelve aeons emitted by Human Being and Church are Advocate and Faith, Paternal and Hope, Maternal and Love, Praise and Understanding, Ecclesiastic and Blessedness, and Desired and Wisdom.

31. In the Platonic-Pythagorean tradition, the term *Limit* (πέρας) describes the process in which unlimited matter was kept in check. In Valentinian theology, this principle was called the Boundary (ὅρος) but also the Cross (σταυρός), the Redeemer (λυτρωτής), the Emancipator (καρπιστής), the Boundary-setter, (ὁροθέτης), and the Guide (μεταγωγεύς). Irenaeus maintains in *Haer.* 1.3.5 that its function of the limiting principle is twofold: when it strengthens the unity, it is called σταυρός, but when it separates from multiplicity, it is called ὅρος (see also *Exc.* 42.1–3). The fan mentioned by John the Baptist (Matt 3:12) is explained to be the Cross, which both purifies the saved and consumes the wicked. These notions are based on an allegorical reading of the Gospel of Matthew. The strengthening power of the Cross is depicted in the words of Jesus, according to which "whoever does not take his cross cannot be my disciple" (Matt 10:38), and the separating power of the Savior is depicted when Jesus says "I came not to send peace, but a sword"—i.e., the Cross (Matt 10:34). The Cross and the Crucifixion were thus associated with the Pythagorean metaphysical principle of separation and unification. In this process, the Cross became a symbol of the twofold process in which the lower essences (i.e., the Dyad) are separated from the higher ones, and at the same time the purer essences are strengthened into a unity (i.e., the Monad). At the protological level, the separation of Sophia's erroneous thought from the Pleroma was seen as a crucifixion. Matter was crucified out of the Pleroma, but at the same time the Pleroma was unified through the Cross. In the same vein, Jesus's crucifixion was not seen in the gospel narratives as an atonement for sins but as a separation of the spiritual and psychic essences from the Savior's material existence. The Valentinians thus transformed the Pauline theology of the cross into a metaphysical theory of separation.

tion to Sophia under the pretense of love directed at the Father without her conjugal partner.

6. Sophia's presumptuous Intention (ἐνθύμησις) is separated from her and is cast out of the Pleroma by the Boundary. In the realm below the Pleroma, the Intention becomes the lower Sophia, called Achamoth. After the separation in the divine realm, the Only Begotten produces another conjugal pair, Christ and the Holy Spirit (Χριστός, Πνεῦμα τὸ ἅγιον), whose task is to inform the other aeons that the First Father is not able to be comprehended except by the Only Begotten (Mind) alone.

7. Finally, all the aeons are strengthened and rectified by Christ and the Holy Spirit, and the whole Pleroma is brought to rest. "The aeons are made equal in form and mind" (μορφῇ καὶ γνωμῇ ἴσους κατασταθῆναι τοὺς Αἰῶνας): all become Mind, Logos, Truth, Life, and so on. As a result, all the aeons emanate the perfect fruit of the Pleroma, Jesus, who contains the Pleroma, that is, the Fullness, within himself. Jesus is called the Savior, Christ, Logos, and All. At the same time, the aeons emanate angels to be the bodyguards of the Savior.

8. Sophia Achamoth, who is now outside the Pleroma, is saved in two subsequent phases that parallel the rectification of Sophia in the Pleroma (see stages 5–6 above). In the first phase, Christ gives form to Sophia, who is amorphous and shapeless, but he does so without recourse to perfect knowledge. However, Christ leaves with Sophia the fragrance of immortality and perfection. After Christ leaves her, she starts to feel various emotions, such as fear, consternation, perplexity, and ignorance, but also the passion of repentance, as she will to turn back (ἐπιστροφή) to the Light, who had deserted her.[32] In the second phase of salvation, the Savior

---

32. The term ἐπιστροφή ("conversion") not only is an essential soteriological term used in the gospels and religious texts in general, but in the Valentinian system it becomes a key technical term that also appears in the texts of later Neoplatonists. Sophia's will to return to the Light became the source of all psychic essences of the world that have an innate desire to return to the Light and to know God. In Neoplatonic epistemology, all souls that have come into being from the One have an innate desire to revert (ἐπιστροφή) to that from which they have proceeded (see Proclus, *Elem.* 31–32; Simplicius, *In Arist. phys.* 147.9: "But soul and the highly valued intellect have come out from what is remaining and turned back to it"). See Pamela Huby

descends to her and gives her form according to the knowledge and heals her passions.

9. The Savior separates the emotions from Sophia, which become the origin of incorporeal matter. The psychic and luminous essence is created out of Sophia's will to return to the Light, and the four cosmic elements (earth, water, air, fire) are created out of Sophia's negative emotions. Sophia herself is transformed from the hylic-psychic stage into a spiritual being. She begins to feel joy as she contemplates the Savior and his angels. As a product of joy, she produces offspring according to the images of the angels of the Savior. Sophia also emitted God as an image of the Father of All, the Demiurge, whose task is to separate psychic and earthly essences and form cosmic elements of the visible cosmos from the unorganized matter. The Demiurge, in turn, emitted the psychic Christ as an image of the Son, and angels as images of the aeons.

Figure 4.1 presents the general structure of the cosmological system described above including also realms of psychic and material essences.

4.3. The Origin of Valentinian Protology

Thomassen observes that the Valentinian protologies can be divided into two main groups. There are theories that give the aeons an existence in the supra-mundane divinity but do not name the particular aeons. The aeons are derived from the primal unity in two consecutive phases: first, in the thought of the Father; second, as independent beings, when they are manifested from him. The same idea of generative exteriorization is the basis for the theories of the second group, but in these accounts the names and the number of the aeons are explicated in detail, and the totality of the aeons is organized according to pairs of syzygies. The protological system described above (*Haer.* 1.1.1–3) belongs to the latter model. The main representative of the former system is the Tripartite Tractate, alongside the Gospel of Truth and other so-called Eastern Valentinian documents.[33]

---

and Christopher C. W. Taylor, trans., *Simplicius: On Aristotle Physics 1.3–4* (London: Bloomsbury, 2011), 56–57.

33. Thomassen maintains that the other writings whose protology can be placed together with Irenaeus's account (*Haer.* 1.1.1–3) in the same group include *Haer.* 1.8.5; Hippolytus, *Haer.* 6.29.2–30.5; Epiphanius, *Pan.* 31.5–6; *Exc.* 6–7.3. The variations

4. Protology: The Creation of the Intelligible Cosmos 103

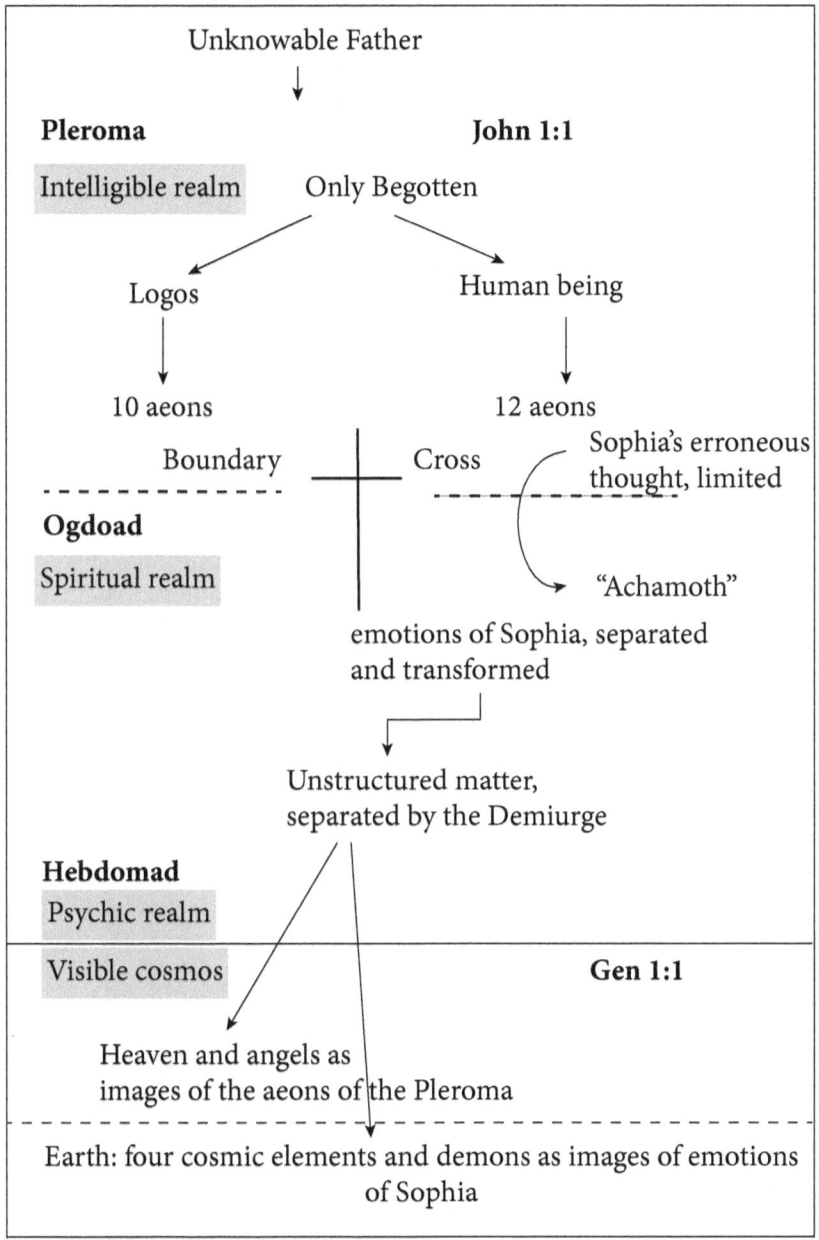

Fig. 4.1. Cosmological System

The difference between the various protological versions lies mainly in the concepts chosen for the description of the same generation of the first principles from the unitary source. Thomassen points out, however, that the Valentinian protologies seek to express the one and the same truth—namely, how the world of multiplicity could be generated from the unitary whole.[34] This means that the Father of All externalized his intention to be known in the form of emanations—that is, intellectual beings called

---

described by Irenaeus in *Haer.* 1.11–12 also represent the same group. The Valentinian Exposition (NHC XI 2) is the only extant document of a protology similar to *Haer.* 1.1.1–3. It belongs, however, to the phase of the Valentinian tradition in which the different Valentinian protologies began to merge: Val. Exp. 29–30 parallels *Haer.* 1.1.1–3, whereas the system described in Val. Exp. 17–24 is closer to the Tripartite Tractate. These notions indicate the enduring significance of the system described by Irenaeus well into the latter part of the third century, when the Valentinian Exposition was presumably written. For details, see Thomassen, *Spiritual Seed*, 194, 236–41.

34. Thomassen is of the opinion that the protology of Irenaeus's system represents a secondary elaboration of a more primitive Valentinian pleromatology. The theories expressed in the Tripartite Tractate and the Gospel of Truth come close to this primitive theory, though there are passages in the former document that "resonate with Origen, Trinitarian debates and Plotinus, and thus with a third century context" (see Thomassen, *Spiritual Seed*, 200; citation from Thomassen, "Relative Chronology," 27). Also, John Kenney observes in the Tripartite Tractate clear influences drawn from third-century Neoplatonic philosophy. See Kenney, "The Platonism of the Tripartite Tractate (NHC 1,5)," in Wallis and Bregman, *Neoplatonism and Gnosticism*, 199, 201–3. It should be noted that the Valentinian systems attested in Irenaeus, *Haer.* 1.1–8, and *Excerpta* C were written at the latest only a few decades after the death of Valentinus. This would mean that the elaboration of the Valentinian protology according to Neopythagorean arithmology was made at a rather early phase, possibly in Rome, in the circle of the disciples of Ptolemy. It is of note that the protological system of the Tripartite Tractate contains only general allusions to the biblical texts, whereas the protology in *Haer.* 1.1–8; *Excerpta* C; and *Exc.* 6–7 contains explicit references to John's prologue and Gen 1–2. This indicates that the Valentinians behind these accounts were more interested in the biblical formulations of the Platonizing cosmic myth. In my opinion, the incarnation theology in the Tripartite Tractate, which Thomassen interprets as representing a primitive version of Valentinianism, reflect a later tendency to revise docetic Valentinian Christology in light of third-century proto-orthodox dogma. Pheme Perkins argues that the Platonic features of the gnostic myth came from the church fathers, who strove to make Valentinians look like Platonists. See Perkins, "Christologies in the Nag Hammadi Codices," *VC* 35 (1981): 379. Perkins's view is not compelling. It would mean that both Irenaeus and Clement would have independently chosen the same rhetorical strategy of labeling the Valentinian system as a deviation from Platonism. It is also notable that Platonic and

4. Protology: The Creation of the Intelligible Cosmos

aeons, who have their origin in the mind of God as his thoughts. These aeons desired to see the one who emitted them and to be informed about their roots, which was without beginning (Irenaeus, *Haer.* 1.2.1; see also Tri. Trac. 54.35–57.23).

It seems that the protological model in *Haer.* 1.1.1–3 is based on the commentary on the prologue of the Gospel of John attested in *Haer.* 1.8.5, having a parallel in Clement's *Exc.* 6.1–7.3. I begin my examination of this primitive version of the Valentinian myth with Clement's account, which represents, in my opinion, a more original version of the Valentinian commentary on John's prologue:

> The passage "In the beginning was the Logos and the Logos was with God and the Logos was God" (John 1:1) the Valentinians accept in this way: They say that "Beginning" is the Only Begotten, whom they also call God, just as he (John) plainly calls him God in what follows: "The Only Begotten God, who is in the bosom of the Father, he has made him known" (John 1:8). The Logos that is "in the Beginning,"—that is, in the Only Begotten, in the Mind and the Truth—he (John) makes known as the Christ, the Logos and Life. Therefore, suitable he says that he is God who is in God and in the Mind. "What came into being in him"—the Logos—"was Life"—his consort [σύζυγος]. Therefore, the Lord also says. "It is I who am the Life." (*Exc.* 6.1–3)[35]

The starting point for the protological theory is the allegorical reading of the prologue of the Gospel of John. The expression "in the beginning was the Logos" (ἐν ἀρχῇ ἦν ὁ λόγος) is an ontological rather than a temporal definition: it depicts how the Logos, as a transcendent being, had its origin in the Beginning or was inside the Beginning. At the same time, the Beginning is personified as the Only Begotten, which was produced by the Father. The Only Begotten contains within himself the Logos

---

Pythagorean opinions were not markers of a heresy for Clement, who admired Philo as a Pythagorean.

35. Trans. Brakke and Layton, *Gnostic Scriptures*, 507; my modifications: Τὸ "ἐν ἀρχῇ ἦν ὁ λόγος καὶ ὁ λόγος ἦν πρὸς τὸν θεὸν καὶ θεὸς ἦν ὁ λόγος" οἱ ἀπὸ Οὐλεντινίνου οὕτως ἐκδέχονται. ἀρχὴν μὲν γὰρ τὸν Μονογενῆ λέγουσιν, ὃν καὶ θεὸν προσαγορεύεσθαι, ὡς καὶ ἐν τοῖς ἑξῆς ἄντικρυς θεὸν αὐτὸν δηλοῖ λέγων· "ὁ μονογενὴς θεὸς ὁ ὢν εἰς τὸν κόλπον τοῦ πατρός, ἐκεῖνος ἐξηγήσατο." τὸν δὲ λόγον τὸν ἐν τῇ ἀρχῇ, τοῦτον τὸν ἐν τῷ Μονογενεῖ, ἐν τῷ Νῷ καὶ τῇ Ἀληθείᾳ, μηνύει τὸν Χριστόν, τὸν Λόγον καὶ τὴν Ζωήν· ὅθεν εἰκότως καὶ αὐτὸν θεὸν λέγει τὸν ἐν τῷ θεῷ τῷ Νῷ ὄντα. "ὃ γέγονεν ἐν αὐτῷ" τῷ λόγῳ, "ζωὴ ἦν," ἡ σύζυγος· διὸ καί φησιν ὁ κύριος· "ἐγώ εἰμι ἡ ζωή."

and the Life, which came into being as a partner (σύζυγος) of the Logos. Moreover, the Only Begotten is called the Mind and has as his partner the Truth. The relationships between these beings are then explained in the following manner:

> So, because the Father was unknown, he wanted to be become known to the aeons. And through his own Intention, as one who is known by himself, he emitted the Only Begotten, the spirit of knowledge, which is in knowledge.[36] Therefore, even he who comes forth from knowledge, that is from the Father's Intention, is knowledge, that is, the Son, for "it is through the Son the Father is known" (John 1:18). But the Spirit of love has been mixed with that of knowledge, as the Father with the Son and Intention with Truth, because it proceeds from Truth as knowledge from Intention. On the one hand, he who remained "the Only Begotten Son in the bosom of the Father" explicated Intention to the aeons through knowledge, because he had indeed emitted from his bosom. On the other hand, he who appeared here is no longer called by the Apostle "the Only Begotten," but "as an Only Begotten." (*Exc.* 7.1–3)[37]

Valentinian protology also contains an epistemological dimension: the unknown God desired emanated intellectual beings, because he wanted to be known through them.[38] The Father possessed an "intention" (ἐνθύμησις) to be known, which caused the generation of the entirety of the intellectual

---

36. Thomassen translates, "And through his own Thought, knowing himself as it were, a spirit of knowledge acting in knowledge, he emitted the Only-begotten" (*Spiritual Seed*, 211). The text in question is difficult. It is evident, however, that the Only Begotten is not equated with the Spirit, but the spirit of knowledge is an *instrument* through which the Father emitted the Only Begotten.

37. Trans. Brakke and Layton, *Gnostic Scriptures*, 507; my modifications: Ἄγνωστος οὖν ὁ πατὴρ ὢν ἠθέλεσεν γνωσθῆναι τοῖς αἰῶσι, καὶ διὰ τῆς ἐνθυμήσεως τῆς ἑαυτοῦ, ὡς ἂν ἑαυτὸν ἐγνωκώς, πνεῦμα γνώσεως οὔσης ἐν γνώσει προέβαλε τὸν Μονογενῆ. γέγονεν οὖν καὶ ὁ ἀπὸ γνώσεως, τουτέστι τῆς πατρικῆς ἐνθυμήσεως, προελθὼν γνῶσις, τουτέστιν ὁ υἱός, ὅτι "δι' υἱοῦ ὁ πατὴρ ἐγνώσθη." τὸ δὲ τῆς ἀγάπης πνεῦμα κέχραται τῷ τῆς γνώσεως, ὡς πατὴρ υἱῷ καὶ ἐνθύμησις Ἀληθείᾳ, ἀπ' ἀληθείας προελθὼν ὡς ἀπὸ ἐνθυμήσεως ἡ γνῶσις. καὶ ὁ μὲν μείνας "μονογενὴς υἱὸς εἰς τὸν κόλπον τοῦ πατρὸς" τὴν ἐνθύμησιν διὰ τῆς γνώσεως ἐξηγεῖται τοῖς αἰῶσιν, ὡς ἂν καὶ ὑπὸ τοῦ κόλπου αὐτοῦ προβληθείς, ὁ δὲ ἐνταῦθα ὀφθεὶς οὐκέτι "μονογενής," ἀλλ' "ὡς μονογενής."

38. Casey and Thomassen translate Ἐνθύμησις as Thought, assuming it parallels Ἔννοια in *Haer.* 1.1.1; 12.1; 12.3. Describing Sophia's fall in *Haer.* 1.2.2, Thomassen translates Ἐνθύμησις not as "thought," as in *Exc.* 7.1–4, but as "desire." In *Gnostic Scriptures*, David Brakke also translates Ἐνθύμησις as "thought." In my translations I prefer

4. Protology: The Creation of the Intelligible Cosmos

beings. The intelligible realm was not, however, an archetype of the visible world but an instrument through which the Father could be known with the help of the two Spirits proceeding from him and mingling with each other. These spirits were the "Spirit of knowledge" (πνεῦμα γνώσεως) and the "Spirit of love" (πνεῦμα ἀγάπης).[39] A distinction is made, however, between Jesus's earthly appearance and his archetypal identity in the Pleroma. Jesus is not the Only Begotten but appears as the Only Begotten, as is explicitly stated in John 1:14. The separation of Jesus, Christ, Logos, and the Only Begotten into distinct beings is one of the reasons Clement condemns Valentinian Christology (*Exc.* 7.3–8; see also *Haer.* 4; preface, 3).

Irenaeus's version of the protological commentary in *Haer.* 1.8.5 mainly follows the same logic as Clement's account, but its author has made some modifications. The interaction between the two Spirits is lacking, and the emission of the beings is described using metaphors of sexual union: the Father begot the Son called the Only Begotten "by whom the Father emitted all things as through a seed" (ἐν ᾧ τὰ πάντα ὁ Πατὴρ προέβαλε σπερματικῶς). As in Clement's commentary, the phrase "he was at the beginning with God" is not taken as a temporal expression but "shows the order of emanation" (ἔδειξε τὴν τῆς προβολῆς τάξιν). A distinction is made, however, between the things made *through* the Logos and those made *in* the Logos (John 1:3). The Logos formed all the aeons after him and became their cause, but what was made *in* the Logos was the Life (Ζωή). Thus, the Life is the conjugal partner of Logos, and they emit the last pair of the second Tetrad—that is, the Human Being and the Church. Furthermore, the Life is associated with the Light (John 1:4), but the Light is not a distinct being, for the whole intelligible cosmos can be depicted as Light. The Savior is the fruit and an image of the whole Pleroma, that is, the Fullness, who shines in the darkness, that is, in the realm outside the Pleroma.[40]

"Thought" for Ἔννοια but "Intention" for Ἐνθύμησις because it describes volitional aspect of the intelligible realm. See also note 29 above.

39. The conceptual background of the primitive Valentinian protology is more Aristotelian than Platonic, because it stresses the synergy of intention and knowledge, not merely knowledge. In Irenaeus's account, Sophia intended to know the Father, acting under the pretense of love, but, in reality, in temerity (τόλμη) without union with his consort Desired (*Haer.* 1.2.2.) Thus, Sophia did not function according to the Spirit of knowledge and the Spirit of love but only according to her own intention to love.

40. The speculation concerning the metaphysical structure of the prologue of the Gospel of John was hotly debated among Alexandrian exegetes. Origen criticizes

In *Exc.* 6–7, the principal Tetrad consists of the Mind, the Truth, the Logos, and the Life, but it is not clear whether the Father and his Intention are counted as members of the Pleroma. In *Haer.* 1.8.5 (see also *Haer.* 1.1.1–3), the "Thought" ('Έννοια), referred to as the "Grace" (Χάρις), is mentioned as the conjugal pair of the Father, forming the first Tetrad with the Mind and Truth. In addition to the Logos and the Life, another pair—that is, the Human Being and the church—must be added to generate the second Tetrad. Consequently, the whole Ogdoad is completed, and it serves as the Mother of all aeons, whereas the Savior is the fruit and the offspring of the entire Pleroma.

It is likely that *Exc.* 6–7.3 and *Haer.* 1.8.5 are two different reworkings of the same protological commentary that served also as the basis for the elaborated version of the protology in *Haer.* 1.1.1–3. As noted, it is rather likely that the same protological system forms the basis for *Excerpta* C. Although *Exc.* 6–7 may be closer to the original version of the commentary, it is not clear whether Clement presents it accurately. Figure 4.2 illustrates the Valentinian model system attested in Irenaeus, *Haer.* 1.1.1–3, which develops from an allegorical reading of the prologue of the Gospel of John. I have highlighted elements that overlap with the protology of *Exc.* 6–7 in gray, and the elements that were added in Irenaeus, *Haer.* 1.8.5 are indicated in bold.

Hans Krämer points out that, in the Valentinian system described above, the aeons of the Pleroma correspond with the world of Platonic ideas, conceived as paradigmatic virtues (Σοφία, Σύνεσις, Πίστις, Ἐλπίς, Ἀγάπη) and qualities (Μίξις, Ἕνωσις, Ἀκίνητος, etc.). The things outside the Pleroma, separated by the Boundary (Ὅρος), are called images or shadows of the Pleromatic realities. It seems that the Valentinian system derives from a Pythagorean-Platonic doctrine of personified ideal numbers and arithmetical progression.[41] In *Haer.* 1.1.1–3, the names of the "unknown

---

Heracleon, who interprets "all things" in John 1:3 as denoting the visible cosmos made by the Logos. This implies that the Logos is not the cause of the intelligible cosmos but the material world only. In *Comm. Jo.* 2.72–99, Origen identifies the Beginning with the divine Wisdom, which precedes the Logos. As in *Haer.* 1.8.5, the life and light are inside the Logos, which means that these cannot be created through the Logos. Strikingly, Origen's interpretation parallels the Valentinian interpretation, according to which a distinction is made between things made *through* the Logos and those made *in* the Logos (John 1:3; *Haer.* 1.8.5).

41. Hans Joachim Krämer, *Der Ursprung der Geistmetaphysik: Untersuchungen zur Geschichte des Platonismus zwischen Platon und Plotin*, 2nd ed. (Amsterdam: Grüner, 1967), 241–49; Turner, *Sethian Gnosticism*, 34–36.

4. Protology: The Creation of the Intelligible Cosmos

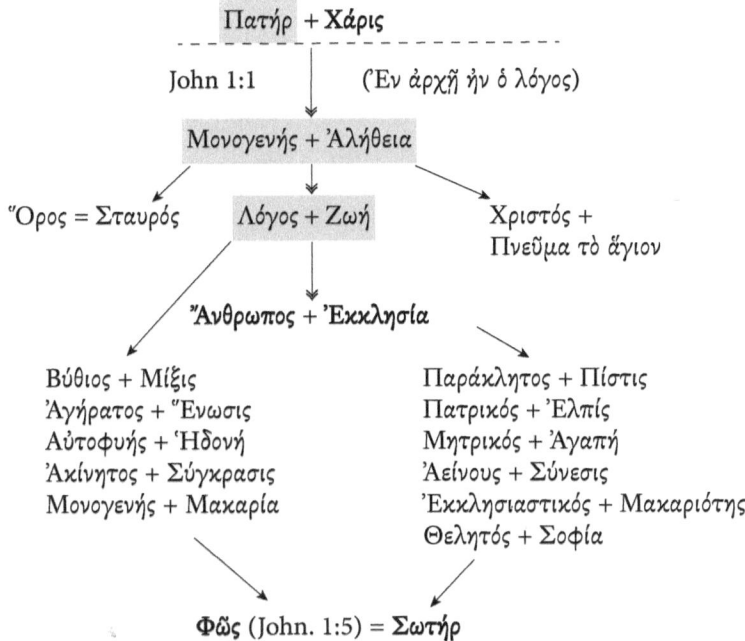

Fig. 4.2. Valentinian Allegorical Reading of the Prologue of the Gospel of John

God" are the First Father (Προπάτωρ) or the First Beginning (Προαρχή), which are derived from the primitive version of the protological account. In *Exc.* 6–7 and *Haer.* 1.8.5, the Only Begotten is called the Beginning (ἀρχή), which would mean that God, out of which the Only Begotten was emitted, can be called the First Beginning (Προαρχή). In *Haer.* 1.1.1, the conjugal partner of the First Father is called the "Grace" (Χάρις), who also appears in the commentary, in *Haer.* 1.8.5. She is also called the Silence (Σιγή), a term that frequently appears in the Valentinian sources to designate the conjugal partner of the Father. The First Father is also called the Profundity or Depth (Βυθός). In the more elaborated model in *Haer.* 1.1.1–3, the aeons are, in the first place, the thoughts of the Father, as in the womb from which they were generated as the seeds.[42]

Thomassen points out that this embryological trope goes back to neo-Pythagorean sources (see Nicomachus's *Introduction to Arithmetic*, Iamblichus's *Introduction to Nicomachus' Arithmetic*, Pseudo-Iamblichus's

---

42. See Thomassen, *Spiritual Seed*, 295–98.

The Theology of Arithmetic, and Theon of Smyrna's *Exposition of Mathematics*), according to which the Monad contains within itself potentially all numbers, like the seed inside a womb.[43] These neo-Pythagorean sources also form the basis of Neoplatonist Syrian's commentary on Aristotle's *Metaphysics*: "For the divine number 'proceeds from the hiding-place of the pure Monad, until one comes to the sacred Tetrad; she, then, bore the mother of all things, all-containing, old, setting a boundary around all things, unchangeable, inexhaustible; they call her pure Decad, the immortal gods and earthborn men.'"[44] A similar embryological model can also be found in the Chaldean Oracles, which speaks about the Monad as the Father and the womb that contains the "all." The name "Depth" (Βυθός) for the Father also appears in the Chaldean Oracles, which speaks about the "Fatherly Depth" (πατρικὸς βυθός). In addition, the name "Silence" (Σιγή), which is attested in many Valentinian sources, occurs also in the Chaldean Oracles, referring to the womb from which the aeons are born.[45] It has been

---

43. Thomassen, *Spiritual Seed*, 293–94. For details on the embryological model in Tri. Trac. 60.5–62.5, see *Spiritual Seed*, 307–13.

44. Syrianus, *In Arist. metaph.* M 4, 1078b12, 106.17, quoted in Arco den Heijer, "Cosmic Mothers in Philo of Alexandria and Neopythagoreanism," *SPhiloA* 27 (2015): 64.

45. See Chaldean Oracles frags. 16, 18, 30. The protological system of the Chaldean Oracles is similar to that of Numenius. In the Chaldean Oracles, the role of the feminine principle Hecate is an emanation of the Father; the demiurgic intellect finds parallels in not only the Valentinian protologies but some Sethian texts (e.g., Three Steles of Seth, Allogenes the Blessed, Zostrianos, and Marsanes). Chaldean theology may have formed the background for the unknown commentary on the *Parmenides*. Pierre Hadot argues that Porphyry was the author of the commentary. According to Hadot, Porphyry did not only repeat the teachings of Plotinus; he combined them with Chaldean theology in an innovative manner by creating a triadic hierarchy of father–power–intellect. See John D. Turner, "The *Chaldean Oracles* and the Metaphysics of the Sethian Platonizing Treatises," in *History and Interpretation from the Old Academy to Later Platonism and Gnosticism*, vol. 1 of *Plato's Parmenides and Its Heritage*, ed. John Turner and Kevin Corrigan, WGRWSup 2 (Atlanta: Society of Biblical Literature, 2010), 213–33. Tuomas Rasimus points out that the anonymous commentary on the *Parmenides* contains fragments that parallel some pre-Plotinian Sethian texts, such as the Secret Book of John and Zostrianos. Rasimus concludes, "In light of the Sethian evidence, we must reassess Pierre Hadot's theory and conclude that it was the Sethian Gnostics rather than Porphyry who were the innovators and that the role of the Sethian Gnostics in the development of Neoplatonism has been greatly underestimated in previous scholarship." For the detailed investigation of the Sethian material and its relationship to the Neoplatonic system of thought, see Rasimus, "Porphyry and the Gnostics: Reassessing Pierre Hadot's Thesis in Light of the Second- and

commonly noted that the Valentinian protological system parallels classic gnostic texts such as the Secret Book of John (BG 2 24.20–25.1), Zostrianos (64.14–16), and Allogenes (49.26–38; 65.32–36). The name "Depth" (Βυθός) also occurs in Eugnostos (V 6.20) and Irenaeus's description of Ophite mythology in Irenaeus, *Haer.* 1.30.1. The Silence (Σιγή) is found in Eugnostos (V 15.21; III 88.8–9) as well as in the related Wisdom of Jesus Christ (III 112.8; 117.17, 21) and the Secret Book of John (III 10.15).[46] In these texts, the first principle is depicted in an apophatic manner, existing beyond being or having undetermined essence.[47] Although it became common among the Middle Platonic philosophers to use apophatic language to describe the radical transcendence of the first principle, the Secret Book of John and some other gnostic texts also used kataphatic language to stress the gulf between the divine world and material creation. The creator-God, called Yaldabaoth, was no longer the representative of the good and ordered cosmos whose providence guided the rational souls of the planetary gods, but an amorphous and chaotic figure who made creations for the sake of deception and whose fiery rulers of heaven aimed to enslave humanity.[48]

The Valentinian cosmological model represents a more positive worldview than the Sethian gnostic accounts mentioned above.[49] Although the material world originated as a result of the conflict in the divine world, the creator-God and the heavenly rulers were created as images of the aeons longing for the heavenly light. Hence, the Valentinian theologians were closer to the cosmological dualism of Plato's *Timaeus* and the protological teachings attested in Philo's works than those of the gnostics. The Marcosians, who formed a distinct group

---

Third-Century Sethian Treatises," in *Its Reception in Neoplatonic, Jewish, and Christian Texts*, vol. 2 of *Plato's Parmenides and Its Heritage*, ed. John Turner and Kevin Corrigan, WGRWSup 3 (Atlanta: Society of Biblical Literature, 2010), 81–110. Thomassen is of the opinion that Valentinian theologians were dependent on the same sources as Porphyry and the later Neoplatonists, Marius Victorinus, Synesius, and the Platonizing Sethians (*Spiritual Seed*, 298–307). It seems, in my opinion, that the manifold relationships of these sources is beyond any historical study.

46. See Rasimus, "Ptolemaeus and the Valentinian Exegesis," 164.
47. Rasimus, "Ptolemaeus and the Valentinian Exegesis," 159 n. 60.
48. See King, *Secret Revelation*, 199–214.
49. It is not clear, however, whether the pessimistic worldview was part of the gnostic myth that was reformed by the Valentinian theologians or whether the pessimistic motif in the gnostic myth resulted from its later Sethianization.

within Valentinian tradition, taught that the creation of the visible world in Gen 1 follows the arithmological order of the Pleroma. Not only the intelligible cosmos but the dry land, the sea, the plants, and the animals are manifestations or shadows of the Tetrad, the Ogdoad, the Decad, and the Dodecad (see *Haer.* 1.18).

Although the Latin manuscript of Irenaeus's *Adversus Haereses* indicates that the protological myth in *Haer.* 1.8.5. comes from Ptolemy, it is more likely that it originated among his disciples.[50] Interestingly, *Exc.* 6–7 parallels also the protology in *Haer.* 1.12.1, which, according to Irenaeus, goes back to "the more knowledgeable followers of Ptolemy."

> Now, the more knowledgeable followers of Ptolemy claim that Bythos has two consorts, which they also call dispositions [διαθέσεις], Thought ["Εννοια] and Volition [Θέλησις], because first he thought of what he would emit, as they say, then he willed it. Hence from these two dispositions and powers, Thought and Volition, which had formed a kind of union, there came forth as from a conjugal union the emission of Only Begotten and Truth. These two proceeded as types and images of Father's two dispositions, the visible of the invisible, Mind of Volition, and Truth of Thought. So the image of supervenient Volition was masculine, but the image of ingenerate Thought was feminine, since Volition became a kind of power of Thought. For Thought was always thinking of the emission but was not able by herself to bring forth what she thought of. When, however, the power of Volition supervened, then she emitted what she was thinking of. (Unger, modified)

The union of two dispositions, Thought and Volition, in *Haer.* 1.12.1 recalls the system in *Exc.* 6–7, in which the Father has an "intention" (ἐνθύμησις) to become known to the aeons through the "mingling" (κρᾶσις) of the "Spirit of knowledge" and the "Spirit of love," out of which the Only Begotten and Truth came into being. It stands to reason that the elaborated protological model systems in *Haer.* 1.1.1–3 and its variant in *Haer.* 1.12.1 were both created in the circle of Ptolemy's disciples. They revised earlier traditions depicted in *Exc.* 6–7 and *Haer.* 1.8.5, which are based on allegorical interpretations of the prologue of the Gospel of John. These Valentinian sources also contain significant parallels with Philo's exegesis on Gen 1:1–5, which I treat next.

---

50. See pages 83–84.

4.4. Philo, *Excerpta* C, and the Prologue of the Gospel of John

The origin of the Valentinian myth of Sophia lies in Middle Platonic transcendental monotheism. The biblical narratives, both in the Jewish Scriptures and early Christian literature, were incorporated into the myth by transforming biblical figures, themes, and ideas into symbols of the pleromatic reality. In Prov 8:22–36, Wisdom is depicted as God's first creation, who existed beside God before the foundation of the world. In the Valentinian revision of the biblical narrative, Wisdom is equated with the Platonic world soul, having fallen from her elevated status as the result of temerity, because she attempted to know what was not knowable and imitate God's creative power. Stead also argues that behind the fall of Sophia lies the idea of the fallen world soul: "something like the Valentinian myth could be reached simply by combining this doctrine with the dualistic picture given to us by Plutarch and representing the disorderly passions of the bad world-soul, not as eternally pre-existing conditions, but as themselves the result of a prior act of disobedience or defection from the highest Good."[51]

Although the fall of heavenly Wisdom can be seen as a Platonizing revision of the Jewish Wisdom theology, the salvation of Sophia by the Savior clearly requires Christian influences. The Valentinian commentators intended to show that their philosophical-cosmological myth enjoyed apostolic authority, because it could already be found in the writings of the New Testament. However, the Johannine prologue was not unintentionally chosen as a basis for the protological myth. Valentinian commentators—and their gnostic predecessors—may have had good reason to believe that it was written originally as a Platonizing description of the creation of the intelligible world.

Sterling points out that the prologue of the Gospel of John can be placed together with Philo's *Opif.* 26–35 in the same tradition of Platonizing interpretations of Gen 1:1–5.[52] Sterling notes that the author of John's

---

51. See Stead, "Valentinian Myth of Sophia," 101, 103.

52. Gregory E. Sterling, "Day One: Platonizing Exegetical Traditions of Genesis 1:1–5 in John and Jewish Authors," *SPhiloA* 17 (2005): 123–30. See also Peder Borgen, "Observations on the Targumic Character of the Prologue of John," *NTS* 16 (1970): 288–95; Thomas Tobin, "The Prologue of John and Hellenistic Jewish Speculation," *CBQ* 52 (1990): 262; John Painter, "Rereading Genesis in the Prologue of John?," in *Neotestamentica et Philonica: Studies in Honor of Peder Borgen*, ed. David E. Aune,

prologue repeats certain catchwords (ἐν ἀρχῇ – ἦν – ὁ θεός – ἐγένετο – τὸ φῶς – τὸ σκότος) in the same order they appear in Gen 1:1–5. In addition, he uses a Semitic staircase parallelism to interlock the pairs of clauses in the prologue poetically. A comparison between Gen 1:1–5 and John 1:1–5 is presented below, the keywords in common indicated by underlining:

Ἐν ἀρχῇ ἐποίησεν ὁ θεὸς τὸν οὐρανὸν καὶ τὴν γῆν ἡ δὲ γῆ ἦν ἀόρατος καὶ ἀκατασκεύαστος, καὶ σκότος ἐπάνω τῆς ἀβύσσου, καὶ πνεῦμα θεοῦ ἐπεφέρετο ἐπάνω τοῦ ὕδατος. καὶ εἶπεν ὁ θεός Γενηθήτω φῶς. καὶ ἐγένετο φῶς. καὶ εἶδεν ὁ θεὸς τὸ φῶς ὅτι καλόν. καὶ διεχώρισεν ὁ θεὸς ἀνὰ μέσον τοῦ φωτὸς καὶ ἀνὰ μέσον τοῦ σκότους. καὶ ἐκάλεσεν ὁ θεὸς τὸ φῶς ἡμέραν καὶ τὸ σκότος ἐκάλεσεν νύκτα. καὶ ἐγένετο ἑσπέρα καὶ ἐγένετο πρωί, ἡμέρα μία. (Gen 1:1–5)

Ἐν ἀρχῇ ἦν ὁ λόγος, καὶ ὁ λόγος ἦν πρὸς τὸν θεόν, καὶ θεὸς ἦν ὁ λόγος. οὗτος ἦν ἐν ἀρχῇ πρὸς τὸν θεόν. πάντα δι' αὐτοῦ ἐγένετο, καὶ χωρὶς αὐτοῦ ἐγένετο οὐδὲ ἕν ὃ γέγονεν. ἐν αὐτῷ ζωὴ ἦν, καὶ ἡ ζωὴ ἦν τὸ φῶς τῶν ἀνθρώπων· καὶ τὸ φῶς ἐν τῇ σκοτίᾳ φαίνει, καὶ ἡ σκοτία αὐτὸ οὐ κατέλαβεν. (John 1:1–5)

In John's prologue, there is certainly a distinction between the use of the verbs ἦν ("to be") and ἐγένετο ("to become"), the same verbs that mark in Plato's *Tim.* 27d–28b the distinction between the eternally existing intelligible world of being (τὸ ὂν ἀεί) and the visible world of becoming (τὸ γιγνόμενον μὲν ἀεί). The four repetitions of ἦν are contrasted with two of ἐγένετο. It is of note that a temporal distinction is made in verse 3, dividing the prologue into two sections: verses 1–2 describe the genealogy of the Logos, whereas verses 4–5 depict the manifestation of the Logos in the

---

Torrey Seland, and Jarl Henning Ulrichsen, NovTSup 106 (Leiden: Brill, 2003), 179–201. Platonizing reading of John's prologue has been recently challenged by Troels Engberg-Pedersen. He argues that the functions of the Logos and the *pneuma* in John's Gospel are closer to Stoic cosmology than Philo's Platonizing views. The Logos and the pneuma "constitute the two sides of the same coin, where the Logos stands for the cognitive side and the *pneuma* for the purely material one. Both were present at creation, moreover, both were operative in it. Both also came to be present—in a uniquely forceful manner— in the individual human being of Jesus of Nazareth when he received the *pneuma*. As a result, he became the bearer of the whole point of creation, which is life and light. He became 'the light of the world' (8:12) so that 'whoever follows me will never walk in darkness but will obtain the light of life' (8:12)." See Troels Engberg-Pedersen, *John and Philosophy: A New Reading of the Fourth Gospel* (Oxford: Oxford University Press, 2017), 72.

creation. The author also adapted the *terminus technicus* from the Middle Platonic tradition in assigning the role of instrumentality to the Logos through which (δι' αὐτοῦ) the world came into being.[53]

The Valentinian interpreters evidently noticed the aforementioned Platonic elements in John's prologue. It was thus not a coincidence that they selected it as a scriptural basis for the genealogy of the aeons of the Pleroma. It is not clear, however, whether the Valentinian teachers invented their peculiar interpretation of John's prologue or whether it was already a part of the preceding Sethian gnostic myth. Nevertheless, the Valentinian exegetes modified the temporal and ontological structure of the prologue in a way that indicates that they may have been also familiar with Philo's allegorical interpretation of Gen 1:1–5.[54]

In *De opificio mundi*, Philo says that God created the intelligible cosmos, that is, the Ideas, during day one (Gen 1:1–5), whereas the creation during the following days was of the visible copies of them (Gen 1:6–2:4).[55] In *Opif.* 17–19, he explains that God acted like an architect who was about to build a city. First, an architect makes a model in his mind, which will be given to the building master in charge of the building program. In the same manner, the Ideas were first drawn up in the mind of God before they were conveyed to the Logos, through which the visible

---

53. Prepositional metaphysics goes back to the distinction between different kinds of causes in Aristotelian logic. The Hellenistic philosophers elaborated these causes, assigning prepositions to them. Philo of Alexandria is an important witness to the Middle Platonic metaphysics of prepositions (see esp. *Cher.* 124–127). Philo connected the instrumental cause of creation to the Logos, through which (δι' οὗ) the cosmos came into being. The metaphysics of prepositions and their relationship to Christ are attested also in 1 Cor 8:6; Col 1:16; Heb 1:2. See Gregory E. Sterling, "Prepositional Metaphysics in Jewish Wisdom Speculations and Early Christian Liturgical Texts," *SPhiloA* 9 (1997): 219–38; Tobin, *Creation of Man*, 66–70. Engberg-Pedersen argues that Platonizing reading of John 1:1–3 fails to notice that the Logos is not only an instrument but a "Stoic-like" directly active, material force in creating the world (*John and Philosophy*, 60).

54. Raymond E. Brown suggests that the original protological hymn behind John's prologue is found in John 1:1–5, 10–12b, 14, 16. The verses about John the Baptist clearly disrupt the content and style of the text. Brown points out that the first reference to the incarnation of the Logos is found in John 1:14. See Brown, *The Gospel according to John*, AB 29 (Garden City, NY: Doubleday, 1966–1970), 1:3–37.

55. Philo also knew of another tradition that divided the intelligible cosmos from the visible world in Gen 2:4 (see Tobin, *Creation of Man*, 20–35, 59–60; Runia, *On the Creation*, 19–20).

world came into being. In this sense, Philo calls the Logos in *Opif.* 25 an "idea of ideas" (ἰδέα ἰδεῶν) because it contains all the Ideas within himself.[56] Thus, the sum total of ideas, which God placed in the Logos, constitutes "the intelligible cosmos" (κόσμος νοητός), which was distinguished from the "sense-perceptible cosmos" (κόσμος αἰσθητός).[57]

A special feature of *De opificio mundi* is the role of number symbolism. The order of the creation follows a certain arithmological pattern.[58] The expression ἐν ἀρχῇ in Gen 1:1 is not, according to Philo, a temporal definition, because time was created together with the cosmos. Time is related to the motion of the celestial bodies, and there cannot be motion before they are created. Therefore, "in the beginning" has to be understood as "according to the number" (κατ' ἀριθμόν), which depicts the ontological

---

56. Runia notes that a similar theory about an "idea which includes in itself all ideas" is attested in Arius Didymus, mentioned in Eusebius, *Praep. ev.* 11.23.6 (see Runia, *On the Creation*, 151). Wolfson sees the expression of Logos as "the idea of ideas" as being based on Aristotle's description of the human mind as the form of forms, εἶδος εἰδῶν (Aristotle, *De an.* 3.432a.1–2 [Hett]): "The soul, then, acts like a hand; for the hand is an instrument which employs instruments, and in the same way the mind is a form which employs forms, and sense is a form which employs the forms of sensible objects" (see Wolfson, *Philo* 1:233).

57. Philo was the first philosopher to explicitly use the term κόσμος νοητός, but it has nevertheless some Platonic antecedents. In *Tim.* 39e, Plato speaks about "the intelligible living being" (τὸ νοητὸν ζῷον) as a model for the sensible world and, in *Resp.* 508b13 draws an analogy between the sun and the idea of the Good, which is in the "noetic place" (ἐν τῷ νοητῷ τόπῳ). A similar phrase occurs in the *Timaeus Locrus*, which speaks about ὁ ἰδανικὸς κόσμος. See David Runia, "A Brief History of the Term *Kosmos Noētos* from Plato to Plotinus," in *Traditions of Platonism: Essays in Honour of John Dillon*, ed. John J. Cleary (Aldershot: Ashgate, 1999), 152–58; Runia, *On the Creation*, 136.

58. Philo refers in his writings to his work *On Numbers*, which is also mentioned by Eusebius in his catalogue on Philo's works. Runia is of the opinion that Philo's arithmological work was a collection of material from various sources for allegorical purposes. In *De opificio mundi*, the numbers 5 and 6 are related to the creation narrative, but, in the case of the numbers 4 and 7, he speaks only about their arithmological importance, without any explicit references to the days of creation. Philo even devotes a long excursus in *Opif.* 89–128 to the significance of the number 7 but does not handle its significance for the seventh day (see Runia, *On the Creation*, 25–29). Irenaeus describes the Marcosian system, which is based on the mystical union of numbers and letters. Unlike the Valentinian accounts in *Excerpta* C and *Haer.* 1.1-8, the Marcosians saw the whole creation narrative in Gen 1 as a visible manifestation of the Tetrad, the Ogdoad, the Decad, and the Dodeced (see *Haer.* 1.13–21).

4. Protology: The Creation of the Intelligible Cosmos

predominance of the creation during day one, compared with the creation of the visible cosmos during days two through six. Therefore, the first day of creation is in *Opif.* 35 called "not the first day, but day one" (ἡμέραν οὐχὶ πρώτην, ἀλλὰ μίαν), because the intelligible cosmos "has the nature of the unit" (μοναδικὴν ἔχοντος φύσιν).

The aforementioned Valentinian interpretations of John's prologue coincide with the views expounded by Philo. As noted above, the phrase "in the beginning" (John. 1:1) is seen in *Exc.* 6–7 and *Haer.* 1.8.5 as a non-temporal ontological expression. "The Beginning" (ἀρχή) refers to the Only Begotten, who is emitted from the Father of All. Thus, the Beginning is hypostasized, and the preposition (ἐν) interpreted as a reference to its ontological relationship with the Logos and subsequently the other intelligible beings who have their origin in the Only Begotten. Thus, the expression "in the beginning" does not refer to the temporal order but to the "the order of emanations" (ἔδειξε τὴν τῆς προβολῆς τάξιν). This reading parallels that of Philo, who argues that "in the beginning" (Gen 1:1) does not refer to a temporal order but to the ontological predominance of the creation of the intelligible cosmos over the visible cosmos.[59]

While in Philo the ontological predominance of the first day of creation concerns the relationship between the intelligible cosmos (day one) and the rest of the creation, in the Valentinian protology "in the Beginning" (ἐν ἀρχῇ) refers to the order of emanations in the intelligible realm. According to the Valentinian interpretation, the Logos was "in the Beginning," through which "all things" in the intelligible cosmos were created.[60] While in John's prologue the demarcation line between the ideal world and the visible cosmos is between verses 2 and 3, the Valentinian commentators saw the whole passage (John 1:1–5) as a description of the genesis of the beings in the intelligible cosmos. The Logos was the instrument through which the whole intelligible cosmos was created "in the Beginning."

---

59. In Gen 1, the terms that define the order, according to Philo, suggest that everything should develop in the right sequence (see Runia, *On the Creation*, 160).

60. Irenaeus attacks this Valentinian interpretation in *Haer.* 3.11.7, arguing that "all things" in John 1:3 cannot refer to the generation of the aeons of Pleroma but to "this world and to everything in it." As noted in ch. 3, Ptolemy offers an interpretation of John 1:3 in his *Letter to Flora* that is similar to Irenaeus's view. Clement also saw the Valentinian interpretation of John's prologue as untenable, but he did not criticize the Valentinian exegesis as such but only its metaphysical teaching, which threatened the oneness of God (see *Exc.* 8.1).

It is clear that the Valentinians could have found the terms "the Beginning," "the Only Begotten," "the Logos," and "the Light" directly by reading John's prologue without recourse to Philo's writings. However, in Valentinian interpretation, these terms are given a logical pattern that cannot have been derived directly from the Gospel of John. The Beginning is hypostasized as referring to the Only Begotten, and the Logos is seen as an instrument of the creation, not the visible cosmos but the intelligible world of aeons. This parallels Philo's view, according to which the Logos contains the Ideas within himself as thoughts of God (see *Opif.* 25).

In *Exc.* 43.2, the Savior is sent to the suffering Sophia. The Savior is also called as "the angel of the counsel" (ὁ τῆς βουλῆς ἄγγελος) and associated with the Logos and the Only Begotten, because the whole Pleroma, that is, the Fullness, is contained within himself (see *Haer.* 1.2.6; 8.5; Col 1:16). Strikingly, these terms related to the Savior can also be found in Philo's *Conf.* 146: "But if there be any as yet unfit to be called a Son of God, let him press to take his place under God's First-born, the Logos, who holds the eldership among the angels, their ruler as it were. And many names are his, for he is called, 'the Beginning,' and 'the Name of God,' and 'His Logos,' and 'the Human being after His image,' and 'he that sees,' that is Israel" (*Conf.* 146, modified).[61] For Philo, the Beginning, the First-born, the Logos, the Eldest of angels, and the Name of God all refer to the same intellectual being generated from the transcendent One.[62] Although these names do not depict exactly the same intellectual being in the Valentinian protology, they are ontologically interrelated with each other. The Logos is "inside" the Beginning, that is, the Only Begotten, who serves as the root for the rest of the aeons of the Pleroma. The Savior, who is emanated by the aeons, is the star and fruit of the entire Pleroma, that is, the Fullness, and he shines in the darkness, that is, in the realm outside the Pleroma. These

---

61. κἂν μηδέπω μέντοι τυγχάνῃ τις ἀξιόχρεως ὢν υἱὸς θεοῦ προσαγορεύεσθαι, σπουδαζέτω κοσμεῖσθαι κατὰ τὸν πρωτόγονον αὐτοῦ λόγον, τὸν ἀγγέλων πρεσβύτατον, ὡς ἂν ἀρχάγγελον, πολυώνυμον ὑπάρχοντα· καὶ γὰρ ἀρχὴ καὶ ὄνομα θεοῦ καὶ λόγος καὶ ὁ κατ' εἰκόνα ἄνθρωπος καὶ ὁ ὁρῶν, Ἰσραήλ, προσαγορεύεται.

62. For the allegory of Israel in *Excerpta* C, see the discussion in ch. 7. The transcendent realm is also called "the Name" by Theodotus. When Sophia wished to grasp that which is beyond knowledge, she rushed into the "void of knowledge" (κένωμα γνώσεως) and the "shadow of the Name" (σκιὰ τοῦ ὀνόματος). The invisible part of Jesus is also equated both with the Only Begotten and the Name, and those who receive the baptism of the angels by proxy will participate in the same Name. See *Exc.* 22, 26, and 32, which go back to Theodotus.

4. Protology: The Creation of the Intelligible Cosmos 119

notions can be derived from Philo, who explains that the creation of light in Gen 1:3 depicts the creation of the Logos, which has God, that is, the Savior as his archetype:

> In the first place: God is light, for there is a verse in one of the psalms, "the Lord is my illumination and my Savior." And He is not only light, but the archetype of every other light, nay, prior to and high above every archetype, holding the position of the model [of a model]. For the model or pattern was the Logos, which contained all His fullness—light, in fact; for, as the Lawgiver tells us, "God said 'let light come into being,'" whereas He Himself resembles none of the things which have come into being. Secondly: as the sun makes day and night distinct, so Moses says that God kept apart light and darkness; for "God," he tells us, "separated between the light and between the darkness." And above all, as the sun when it rises makes visible objects which had been hidden, so God when He gave birth to all things, not only brought them into sight, but also made things which before were not, not just handling material as an artificer, but being Himself its creator. (*Somn.* 1.75)[63]

Philo makes a distinction between God as Light and its perfect model, the Logos, which contained all his fullness. Thus, God creates Light, that is, the Logos, which refers to the intelligible cosmos in its entirety. It is notable, that the Pleroma, that is, the Fullness (πλήρωμα), is another key technical term in Valentinian protology.[64] As noted, the whole Fullness,

---

63. ἐπειδὴ πρῶτον μὲν ὁ θεὸς φῶς ἐστι "κύριος γὰρ φωτισμός μου καὶ σωτήρ μου" ἐν ὕμνοις ᾄδεται καὶ οὐ μόνον φῶς, ἀλλὰ καὶ παντὸς ἑτέρου φωτὸς ἀρχέτυπον, μᾶλλον δὲ παντὸς ἀρχετύπου πρεσβύτερον καὶ ἀνώτερον, λόγον ἔχων παραδείγματος <παραδείγματος>. τὸ μὲν γὰρ παράδειγμα ὁ πληρέστατος ἦν αὐτοῦ λόγος, φῶς "εἶπε" γάρ φησιν "ὁ θεός· γενέσθω φῶς", αὐτὸς δὲ οὐδενὶ τῶν γεγονότων ὅμοιος ἔπειθ' ὡς ἥλιος ἡμέραν καὶ νύκτα διακρίνει, οὕτως φησὶ Μωυσῆς τὸν θεὸν φῶς καὶ σκότος διατειχίσαι· "διεχώρισε γὰρ ὁ θεὸς ἀνὰ μέσον τοῦ φωτὸς καὶ ἀνὰ μέσον τοῦ σκότους" ἄλλως τε ὡς ἥλιος ἀνατείλας τὰ κεκρυμμένα τῶν σωμάτων ἐπιδείκνυται, οὕτως καὶ ὁ θεὸς τὰ πάντα γεννήσας οὐ μόνον εἰς τοὐμφανὲς ἤγαγεν, ἀλλὰ καὶ ἃ πρότερον οὐκ ἦν, ἐποίησεν, οὐ δημιουργὸς μόνον ἀλλὰ καὶ κτίστης αὐτὸς ὤν (my modifications). The insertion παραδείγματος comes from Colson. I do not think that the insertion is necessary, though it may be compatible with what Philo says elsewhere about the Logos as a paradigm. Brackets added by me. I also use the term *Logos* instead of *Word*.

64. The Pleroma contains the perfect number of aeons deriving from the Monad and the first Tetrad. The realm of aeons became perfect, as the number of intelligible beings was fulfilled. Sophia was the last aeon of the Dodecad (2 + 4 + 6) as well as the Triacontad (2 + 4 + 6 + 8 + 10 = 30). This was the reason Sophia's novel creation was

that is, the Light, dwells in the Savior, which is a reference to Col 1:16: "For in him all the fullness of God was pleased to dwell" (ἐν αὐτῷ εὐδόκησεν πᾶν τὸ πλήρωμα κατοικῆσαι).[65] The fullness is also mentioned in John 1:16: "And from his fullness have we all received, grace upon grace" (ὅτι ἐκ τοῦ πληρώματος αὐτοῦ ἡμεῖς πάντες ἐλάβομεν καὶ χάριν ἀντὶ χάριτος).

It is not likely that the term *Pleroma* in the Valentinian myth would have been *derived* from John's Gospel, pseudo-Pauline literature, or Philo's texts. In Valentinian theology, the Pleroma has its basis in Pythagorean arithmological speculations. It refers to the perfection of the divine realm but also to the fulfillment of the number of intelligible beings: the divine realm became perfect as the number of aeons was fulfilled. Valentinian exegetes could find these Pythagorean notions and terms in the Gospel of John and the Colossians, which permitted a protological interpretation of these passages.[66] In Philo, the term *fullness* (πλήρωμα) refers in some cases to God's omnipresence in the world (*Gig.* 27, 47), his unity (*Her.* 187), and harmonious essence (*Her.* 217). Philo says that God's fullness is based on his unity, because he "admits neither addition nor subtraction." Thus, the "fullness" and "unit" has in Philo's thinking certain arithmological basis. "For the whole series of numbers to infinity multiplied by infinity ends when resolved in the unit and begins with the unit when arranged in an unlimited series. And therefore those who study such questions declare that the unit is not a number at all, but the element and source from which number springs" (*Her.* 190). It is of note, however, that Philo remarks in *Somn.* 1.75 that God not only revealed the image of Light—that is, the Logos—but he also separated light from darkness. Although this distinction may refer to the division between an intelligible light, that is, the Logos, and visible lights (or the whole visible cosmos), Philo's exegesis in *Opif.* 29–35 indicates that it also describes the conflict within the intel-

---

impossible and erroneous; the number of aeons was perfect. See Jean-Marc Narbonne, "The Neopythagorean Backdrop to the Fall of the Soul," in *Gnosticism, Platonism and the Late Ancient World: Essays in Honour of John D. Turner*, ed. Kevin Corrigan and Tuomas Rasimus, NHMS 82 (Leiden: Brill, 2013), 414–19. The intention of the last aeon was fatal. The arithmological basis of Sophia's fall is also attested in the allegory of the parable of the lost sheep (Luke 15:4–7) by Marcus (see *Haer.* 1.16.1; see Narbonne, "Neopythagorean Backdrop to the Fall," 414–19).

65. The parallels between Philo's *Somn.* 1.75, John 1:16, and Col 2:16 are also noted in Matthew E. Gordley, *The Colossian Hymn in Context*, WUNT 2/228 (Tübingen: Mohr Siebeck, 2007), 224–25.

66. See 69 n. 60 above.

ligible realm. This parallels Valentinian protology, in which the Light, that is, the Savior, that shone in the darkness (John 1:5) does not refer to the earthly darkness but to the darkness in the intelligible realm, which was separated out of the Pleroma by the Boundary, before the foundation of the visible cosmos.

I next investigate more thoroughly Philo's exegesis on the creation of the intelligible cosmos during day one in *Opif.* 29–35 to present a more detailed description concerning the similarities and dissimilarities in the protological systems of Philo and the Valentinians.

4.5. Philo's Interpretation of Day One and Traditions of Cosmic Creation

Philo's description of the creation of the ideal world begins in *Opif.* 26–28, which explicates the meaning of the phrase "in the beginning" and the predominance of day one. I have investigated these subjects and the parallels with the Valentinian accounts above. In *Opif.* 29–30, Philo gives an allegorical account of the structure of the intelligible realm, which God placed in the Logos. Although Philo says that the number of ideas is uncountable, he nevertheless sets out to find in Gen 1:1–5 the most fundamental ideas based on the sacred number seven. Philo maintains that, on day one, God created the incorporeal heaven, the invisible earth, the idea of air, the idea of void, the incorporeal substance of water, the incorporeal substance of the spirit, and the incorporeal light that served as a paradigm for all celestial lights. In *Opif.* 30, Philo maintains that the ideas of spirit of God and light are given predominance in the intelligible cosmos: "The former he named of God, because spirit is highly important for life and God is the cause of life. Light he describes as exceedingly beautiful, for the intelligible surpasses the visible in brilliance and brightness" (Runia).

Runia points out that professional philosophers may find Philo's description of the intelligible cosmos peculiar.[67] The content of the ideal world and the relationship between its elements seem to be composed artificially, on the grounds of the biblical narrative. Harry Wolfson proposes, however, that Philo was trying to describe the creation of the ideas of the four cosmic elements (water, air, earth, and heaven [i.e., fire]) and the ideas of the void (= the Receptacle), spirit (= mind), and light.[68] Wolf-

---

67. Runia, *On the Creation*, 163–64.
68. Wolfson, *Philo*, 1:309–10.

son's interpretation has not gained much support. It is not likely that the ideas of heaven, earth, air, and water refer to the four cosmic elements, as Wolfson proposed, but rather to the regions of the cosmos. The view that heaven depicts the element of fire contradicts what Philo teaches elsewhere about the essence of heaven. In most cases, Philo agrees with the common Middle Platonic view that the heavenly sphere is made out of ether or some other unknown matter. Also, the idea of the void does not refer to the Platonic Receptacle, as Wolfson suggests, but to the region between the moon and earth, which is filled with air. With this, Philo may have been criticizing the Epicureans, who postulated that a cosmic void existed between moon and earth (see *Opif.* 32).[69]

It is of note that Philo offers contradictory exegeses of Gen 1:3 concerning the creation of light in *De opificio mundi*. As we noted above, in *Somn.* 1.75, Philo interprets the creation of light (Gen 1:3) as signifying the creation of the Logos, which is an image of God, that is, the archetypal Light. In *Opif.* 29, the idea of light is the seventh to be created during day one. This implies that the idea of light is part of the intelligible cosmos, that is, the Logos. In *Opif.* 31, however, Philo gives another interpretation, that "the invisible and intelligible light" (τὸ ἀόρατον καὶ νοητὸν φῶς) in Gen 1:3 is "an image of the divine Logos, which communicated its genesis." This evidently refers to God's words "Let there be light." Thus, it is not the Logos that is created in Gen 1:3 but the image of the Logos made by the Logos himself.

It is possible that in *Opif.* 31 Philo is dependent on an exegetical tradition that is not logically compatible with his description of the creation of the noetic cosmos: the light in Gen 1:3 does not refer to the idea of light as the model of the light-bearing heavenly bodies but to the idea of the *essence* of the light from which the heavenly realm draws their illumination.[70] The idea of light in *Opif.* 31 is not the "paradigm" (παράδειγμα), as in *Opif.* 29, but the "source" (πηγή) of all cosmic lights. Additionally, in *Opif.* 31, the intelligible light is a star that transcends the heavenly realm,

---

69. See Runia, *On the Creation*, 171–72. Runia maintains that the idea of spirit may refer to the *pneuma* in its Aristotelian sense, as the instrument which allows the soul to affect the body (166). For a criticism of Wolfson's interpretation, see also Winston, *Philo of Alexandria*, 9–13. The problem of the creation of matter in Philo is investigated in detail in ch. 5.

70. Runia refers to Boyancé, who suggested that Philo must be dependent on some philosophical source in *Opif.* 31, but is himself skeptical (see Runia, *On the Creation*, 169).

and it is called "all-brightness" (παναύγεια), which does not appear elsewhere in Philo's texts. These differences are important for a comparison of *Opif.* 31 with the Valentinian cosmological account, which I investigate in the following chapter.

After a short reference to the ideas of air and void in *Opif.* 32, Philo returns to his main topic, explaining in *Opif.* 33–34 the consequences of the manifestation of the intelligible light—that is, the Logos—and its rival, darkness. Although the manifestation of light, the yielding of darkness, and the setting of morning and evening are events in the visible cosmos in Genesis, in Philo's exegesis, they become processes within the intelligible realm. In *Opif.* 34, Philo has to stress that these elements and boundaries belong to the class of incorporeal things and are entirely "ideas, symbols and seals" (ἰδέαι καὶ τύποι καὶ σφραγῖδες). Strikingly, according to Philo, there is discord within the intelligible cosmos between the Logos and its rival—that is, darkness. The passage in *Opif.* 33 is worth quoting in its entirety:

> As soon as the intelligible light, which existed before the sun, was ignited, its rival darkness proceeded to withdraw. God built a wall between them and kept them separate, for he well knew their oppositions and the conflict resulting from their natures. Therefore, in order to ensure that they would not continually interact and be in strife with each other, and that war would not gain the upper hand over peace and bring about disorder in the cosmos, he not only separated light and darkness, but also placed boundaries in the extended space between them, by means of which he kept the two extremes apart. (trans. Runia)

In *Opif.* 34, Philo says that the intelligible "boundaries" (ὅροι) between the light and darkness are called evening and morning.[71] They are set in the middle, which may mean that they are two sides of the same boundary. The intelligible darkness must be fenced off with and controlled by the boundaries between them. That darkness is mentioned twice in Gen 1:1–5 gives occasion for allegorical speculation. The first instance, in Gen 1:2, refers, according to Philo's allegorical interpretation, to the idea of air, because air is by nature dark. The second instance, in Gen 1:4, refers to

---

71. The conflict between light and darkness may parallel Plato's description of the relationships between the ideas in the intelligible realm. In *Soph.* 254–256, Plato lists five major relations—namely, being, similarity, difference, movement, and rest. Runia points out that four of these kinds are opposites, which may reflect a similar tension between light and darkness, as attested in Philo (Runia, *On the Creation*, 164).

some other darkness, because it comes into being as a rival to light, that is, the Logos. It seems that the conflict within the intelligible realm in Philo's account reflects Middle Platonic speculations concerning Plato's list of opposites in *Soph.* 254d–255a (same, different, movement, and rest). In Plato, these opposites describe the characteristics of two distinct realms of creation (the world of being and the world of becoming), but Philo follows the Middle Platonic teachers and projects this distinction also onto the intelligible cosmos.[72]

The conflict within the intelligible realm and the separation of darkness in Philo's exegesis of day one parallel Valentinian protological accounts, though the biblical basis in the latter is not Gen 1:1–5, as in Philo, but John 1:1–5. According to the Valentinians, the principle of matter and the creation of the visible cosmos were the outcome of conflict within the divine world. In *Haer.* 1.1.3–4.1, the separation of the erroneous Intention of Sophia from the realm of Light and banishment into the realm of "shadow and the void" parallels the separation of intelligible light and darkness in Philo's account.[73] In the Valentinian accounts, it is the Savior, who is called as the Light and the image of the Pleroma, that is, the Fullness, who shines in the darkness, but darkness—that is, the realm of Sophia outside the Pleroma—cannot understand it. In Philo, the archetypal Light is God and the

---

72. In Numenius (frag. 15), the difference between the first and the second God is related to movement. Whereas the essence of the first God is in rest, movement is related to that of the second God. The distinction between rest and movement does not reflect the distinction between the intelligible realm and the visible cosmos, as in Plato's *Sophist*; rather, the distinction is already made between beings in the intelligible cosmos (see Dillon, "Numenius," 198–99).

73. In *Haer.* 6.25, Hippolytus also refers to Gen 1:2 as a prooftext for the amorphous nature of Sophia's creation, which was cast out of Pleroma: "Sophia, therefore, prepared to project that only which she was capable, viz., a formless and undigested substance. And this he says is what Moses asserts: 'The earth was invisible and unfashioned' (Gen 1:2)" (MacMahon, *ANF* 5). The conception that it was not Sophia's erroneous thought—as in Irenaeus's and Clement's accounts, described above—but her amorphous creation that was separated from the Pleroma comes from a distinct source. In one passage, Irenaeus refers to this same teaching (see *Haer.* 1.2.3). Ismo Dunderberg, however, is skeptical that Hippolytus's biblical allusions are drawn from a Valentinian source at all. Dunderberg points out that Hippolytus has a tendency to add biblical references to his descriptions of Valentinian teachings. It is possible that the reference to Gen 1:2 as a prooftext for the expulsion of Sophia's creation from the Pleroma in Hippolytus, *Haer.* 6.25, comes from Hippolytus's pen, not from a Valentinian source (see Dunderberg, *Beyond Gnosticism*, 199–201).

Savior, whose model, the Logos, contains all his fullness (see *Somn.* 1.75 above). Both in Philo and in Valentinian accounts, the rivalry of the Logos and the Light is fenced off by the boundary or boundaries, which is a standard Pythagorean term for the separation of the principle of multiplicity and matter from the One.[74] In *Haer.* 1.3.5, the boundary serves a double role: on the one hand it separates and on the other hand it strengthens.[75] The duality of the boundary parallels Philo's account, according to which the boundary serves the double function of morning and evening.

In the Valentinian protology, the conflict within the intelligible cosmos is the basis for the creation of matter and the visible cosmos. The erroneous intention of Sophia is separated from the intelligible realm, that is, the realm of Light, and transformed into cosmic matter. Philo does not explicitly equate the intelligible darkness with matter. However, the intelligible boundary has its cosmic counterpart in the creation of the heaven, which separates the visible cosmos from the Ideas (see *Opif.* 37). It is possible, however, that in Philo's system the principle of matter has its origin in conflict within the intelligible realm, although Philo does not explicate his thinking. This means that matter came into being as a by-product of the creation of the intelligible cosmos through the Logos.

4.6. Conclusions

It is rather likely that the Valentinian protological model system in *Excerpta* C and *Haer.* 1.1.1–3 is based on the exegesis of the prologue of the Gospel of John attested in *Exc.* 6–7 and *Haer.* 1.8.5. These teachings were elaborated by the Valentinian teachers in Alexandria and Rome who noticed that John's prologue was written as a Platonizing commentary on Gen 1:1–5, similar to Philo's account in *Opif.* 25–36. It was therefore not a coincidence that the Valentinians selected John's prologue as a biblical basis for their protological myth.

The Valentinian protological system was not solely derived from the Gospel of John. The myth of Sophia has its basis in Middle Platonic protological theories and may have been a part of a preceding gnostic myth that the Valentinians had adopted. The parallels with Philo imply that the Valentinian theologians were also familiar with the Hellenistic Jewish exe-

---

74. See, e.g., Simplicius, *In Arist. phys.* 231.15–22, and the discussion concerning the derivation of matter on pages 137–38 below.

75. See also note 100 n. 31 above.

getical traditions attested in Philo's works. It seems reasonable, then, to suggest that protological teachings attested in *Opif.* 25–36, *Conf.* 146, and *Somn.* 1.75 were part of the intellectual source material for their commentaries on John's prologue.

In addition to the similarities between protological allegories of Philo and the Valentinians, there are also remarkable differences. In Philo, the creation of the intelligible world serves as an archetype for the creation of the visible cosmos. In the Valentinian accounts, on the other hand, the Father of All does not create the intelligible realm as an archetype for the visible cosmos but creates intellectual beings in order to be known and loved by them. The visible cosmos is an outcome of an error in the precosmic creation. This mythological feature is lacking in Philo's texts.

It is notable that in Philo the intelligible cosmos already contains a conflict between intelligible light, that is, the Logos, and intelligible darkness, which must be confined to sustain the harmony of the cosmos. Thus, the monadic and dyadic aspects of divinity are already present in Philo's exegesis of day one. Although Philo does not discuss this conflict further in his text, these motifs were elaborated on by the Valentinian teachers, who considered the separation of light from darkness to indicate the separation of the principle of matter from the intelligible realm. These notions are further investigated in chapter 5.

It is possible that the Valentinian teachers in Rome got to know some of Philo's exegetical innovations in *De opificio mundi* via Ptolemy. As noted in chapter 3, Ptolemy was familiar with the moderate exegetical interpretations in Philo's Exposition of the Law and may have had access to Philo's works. However, the protological parallels with Philo are also attested in *Exc.* 6–7, which can be located in Alexandria. Thus, it is more likely, then, that some of the allegorical traditions related to the creation of the world in Gen 1:1–5 were still extant in Alexandria among Valentinian exegetes during the latter part of the second century. These allegorical traditions were brought to the disciples of Ptolemy in Rome by the Valentinian teachers of Alexandria.

5
The Wisdom of God and the Creation of Matter

In the preceding chapter, I investigated the generation of the intelligible world in the systems of the Valentinians and Philo. In both traditions, the divine world generated by the transcendent One is seen in light of the Platonic ideal world. While Philo uses Gen 1:1–5 as the basis for discussing the creation of the intelligible cosmos, Valentinians use the prologue of John's Gospel as a base text for their protological account. The creation narrative in Gen 1:1–5 was seen by the Valentinians as a description of the creation of the visible cosmos. In the Valentinian myth, the intelligible cosmos is not an archetype of the visible world, as in Philo's system. Instead, the unknown God created it to be known by intelligible beings called aeons. The creation of the visible cosmos has its origin in the rupture among the divine beings, ensuing in the fall of the youngest of the aeons, called Sophia. However, the chasm between the intelligible cosmos and the visible world is not absolute: the psychic heaven—that is, the realm of the heavenly bodies—ruled by the psychic intellects, have their archetypes in the Pleroma.

The origin of matter was one of the most hotly debated questions within Hellenistic philosophical schools. The Valentinian teachers' theory of matter was indebted to neo-Pythagorean tradition, in which the principle of multiplicity and matter was derived from the transcendent One through deprivation. Although Philo does not present a detailed theory about the origin of matter, the most logical conclusion is that he leaned on a metaphysical-ontological interpretation of Plato's *Timaeus* that went back to Eudorus of Alexandria. Thus, Philo and the Valentinians can be located in a scholarly tradition that interpreted Plato's *Timaeus*, as well as the creation narrative of Genesis, metaphorically in light of Pythagorean and Aristotelian views.

5.1. The Philosophical Background of the Creation of Matter

Plato's *Timaeus* formed the cosmological basis for further speculations among Middle Platonic philosophers. In *Tim.* 29–30, the basic causes of the universe are the "mind" (νοῦς) and "necessity" (ἀνάγκη), which interact with each other as the Demiurge creates the visible copies of "noetically living beings" (τὰ νοητὰ ζῷα).[1] In addition to the eternal model, that is, the world of Ideas, and the Demiurge, there exists, according to Plato, the Receptacle, which is able to receive the images of the cosmic elements—namely, earth, water, air, and fire. In *Tim.* 50, Plato explains that the Receptacle is like a mirror that reflects images of the cosmic elements, without having qualities of its own. He also compares the Receptacle with an ointment that is used as a neutral base for various fragrances. Although the Receptacle itself is neutral, the "powers" (δυνάμεις) of the elements start to interact with one another. They put the Receptacle into chaotic motion, which generates the cosmic principle of "necessity" (ἀνάγκη).[2] According to Plato, the qualities of the four cosmic elements in the Receptacle are in constant motion, like seeds that shake and sway in a "winnowing-basket" (πλόκανον).[3]

The task of the Demiurge, who functions as the cosmic Mind, is to bring order to this precosmic chaos by contemplating the eternal Ideas as models. For that reason, the Demiurge creates the World Soul as a mediating entity, which forces the randomly moving elements of the Receptacle to rest according to divine reason. The visible cosmos is thus a combination of necessity and *nous*, that is, chaos and rest. On the one hand, the Receptacle is a neutral recipient in which genesis takes place; on the other, it is a chaotic essence out of which the four elements of the world are brought

---

1. Plato's *Timaeus* is divided into three sections, examining the premises of mind and necessity from three different points of view. The first section (29d–47e) describes the ordering of the universe through the mind (νοῦς); the second section (47e–69a), the same process from the point of necessity (ἀνάγκη); and the third (69a–92c), the interaction of the mind and necessity, especially at an anthropological level. See Thomas Tobin, ed., *Timaios of Locri, On the Nature of the World and the Soul: Text, Translation and Notes*, SBLTT 26 (Chico, CA: Scholars Press, 1985), 11–12.

2. See Francis Cornford, *Plato's Cosmology: The Timaeus of Plato* (repr., Cambridge: Hackett, 1997), 197–210.

3. For Plato's analogy of the winnowing basket, see *Tim.* 52e. Since bodily motion cannot exist without the self-motion of the soul, some commentators of Plato (e.g., Plutarch) postulated that an irrational world soul was responsible for precosmic chaos.

forth by the Demiurge. However, the Receptacle in its chaotic stage is not corporeal until the Demiurge persuades the four cosmic elements to rest.

Some Middle Platonic teachers reformed the creation narrative in the *Timaeus* by combining it with the transcendental monism of Aristotle and the Neopythagorean first principles. This means that the primary bases for the genesis of the cosmos are no longer *nous* and necessity but the triad of the principles: the Ideas, matter, and God.[4] The Ideas of the cosmic elements no longer exist independently but are seen as the thoughts of God, who is identified as the prime mover of Aristotle. The term *matter* (ὕλη) was adopted from Aristotle, but it was not connected to the Platonic Receptacle in its neutral form, only in its chaotic stage. The femininity of matter was postulated also by Aristotle, who says that matter desires form as the female desires the male and the ugly the beautiful (*Phys.* 192a.31, 209b.11–17).[5] However, chaotic matter is not fundamentally evil but has the innate tendency to escape rationality. It becomes the principle of disorder and "necessity" (ἀνάγκη), which must be persuaded by the Logos.[6] Other Middle Platonic writers, such as Plutarch, retained the former dualistic model, postulating that an evil world soul was responsible for disorder in the world.[7]

---

4. The doxological pattern of the three ἀρχαί is attested, e.g., in *Placita* of Aëtius (1.3.20) and *Timaios of Locri*, according to which "before the heaven came to be, the idea and matter, as well as the God, who is the fashioner of the better, already existed" (94c). Runia points out that the system of three *archai* (God, matter, ideas) attested in the various Middle Platonic texts was an elaboration of the preceding model, which consisted of only the two first principles (*nous*-ideas and matter). Runia refers to the information in Theophrastus's fragment (230) and the Platonic doxography of Diogenes Laertius (3.67–80), where only two *archai* are mentioned. See Runia, "Philo and Middle Platonism Revisited," 135; see also Tobin, *Timaios of Locri*, 14–16.

5. Aristotle associates Plato's notion of space with his concept of matter (ὕλη), which is a recipient (τὸ ὑποκείμενον) of each thing and has the capacity to receive form. Aristotle maintains that "when the boundary and attributes of a sphere are taken away, nothing but matter is left." It is possible that the identification of matter and Plato's Receptacle was not invented by Aristotle but came from the scholastic tradition of the Old Academy. See Dillon, *Middle Platonists*, 14; see also Kevin Corrigan, "Positive and Negative Matter in Later Platonism: The Uncovering of Plotinus' Dialogue with the Gnostics," in Turner and Majercik, *Gnosticism and Later Platonism*, 19–56.

6. It should be noted that the term *necessity* (ἀνάγκη) does not mean some deterministic natural law in its modern scientific meaning but instead refers in Plato to contingent and irrational motion without purpose or intention. See Cornford, *Plato's Cosmology*, 159–77; also Tobin, *Timaios of Locri*, 14–16.

7. See Dillon, *Middle Platonists*, 202–4.

The existence of matter was also related to the question of the eternity of the cosmos. In *Tim.* 28b, Plato maintains that the "primary question which has to be investigated at the outset in every case is, whether it [the cosmos] has always existed, having no beginning of generation, or whether it has come into existence, having begun from some beginning" (Bury). The latter option seems to be compatible with the narrative in the *Timaeus*, which describes how the Demiurge creates the cosmos out of the preexistent matter. This view conflicts, however, with Plato's view, that time itself came into being together with the creation and movement of the heavenly bodies. If time did exist before the world came into being, then how should the chronologically definable beginning of the cosmos in the *Timaeus* be understood?

One solution to the aforesaid problems was to interpret Plato's cosmological narrative in the *Timaeus* metaphorically.[8] Some Platonists assumed that Plato described the creation of the world by the Demiurge out of preexistent chaotic matter for pedagogical reasons, only to explain the logical structure of the world. Rather than a historical and actual divine being or God, the Demiurge can rather be understood as a symbolic figure, which can in reality be identified with the cosmic Nous or the rational part of the world soul.[9] This would mean that the one definitive point of time in the creation in the *Timaeus* is also part of the metaphorical cosmic myth. In reality, both the realm of being—that is, the world of ideas—and the realm of becoming—that is, the visible cosmos—have always existed ever since without a beginning or an end.[10]

---

8. This was the view of some prominent teachers of the Old Academy, such as Speusippus (ca. 407–339 BCE), Xenocrates (ca. 396–314 BCE), and Crantor (ca. 335–275 BCE).

9. In some cases, Plato identifies the Demiurge with the *nous* explicitly. In *Leg.* 967b.5–6, he maintains that it is *nous* that has ordered everything in heaven. Likewise, in *Phileb.* 29c.6–8, Plato suggests that all agree that Nous is king of heaven and earth and that *nous* cannot exist without a soul. Therefore, the Demiurge-Nous could be identified with the rational part of the world soul in the light of Plato's dialogues. See Reginald Hackforth, "Plato's Theism," in *Studies in Plato's Metaphysics*, ed. Reginald E. Allen (London: Routledge & Kegan Paul, 1965), 439–47; see also Stephen Menn, *Plato on God as Nous*, ed. Richard A. Watson and Charles M. Young, JHPS (Carbondale: Southern Illinois University Press, 1995), 6–13.

10. In addition to Eudorus of Alexandria (ca. first century BCE), the second-century (CE) proponents of *creatio aeterna* were Alcinous, Apuleius, Albinus, and an Athenian Platonist named Calvenus Taurus. The notion of an eternal cosmos is

5. The Wisdom of God and the Creation of Matter

The symbolic interpretation of the *Timaeus* may have been a reaction to Aristotle's criticism of Plato's cosmic myth.[11] Aristotle takes the *Timaeus* literally, arguing that it would be absurd to suppose that the immaterial Demiurge could have created the material world. For Aristotle, causation between beings at ontologically different levels is impossible. Also, the notion that the world is both created and eternal is irrational, because all things that are created are also destructible. Therefore, Aristotle says that the world must be uncreated and indestructible: the cosmos is a closed system in which the elements of the world are constantly changing their accidental qualities and forming the next generation of bodies.[12] Thus, the term *genesis* describes the process of change and generation within an eternal and nonchanging substratum.[13]

Some Middle Platonic philosophers revitalized the nonliteral reading of the account of the creation of the world in the *Timaeus* by combining it with Aristotelian transcendental theology and Pythagorean first principles. A theory of the creation of the world began to emerge according to

---

also attested in the pseudo-Pythagorean Timaois of Locri (ca. first century CE). Also, the Neopythagorean Proclus adopted the theory of eternal creation, maintaining that the world is "constantly in a process of creation" (ἀεὶ γιγνόμενον καὶ γεγενημένον; see Proclus, *In Plat. Tim.* 209.3–25). Like Philo, Proclus criticized the teachers of the Old Academy for their conceptual and figurative interpretation of Plato's *Timaeus*. Proclus says that, if the creation were only taken symbolically, then the Demiurge would also only be a symbolic being. There were, however, some Middle Platonic commentators—such as Plutarch (ca. 45–120 CE) and Atticus (ca. 150–200 CE)—who took Plato's cosmological myth literally: the visible world came into being at some point of time when the Demiurge started to shape chaotic, preexistent matter. The literal interpretation of the *Timaeus* was the dominant view mainly of the dualistic systems. See Winston, *Philo of Alexandria*, 14; Gregory Sterling, "Creatio temporalis, aeterna, vel continua? An Analysis of the Thought of Philo of Alexandria," *SPhiloA* 4 (1992): 28–29; Dillon, *Middle Platonists*, 242–44.

11. Aristotle mentions the nonliteral reading of the *Timaeus* in *Cael.* 279b30. Aristotle says that some teachers of the Old Academy—e.g., Speusippus and Xenocrates—suggested that Plato's description of creation in the *Timaeus* can be interpreted "didactically," like a mathematician using diagrams to explain mathematical rules. The nonliteral reading of Plato's *Timaeus* must have been popular, since Aristotle's disciple Theophrastus opposed his teacher, reading the *Timaeus* nonliterally in harmony with the teachers of the Old Academy (see Sterling, "Creatio temporalis," 15–41).

12. For the view that the world is uncreated and indestructible, see Aristotle, *Cael.* 1.10–12.

13. For Aristotle's view on *genesis*, see *Gen. corr.* 1.317a; 2.331a, 334–335a, 337a.

which God is not solely a symbolical figure but the source of the Ideas (the Monad) and the principle of multiplicity and matter (the Dyad) as well. According to this model, "to be created" necessitates a metaphysical-ontological dependency on the transcendent One. Also, matter could not exist independently as an *arche*—like the Receptacle in the *Timaeus*—but must be derived from God. As the Ideas are located within God's mind as his thoughts, the principle of matter had to have its origin in the transcendent One as a dyadic shadow projection of the Monad or a deprived aspect of the monadic Logos. These philosophical foundations were later accepted by both Philo and the Valentinian teachers in Alexandria.

5.2. The Creation of Matter in the Writings of Philo

Unfortunately, Philo does not give a clear answer as to whether he supports the doctrine of creation *ex nihilo* or creation out of preexistent matter and whether he sees creation as a temporal act (*creatio temporalis*) or an eternal process (*creatio aeterna*).[14] On the one hand, Philo seems to assume that matter existed before the Creator started to form the elements of the world. In *Opif.* 7–9 (see also 21–22), Philo states that there are two basic principles out of which the world is created: one is the pure universal and active *nous*, the other the passive, lifeless, and motionless principle, which is full of discord and disharmony. The passive element of creation is depicted as matter (ὕλη) or "substance" (οὐσία), or simply "nonbeing" (μὴ ὄν).[15] On the other hand, Philo says in *Somn.* 1.76 that "as the sun when it rises makes visible objects which had been hidden, so God when He gave birth to all things, not only brought them into sight, but also made things which before were not, not just handling material as an artificer [δημιουργός] but being Himself its creator [κτίστης]."[16]

---

14. See Gregory Sterling, "'The Most Perfect Work': The Role of Matter in Philo of Alexandria," in *Creation ex nihilo: Origins, Development, Contemporary Challenges*, ed. Gary A. Anderson and Markus Bockmuehl (Notre Dame, IN: University of Notre Dame Press, 2017), 99–118.

15. Philo compares "nonbeing" to manna, or children, which were brought from nonbeing to being from preexistent matter. The former had its origin in the element of air, when God brought forth miraculously nourishment to Israel in the desert (see *Mos.* 2.267). In the latter case, parents were the midway between divine and human nature when a child is born (see *Spec.* 2.225; see Winston, *Philo of Alexandria*, 7–8).

16. See Winston, *Philo of Alexandria*, 8; Drummond, *Philo Judaeus*, 1:303–4.

Wolfson tried to prove that Philo was the first religious-philosophical teacher to teach about creation *ex nihilo*.[17] He argues that Philo postulated in *Opif.* 29 the creation of the ideas of the four cosmic elements—that is, the ideas of earth, water, air, and fire (= heaven). The abyss in Gen 1:2 refers to the "idea of the void," which Wolfson equates with the idea of the Platonic Receptacle. Moreover, Wolfson suggests that God not only creates the Ideas but the cosmic copies of them, which means that God also creates the cosmic copy of the idea of the Receptacle.[18]

However, Wolfson's analysis of the content of the intelligible cosmos is not compelling. Rather than ideas of the cosmic bodies, in *Opif.* 29 Philo is explaining archetypical paradigms of the regions of the cosmos. The idea of the void refers to the region between the moon and earth, which is filled with air, not to the idea of the Platonic Receptacle.[19] It is also unreasonable to think that God would have created something that he could not himself contact without intermediaries. Philo explicitly mentions in *Spec.* 1.328 that God creates all things in the world out of matter "without laying hold of it himself, since it was not lawful for the happy and blessed One to touch limitless chaotic matter." In *Her.* 134–140, the separation of preexistent matter into four cosmic elements (air, fire, earth, water) is delegated to the Logos. Philo's statement in *Aet.* 5, according to which "nothing comes into being from the nonexistent and nothing is destroyed into the nonexistent," seems then to oppose the theory of creation *ex nihilo*.[20]

If creation *ex nihilo* is rejected, there are two remaining options that could explain Philo's theory concerning the origin of matter. These options are (1) that matter has existed eternally as an independent principle besides God, or (2) that matter came into being indirectly as a result of the process of creation. The former option is related to the theory of *creatio temporalis*, according to which the world came into being at the moment that God began to shape preexistent matter.[21] The latter represents *creatio aeterna*,

---

17. Wolfson, *Philo* 1:308–9.

18. For a similar interpretation, see Richard Sorabji, *Time, Creation, and the Continuum: Theories in Antiquity and the Early Middle Ages* (Ithaca, NY: Cornell University Press, 1983), 203–9. Winston remarks that creation *ex nihilo* was an unknown doctrine within Judaism during the time of Philo. See note 27 below.

19. See Runia, *On the Creation*, 171–73; Winston, *Philo of Alexandria*, 9–13.

20. See Winston, *Philo of Alexandria*, 11–13.

21. Gerhard May argues that Philo interpreted the *Timaeus* literally. This would mean that the cosmos came into being at a definite point of time as the result of God's will and would last eternally on the grounds of God's omnipotence. Thus, Philo would

which became, as I noted above, the standard view among the Middle Platonists since Eudorus of Alexandria. According to the theory of *creatio aeterna*, the temporal expressions in the creation myth of the *Timaeus* describe the ontological dependence of the world on its primary *arche*.

Philo was evidently aware of the philosophical discussion and the different views concerning the creation of the world and the origin of matter. In *De aeternitate mundi*, Philo enumerates three philosophical solutions concerning the creation of the world: (1) the Aristotelian view, according to which the world is uncreated and indestructible; (2) the Stoic view, which postulates a succession of created and destructible worlds; and (3) the Platonic view, which, according to Philo, was anticipated by Moses: the world is created, but its indestructibility is sustained by God's providence.[22]

In *Aet.* 13-14, Philo is not wholly pleased with the various Platonic interpretations of the *Timaeus*.[23] On the one hand, he rejects the sophisticated Platonic interpretation that apparently refers to the symbolical

---

have agreed with Plato that matter exists eternally beside God as the second *arche*. See Gerhard May, *Creatio ex nihilo: The Doctrine of Creation Out of Nothing in Early Christian Thought*, trans. A. S. Worral (Edinburgh: T&T Clark, 1994), 6-21. See also Hans-Friedrich Weiss, *Untersuchungen zur Kosmologie des hellenistischen und palästinischen Judentums*, TU 97 (Berlin: Akademie, 1966), 18-74. For a similar interpretation, see Drummond, *Philo Judaeus* 1:297-307; Salvatore Lilla, *Clement of Alexandria: A Study in Christian Platonisim and Gnosticism* (Oxford: Oxford University Press, 1971), 193-99. Runia is of the opinion that Philo does not give a clear answer to the problem of the matter, because his primary aim is exegetical and ethical. Philo may have taught the preexistence of matter, which existed independently of God. Matter is not, however, the second *arche*, similar to God, because God is constantly forming it (see Runia, *Philo of Alexandria*, 435-55).

22. David Runia suggests that *De aeternitate mundi* has as its formal basis the genre of the θέσις. It can be divided into three parts, which are demarcated by two transitional sentences (*Aet.* 20, 150). Notably, *Aet.* 20-149 does not present Philo's own views but arguments of others. The final part of the work is missing, which means that Philo's own view remains unclear. Runia suggests, in the light of the structure of the work, that the final part may have contained a detailed defense of the theory that posits that the world is both created and indestructible. See Runia, "Philo's 'De aeternitate mundi': The Problems of Its Interpretation," *VC* 35 (1981): 105-51.

23. Philo points out that the view that the world is uncreated and indestructible was not an invention of Aristotle but the Pythagoreans. He mentions in *Aet.* 12 a work of Ocellus, *A Treatise on the Nature of the Universe* (Περὶ τῆς τοῦ παντὸς φύσεως), in which the author asserts that the world is indestructible and offers some demonstrative proofs. Philo does not explicitly reject this possibly Neopythagorean teaching concerning the eternity of the world. Instead, he argues (*Aet.* 21-22) that the world can be

reading of the *Timaeus* by the teachers of the Old Academy. However, Philo does not say that he *accepts* the literal interpretation, but he does describe it as being "better and truer" (βέλτιον καὶ ἀληθέστερον) than the metaphorical theory, because it does not challenge the active role of God in the creation.[24] Although Philo's own view remains ambiguous in the *De aeternitate mundi*, he formulates his own thesis more clearly in *Prov.* 1.7 as follows:

> God is continuously ordering matter by his thought. His thinking was not anterior to his creating, and there never was a time when he did not create, the ideas themselves having been with him from the beginning. For God's will is not posterior to him, but is always with him, for natural motions never give out. Thus ever thinking he creates, and furnishes to sensible things the principle of their existence, so that both should exist together: the ever-creating Divine Mind and the sense-perceptible things to which beginning of being is given.[25]

Sterling points out that Philo may have modified his thoughts in *Prov.* 1.7 concerning what he writes about the creation of the world in *Opif.* 7, 9–11, which is closer to Plato's view in the *Timaeus*.[26] Philo states that the visible world cannot be distinguished from the "ever-creating Divine Mind." There is only one *arche* of the world, which means that God must be at least indirectly also the *arche* of matter. The creation of the visible world is eternal (*creatio aeterna*) because God continually preserves its existence by thinking about its eternal Ideas. Thus, the existence of the world is dependent on God's active and all-pervasive will to create through his Logos (see also *Sacr.* 65–68). Primordial matter does not have an independent and real existence of its own, as in the Receptacle in the *Timaeus*,

---

destroyed only by external causes or by the powers within itself. Both of these causes are not compelling for Philo, and he thus concludes that the world is indestructible.

24. The argumentation in *Aet.* 8–19 is rather complicated. Sterling agrees with Baltes that Philo may have used some Peripatetic source, as he presents views from different philosophical schools of thought ("Creatio temporalis," 36–37). In my opinion, Philo's view was not absolutely Platonic, and it was not absolutely anti-Aristotelian, either, resulting in the tension in Philo's statements in *Aet.* 8–19. For Philo, the main problem in various philosophical theories is that they are infected by the charge of the inactivity of God.

25. Trans. Winston, *Philo of Alexandria*, 15.

26. See Sterling, "Creatio temporalis," 39–41.

nor is God merely ordering it. Rather, matter has come into being as a by-product, or shadow reflection, of the creation of the intelligible world. Winston points out that, for Philo, matter is "a logical moment rather than a temporal reality."[27]

It thus seems that Philo did not accept either the Platonic or the Aristotelian theories of creation uncritically. Although he drew his teaching from the neo-Pythagorean and Platonic tradition and seems to interpret the *Timaeus* metaphorically, these tenets ought not to diminish the activity of God in the process of creation, as is the case in the purely symbolic view of some "sophisticated Platonists."[28] The term *genesis* is not, according to Philo, a temporal expression or pedagogical symbol but denotes metaphysical-ontological dependence on God's creative activity. Philo (*Opif.* 26) follows Plato in saying that "time was not created before the cosmos, but that time was either created together with the cosmos or after" (χρόνος γὰρ οὐκ ἦν πρὸ κόσμου, ἀλλ' ἢ σὺν αὐτῷ γέγονεν ἢ μετ' αὐτόν). The six days of creation do not mean that God needed time for the creation but that he created the whole world instantaneously by thinking about it.[29] The number of days represents the logical structure of the visible world that is made simultaneously as a copy of the intelligible model, not the chronological interval between the days of creation.[30]

The consensus among the Philonic scholars is that matter does not have an intelligible archetype in the world of ideas. Wolfson's thesis,

---

27. Winston, *Logos*, 17–18. According to the Wisdom of Solomon, another representative text of Alexandrian Hellenistic Judaism, God "created the world out of formless matter" (Wis 11:17), without there being any mention of the origin of matter. Winston stresses that there is no evidence for the doctrine of *creatio ex nihilo* in Jewish or Greek tradition at the time of Philo. Creation in the Wisdom of Solomon was understood as a continuous process. Winston suggests that the Wisdom of Solomon may be dependent on Philo: matter was not created out of nothing but came into being as a by-product of creation. See David Winston, *The Wisdom of Solomon: A New Translation with Introduction and Commentary*, AB 43 (New York: Doubleday, 1979), 39–40.

28. See Sterling, "Creatio temporalis," 40–41.

29. Philo says in *Opif.* 13: "He says that the cosmos was fashioned in six days, not because the maker was in need of a length of time–for God surely did everything at the same time, not only in giving commands but also in his thinking—, but because things that come into existence required order" (trans. Runia).

30. Philo argues that the number six is an arithmetically perfect number containing the male (number 3) and female (number 2) aspects of creation ($2 + 2 + 2 = 6$; $3 + 3 = 6$). Thus, the creation in six days describes the perfection of the created cosmos metaphorically.

according to which God also created the idea of the Receptacle, is apparently erroneous. There are, however, as I noted in chapter 4, some elements in Philo's protological accounts that may refer to a principle of matter in the intelligible world. In *Opif.* 33–34 (see also *Somn.* 1.75), Philo describes how darkness came into being as a rival to light, when the intelligible cosmos—that is, the Logos—was created. Darkness must be fenced off by the boundaries, that is, the morning and the evening, which according to Philo belong to the intelligible cosmos. As noted, the boundary is a standard neo-Pythagorean principle that functions as a control on the principle of multiplicity and matter. This would mean that God did not create matter; it came into existence as a counterelement to the Logos and opposed the ordered cosmos.

Matter is, however, a necessary cosmic element for the creation of the visible world. In Philo's cosmological system, matter is not evil, though it may become the source of evil, if rationality does not take control of it. There is not such a thing as cosmic evil or chaotic matter in Philo's cosmology, which has an existence of its own. God sends even chaotic natural catastrophes to benefit humankind in general, and if something evil happens as a result of them, it is not caused by God's will, but these effects are produced by their natural causes (*Prov.* 42–44, 52–54). It seems, then, that chaotic materiality can be experienced in the world only in the microcosmic realm, where the human mind loses its rationality and is captured by irrational passions and a love for material things.[31]

5.3. The Creation of Matter in the Valentinian Sources

The generation of matter in *Haer.* 1.2–4 and the parallel section in *Excerpta* C resembles theories in the school tradition of the neo-Pythagorean Moderatus of Gades.[32] According to Moderatus's theory described in Simplicius, *In Arist. Phys.* 230.34–231.27, "quantity"—that is, the principle of multiplicity and matter—is derived from the "unitary Logos" by depriving

---

31. As we will notice in chapter 6, Philo suggests that the soul of Adam was made in Gen 2:7 "out of dispersed matter" (ἐκ σποράδος ὕλης), which depicts its mixing with irrationality and passions (see *Leg.* 1.31–32).

32. For Moderatus's role in the first-century CE Pythagorean tradition, see Trapp, "Neopythagoreans," 355–58. Moderatus came from the city of Gades in Spain, but according to Plutarch's information he was also active in Italy (356). See also Dillon, *Middle Platonists*, 344–46.

it of its rationality.³³ Thomassen notes that, in the Valentinian cosmological myth, the whole Pleroma—that is, the sum total of aeons below the primal God—can be equated with the second Monad, or unitary Logos, of Moderatus's system, and Sophia with Quantity, which is deprived of its rationality.

Thomassen lists some vocabulary that is common to the Valentinian protology and that of Moderatus. In *Haer.* 1.2.2–4, "Extension" (ἐκθείνεσθαι, ἔκτασις) is employed to describe Sophia, as with Quantity in Moderatus's account. Sophia extends herself to reach the One, and she would have been dissolved into universal essence had she not encountered the power—that is, the Boundary—that supports the Pleroma. In Moderatus (Simplicius, *In Arist. phys.* 231.15–22), Quantity is likewise restricted by boundaries. Sophia's intention to extend herself is also "separated" (χωρισθεῖσα) and "excluded" (ἀφορισθῆναι) in the same way that "Quantity" (ποσότης) is derived through "privation" (στέρησις), "loosening" (παράλυσις), "extending" (ἔκτασις), and "spreading out" (διασπασμός). According to Moderatus, Quantity exists "because of deviation [παράλλαξις] from being, for which reason matter is also thought to be evil since if flees away from the good."³⁴

Although the Valentinian protological model fits nicely with Moderatus's description of the derivation of matter, there are also various allusions in the Valentinian accounts that connect them directly to Plato's *Timaeus*, in which the creation of the cosmos results from the synergy of *nous* and necessity. In *Haer.* 1.1.1–3, the Mind (Νοῦς) emanates from God, con-

---

33. The quotation of Moderatus by Simplicius is based on information attested in Porphyry's lost work Περὶ ὕλης. See Thomassen, *Spiritual Seed*, 270–75; Einar Thomassen, "The Derivation of Matter in Monistic Gnosticism," in Turner and Majercik, *Gnosticism and Later Platonism*, 4. On the system of Moderatus, see also Dillon, *Middle Platonists*, 347; Philip Merlan, "Greek Philosophy from Plato to Plotinus," in *The Cambridge History of Later Greek and Early Medieval Philosophy*, ed. Arthur H. Armstrong (Cambridge: Cambridge University Press, 1967), 91–92.

34. See Han Baltussen et al., trans., *Simplicius: On Aristotle Physics 1.5–9*, (London: Bloomsbury, 2011), 113. It is notable, however, that in the Valentinian system it was the last aeon, Sophia, who became the source of matter, though it is stated that the intention to know the unknown Father had infected the other aeons too (*Haer.* 1.2.2). As noted, the intention of the last aeon was fatal. This was based on the Pythagorean theory of the number thirty (2 + 4 + 6 + 8 + 10 = 30), which is also the total number of aeons in the Pleroma. Sophia was the last aeon of the Dodecad as well as the Triacontad, which implies that the novel creation of Sophia moved necessarily beyond the Limit/Boundary (ὅρος) of the Pleroma, and it was therefore imperfect.

5. The Wisdom of God and the Creation of Matter

taining all the aeons as the seed. However, in *Haer.* 1.4.1, the intention of the youngest of the aeons, Sophia, is cast out "by necessity into the places of shadow and emptiness" (ἐν σκιᾶς καὶ κενώματος τόποις ἐκβεβράσθαι κατὰ ἀνάγκην). Thus, Valentinian theologians followed Plato in thinking of the generation of the intelligible world as "things fashioned through the *nous*" (τὰ διὰ νοῦ δεδημιουργημένα), whereas the creation of the visible world that follows from Sophia's exclusion from the Pleroma is "what came through necessity" (τὰ δι' ἀνάγκης γινομένα; see *Tim.* 47e–48a). The intention of Sophia is personified and depicted as "shapeless and devoid of form" (ἄμορφος καὶ ἀνείδεος), paralleling Plato's description of the Receptacle in the *Timaeus*, which is similarly "some form that is invisible and unshaped" (ἀνόρατον εἶδός τι καὶ ἄμορφον; see *Tim.* 51b).

It is noteworthy that Sophia's "intention" (ἐνθύμησις) is also connected with ignorance. It is shapeless, because Sophia did not understand that the Father of All is incomprehensible. Therefore, the fall of Sophia from the divine realm has an epistemological origin. The reference to "the places of shadow and emptiness" (ἐν σκιᾶς καὶ κενώματος τόποις) into which Sophia's intention is thrown is an allusion to Plato's allegory of the cave (see *Resp.* 514–518).[35] Like prisoners in a cave looking at shadows projected on the wall in Plato, Sophia is bound to the realm of the emptiness of knowledge and mere shadows, until the Savior comes from above and enlightens her with perfect knowledge.[36] The salvation of Sophia living in the place of

---

35. In Plato's famous allegory, the prisoners in the subterranean cave see only shadows and reflections on the wall coming from the puppet images. One of prisoners is freed and can make a laborious journey from the cave of darkness to the real world, where the idea of good sheds light on objects seen through the eye of the soul. Plato's point is that the real knowledge is based on the vision of the ideal world, especially the idea of good, which is "the cause for all things of all that is right and beautiful, giving birth in the visible world to light, and the author of light and itself in the intelligible world being the authentic source of truth and reason, and that anyone who is to act wisely in private or public must have caught sight of this" (*Resp.* 517c [Shorey]). In the Valentinian version of the myth, Sophia is cast into the world of shadows. She is living in the darkness until the advent of Light, referred to as Christ. Sophia could not ascend to the light, because she lacked understanding, because her eye of the soul is blinded. Therefore, Sophia began to feel bad emotions until the advent of the Savior, who provided Sophia a perfect understanding concerning the Father of All and the world of the aeons, which parallels Plato's transcendent idea of good.

36. These notions are also attested in *Exc.* 31, which goes back to Theodotus. In this version, Sophia—although the text does not mention her name explicitly—"fell into ignorance and formlessness" (ἐν ἀγνωσίᾳ καὶ ἀμορφίᾳ ἐγένετο), when she wished

shadows and the cave of ignorance is actualized in two subsequent phases, which parallel the salvation of the prisoners in Plato's allegory. In the first phase, Christ descends from the intelligible realm of Light, visits Sophia Achamoth, and bestows form on her, but not in accordance with perfect knowledge. Christ leaves her only a fragrance of immortality and a desire to return to the Light. When Sophia tries to follow Christ to the Pleroma, she is prevented by the Boundary. Therefore, Sophia begins to experience various kinds of emotions, such as fear, perplexity, consternation, distress, and ignorance, which serve as the basis for incorporeal matter. It is notable that Sophia did not experience bad emotion when she lived in the world of shadows but only after she got to know that something better exists: it is the light of Christ that reveals to Sophia her fallen condition and activates her emotions. In the second phase, the Savior—that is, the Light—descends on Sophia and gives her form according to knowledge. The Savior teaches Sophia the emanations of the Father of All and that the Father is beyond understanding.[37]

The salvation of Sophia from the shadows of ignorance is part of the cosmic drama that leads to the creation of matter and the visible cosmos. The Savior not only heals Sophia's emotions through knowledge but separates them and converts them "from incorporeal passion to incorporeal matter" (ἐξ ἀσωμάτου πάθους εἰς ἀσώματον τὴν ὕλην). The Savior bestows capability on matter to be later formed by the Demiurge into bodily structures and compounds (see *Exc.* 46.1; *Haer.* 1.4.5).

In the *Timaeus*, Plato says that the projection of the ideas of the cosmic bodies into the Receptacle is "most perplexing and very hard to apprehend." The Receptacle is the "all-receiver," which reflects like a mirror the random to-ing and fro-ing of the qualities of the four cosmic elements, but Plato

---

to grasp that which is beyond knowledge. This led Sophia into a "void of knowledge" (κένωμα γνώσεως) and the "shadow of the Name" (σκιὰ τοῦ ὀνόματος)—i.e., the perfect form of the aeons. It is of note that the Logos is called "the name of God" also by Philo in *Conf.* 146.

37. There is no consensus in the Valentinian sources concerning which emotions Sophia experience. It seems, however, that Sophia's emotions parallel each other in *Haer.* 1.5.4 and *Excerpta* C. In these passages, fear and grief are seen as the sources of irrational souls and evil spirits, and the elements of the world (earth, water, air) are based on terror and perplexity. As noted, the conversion or repentance of Sophia as the source of psychic essence is not mentioned in *Excerpta* C. It is likely, as I have pointed out earlier, that this was an innovation of the Valentinian teaching that went back to the disciples of Ptolemy in Rome.

cannot explain the cause of these reflections (see *Tim.* 51b). The Valentinians obviously intended to give an answer to this "perplexing problem," as they offered explanations as to how precosmic matter was derived from the transcendent One and how the cosmic elements are projected into incorporeal matter. Just as the Platonic Receptacle has no qualities of its own before the cosmic bodies were projected into it, so does the Valentinian Sophia lack any qualities of her own, until Christ—that is, the Light—deserts Sophia, setting her emotions into chaotic motion. These passions of Sophia become the basis for incorporeal matter and the elements of the world. They can be equated with the randomly reflecting "qualities" (ἴχνη) of the cosmic elements in the Receptacle described in the *Timaeus*.

The Valentinian myth thus affirms that matter does not have its origin in the noetic world. Rather, it has its basis in the emotional surplus that resulted from the fixation of the ignorance of the one corrupted aeon. This waste product was transformed into precosmic matter, out of which the visible cosmos was created. The finest part of matter possesses, however, an inclination toward incorruptibility, which has its origin in Sophia's will to escape from the cave of ignorance and return to the Light. This part of matter is called psychic, serving as raw material not only for the psychic part of the human soul but also for the heavenly cosmos. The ruler of the seven heavens, the Demiurge, and his angelic powers were also made out of this psychic and luminous essence (see *Haer.* 1.5.1; *Exc.* 47–48).

5.4. Wisdom as Mother and Matter in Philo and Valentinian Sources

In the Valentinian protological narrative, precosmic matter and the principle of multiplicity are associated with biblical Wisdom, that is, Sophia. This view can be found already in Philo, who describes the role of the Logos in almost all senses as Wisdom in Jewish wisdom literature. Wisdom exists before the creation of the world (Prov 8:22–31), establishes the world (Jer 10:12, Prov 3:19), and is means by which all the works of God are performed (Ps 104:24). Moreover, Wisdom is imparted to humans by God (Prov 2:6), is personified (Prov 8:1), and is identified with the Torah (Sir 24:23) and linked to the reasoning of God (Wis 9:9). All these characteristics of Wisdom are also applied to the Logos in Philo's writings.[38]

---

38. Plato also speaks in *Phileb.* 30c about wisdom (σοφία) and mind (νοῦς) as equivalent terms, which may have supported Philo's tendency to assimilate the Logos (= *nous*) to Wisdom (see Wolfson, *Philo* 1:254–56; Winston, *Logos*, 14–16).

Although in most cases the Logos is substituted for Wisdom in Philo, it does not exhaust all the characteristics of personified Wisdom. In some cases, the Logos and Wisdom seem to be causally linked to each other. In *Fug.* 97, the Logos is said to be the fountain of Wisdom, but, in *Fug.* 109, Wisdom is said to be the mother of the Logos. In the allegory of the river of Eden and its four heads, Philo says, in *De somniis* 2.242–3, that it is "divine Logos" (ἱερὸς λόγος) that descends from the fountain of Wisdom like a river and waters the "virtue-loving souls." In *Leg.* 1.65, however, Philo offers a different interpretation of the river of Eden: it is the "idea of virtue," which comes forth from the Wisdom of God that is *identified* with the Logos.

It is rather difficult to make sense of these contradictory statements of Philo concerning the relation between the Logos and Wisdom. Wolfson proposes that the relationship between Wisdom and the Logos describes God's thinking power from different points of view. In the instances where the Logos is said to spring forth from Wisdom, the Logos represents the immanent stage of the Logos, whereas Wisdom represents its precosmic stage. In the instances where the Logos is the fountain of Wisdom, on the other hand, the situation is reversed: Wisdom is an immanent representation of the precosmic Logos. It is, however, the same stream of Logos-Wisdom that is depicted in some cases as the Logos and in some other cases as Wisdom.[39]

Another difference between Logos and Wisdom lies in how Philo refers to the latter. In *Fug.* 109, Wisdom is called "mother" (μήτηρ), "through which all came into existence" (δι' ἧς τὰ ὅλα ἦλθεν εἰς γένεσιν), and, in *Det.* 54, Wisdom is the "mother through which everything was brought to completion" (μητέρα δὲ τὴν σοφίαν, δι' ἧς ἀπετελέσθη τὸ πᾶν). Thus, Wisdom is not only called the instrument, like the Logos, but also mother. In *De ebrietate* 30–31, Philo describes Wisdom also as "the mother and nurse" (μήτηρ καὶ τιθήνη), who is made fertile by the seed of God and gives birth to her son, the visible world:

> Now "father and mother" is a phrase which can bear different meanings. For instance, we should rightly say and without further question that the Craftsman who made this universe was at the same time the father of what was thus born, while its mother was the knowledge possessed by its Maker. With His knowledge God had union, not as men have it, and

---

39. See Wolfson, *Philo*, 1:258–61.

5. The Wisdom of God and the Creation of Matter

begat created being. And knowledge, having received the divine seed, when her travail was consummated bore the only beloved son who is apprehended by the senses, the world which we see. Thus, in the pages of one of the inspired company, wisdom is represented as speaking of herself after this manner: "God obtained me first of all his works and founded me before the ages" (Prov 8:22). True, for it was necessary that all that came to the birth of creation should be younger than the mother and nurse of the All. (*Ebr.* 30–31, modified)

It is evident that Philo derives these characteristics from Plato's *Timaeus*, which likewise calls the Receptacle the "mother and nurse" (see *Tim.* 49a, 51a).[40] Generative terminology is used by Plato to depict the Receptacle in which the creation takes place. This idea goes back to the ancient theory that the mother does not produce the child but only gives nutrition and "space" (τόπος) for an embryo, as reported, for instance, in Aristotle.[41] In *Tim.* 50c–d, the Father is the model (i.e., the world of forms), the mother is the Receptacle, and their offspring is the world of Becoming. In Philo, Father is God, who unites with the Mother, and the Son is their offspring, the visible cosmos, which is produced from the seed of the Father.

Although Philo associates Wisdom with the the mother and nurse, which are descriptions of the Receptacle in Plato, Runia suggests that there "is insufficient evidence to prove a philosophical rationale behind the similar description of ὕλη and σοφία." Runia maintains that there is certain plasticity of the symbols and images in Philo. Therefore, the symbols of father, mother, daughter, nurse, and so on are used rather freely by Philo without any need to draw from them any profound conclusions about philosophical thinking.[42] Dillon suggests, however, that Philo may have found the idea of the female life principle in the Platonic-Pythagorean tradition, which he applies to the figure of Wisdom from the Bible. This led, however, to a conflict in Philo's general system of thought, according to which Wisdom and the intelligible cosmos ought to have been virtually

---

40. Philo's interpretation in *Ebr.* 30–31 is an extrapolation from Deut 21:18-21, in which "drunkenness not of the milder but of the most intense sort" is discussed (see *Ebr.* 27). Philo infers that the accusers of such a wicked person are his "mother and father."

41. See Cornford, *Plato's Cosmology*, 187. As noted, the femininity of matter is attested already by Aristotle, who says that matter desires form as the female desires the male and the ugly the beautiful.

42. See Runia, *Philo of Alexandria*, 284–85.

opposite to matter. The notion of wisdom as mother and nurse is therefore not elaborated any further by Philo, because he noticed that it would have led to inconsistencies concerning his overall theory of creation.[43] Winston points out that Philo was indeed aware of a neo-Pythagorean formulation according to which an aspect of the Nous/Logos can be described as the feminine Unlimited Dyad or Intelligible Matter.[44]

The association of biblical Wisdom with matter is exceptional in Hellenistic Jewish and early Christian literature. Evidently, it is also a marginal feature in Philo's oeuvre. It is possible, however, that Philo may have integrated some preceding allegorical traditions into his works that did not fit perfectly into his overall theological system. Significantly, the gnostics and the Valentinian teachers also knew of these traditions and integrated them into the myth of Sophia. The stages of Sophia's precosmic salvation serve not only as the origin of matter but also as the paradigm for the salvation of human beings. At an anthropological level, the *ordo salutis* of Sophia plays a threefold role. First, she is an archetype for the imperfect soul, assimilated with sense perceptions and passions. Second, she is a paradigm for those who are searching for immortality. Third, Sophia is the mother of those whose souls are healed and formed according to perfect knowledge.

A similar discrepancy between Wisdom as a symbol of cosmic matter and the cultivation of the human soul is also attested in Philo. In *Ebr.* 59–61, Philo describes the transformation of the soul of Sarah from the imperfect feminine into the perfect masculine. Philo explains that the words of Abraham in Gen 20:12, "she really is my sister, the daughter of my father though not of my mother," allegorically mean that Sarah does not have Wisdom, that is, the matter, as a mother, because she has rejected the customs of women—that is, the passionate sense perceptions—and become an offspring of the seed of the Father of All. "She is not born of that mate-

---

43. Dillon, *Middle Platonists*, 164. Most recently, Arco den Heijer has argued that Wisdom as mother in Philo is not necessarily linked with the Platonic Receptacle or the Pythagorean unlimited Dyad but has its basis in the Pythagorean Tetrad, which is referred to as "the mother of all." Den Heijer points out that, in Philo, Wisdom as mother is not a passive all-receiver but plays an active and emanative role in the cosmic harmony as well as in the harmony of the soul. See den Heijer, "Cosmic Mothers in Philo."

44. Winston, *Logos*, 20–21. Winston refers to Plutarch (*Is. Os.* 371e, 374a), who fused Egyptian mythology with Platonic philosophy by allegorizing the Receptacle in the *Timaeus* as the goddess Isis.

rial substance perceptible to our senses, ever in a state of formation and dissolution, the material which is called mother or foster-mother or nurse of created things by those in whom first the young plant of wisdom grew; she is born of the Father and Cause of all things" (*Ebr.* 61).[45] It cannot be a coincidence that Philo depicts sense-perceptible matter (ὕλη ἡ αἰσθητή) in the same terms used by Plato in the *Timaeus* for the Receptacle: μήτηρ (50d3), τιθήνη (49a6, 52d5, 88d6), τροφός (88d6). It is of note that Philo says that the young plant of wisdom grew from matter, which is contrasted to Sarah, who is born from the seed of the Father of All. We can infer from this that Philo is comparing the imperfect soul to sense-perceptible matter associated with Wisdom.

The association of Wisdom with matter does not necessarily have a negative connotation in Philo. The earthly soul is the neutral all-receiver or the nurse of becoming, in which the formation of the perfect soul can be actualized. At an anthropological level, the earthly soul is depicted negatively only if the right reason does not control it and the soul dissolves into the realm the sense perceptions and passions. Without the right reason, the soul is comparable to restless matter, which randomly reflects the images of the sense perceptions, causing vicious passions. It is, however, the earthly soul in which the formation of the perfect soul can take place and which can therefore also be depicted as mother and nurse in a positive way. In *Det.* 115, the Platonic terminology of Receptacle is associated with the education of the human soul. Philo says that in Deut 32:13 ("suck honey out of the rock and oil out of the hard rock") Wisdom is referred to as "the solid and indestructible wisdom of God, which feeds and nurses and rears to sturdiness all who yearn after imperishable sustenance."[46] Similarly, in *Her.* 53, Philo personifies Wisdom, calling her the mother of all who are really living to God: "'For Adam,' it says, 'called the name of his wife "Life," because she is the mother of all things living,' that is doubtless of those who are in truth dead to the life of the soul. But those who are really living have Wisdom for their mother, but Sense they take for a bond-woman, the handiwork of nature made to minister to knowledge" (*Her.* 53). Thus, Philo does not associate Wisdom solely with the soul that

---

45. οὐ γὰρ ἐξ ὕλης τῆς αἰσθητῆς συνισταμένης ἀεὶ καὶ λυομένης, ἣν μητέρα καὶ τροφὸν καὶ τιθήνην τῶν ποιητῶν ἔφασαν, οἷς πρώτοις σοφίας ἀνεβλάστησεν ἔρνος, ἀλλ' ἐκ τοῦ πάντων αἰτίου καὶ πατρός.

46. πέτραν τὴν στερεὰν καὶ ἀδιάκοπον … σοφίαν θεοῦ, τὴν τροφὸν καὶ τιθηνοκόμον καὶ κουροτρόφον τῶν ἀφθάρτου διαίτης ἐφιεμένων.

is imperfect and polluted with passions, but also with the soul perfected by the seed of virtue. Those who obey the right reason have Wisdom as their mother, rejoicing like Sarah hearing that the virtue has given birth to happiness, that is, Isaac (see *Leg.* 2.82; *Mut.* 137). They have been formed and made fertile by the seed of Logos, who "makes a woman into a virgin again" (see *Cher.* 43–45, 49–50).

These multiple associations of Wisdom with mother and matter in Philo's texts can also be found in the Valentinian protological myth. On the one hand, Sophia—or her negative emotions—represents the precosmic and immaterial matter out of which the Demiurge creates the visible world. On the other hand, Sophia's negative emotions serve as a paradigm for the irrational soul infected by passions. It seems that the Valentinian myth of Sophia is based on Hellenistic Jewish speculations concerning the relationship of Wisdom and the Platonic Receptacle attested also in Philo's Allegorical Commentary. The Valentinian theologians incorporated these notions more closely into neo-Pythagorean protology. Thus, Sophia becomes the principle of multiplicity and matter, which is derived from the transcendent One.

5.5. The Separation of Matter

In the Valentinian protological myth, the advent of the Savior brings about the healing of Sophia's emotions through knowledge. He separated them from Sophia to become incorporeal matter and bestowed on matter the capability of becoming two essences (hylic and psychic) and the elements of the world (earth, water, air, and fire). However, the Savior left matter in a confused state, to be separated by the Demiurge into structures and bodies. This sequence of events parallels Plato's *Timaeus*, in which chaotic matter does not become stable corporeal structures until the Demiurge starts to organize it using shapes and numbers (see *Tim.* 52d–53c). The formation of matter out of Sophia's emotions is attested in the Valentinian accounts in the following way:[47]

> Πρῶτον οὖν ἐξ ἀσωμάτου πάθους καὶ συμβεβηκότος εἰς ἀσώματον ἔτι τὴν ὕλην αὐτὰ μετήντλησεν καὶ μετέβαλεν. εἶθ᾽ οὕτως εἰς συγκρίματα καὶ σώματα (ἀθρόως γὰρ οὐσίαν ποιῆσαι τὰ πάθη οὐκ ἐνῆν)· καὶ τοῖς σώμασι κατὰ φύσιν ἐπιτηδειότητα ἐνεποίησεν. Πρῶτος μὲν οὖν Δημιουργὸς ὁ Σωτὴρ γίνεται καθολικός.

---

47. Trans. Brakke and Layton, *Gnostic Scriptures*, 516; my modifications.

Therefore, first, out of incorporeal and contingent passion, he (the Savior) transferred and transformed them into still incorporeal matter, and then likewise into compounds and bodies. For it was not possible all at once to make the passions an essence. And he created in the bodies properties according to their nature. Therefore, the Saviour becomes the first and universal creator. (*Exc.* 46.1–47.1)

ἀλλ' ἀποκρίναντα χωρήσει τοῦ συγχέαι καὶ πῆξαι, καὶ ἐξ ἀσωμάτου πάθους εἰς ἀσώματον τὴν ὕλην μεταβαλεῖν αὐτά· εἶθ' οὕτως ἐπιτηδειότητα καὶ φύσιν ἐμπεποιηκέναι αὐτοῖς, ὥστε εἰς συγκρίματα καὶ σώματα ἐλθεῖν, πρὸς τὸ γενέσθαι δύο οὐσίας, τὴν φαύλην τῶν παθῶν, τήν τε τῆς ἐπιστροφῆς ἐμπαθῆ· καὶ διὰ τοῦτο δυνάμει τὸν Σωτῆρα δεδημιουργηκέναι φάσκουσι. Rather he (the Savior) set them apart, poured them together and fixed them and transformed them from incorporeal passion into incorporeal matter. In this way, he bestowed upon them suitable properties and nature to become compounds and bodies so that two essences came into being, a bad one from passions; and a passive one (i.e., psychic) deriving from the turning back.[48] For this reason, they say that the Savior acted virtually as the Creator. (*Haer.* 1.4.5)

The accounts in *Exc.* 46.1–47.1 and Irenaeus's *Haer.* 1.4.5 are not totally identical. In the former, the clause after εἶθ' οὕτως does not speak about bestowing predisposition on the passions of Sophia, as in Irenaeus, but about the generation of "compounds and bodies" (συγκρίματα καὶ σώματα). Irenaeus's account also contains a second result clause (πρὸς τό), concerning the "two essences" (δύο οὐσίαι), which are not mentioned at all in this passage of *Excerpta* C. However, the two essences are mentioned later in *Exc.* 47.1–4, where the separation of the psychic and hylic essences is described. Dunderberg points out that the terms used in these passages refer to potentiality and determination. The term πήγνυμι is used in the passive to denote something that is irrevocably fixed, and the term ἐπιτηδειότης refers to capability.[49] The term συμβεβηκός in Clement's account is a *terminus technicus* in ancient physics—especially in Peripatetic philosophy—that refers to an "accidental attribute" that does not define the essence of the subject (see Aristotle, *Metaph.* 1025a, 1026b; *Top.*

---

48. Layton translates "a bad one, deriving from the passions; and a mixed one tainted with passion, deriving from the turning back" (*Gnostic Scriptures*, 358). Unger prefers "the one, coming from the passions, evil; the other, coming from the amendment, liable to suffering" (*Against Heresies*, 32).

49. See Dunderberg, *Beyond Gnosticism*, 124–25.

1.102b). These notions imply that the passions of Sophia are in an accidental state before the Savior fixes them. The most important difference between these Valentinian accounts is that *Excerpta* C nowhere mentions the theory that Sophia's passion related to her returning is the basis for psychic essence.[50]

Despite the aforesaid differences, the main content of the accounts is similar. In both, the Savior heals the emotions of Sophia by separating them and transmuting them into unstructured precosmic matter to be formed by the Demiurge. However, the Demiurge does not work independently but is controlled by Sophia. Thus, creative activity is shared between three beings: the Savior, Sophia, and the Demiurge. "The Savior becomes the first and universal creator" (Πρῶτος μὲν οὖν Δημιουργὸς ὁ Σωτὴρ γίνεται καθολικός), who creates the material and psychic essences of the world. Through the Savior's instrumentality, Sophia comes into existence, and it is virtually the Savior who creates the world, because he fixes and separates Sophia's emotions.[51] Sophia is the second creator, who builds a house (= the Demiurge) and bases it on seven pillars, which refers to the seven heavenly spheres (see Prov 9:1). The task of the Demiurge, finally, is to separate psychic essence from matter and divide this matter into the four cosmic elements. Figure 5.1 illustrates the relationship of the Savior, Sophia, and the Demiurge in the Valentinian accounts:

In Philo's writings, the Logos is not only the "pattern" (ἀρχέτυπος, παράδειγμα) according to which the world is created or the "place" (τόπος) for the Ideas but also an "instrument" (ὄργανον) "through which" (δι' οὗ) God creates the world. The Logos also functions as a "cutter" (τομεύς) that divides matter and shapes the cosmic elements (earth, water, air, and fire) out of it (see Philo, *Opif.* 25; *Her.* 140).[52] Philo identifies God with the Platonic Demiurge, who uses the Logos as his instrument, whereas in the Valentinian systems it is Sophia who uses the Demiurge as her instrument.

---

50. The psychic essence has its origin in the conversion of Sophia and becomes the origin of the essences of not only the Demiurge and angels but also of the devil, because her conversion contained an element of fear. Unlike the Demiurge, who is ignorant of the spiritual realm, the devil knows of the divine realm above the psychic heaven (see *Haer.* 1.5.4).

51. In the Valentinian Exposition, it is the Savior himself who acts in the role of the "dividing Demiurge" (Val. Exp. 35.30–34; see Thomassen, "Derivation of Matter," 16–17).

52. See Runia, *Philo of Alexandria*, 446–51.

The Savior is a manifestation of the Pleroma,
who is contemplated by

↳ Sophia, who uses

    ↳ the Demiurge as an instrument in:

        1. the creation of heavenly intellects out of psychic essence, according to the model of the aeons, and
        2. the separation of matter into four cosmic elements.

Fig. 5.1. Savior, Sophia, and the Demiurge

The functions of the Logos in Philo as a pattern and an instrument are distributed in the Valentinian myth to the Savior (the pattern) and the Demiurge (the instrument). Although Sophia attempts to do everything in honor of the aeons, it is only the psychic realm that has the capability of reflecting the ideal world of the aeons. The psychic essence has its ontological basis in Sophia's repentance and search for the light. This means that only the beings of the psychic realm, which rule the seven heavens, are copies of the intelligible cosmos.

5.5.1. The Creation as διάκρισις

According to *Haer.* 1.5.1, the creation of heaven and earth in Gen 1:1 does not describe the creation of the ideas of heaven and earth, as in Philo, but the separation of the psychic (= heaven) and hylic (= earth) essences, which were in a state of confusion before the Demiurge began to shape them. In *Haer.* 1.5.2, the separation of heaven and earth is depicted in the following way:

> Thus, they say that he became the Father and God of things outside the Pleroma (i.e., the Fullness), and he is the maker of all psychic and hylic things. He separated the two essences that had been poured together. He made bodies out of incorporeal things and created the heavenly and earthly things. And he became the Demiurge of the hylic and the psychic things, of right and left, of light and heavy, those tending upwards and those tending downwards. He constructed the seven heavens, and they say that the Demiurge is above them, and for that reason they call him Hebdomad, but the mother Achamoth is called Ogdoad, preserving the number of the primal and first Ogdoad of the Pleroma. They say that

that the seven heavens are intellectual, and that they are angels, and the Demiurge himself is an angel, but resembling God. And paradise is above the third heaven and is virtually the fourth archangel, and that Adam received something from him when he passed time within it. (my trans.)⁵³

The Creator God made "heavenly and earthly things" (τά τε οὐράνια καὶ τὰ γήϊνα) by "separating" (διακρινεῖν) the psychic and hylic essences each other. Thus, the creation of heaven and earth in Gen 1:1 is seen as a separation of primordial matter. The Demiurge is called the Father and God outside the Pleroma and the Maker of all psychic and hylic things (Πατέρα οὖν καὶ Θεὸν λέγουσιν αὐτὸν γεγονέναι τῶν ἐκτὸς τοῦ Πληρώματος, Ποιητὴν ὄντα πάντων ψυχικῶν τε καὶ ὑλικῶν). Although the Demiurge gave form to all things that came to exist after him, he was in reality prompted by Sophia.⁵⁴ It is possible that, in *Haer.* 1.5.1, Irenaeus is summarizing Valentinian teachings from various sources. A more nuanced and somewhat different description of the separation of the psychic and hylic essences is found in *Excerpta* C, which contains a detailed allegorical commentary on Gen 1:1–3. The text in *Exc.* 47–48 is as follows:

> Therefore, the Savior becomes the first universal Demiurge. "But Sophia" is the second, and she "built a house for herself and erected seven pillars" (Prov 9:1). And first of all, she emitted an image of the Father, a God, and through him she "created the heaven and the earth"—that is, the heavenly and earthly, the things on the right and the things on the left. He, as an image of the Father, became a father, and he first emits the

---

53. Πατέρα οὖν καὶ Θεὸν λέγουσιν αὐτὸν γεγονέναι τῶν ἐκτὸς τοῦ Πληρώματος, Ποιητὴν ὄντα πάντων ψυχικῶν τε καὶ ὑλικῶν· διακρίναντα γὰρ τὰς δύο οὐσίας συγκεχυμένας, καὶ ἐξ ἀσωμάτων σωματοποιήσαντα, δεδημιουργηκέναι τά τε οὐράνια καὶ τὰ γήϊνα, καὶ γεγονέναι ὑλικῶν καὶ ψυχικῶν, δεξιῶν καὶ ἀριστερῶν δημιουργὸν, κούφων καὶ βαρέων, ἀνωφερῶν καὶ κατωφερῶν· ἑπτὰ γὰρ οὐρανοὺς κατεσκευακέναι, ὧν ἐπάνω τὸν Δημιουργὸν εἶναι λέγουσι· καὶ διὰ τοῦτο ἑβδομάδα καλοῦσιν αὐτόν, τὴν δὲ μητέρα τὴν Ἀχαμὼθ Ὀγδοάδα, ἀποσώζουσαν τὸν ἀριθμὸν τοῦ ἀρχεγόνου, καὶ πρὸ τῆς τοῦ πληρώματος Ὀγδοάδος. Τοὺς δὲ ἑπτὰ οὐρανοὺς νοεροὺς φασιν· Ἀγγέλους δὲ αὐτοὺς ὑποτίθενται, καὶ τὸν δημιουργὸν δὲ καὶ αὐτὸν ἄγγελον Θεῷ ἐοικότα· ὡς καὶ τὸν Παράδεισον ὑπὲρ τρίτον οὐρανὸν ὄντα, τέταρτον Ἄγγελον λέγουσι δυνάμει ὑπάρχειν, καὶ ἀπὸ τούτου τι εἰληφέναι τὸν Ἀδὰμ διατετριφότα ἐν αὐτῷ.

54. Philo also uses the demiurgic (technical) and procreative (biological) metaphors of the creation. In *Opif.* 7, 10, Philo stresses that the Creator of the universe is not only the Maker but also the Father who cares about the safety of his children (see Runia, *Philo of Alexandria*, 421–23; Runia, *On the Creation*, 113–14).

psychic Christ as an image of the Son; then the archangels, as images of the aeons; then angels of the archangels, out of psychic and luminous essence, about which the prophetic word says: "And the Spirit of God was borne above the waters." [Gen 1:2] This speaks of the intertwining of the two essences, those which are obedient to him;[55] the unmixed "was borne above" and the heavy and material, the dirty and coarse were borne under it. But it is suggested that it (mixture) was in the beginning incorporeal by saying "invisible," for it was never invisible to any human, which did not yet exist, nor to God, for he created it. Rather, in this way it somehow expresses its unformed, unshaped, and undesigned character. As the Demiurge discriminated pure things from the coarse (heavy), since he perceives each nature, he made light—that is, he manifested and brought forth the idea of light—the light of the sun and of the heaven was made much later." (my trans.)

The content of the allegorical commentary becomes clearer if read alongside the Greek text of Gen 1:1-3, which I present in the following table, with the key words indicated by underlining:

Gen 1:1-3	Exc. 47-48
Ἐν ἀρχῇ ἐποίησεν ὁ θεὸς τὸν οὐρανὸν καὶ τὴν γῆν.	Πρῶτος μὲν οὖν Δημιουργὸς ὁ Σωτὴρ γίνεται καθολικός. "ἡ δὲ Σοφία" δευτέρα "οἰκοδομεῖ οἶκον ἑαυτῇ καὶ ὑπήρεισεν στύλους ἑπτά." Καὶ πρῶτον πάντων προβάλλεται εἰκόνα τοῦ Πατρὸς Θεόν, δι' οὗ ἐποίησεν τὸν "οὐρανὸν καὶ τὴν γῆν", τουτέστι τὰ οὐράνια καὶ τὰ ἐπίγεια, τὰ δεξιὰ καὶ τὰ ἀριστερά. Οὗτος ὡς εἰκὼν Πατρὸς πατὴρ γίνεται καὶ προβάλλει πρῶτον τὸν ψυχικὸν Χριστόν, Υἱοῦ εἰκόνα. ἔπειτα τοὺς Ἀρχαγγέλους, Αἰώνων εἰκόνας. εἶτα Ἀγγέλους <Ἀρχ>αγγέλων ...

---

55. Casey rejects the words in the manuscript αὐτῶν πεπεισμένων and proposes the emendation "made by him" αὐτῷ πεποιημένων (see also Smith, *Valentinian Christianity*, 115; Brakke and Layton, *Gnostic Scriptures*, 517). In my opinion, there is no reason to emend the text. See page 54 below.

ἡ δὲ γῆ ἦν ἀόρατος καὶ ἀκατασκεύαστος, καὶ σκότος ἐπάνω τῆς ἀβύσσου, καὶ πνεῦμα θεοῦ ἐπεφέρετο ἐπάνω τοῦ ὕδατος.	... ἐκ τῆς ψυχικῆς καὶ φωτεινῆς οὐσίας ἥν φησιν ὁ προφητικὸς λόγος. "Καὶ Πνεῦμα Θεοῦ ἐπεφέρετο ἐπάνω τῶν ὑδάτων," κατὰ τὴν συμπλοκὴν τῶν δύο οὐσιῶν τῶν αὐτῶν πεπεισμένων τὸ εἰλικρινὲς "ἐπιφέρεσθαι" εἰπών, τὸ δὲ ἐμβριθὲς καὶ ὑλικὸν ὑποφέρεσθαι, τὸ θολερὸν καὶ παχυμερές. Ἀσώματον δὲ καὶ ταύτην ἐν ἀρχῇ αἰνίσσεται τὸ φάσκειν "ἀόρατον." οὔτε γὰρ ἀνθρώπῳ τῷ μηδέπω ὄντι ἀόρατος ἦν. οὔτε τῷ Θεῷ· ἐδημιούργει γάρ· ἀλλὰ τὸ ἄμορφον καὶ ἀνείδεον καὶ ἀσχημάτιστον αὐτῆς ὧδέ πως ἐξεφώνησεν.
καὶ εἶπεν ὁ θεός Γενηθήτω φῶς. καὶ ἐγένετο φῶς. 4. καὶ εἶδεν ὁ θεός τὸ φῶς ὅτι καλόν. καὶ διεχώρισεν ὁ θεὸς ἀνὰ μέσον τοῦ φωτὸς καὶ ἀνὰ μέσον τοῦ σκότους. 5. καὶ ἐκάλεσεν ὁ θεὸς τὸ φῶς ἡμέραν καὶ τὸ σκότος ἐκάλεσεν νύκτα. καὶ ἐγένετο ἑσπέρα καὶ ἐγένετο πρωί, ἡμέρα μία.	Διακρίνας δὲ ὁ Δημιουργὸς τὰ καθαρὰ ἀπὸ τοῦ ἐμβριθοῦς, ὡς ἂν ἐνιδὼν τὴν ἑκατέρου φύσιν, φῶς ἐποίησεν, τουτέστιν ἐφανέρωσεν καὶ εἰς φῶς καὶ ἰδέαν προσήγαγεν, ἐπεὶ τό γε ἡλιακὸν καὶ οὐράνιον φῶς πολλῷ ὕστερον ἐργάζεται.

It is possible that the account in *Exc.* 47–48 is part of a longer commentary on Genesis that is integrated into the protological account. After the Savior separates out Sophia's negative emotions, transforming them into precosmic matter, Sophia creates the Demiurge, through whom she divides heaven and earth. This parallels Irenaeus's account, according to which Sophia cannot give form to anything spiritual, but she endeavors still to make something, which she is capable of doing. She begins to form beings out of psychic essence to honor the aeons, though in fact they are made through her by the Savior (see *Haer.* 1.5.1 above). In Clement's account, Sophia emits the Demiurge as an image of the Father of All, who in turn emits the psychic Christ as an image of the Only Begotten Son and the angels and archangels out of "psychic and luminous essence" as images of the rest of the aeons.[56]

---

56. In Irenaeus's version, Sophia imitates the invisible Father, keeping herself concealed from the Demiurge, who is identified with the Only Begotten (*Haer.* 1.5.1). I suggest that this statement originates with Irenaeus, because it contradicts what he says elsewhere in his account about the relationship of the Father and the Son in the

Notably, Sophia is not identified explicitly anywhere in Irenaeus's account with biblical Wisdom. However, in *Exc.* 47.1, it is stated that "Sophia built a house for herself and erected seven pillars," which refers to Wisdom in Prov 9:1: "Wisdom has built herself house, she has set up her seven pillars" (ἡ σοφία ᾠκοδόμησεν ἑαυτῇ οἶκον καὶ ὑπήρεισεν στύλους ἑπτά). In the Valentinian allegory, this house represents either the cosmic house—that is, the psychic region of the Demiurge—or the Demiurge himself, who is in many Valentinian sources called "place" (τόπος).[57] These seven pillars represent the seven heavenly spheres, which are ruled by the Demiurge and his angels, the latter of whom the Demiurge is placed above. The seven heavens are intellectual beings, and they form the invisible psychic heaven, which was created first by Sophia through the Demiurge (Gen 1:1; see Irenaeus, *Haer.* 1.5.2).

In *Exc.* 48.1, the Demiurge made the other intellectual beings—that is, the Christ and the angels—"out of psychic and luminous essence" (ἐκ τῆς ψυχικῆς καὶ φωτεινῆς οὐσίας), which is referred to in the context of the "prophetical word" in Gen 1:2: καὶ Πνεῦμα Θεοῦ ἐπεφέρετο ἐπάνω τῶν ὑδάτων. This is taken as an allegorical description of the "intertwining (or combination) of the two essences," before the Demiurge separates them (see also *Haer.* 1.5.2; 4.5). Although the temporal sequence is unclear, the most logical interpretation is that the separation of the two essences by the Demiurge reveals the idea of light and brings forth its cosmic image—that is, the psychic essence—which also serves as the basis for the luminous soul-bodies of the psychic beings; the light of the

---

Pleroma. It is explicitly stated that the Son—i.e., the Only Begotten—is the only aeon who knows the Father and is *not* concealed by him. Therefore, the idea that Sophia would imitate the Father by concealing herself from the Demiurge does not make any sense.

57. *Topos* has more than one meaning in the Valentinian accounts. It can refer to the region of Sophia—i.e., the Ogdoad—which in Irenaeus's account is also called ὁ μεσότητος τόπος (see also Tri. Trac. 92.26; Irenaeus, *Haer.* 1.5.3). In some Valentinian texts, it is also depicted as the final place of salvation for the Demiurge and the righteous ones (Irenaeus, *Haer.* 1.7.1). *Topos* can, however, also refer to the Demiurge himself or to the Hebdomad—i.e., the region of the Demiurge—as is the case in Hippolytus, *Haer.* 6.32.7–9. There, Hippolytus describes the Valentinian teaching that the essence of the Demiurge is of a "fiery nature and is also termed by them the supercelestial *Topos*, and *Hebdomad*." The identification of the Demiurge with the *Topos* is also attested in Heracleon, frag. 35 (see Thomassen, *Spiritual Seed*, 116).

cosmic bodies was made much later.⁵⁸ The psychic essence also bears soteriological significance, because it is created from Sophia's longing for the eternal Light. The psychic essence thus possesses intellectuality, albeit in a potential stage, and therefore the psychic angels who ruled the seven heavens are also called intellects.

5.5.2. The Visibility of Earth and the Ancient Theory of διάκρισις

As clarified above, the Valentinian commentators understood the creation of heaven and earth in Gen 1:1 as a result of the separation of the psychic and hylic essences by the Demiurge. This work of the Demiurge recalls Plato's *Timaeus*, in which the visible world is explained to be the outcome of the cooperation of Reason and Necessity, that is, the Logos and an Errant Cause. The Demiurge has to "persuade" (πείθειν) the Receptacle, which is associated with disorder and random change, to come to order. Plato writes: "And inasmuch as Reason was controlling Necessity by persuading her to conduct to the best and the most part of the things coming into existence thus and thereby it came about, through Necessity yielding to intelligent persuasion, that this Universe of ours was being in this wise constructed at the beginning" (*Tim.* 48a [Bury]).⁵⁹ In the Valentinian myth, the psychic realm, which was separated from matter, consisted of the seven heavens, ruled by the Demiurge, called Hebdomad, and his angels. These psychic intellects do not belong to the world of aeons, though they are created as images of them. However, the Valentinians understood the earth of Gen 1:1 to belong to the visible and material world, as discussed in *Exc.* 47.4: "But it is suggested that it (mixture) was in the beginning incorporeal by saying 'invisible,' for it was never invisible to any human, which did not yet exist, nor to God, for he created it. Rather, in this way it somehow expresses its unformed, unshaped, and undesigned character." Unlike the invisibility of the psychic essence, the Valentinian teachers emphasized that the earth in Gen 1:1 is visible: the term *invisible* (ἀόρατος) signifies that the earth was "unformed, unshaped, and undesigned" (ἄμορφον καὶ ἀνείδεον καὶ ἀσχημάτιστον). It would seem,

---

58. Although the essence of the Demiurge and other psychic beings is basically "invisible and incorporeal" (ἀόρατος καὶ ἀσώματος), it may take visible manifestations in the world, as is the case when the visible body of the Savior is spun "from unseen psychic essence" (ἐκ τῆς ἀφανοῦς ψυχικῆς οὐσίας; see *Exc.* 50.5, 59.4).

59. See Cornford, *Plato's Cosmology*, 159–77.

then, that there had been some commentators of Genesis who argued that the creation of the earth in Gen 1:1 described the creation of the invisible cosmos, because the earth was "unseen" (ἀόρατος). The Valentinian allegorists explicitly reject this view, claiming that the precosmic matter has never been unseen; *invisibility* refers instead to its formlessness. This interpretation recalls *Haer.* 1.5.2, according to which matter was in a state of confusion before the Demiurge began to "make bodies out of incorporeal essences" (ἐξ ἀσωμάτων σωματοποιήσαντα). Thus, the term *incorporeal* (ἀσωματός) can be interpreted also in this context to denote matter, which is formless or in a state of confusion.

It is rather likely that the criticism in *Exc.* 47.4 was directed toward a Platonizing reading of Genesis, which treats Gen 1:1–2 as a description of the creation of the invisible and intelligible realm. This might then be taken as an explicit counterargument to Philo, who maintains in *Opif.* 29 (see also 34) that the earth of Gen 1:1 refers to the intelligible earth. Philo's view, however, was rather rare among the early Christian writers. Quoting Gen 1:2 in *Strom.* 5.93.5–94.5, Clement claims that the words of Genesis inspired Plato and Aristotle to postulate that the existence of matter was among the first principles, but the invisible earth was, according to Moses, a part of the archetypal monadic world.[60] It is unclear whether *Exc.* 47.4 was directed at Philo or Christian Platonists who, like Clement, adhered to Philo's theory about the creation of the intelligible cosmos during day one (Gen 1:1–5). If Valentinian teachers were familiar with Philo's exegetical theory concerning the creation during day one, they explicitly rejected it, as they interpreted the creation narrative in Gen 1:1–5 as a description of the creation of the visible cosmos.

The creation of the visible lights of heaven is not explicitly described in the Valentinian accounts. It is only mentioned in passing that the "light of the sun and of the heaven" (ἡλιακὸν καὶ οὐράνιον φῶς) was created after the separation of the psychic and luminous essence from hylic matter by the Demiurge. Thus, it would seem that the Valentinian interpreters followed the temporal order of Genesis, according to which the firmament and the visible lights of heaven were created during the second and fourth days.

---

60. In addition to Clement's *Strom.* 5.93.5, the other explicit reference to the Mosaic theory of ideas occurs in Eusebius, *Praep. ev.* 11.24.7–12. Whether Clement was the source of Eusebius or whether he had read this statement directly from Philo is uncertain (see Van den Hoek, *Clement of Alexandria*, 196–97; Lilla, *Clement of Alexandria*, 189–92).

In *Opif.* 36–38, Philo explains how, during the second day (Gen 1:6–8), God made heaven, that is, the firmament, which was the first among the visible things to be made. The earth and water were still in a state of confusion, before God began to shape the earth during the second day of creation. The origin of this watery matter is not explained. It is simply assumed in *Opif.* 38 to be raw material for the Demiurge to create from. Philo maintains that earth and water are mixed with each other, forming "one undistinguishable and shapeless nature" (μία ἀδιάκριτος καὶ ἄμορφος φύσις). The heaven is then set as a boundary that separates confused matter from the higher cosmic spheres, as is also related in *Plant.* 3:

> When the world fashioner commenced his formative activity, he took the material which of itself was confused and lacking order and led it from disorder to order and from confusion to separation. He fixed earth and water as roots in the middle, drew up the trees of air and fire from the middle towards the upper part, and fortified the encircling ethereal region by making it into a border [*horos*] and guard post for that which lay within. From this the heaven [*ouranos*] also appears to have received its name. (Geljion and Runia)[61]

Philo here describes how God "began to shape (precosmic matter) and bring it from confusion to separation" (ἐκ συγχύσεως εἰς διάκρισιν ἄγων ὁ κοσμοπλάστης μορφοῦν ἤρξατο). Heaven is not separated from matter but is instead set by God as ethereal region between the visible and the invisible world. Heaven, that is, the firmament, is arranged as a "boundary" (ὅρος) and "container" (φυλακτήριον) that separates the material creation and the regions of earth, water, air, and fire from the divine world. As noted above, the visible heaven as a boundary has its intelligible archetype in the intelligible realm, when God separated the Light, that is, the Logos, from the darkness by setting of "boundaries" (ὅροι), that is, morning and evening between them (see *Opif.* 33–34, 37; *Somn.* 1.75; see ch. 4.5 above).

The separation of matter and the formation of the cosmic bodies (earth, water, air, and fire) are not described in detail in *Opif.* 36 or *Plant.* 3–4, only in *Her.* 133–236, where Philo investigates the principle of equality in the creation and the role of Logos. In *Her.* 133–134, Philo explains

---

61. The derivation of οὐρανός from ὅρος connects the term with with ὡρεύειν ("to take care of"). See Cornutus (*Nat. d.* 1.1–2) and Pseudo-Aristotle, *Mund.* 6, 400a8. In *Opif.* 37, Philo links the word οὐρανός with ὁρατός ("visible"). See Geljon and Runia, *On Planting*, 100; Runia, *On the Creation*, 176–77.

how the Logos divides matter according to its physical characteristics into four cosmic elements:[62]

> The subject of division into equal parts and of opposites is a wide one, and discussion of it essential. We will neither omit not protract it, but abridge it as far as possible and content ourselves with the vital points only. Just as the great Artificer divided our soul and limbs in the middle, so too, when He wrought the world, did He deal with the being of all that is. This He took and began to divide as follows. First He made two sections, heavy and light, thus distinguishing the element of dense from that of rare particles. Then again He divided each of these two, the rare into air and fire, the dense into water and land, and these four he laid down as first foundations, to be the sensible elements of the sensible world. (*Her.* 133–134)

The biblical basis for the separation of the cosmic elements out of preexistent matter is Gen 15:7–21, which describes the dividing up of the covenant animals. Philo allegorizes the phrase "and he divided them in the middle" (διεῖλεν αὐτὰ μέσα), claiming that God divides in this way all the bodies and the cosmic elements "according to the principle of equality" (περὶ τῶν ἴσων). The birds flying on high are left undivided, which means that heaven, that is, the firmament, is left undivided, because it is the representation of the dividing Logos itself (see *Her.* 227–236).

Philo's theory of separation is based on the well-known ancient theory of *diakrisis*. The Logos first divides up the "heavy" (τὸ βαρύ) and the "light" (τὸ κοῦφον) essences of matter. After that, both of these essences are divided in turn into the "sparse" (τὸ λεπτομερές) and the "dense" (τὸ παχυμερές). In that way, fire is separated from air and earth from water, the four cosmic elements being created according to the divine model. As noted, heaven is not divided or separated from matter, but God places it as a boundary between the earthly region and the intelligible cosmos. The following diagram illustrates the *diakrisis* theory used by Philo in his allegorical exegesis:[63]

---

62. For *diakrisis*-cosmogonies, see Walter Spoerri, *Späthellenistische Berichte über Welt, Kultur und Götter* (Basel: Reinhardt, 1959); see also Thomassen, *Le Traité Tripartite (NH I, 5)*, 368–69; Thomassen, "Derivation of Matter," 16–17; Dunderberg, *Beyond Gnosticism*, 124–25.

63. In *Gig.* 22, Philo presents another theory of the separation of matter: "The pneuma of God means according to one sense the air that flows up from the earth, the

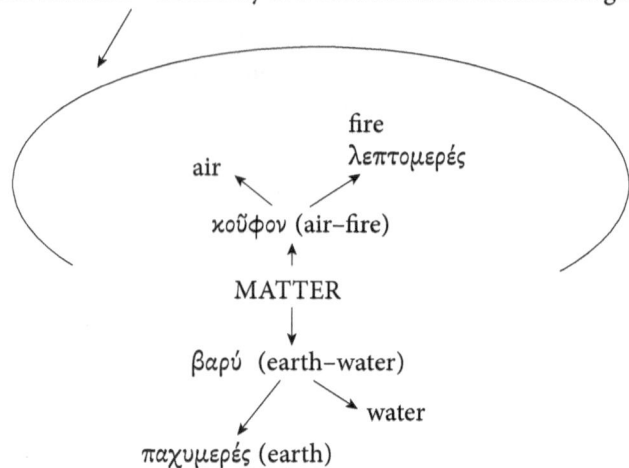

Fig. 5.2. The *Diakrisis* Theory of Philo

As noted above, the Valentinian teachers used the same theory of *diakrisis* to describe the separation of matter by the Demiurge.

> Thus, they say that he became the Father and God of things outside the Pleroma, and he is the maker of all psychic and hylic things. He sepa-

---

third element that rides on the water, for which reason he says in the creation account, 'the spirit of God was borne above the water' (Gen. 1:2), for the air, which is light, rises and is borne upward, using the water as its base. In another sense it is pure knowledge that every wise man duly shares" (trans. Winston, *Philo of Alexandria*, 64). In this passage, Philo maintains that the spirit, which refers to the cosmic element of air, has its basis in the element of water: the air is separated from the watery earth through evaporation and tends upward. This passage differs from *Opif.* 26–35, according to which Gen 1:2 describes the contents of the intelligible cosmos. In addition, the spirit in *Opif.* 29–30 is not described as an archetype of air but an idea of the life of all living beings, whereas the idea of air is established in the creation of darkness. Philo is therefore, in *Gig.* 22, dependent on an exegetical tradition that differs from that of *Opif.* 26–35 but may be compatible with Prov 1:22, according to which water, darkness, and the abyss constitute, besides God, the first principles from which the world comes into being. These notions indicate that Philo was working with an existing exegetical tradition, though in some cases it is impossible to form a coherent view, if all conflicting teachings are brought together (see Runia, *Philo of Alexandria*, 119).

rated the two essences that had been poured together. He made bodies out of incorporeal things and created the heavenly and earthly things. And he became the Demiurge of the hylic and the psychic things, of right and left, of light and heavy, those tending upwards and those tending downwards. (*Haer.* 1.5.2)

"And the Spirit of God was borne above the waters." (Gen 1:2) This speaks of the intertwining of the two essences, those which are obedient to him; the unmixed "was borne above" and the heavy and material, the dirty and coarse were borne under it.... As the Demiurge discriminated pure things from the coarse (heavy), since he perceives each nature, he made light—that is, he manifested and brought forth the idea of light—the light of the sun and of the heaven was made much later. (*Exc.* 47.3–48.1)

The terms used in the accounts of Philo, Irenaeus, and *Excerpta* C concerning the essences of the elements of the world are as follows:[64]

Essence	Philo, *Her.* 133 (*Opif.* 31)	Irenaeus, *Haer.* 1.5.2	*Exc.* 47–48
heaven	(εἰλικρινής, καθαρά) αἰθέριον	psychic	psychic εἰλικρινές, καθαρόν
subtle: fire	λεπτομερές	ἀνωφέρειν	
light: air	κοῦφον	κοῦφον	
heavy: water	βαρύ	βαρύ	θολερόν
dense: earth	παχυμερές	κατωφέρειν	παχυμερές

It is likely that the accounts in *Exc.* 47–48 and *Haer.* 1.5.2 are dependent on a similar *diakrisis* theory to that attested in Philo. The source used by Irenaeus contains a more detailed version of the separation of matter than that attested in the allegorical commentary of *Excerpta* C. Irenaeus omits some parts of that account, which explains the differences between *Exc.* 47–48 and *Haer.* 1.5.2. In Irenaeus's account, precosmic matter—out of which the psychic essence was already separated—is divided by the Demiurge first into the "heavy" (βαρύ) and the "light" (κοῦφον), and after

---

64. The term "pure" (εἰλικρινής) does not appear in *Her.* 133, but I have included it in the table for the sake of comparison, because it does appear in *Opif.* 31, referring to the idea of the essence of light.

that into the elements that "tend upward" (ἀνωφέρειν) and those that "tend downward" (κατωφέρειν). Although the cosmic elements are not mentioned in this passage, it seems evident that the elements that tend upward denote fire, which is distinguished from air. The elements tending downward then denote earth, which the Demiurge separates from the water.

This description of the separation of matter in the Valentinian sources also fits with the *diakrisis* theory attested in Philo. It is notable that the terms used in Clement's and Irenaeus's accounts differ from each other, but both have parallels in Philo's theory of *diakrisis*. *Excerpta ex Theodoto* 47–48 distinguishes the psychic essence from hylic matter, which is depicted as the "dense" (παχυμερές) portion of "thick" (θολερόν) matter. The term "dense" (παχυμερές) is used by Philo to distinguish earth from water. Strikingly, in *Excerpta C*, the psychic essence, which is a manifestation of the idea of light, is called "pure" (καθαρά) and "unmixed" (εἰλικρινές). These terms refer in Philo's *Opif.* 31 to the idea of the essence of light created in Gen 1:3, which I handled already in chapter 4. I next analyze the significance of these parallels.

5.5.3 Creation of the Pure Light and the Psychic Essence

In *Opif.* 31, Philo interprets Gen 1:3 as denoting the creation of the idea of light by the Logos. While *Opif.* 29 describes the idea of light as the model for the heavenly bodies (sun, moon, stars, and planets), *Opif.* 31 seems to refer to the essence of light, that is, brightness from which the sun and other planets derive their light. The passage in *Opif.* 31 is as follows:

> That invisible and intelligible light [τὸ δὲ ἀόρατον καὶ νοητὸν φῶς] has come into being as the image of the divine Logos, which communicated its genesis. It is a star that transcends the heavenly realm [ὑπερουράνιος ἀστήρ], source of the visible stars, and you would not be off the mark to call it "all-brightness" [παναύγειαν]. From it the sun and moon and other planets and fixed stars draw the illumination that is fitting for them in accordance with the capacity they each have. But that unmixed and pure gleam [τῆς ἀμιγοῦς καὶ καθαρᾶς αὐγῆς] has its brightness dimmed when it begins to undergo a change from the intelligible to the sense-perceptible [ἐκ νοητοῦ πρὸς αἰσθητὸν μεταβολήν], for none of the objects in the sense-perceptible realm is absolutely pure [εἰλικρινές]. (Runia)

Philo explains that the intelligible light in *Opif.* 31 is "pure" (καθαρά) and "unmixed/pure" (εἰλικρινής), though its brightness weakens when it begins to undergo a change from the intelligible to the sense-perceptible cosmos.⁶⁵ This passage becomes comprehensible in light of two important distinctions that Philo makes concerning the nature of light. First, Philo distinguishes between the visible light and the intelligible light. The former is the light through which sense-perceptible objects can be seen. The latter is the intelligible light through which God's presence in the world can be comprehended. In *Mut.* 6, Philo claims that God is the source of the purest light, through which the human mind can comprehend God's presence and actions in the world (see also *Somn.* 1.115–116). In *Abr.* 157, Philo makes another distinction between the perishable and the everlasting lights. Perishable light proceeds from fire, whereas everlasting light descends from heaven, as if the stars were pouring down their beams "from everlasting springs" (ἀπ᾽ ἀενάων πηγῶν). It seems, then, that the creation of light in *Opif.* 31 especially refers to the idea of the everlasting and pure light, which descends into the visible cosmos through the heavenly bodies.

The terms associated with the pure light in *Opif.* 31 also appear in the aforementioned Valentinian description of the creation of light (Gen 1:3) in *Exc.* 47.3–48.1. In this passage, the psychic (= heaven) and hylic (= earth) essences are said to be intertwined with each other before the Demiurge separates them. The psychic essence, which is also depicted as "luminous" (φωτεινή), differs from the rest of matter, because it is not mixed but intertwined with matter. Thus, when the Demiurge separates the psychic essence from matter, "he made light—that is, he manifested and brought forth the idea of light" (φῶς ἐποίησεν, τουτέστιν ἐφανέρωσεν καὶ εἰς φῶς καὶ ἰδέαν προσήγαγεν), meaning that the separation of the matter reveals the light, which is depicted as "pure" (καθαρά) and "unmixed" (εἰλικρινής). This parallels Philo's description of the everlasting light in *Opif.* 31.⁶⁶ In

---

65. The term εἰλικρινής (sometimes in the form εἰλικρινές) appears thirty times in Philo, in various contexts. In some cases, εἰλικρινές refers to the pure human mind that alone can comprehend God (*Leg.* 1.88; *Post.* 134; *Ebr.* 101, 189; *Her.* 98; *Praem.* 46) or the pure mind that is not infected by the senses (*Leg.* 3.111). The term εἰλικρινές can also refer to the pure intellect of God (*Opif.* 8–9; *Praem.* 40; *Contempl.* 2) or the stars (*Spec.* 1.39–40). In these instances, Philo was clearly influenced by Plato. The term εἰλικρινές is used in *Phaed.* 66a.3 (see also 67b.1) in the sense of pure thought that is not mixed with the senses. In *Tim.* 45b.7, the term is related to the mechanism of pure vision that involves the pure fire of the sun, not mixed with any of the other primary bodies.

66. It is possible that the idea in the aforementioned Valentinian passage represents the whole intelligible cosmos—i.e., the world of aeons as Light, which serves

Philo, the everlasting light can be associated with ether, which is also referred to as the finest essence of the visible cosmos in Valentinus's psalm *Harvest*.[67] Thus, it is likely that in *Excerpta* C the psychic and luminous essence also parallels the cosmic element of ether.

5.6. Heaven as a Boundary in Philo and Valentinian Writings

In *Opif.* 36–37, Philo writes that the first thing to be created in the visible cosmos is heaven, which is called the "firmament" (στερέωμα), referring to the three-dimensional and solid feature of the visible world. As in *Plant.* 3–4, heaven is also called a "boundary" (ὅρος), because it separates the visible cosmos from the ideal world having its model in the separation of light and darkness during day one (see *Opif.* 33–34). In *Mos.* 2.194 Philo says that, unlike the Egyptians who honor earth, Moses regards heaven as a "palace of the highest sanctity," an ethereal region having no mixture of evil (see also *QG* 4.57). In describing the creation of the cosmos, Philo tries to follow the biblical creation narrative as closely as possible. Thus, heaven is created before the creation of the heavenly bodies; the whole is created without its parts.

In *Opif.* 45–61, Philo describes the creation of the visible lights of heaven—the sun, the moon, and the stars—during the fourth day. Although Philo describes these cosmic intellects as "without bodies," they are not totally incorporeal. They only lack an earthly body similar to human bodies and then are free from irrational impulses.[68] In *Opif.* 73, Philo maintains that the heavenly bodies are living beings with intelligence, or rather each of them is an intellect, insusceptible to any kind of wickedness.[69] Following Plato's teachings in the *Timaeus*, Philo indicates

---

as an archetype for the intellect beings (νοητοί) of the psychic realm ruled by the Demiurge, as well as their luminous essence. The term *idea* in the singular evokes the common Middle Platonic usage of the term *idea* as a substitute for all ideas. It was a part of the doxological pattern in the Middle Platonic systems to describe the three ἀρχαί of the world: God, the Idea, and the matter. The Idea is mentioned in the singular, e.g., in Timaios of Locri 94c; Alcinous, *Epit.* 9–10; 14; Numenius, frag. 16.

67. See ch. 6.4. In *Excerpta* C the psychic essence also forms the soul-body for the spiritual seed, which is in harmony with a common Middle Platonic view concerning the ethereal soul-body of the intellect.

68. See Winston, *Logos*, 33–34.

69. See Runia, *On the Creation*, 65. The purest kind of substance out of which the stars and other cosmic bodies were created may denote ensouled fire or ether.

in *Opif.* 55 that God locates "divine images" (ἀγάλματα θεῖα) in heaven "as though in a temple" (ὥσπερ ἐν ἱερῷ), which is made of the "purest part of a bodily substance" (καθαρωτάτῳ τῆς σωματικῆς οὐσίας).⁷⁰ Philo also declares in *Spec.* 1.166 that heaven is the sanctuary of the visible cosmos, which is called the highest and truest temple of God, "having for its sanctuary the holiest part of all existence, namely heaven, for its votive offerings the stars, for its priests the angels, who are servitors of his powers, unbodied souls, not mixtures of rational and irrational nature as ours are, but with the irrational eliminated, completely mind, pure

---

Although Philo discusses in *Opif.* 27 the creation of the intelligible cosmos, he mentions heaven as the most excellent thing in the visible cosmos, because it is composed of the purest substance and serves as the dwelling place for the visible gods, i.e., the heavenly bodies. In *Plant.* 3–4 and *Her.* 227–236, Philo explicates that heaven is the boundary from the realm of the four cosmic elements, meaning that heaven was made from some other substance. In *Somn.* 1.14–39, however, Philo speculates that the "the well of the oath" (Gen 28:12) is an allegory of the fourth cosmic element—i.e., fire—and could be identified with heaven. However, Philo also claims that the essence of heaven is incomprehensible. Therefore, it would be as fruitless to seek its substance as it is to understand the essence of the human mind. See Tobin, *Creation of Man*, 82–84; Winston, *Logos*, 64–65; Runia, *On the Creation*, 174–75; Geljon and Runia, *On Planting*, 99–100. It seems that Philo hesitates between the system of four elements and the acceptance of a fifth element, the ether, which can be seen as a special kind of fire, or perhaps the purest form of light.

70. See Runia, *On the Creation*, 204; Runia, *Philo of Alexandria*, 224. In the *Timaeus*, the Father and Maker of the world is said to make a cosmic sanctuary (ἄγαλμα) for the everlasting gods, who are called the "gods of gods" (θεοὶ θεῶν), the term ἄγαλμα being a common phrase for a cult statue, shrine, or objects of worship in which the gods dwells. The eternal gods that dwell in the cosmic sanctuary are evidently the planetary gods who obey the motions of the ideal world. Thus, the sanctuary in question is not the visible world as such but the celestial sphere, the living and moving ἄγαλμα of the noetic world. See *Tim.* 37c–d, 41a–d; Cornford, *Plato's Cosmology*, 99–101. Some Platonists understood the phrase "gods of gods" in the *Timaeus* as a reference to the Ideas (= gods), which serve as archetypes for the planetary gods. Plotinus maintains that the intellectual level consists of "divine beings," drawing a distinction between celestial gods and the gods of the intellectual realm—i.e., divine ideas (*Enn.* 1.8.2; 3.5.6; 5.8.3, 5). Proclus says that the cosmos is the ἄγαλμα of the everlasting gods. The presence of gods in the cosmos channels the radiance emanating from the intelligible gods—i.e., the Ideal world. Proclus calls the Demiurge ἀγαλματοποιὸς τοῦ κόσμου. On heaven as a shrine for the heavenly gods, see also Seneca, *Ep.* 90.28; Aristotle, *On Philosophy*, frags. 14, 18 (discussed in Runia, *On the Creation*, 204).

intelligences, in the likeness of the monad."[71] Philo stresses, however, that the godlike heavenly bodies and angels should not be worshiped but only God, who is the ruler of the heavenly spheres.

In the Valentinian cosmological model, the psychic heaven, which is made out of luminous essence, parallels the view held by Philo described above. In *Excerpta* C and related passages in Irenaeus's account, the psychic realm is described as a cosmic copy of the Pleroma. The heavenly intellects are images of the aeons: the Demiurge is an image of the Father of All, the psychic Christ is equated with the Son, and the archangels and angels are made as images of the rest of the Pleroma. Although the Demiurge thought that he was the Father (Πατήρ) and Maker (Ποιητής) who fashioned the psychic Christ, the seven heavens, and the angelic intellects, it was in fact Sophia who made these things through him. Thus, the whole psychic realm is ruled by the intellects, who have their archetypes in the Pleroma, that is, the Fullness. This means that the visible cosmos created by the Demiurge reflects the harmony of the Pleroma at least in some extent, and human beings can reach some knowledge of the Pleroma through the contemplation of the heavenly realm. It is noteworthy that the Tripartite Tractate describes the etymology of the term *aeon* in the light of the order of the annual seasons: "For just as the present aeon is single, yet divided into ages, ages into years, years into seasons, seasons into months, months into days, days into hours, and hours into moments, in the same way, the true aeon also is single yet multiple" (Tri. Trac. 73.18–74.18). According to the Tripartite Tractate, the order of the seasons of the year is an image of the order in the intelligible realm. This idea was a commonplace in the Platonic-Aristotelian worldview. It is also mentioned by Philo, who says that the annual seasons are the outcome of the rational circuits of the heavenly bodies, which reflect the harmony of the intelligible cosmos (see *Opif.* 47, 55, 112–117).[72] Philo, however, does not make strict distinctions

---

71. Trans. Winston, *Philo of Alexandria*, 279. The earliest reference in Greco-Roman literature to the notion of the cosmos as a temple is in Pseudo-Plato, *Epin.* 983e–984b. See also Plutarch, *Mor.* 477C; Seneca, *Ep.* 90.28.

72. See Runia, *On the Creation*, 284–85. For Philo, the cosmic heaven was a living image of the intelligible cosmos. God created it on the fourth day, which in arithmology is related to the sacred number ten ($1 + 2 + 3 + 4 = 10$). Although there are beings in the world whose essences are mixed with imperfection and evil, the heavenly sphere represents perfection, harmony, and beauty in the cosmos. Philo did not, however, accept the common Hellenistic religious model of the cosmos, which can be found in the Hermetic writings, in Stoic theology, and even in the transcendent

5. The Wisdom of God and the Creation of Matter 165

between the intelligible cosmos, heaven, and the material realm, because the power of God's Logos sustains all of creation. Rather, Philo interprets the Logos of God as the cosmic bond, uniting all things to God. It seems that the accounts in *Haer.* 1.1–7 and *Excerpta* C limit the sympathy of the cosmos to the realm of the psychic heaven, which reflects the harmony of the Pleroma. The heavenly spheres are not ruled by malevolent archons, as in some Sethian gnostic sources, but by rational intellects, who imitate the harmony of the Pleroma. It is only the material creation, which is made from Sophia's chaotic and random emotions, that lacks a relation to the divinity.

The parallelism between the intelligible cosmos and the visible cosmos is also attested in a fragment of Valentinus that describes the creation of the visible cosmos according to the heavenly model:

> As much as the image is inferior [ἐλάττων] to the living person [ἡ εἰκὼν τοῦ ζῶντος προσώπου], so is the world inferior to the living aeon [ὁ κόσμος τοῦ ζῶντος αἰῶνος]. What is the cause of the image? The greatness of the person who provided the model for the painter, so that he might be honored through his name. For the form was not regarded as equal to the original, but the name filled out what was lacking in the artefact. For the invisibility of God as well contributes to faith in the created work. (*Strom.* 4.89.6–90.1)[73]

Evidently, Valentinus's fragment has a parallel in Plato's creation myth in the *Timaeus*, in which the Father and Maker of the world gazes on the eternal model (πρὸς τὸ ἀΐδιον ἔβλεπεν) to fashion the cosmos that contains visible copies of the intelligible living beings (τὰ νοητὰ ζῷα; see *Tim.* 28c–30c).[74] It is notable that the archetypal living aeon in Valentinus's

---

theology of the Middle Platonic tradition. For Philo, the divination of the heavenly bodies should not lead to worship of the cosmos. The visible gods—i.e., the heavenly bodies—are servants of one God apprehended only by the intellect (*Spec.* 1.13–20). On the Hellenistic religious model of the cosmos, see Runia, *On the Creation*, 207–9; Franz Cumont, *Astrology and Religion among the Greeks and Romans* (New York: Putnam's Sons, 1912), 101–38.

73. Trans. Thomassen, *Spiritual Seed*, 465.

74. The comparison between a real model and painting versus ideas and the cosmos is Platonic. For the discussion on the Ideas, earthly representations, and paintings, see Plato, *Resp.* 596a–605c. The planetary spheres as a cult sanctuary for the heavenly gods are comparable to the statues made by Daedalus in Plato, *Euthyphr.* 11b, 15b; *Meno* 97d. Thomassen maintains that, although the Platonic two-world

fragment is in the singular, which evokes the common Middle Platonic usage of the term *idea* as a substitute for all ideas. Thus, the living aeon in this context stands for the entirety of the aeons, that is, the Pleroma.

Although Valentinus says that the cosmos is an inferior copy of the intelligible world, he also maintains that it should be honored for the sake of its divine archetype, as the painting is honored through the name of its model. This would mean that Valentinus means to portray the whole cosmos as a copy of the living aeon, not only the most refined element—that is, the psychic heaven—as in the Valentinian accounts described above. Thus, Valentinus's idea of the cosmic sympathy is closer to Philo's view, which takes the whole creation as a cosmic copy of the noetic cosmos.

5.7. Conclusions

In this chapter, I have investigated issues related to the creation of matter and visible cosmos in Philo and Valentinian sources, which become comprehensible in light of neo-Pythagorean theories. Eudorus of Alexandria was probably the first to present a detailed theory of the derivation of matter from the transcendent One. Eudorus's protological innovations became the standard view among the first- and second-century Middle Platonic teachers, though dualist tendencies persisted among some prominent teachers who postulated the preexistence of matter as the second *arche* besides God. While Philo's theory concerning the creation of matter is compatible with Eudorus's view, the Valentinian teaching (*Excerpta* C, *Haer.* 1.1–4) is closer to the theory of Moderatus of Gades, according to which matter came into being through deprivation from the noetic realm.

It is notable that multiple relationships between the preexistent Wisdom and Plato's Receptacle (namely, matter) are present already in Philo's cosmological allegories, even though they do not fit perfectly with his overall Logos theology. In some cases, Philo associates the Platonic Receptacle with the feminine and dyadic aspect of Wisdom. The Valentinian theologians elaborate these Platonizing speculations, incorporating

---

model obviously influences the parallelism between cosmos and the transcendent world, the choice of the word *living* in Valentinus's fragment was based on the analogy of the painting and its living model (*Spiritual Seed*, 465–66). It was common in Greco-Roman religious tradition to make a distinction between the cult statues and humans as images of gods. A wise human was seen as a "living image" (εἰκὼν ζῶσα) of the gods, whereas the concrete and material images were lifeless.

them into the myth of Sophia's fall and restoration. The stages of Sophia's salvation not only form the origin of matter but also serve as the paradigm for the salvation of human beings.

The Valentinian commentary on Gen 1:1–5 in *Excerpta* C explicitly rejects the Philonic view that Gen 1:1 describes the creation of the invisible and intelligible earth. This implies that the Valentinian teachers knew of a similar interpretation to the one attested in Philo's *De opificio mundi*, which they explicitly were rejecting. Strikingly, the Valentinians also present an interpretation of Gen 1:3 as denoting the revelation of the pure and everlasting light, referring to the psychic essence, which parallels Philo's interpretation in *Opif.* 31. It is not clear, however, whether Valentinians knew of Philo's works directly or whether they had access to pre-Philonic source material that was probably used by Philo in his exegesis of Gen 1:3 and was still extant among Alexandrian Christian exegetes in the latter part of the second century.

I also noted that the Valentinian accounts in *Exc.* 47–48 and *Haer.* 1.5.2 are dependent on the physical theory of *diakrisis*, which describes the division of matter into four cosmic elements (earth, water, air, and fire), according to their physical characteristics. Philo uses the same theory in his description of the separation of matter by the Logos. In the Valentinian accounts, the cosmic elements are linked to the passions of Sophia, which serve as a mythological basis for the separation of the matter by the Demiurge. This feature is evidently lacking in Philo.

Taking into account all these parallels, the derivation of matter, its association with Wisdom, the interpretation of Gen 1:3 as denoting the pure and everlasting light, and the separation of matter on the grounds of the theory of *diakrisis*, it is reasonable to conclude that the Valentinians were working within an allegorical tradition whereby many of Philo's interpretations were alternately adopted, rejected, and reformed.

6
The Creation of the First Human in Allegorical Exegesis

Valentinian anthropology is fundamentally connected to the protological and cosmological accounts discussed in the previous chapters. Valentinians' understanding of the threefold cosmic structure and the division between hylic and psychic essences is incorporated into their interpretation of the creation of the first human being. The creation of Adam is, however, the reverse of the creation of the visible cosmos. Whereas the creation described in Gen 1:1 is seen as a separation of the hylic and psychic essences, the creation of Adam is understood as depicting how these essences were brought together in him and his descendants. The Demiurge created the irrational soul of Adam out of incorporeal matter (Gen 2:7), into which he breathed the likeness of himself—that is, the psychic essence (1:26). At the same time, Sophia deposited into the psychic soul of Adam a seed of her own, which she produced as an image of the Savior's angels (1:27). In the end, Adam is clothed in the garments of skin, which denotes the sense-perceptible material body. As in Philo's Allegorical Commentary, the Valentinian description of Adam's creation is a typological model of humankind. Adam is more a type than a real, historical person: the threefold structure of the soul of the first human being forms the basis for the tripartite division of humankind into the hylic, psychic, and spiritual categories.

6.1. The Philosophical Background to Valentinian Anthropology

Valentinian anthropology drew on Middle Platonic theories of the human soul, which were strongly influenced by Aristotelian transcendental psychology.[1] The origin of these theories was evidently in Plato's dialogues,

---

1. For an excellent summary of the Aristotelian influence on the Middle Platonic and gnostic teachers, see Gerard P. Luttikhuizen, *Gnostic Revisions of Genesis Stories and Early Jesus Traditions*, NHMS 58 (Leiden: Brill, 2006), 37–42.

especially the *Timaeus*, which describes the human soul as a fragment of the world soul. In the famous passage *Tim.* 41d–e, Plato describes how the Demiurge shapes the rational and immortal part of the human soul out of the same substance as the world soul. Yet that rational part is only "second or third in the degree of purity." The creation of the body and those mortal parts of the soul that are connected to the bodily life are left for the "younger gods," who imitate the creative activity of the Demiurge.[2] Thus, the human soul is a mediating principle between the purely rational world of Ideas and the material creation; it is an image of the world soul, which is a harmonious composition of Indivisible ("being") and Divisible ("becoming") kinds of essence (see *Tim.* 35a).[3]

The discussion around Plato's anthropology began already during the Old Academy. The most famous critic of Plato's anthropological conceptions was Aristotle, who found problematic the relationship between the physical body and the nonphysical soul. In *De an.* 412b.4–6, Aristotle maintains that the soul is not an ontologically different entity from the body but the "first actuality of a natural body possessed of organs" (Hett; ἐντελέχεια ἡ πρώτη σώματος φυσικοῦ ὀργανικοῦ). Thus the soul is an inseparable, functional principle of an individual body. Aristotle illustrates the relationship between body and soul by comparing it with an eye and the faculty of sight. If an eye were the body, the faculty of seeing would be its soul. Just as there is no faculty of seeing without the eye, there is no soul without a body.[4]

Although Aristotle's psychology paved the way for the hylomorphic views of the mind-body relationship, some details in his writings imply that he was still working within a dualistic worldview.[5] While the sensible

---

2. See Cornford, *Plato's Cosmology*, 139–47.

3. Cornford, *Plato's Cosmology*, 59–66.

4. Aristotle solved the problem of causation in Plato's psychology by postulating a mediating soul-body between the nonphysical soul and the physical body. This soul-principle does not make contact with the body and its organs directly but through an intermediary entity called *pneuma* that mediates between the soul and the body. The *pneuma* is a vehicle, instrument, or shell of the soul, which is contained in the male semen, before any bodily organs are produced (Aristotle, *Mot. an.* 10.703a4–b2; *De an.* 3.10.433b.19). See Abraham P. Bos, "Aristotelian and Platonic Dualism in Hellenistic and Early Christian Philosophy and Gnosticism," *VC* 56 (2002): 278.

5. On the physicalist and nonphysicalist dimensions of Aristotle's psychology, see Jonathan Barnes, "Aristotle's Conception of Mind," in *Articles on Aristotle*, ed. Jonathan Barnes, Malcolm Schofied and Richard Sorabji (London: Duckworth, 1979),

6. The Creation of the First Human in Allegorical Exegesis

and reasoning parts of the human soul, together with its instrumental soul-body, decay together with the body, the highest part of the human soul, the intellect, "seems to come about in us as being a sort of substance and seems not to be destroyed" (*De an.* 408b.18 [Hett]).[6] This distinction is based on that between passive and active intellects.[7] According to Aristotle, every object of thought consists of passive matter and active form. This distinction also applies to operations of the human mind.[8] The reasonable human soul is capable of reasoning, planning, and imagination, but it also has the capacity to become conscious of itself as thinking. These two aspects—the mind as thinking and the mind thinking of itself as thinking—refer to the passive and active parts of the human mind. The active intellect gives form to the passive mind, just "as the light that makes potential colors into actual colors" (*De an.* 430a.10–25 [my trans.]).

The active mind not only supplies intuitive knowledge but has the capacity to separate itself from the sense-perceptible world and contemplate the transcendent world.[9] There is also one crucial difference between

---

4:32–41. Abraham P. Bos argues against the standard hylomorphic interpretation of Aristotle's *De anima*. He suggests that Aristotle was still working within the dualistic framework, though he made crucial alterations in Plato's teaching. See Abraham P. Bos, *The Soul and Its Instrumental Body: A Reinterpretation of Aristotle's Philosophy of Living Nature* (Leiden: Brill, 2003); Bos, "Aristotelian and Platonic Dualism," 276–84.

6. Plato suggested already in *Tim.* 30b–c that *nous* was an ontologically independent entity from the soul, maintaining that the Demiurge had set "an intellect [*nous*] within the soul and the soul within the body," which can be equated with the cosmos as an "ensouled living being with an intellect" (τὸν κόσμον ζῷον ἔμψυχον ἔννουν). At the microcosmic level, however, *nous* in Plato's texts is identified mainly with the rational part of the soul.

7. Cicero reports that Aristotle considered the immortal part of the soul to consist of a special divine fifth element (*quinta essentia*), similar to that of the celestial bodies. As *pneuma* is the vehicle of the soul, ether is a vehicle of the eternal mind. For the essence of the heavenly bodies, see Aristotle, *Cael.* 269a.31; 270a.12, b.10; 289a.15.

8. Victor Caston argues that the chapter in question "concerns two separate species of mind, and not divisions within a mind." The attributes of the mind described in *De an.* 3.5 parallels those of the cosmic Mind described in *Metaph.* 12.7–9. Thus, it is the cosmic mind, which is described in *De an.* 3.5, not a separate essence of the human mind. See Victor Caston, "Aristotle's Two Intellects: A Modest Proposal," *Phronesis* 44.3 (1999): 199–227.

9. The relationship between the passive mind, i.e., *logos*, and the active mind, i.e., *nous*, is not exclusive. Active thinking cannot exist without logical reasoning based on the sense perceptions, and vice versa. The *nous* is able to be logical, and the *logos* is able to be noetic. The multidimensionality of *nous* and *logos* in Aristotle's epistemology is

the passive and active minds: while the reasoning of the passive mind functions naturally as the human being grows and learns, active intellect is engaged from outside.[10] The active intellect must be awakened by the "cosmic mind."[11] Therefore, Aristotle argues that the active intellect is not a part of the soul but "seems to be a different *genus* [γένος] of the soul" (*De an.* 413b.24–27). Hence, Aristotle draws a distinction between two states of the human soul: one of sleep and one of being awake (*De an.* 412a23–26). When the soul is sleeping, it has only a potential for higher intellectual capacities (*nous*-in-potency), but when it is awakened these capacities are actualized (*nous*-in-action). These two modes of the intellect thus do not denote two separate intellects but one intellect in two separate stages.

In the Middle Platonic tradition, the idea of the awakening of the soul goes back to the aforesaid Aristotelian traditions.[12] In the Valentinian teachings, the awakening of the individual soul has its paradigm in the salvation and awakening of Sophia, which is mentioned in *Exc.* 3.1–2: "When the Savior came, he awakened the soul and kindled the spark. For the words of the Lord are power. Therefore, he said, 'Let your light shine before humans' (Matt 5:16). And after the Resurrection, by breathing the Spirit on the apostles, he blew away the dust like ash and removed it, but he kindled the spark and gave it life" (my trans.).[13] This spiritual awakening is also mentioned in the Valentinian Gospel of Truth (28.32–30.23):

---

described in Richard A. Lee and Christopher P. Long, "Nous and Logos in Aristotle," *FZPhTh* 54.3 (2007): 348–49.

10. Merlan, "Greek Philosophy from Plato to Plotinus," 42–43.

11. Bos, *Soul and Its Instrumental Body*, 226–29; Abraham P. Bos, "Philo of Alexandria: A Platonist in the Likeness of Aristotle," *SPhiloA* 10 (1998): 73–74; Bos, "Aristotelian and 'Platonic' Dualism," 286–91.

12. Bos, "Aristotelian and Platonic Dualism," 286–91. The awakening of the World Soul by the cosmic Intellect was a common motif in Middle Platonism (e.g., Alcinous, *Epit.* 14; Plutarch, *An. procr.* 1026e–f), and it served as a paradigm for the awakening of the human soul through intellectual activity. The awakening of the individual soul from an irrational sleep is also mentioned in the Hermetic sources (see Corp. herm. 1.27, 10.5). See also Rom 13:11, where the awakening metaphor is used relating to the salvation: "Besides this you know what hour it is, how it is full time now for you to wake from sleep."

13. Ἐλθὼν οὖν ὁ Σωτὴρ τὴν ψυχὴν ἐξύπνισεν, ἐξῆψεν δὲ τὸν σπινθῆρα. δύναμις γὰρ οἱ λόγοι τοῦ Κυρίου. Διὰ τοῦτο εἴρηκεν· «Λαμψάτω τὸ φῶς ὑμῶν ἔμπροσθεν τῶν ἀνθρώπων.» Καὶ μετὰ τὴν ἀνάστασιν, ἐμφυσῶν τὸ Πνεῦμα τοῖς Ἀποστόλοις, τὸν μὲν χοῦν καθάπερ τέφραν ἀπεφύσα καὶ ἐχώριζεν, ἐξῆπτε δὲ τὸν σπινθῆρα καὶ ἐζωοποίει.

6. The Creation of the First Human in Allegorical Exegesis

> Such are those who have cast off ignorance from themselves like sleep, considering it to be nothing. Neither do they consider its other products to be real things. Rather, they put them away like a dream in the night and deem the knowledge of the Father to be the light. That is how each person acted while being in ignorance: as though asleep. And the person who has knowledge is like one who has awakened. And good for the person who returns and awakens! And blessed is the one who has opened the eyes of the blind! (trans. Layton, modified)

Philo, too, regards the salvation of the soul as an awakening. In *Abr.* 70, he compares the rejection of the false doctrines of "Chaldean philosophy" with the act of awaking from a deep sleep:[14]

> Having been brought up, then, in this doctrine, and having followed Chaldean beliefs for some considerable time, as if from deep sleep he opened the eye of the soul and, beginning to view pure radiance in place of profound darkness, he followed the light and beheld what he had not seen before, a kind of charioteer and helmsman of the cosmos presiding over and directing in a salutary way His own creation, bestowing care and supervision upon all those parts of it which are deserving of divine concern. (*Abr.* 70 [Birnbaum and Runia])

In addition to the metaphor of awakening, Aristotle's speculations concerning the different kinds of soul-bodies and the twofold intellect had a profound impact on the teachings of Middle Platonic philosophers.[15]

---

14. Deep sleep as a metaphor for foolishness occurs before Philo, in Sir 22:9 (LXX): "The one who teaches a fool … rouses a sleeper from deep slumber." See Birnbaum and Dillon, *On the Life of Abraham*, 216–18; Bos, "Philo of Alexandria," 66–86; also *Somn.* 1.164–165.

15. The strict distinction between the soul and the intellect is also found in Plutarch, who not only drew a distinction between rational and the irrational parts of the soul but also between the rational soul and *nous* (*Fac.* 943a). Plutarch maintained that there were two conjunctions: the first of the soul and the body, and the second of the soul and the mind. There were also, according to Plutarch, three classes of humankind. The first group lacked the mind altogether, being mixed with bodily passions. The second group had a mind, but they struggled with passions and divine impacts. The third group possessed the mind in a perfect fashion, which lifted them above all bodily passions. Plutarch criticized those who regarded the mind as part of the soul. In reality, the mind is a demon that exists outside the soul and the body and whose task is to guide the human soul toward its home in heaven (Plutarch, *Gen. Socr.* 591d). The association of the *nous* with a demon comes from Plato, who says, in *Tim.* 90a,

While the passive mind perishes together with the body and its pneumatic soul-body, the active mind is eternal as it contemplates the supra-cosmic mind, that is, God.[16] It became common in Middle Platonic tradition to think of the soul as experiencing a sort of double liberation during death. In the first stage, the soul, together with its pneumatic body, is liberated from the body. In the second stage, the active mind, the intellect, is separated from the pneumatic soul-body. These notions concerning the afterlife can be found in different versions in the Middle Platonic sources and gnostic writings as well as in the Hermetic tradition.[17]

Plato's view on *theopoiesis*—becoming like God—became a commonplace in various Middle Platonic traditions and was combined with the aforementioned Aristotelian views. In *Theaet.* 176a–b, Plato says that humans should escape from earth to the dwelling of gods and to "become like God as far as it is possible" (ὁμοίωσις θεῷ κατὰ τὸ δυνατόν) for mortal beings. Plato's view concerning the potentialities of soul was rather optimistic, and it could not give a logical answer to the reality of human suffering and erroneous choices.

There thus emerged different theories among the Platonic teachers to try to explain the reality of moral vices. Some Platonists, such as Numenius and some gnosticizing Platonists, taught that the reason for erroneous choices was the precosmic fall of the world soul. The imperfection of the human soul could be derived from the fact that it was a fragment of

---

that a demon is "the most authoritative element of soul," whose task is to raise the human soul to heaven. For an analysis of Plutarch's view, see Dillon, *Middle Platonists*, 211–12.

16. In his lost dialogue *Eudemus*, Aristotle discusses the soul's return home after death, suggesting that at least some part of the soul continues to exist after the death of the individual. It is not clear, however, whether the immortal part of the soul is able to keep its individuality after death. See *Eudemus* frags. 1 and 6 in *Aristotelis fragmenta selecta*, ed. W. David Ross (repr., Oxford: Clarendon, 1964).

17. For the double liberation of the soul in the Hermetic tradition, see Corp. herm. 10.16–17. Aristotle's theory of the soul forms the basis for the Middle Platonic theories concerning different kinds of soul-bodies, enjoying popularity also among early Christian teachers. Irenaeus presupposes, in light of 1 Cor 15:44, the existence of twofold soul-bodies—the animal bodies, which remain in life after death, and the spiritual ones, which are put on after the resurrection (*Haer.* 5.7.1–2). The idea of the instrumental soul-body of the intellect is attested in the writings of Alexandrian theologians Origen and Didymus the Blind (see Origen, *Cels.* 2.60, *Fr. Matt.* 17.30). For an Aristotelian background of the Gnostic Secret Book of John, see Luttikhuizen, *Gnostic Revisions*, 37–42.

the fallen world soul. Some other Platonists taught that the corruptions of the human soul resulted from its embodiment: the soul lost its rationality periodically as a result of incarnation. There was, however, a third option: the human soul was divided, and some part of the soul remained undescended. The theory of the undescended soul is commonly seen as Plotinus's innovation, but there are traces of this teaching already among Middle Platonic teachers. According to his view, human moral weakness is the outcome of the soul's not being able to integrate itself with the higher, undescended part of the soul, which serves as an archetype for the soul.[18] Shaw presents these different views as follows:

1. Gnostics (as described in *Enn.* 2.9)
   (a) The suffering of individual souls is due to the fall of the World Soul
   (b) Individual souls (collectively) = the World Soul
2. Plotinus (A) (against the Gnostics)
   (a) The suffering of individual souls is *not* due to the fall of the World Soul, because the World Soul cannot fall [*Enn.* 2.9.7.9–19]. The relationship of individual souls to their bodies includes a temporary period of suffering and confusion [*Enn.* 2.9.7–18], which can be overcome by education and an increasing mimesis of the gods [*Enn.* 2.9.18.32–35].
   (b) The World Soul *is not equal* to the sum of individual souls [*Enn.* 2.9.8.36–29].
3. Plotinus (B)
   (a) The World Soul does not fall and neither do individual souls. The suffering of individual souls, therefore, is merely the suffering of their "images"; in truth, individual souls remain above, at the level of the World Soul.
   (b) The World Soul = unfallen individual souls.[19]

The anthropological teaching in the Valentinian sources contains features that link it to the first and third positions, which are fused together. Although the irrationality of the soul is the outcome of the fall of Sophia, the rational and spiritual parts of the soul are connected to Sophia's

---

18. For the role of the undescended soul in Platonic anthropology, see John M. Rist, "Integration and the Undescended Soul in Plotinus," *AJP* 88 (1967): 410–22.
19. Shaw, *Theurgy and the Soul*, 65.

repentance and enlightenment. Sophia creates the spiritual seed as images of the Savior's angels after she has been purified of her erroneous thoughts and pernicious emotions. The incarnated part of the spiritual seed have their divine archetypes in the angelic "*ecclesia* above," but these supra-cosmic spiritual identities do not incarnate. They remain intact in the realm below the Pleroma together with Sophia. Thus, the relationship between the spiritual seed and their divine archetypes can be understood on the analogy of the Aristotelian theory of passive and active intellects. In Valentinian anthropology, the passive intellect becomes active when it becomes conscious of its heavenly self—that is, its angelic archetype.

6.2. The Threefold Structure of the Human Soul in Valentinian Sources

I next present the creation of the first human being according to *Exc.* 50–51 and parallel section in *Haer.* 1.5.5–6. The sequence of the creation of humankind is as follows:

1. Sophia generates the spiritual seed as images of the angels of the Savior (see Gen 1:27);
2. The Demiurge and his assistants create the irrational and hylic soul of Adam out of matter (see Gen 2:7);
3. The Demiurge breathes the likeness of himself into the hylic soul, which serves as a soul-body for the rational and psychic soul (see Gen 1:26);
4. Sophia inserts the spiritual seed into the psychic soul of Adam; and
5. The Demiurge clothes the hylic-psychic soul, together with the seed of Sophia, in the garments of skin, which refers to the material body (see Gen 3:21).

6.2.1. The Creation of the Spiritual Seed

In Valentinian anthropologies, the creation of humankind begins at the supra-cosmic level, as the Savior descends to the suffering Sophia, who has removed from the Pleroma. After the Savior purifies Sophia of her erroneous thoughts, she begins to contemplate the angels who accompanied the Savior.[20] The joyful contemplation forms the basis for the creation of the

---

20. In the Pseudo-Aristotelian *De mundo*, the power of God is scattered across a multitude of subordinate executive powers called "bodyguards" (δορυφόροι). This

6. The Creation of the First Human in Allegorical Exegesis

spiritual seed, as images of the angels. The sequence of events is attested in *Haer.* 1.4.5 as follows: "They teach, too, that when Achamoth had been freed from passion and had with joy received the contemplation of the lights which were with him, that is, of the angels that were with him, and had yearned after them, she brought forth fruits after their image, a spiritual offspring, born after the likeness of the Savior's bodyguard" (Unger). There is some confusion concerning the biblical basis in this passage. It seems that the creation of the seed of Sophia is based on Gen 1:26 ("she brought forth fruits *after their image*, a spiritual offspring, born *after the likeness* of the Savior's bodyguards"). The same text is used, however, in *Haer.* 1.5.5, when the Demiurge creates Adam's irrational soul-body (see below). It is rather unlikely that the same biblical text (Gen 1:26) would have served as the basis for the creation of the spiritual seed of Adam and his psychic soul as well. I suggest that Irenaeus paraphrased his source material carelessly. The biblical allusion to Gen 1:26 in describing the creation of the spiritual seed may even have come from Irenaeus himself. It is also noteworthy that Gen 1:26 does not fit well in the description of the creation of the seed of Sophia. Although there is a multiplicity of models, that is, angels, there are not many creators. The spiritual seed is created by Sophia alone. It is more likely that the original basis for *Haer.* 1.4.5 was Gen 1:27, which is more commonly found in other Valentinian sources (Tri. Trac. 90.14–91; *Exc.* 21), as I will show below. Although these examples represent the so-called Eastern tradition, they will shed some light on the interpretation of the accounts in *Excerpta* C and *Haer.* 1.4.5.

The creation of the seed of Sophia as images of the Savior's army is also attested in the Tripartite Tractate. In addition to the Savior, who is the expression of the Father, the aeons produce army of beings as images of themselves (see Tri. Trac. 86.23–87). As the Savior reveals himself to the Logos, he becomes filled with an inexpressible joy, bringing forth living images of the living beings that accompany the Savior (Tri. Trac. 90.14–91). In the Tripartite Tractate, the Logos plays a similar role as Sophia in other Valentinian source. The biblical basis for the creation of the spiritual seed is evidently Gen 1:27, and it is stressed that the spiritual

---

has a parallel in Philo, who states that the powers accompanied God as "bodyguards" (*Sacr.* 59). Also, in *Haer.* 1.4.5, the angels who accompanied the Savior during his descent to suffering Sophia are called "bodyguards" (δορυφόροι; see Bos, "Philo of Alexandria," 77–78).

offspring of Logos are male beings (see Tri. Trac. 94.10–95.16).[21] Clement also preserves in *Exc.* 21.1 a teaching of Theodotus that describes the creation of the seed of Sophia on the grounds of Gen 1:27: "The Valentinians say that the finest emanation of Sophia is spoken of in 'He made them according to the image of God; male and female he made them' (Gen 1:27). The males from this emanation are the election, but the females are the calling, and they call the males angelic and the females themselves, the dispersed spirit [or seed]" (my trans.).[22] The creation of the spiritual seed is depicted in this passage as Sophia's "finest emanation" (προβολὴ ἡ ἀρίστη). This implies that there are some other emanations of lower rank by Sophia. Although the temporal order in Theodotus's fragmentary passages is unclear, it is likely that the lower beings are the powers on the left, which Sophia created earlier, together with the powers on the right (see *Exc.* 34.1–2). The finest emanation of Sophia is depicted as images, but angels as archetypes of Sophia's production are not mentioned. It is stated instead that the seed of Sophia is split into two parts, the male and the female seed. The former part of the seed is depicted as angelic, while the latter part incarnates. It seems, then, that *Exc.* 21.1 does not describe the creation of the seed of Sophia as images of the angels but the creation of angels themselves, which are separated from the unitary seed before its incarnation.[23]

---

21. See Einar Thomassen, "The Tripartite Tractate," in Meyer, *Nag Hammadi Scriptures*, 81 n. 36.

22. Τὸ "κατ᾽ εἰκόνα θεοῦ ἐποίησεν αὐτούς, ἄρσεν καὶ θῆλυ ἐποίησεν αὐτούς" τὴν προβόλην τὴν ἀρίστην φασιν οἱ Οὐαλεντινιανοῦ τῆς Σοφίας λέγεσθαι, ἀφ᾽ ἧς τὰ μὲν ἀρρενικὰ ἡ ἐκλογή, τὰ δὲ θελυκὰ ἡ κλῆσις, καὶ τὰ μὲν ἀρρενικὰ ἀγγελικὰ καλοῦσι, τὰ θελυκὰ δὲ ἑαυτούς, τὸ διαφέρον πνεῦμα [σπέρμα]. The first sentence contains an interesting textual alteration from the text of LXX: the first pronoun, αὐτόν, in the sentence "He created him" (LXX) is changed to αὐτούς ("He created them"). The generation of the sexes in Gen 1:27 is seen as a biblical typology for the twofold emission of the seed by Sophia. The sexes are not understood biologically but as an allegory of the spiritual rupture within Sophia's seed, which is sowed into Adam's soul. In other passages that go back to Theodotus, the female seed, depicted as dispersed seed, is compared with an aborted fetus (*Exc.* 67–68). On the relationship of the Valentinian myth with ancient conceptions of sexual intercourse, birth, and embryology, see Richard Smith, "Sex Education in Gnostic Schools," in *Images of the Feminine in Gnosticism*, ed. Karen L. King (Harrisburg, PA: Trinity Press International, 2000), 345–69.

23. The female part of the seed was sowed into the world, while the angelic male part of the seed was drawn together with the Logos—i.e., the Savior. The angelic part of the seed of Sophia formed the spiritual body of the Savior, as he emptied himself

6. The Creation of the First Human in Allegorical Exegesis

It is not explained in *Excerpta* C how Sophia produces her offspring. Contrary to Irenaeus's account in *Haer.* 1.4.5, the angels as archetypes for Sophia's offspring are also not explicitly mentioned. It is stated, however, that the Savior is accompanied by male angels as he visits the suffering Sophia (see *Exc.* 44.1). The male angels are also mentioned in the context of the implantation of the spiritual seed into Adam's soul (see *Exc.* 53.3). Thus, it would not be unreasonable to think that, also in *Excerpta* C, Sophia produces her seed as images of the angels of the Savior. The biblical prooftext may be Gen 1:27, because Gen 1:26 is used already as the basis for the creation of the hylic-psychic soul of Adam.

The consensus among Valentinian theologians in the aforementioned sources (Theodotus's fragments, the Tripartite Tractate, *Excerpta* C, and *Haer.* 1.4.5) is that the Savior's angels or some other pleromatic beings served as archetypes for Sophia's production of the spiritual seed. In *Haer.* 1.5.6, the seed of Sophia is depicted as the "spiritual beings" and "a corresponding type of the *ecclesia* above" (ἀντίτυπον τῆς ἄνω Ἐκκλησίας), which is associated with the last pair of the Ogdoad in the Pleroma—that is, "the Human Being–*ecclesia*." Thomassen points out that, rather than a separate member of the Pleroma, the Human Being–*ecclesia* may be seen as an aspect of the Pleroma as a whole.[24] The Human Being–*ecclesia* is also included in the Savior, because, leaning on Col 2:9, the whole Pleroma, that is, the Fullness, is said to dwell in the Savior (ἐν αὐτῷ κατοικεῖ πᾶν τὸ πλήρωμα τῆς θεότητος σωματικῶς; see Irenaeus, *Haer.* 1.3.4; also Col 1:15).

We can thus conclude that, in the Valentinian system, the Savior's angels collectively serve as an archetypal human being for Sophia's spiritual

---

and descended to the world to save the dispersed seed (see *Exc.* 26.1–3). Thomassen points out that the accounts in Theodotus and the Tripartite Tractate are in accord in that the seed of Sophia-Logos is divided into two parts. Some remains in the realm of Sophia-Logos, some is incarnated into the world, and the remainder will be incarnated later together with the Savior during his baptism as his spiritual body (see Thomassen, *Spiritual Seed*, 29–58). In *Haer.* 1.1–7 and *Excerpta* C, the angels of the Savior do not incarnate but remain together with Sophia in the Ogdoad, in the realm below the Pleroma.

24. See Thomassen, *Spiritual Seed*, 441. The idea of the creation of humankind as an image of the angels is rarely found in early Christian literature. In appears, however, in some Jewish apocalyptic sources. In 4Q417, Adam is said to be created according to the pattern of the Holy Ones, probably in reference to angels (see van Kooten, *Paul's Anthropology*, 22–27).

emanation.²⁵ Evidently, the Platonic twofold model forms the intellectual background for the Valentinian anthropology. The angels are intelligible models for the seed of Sophia referred to as images. Thus, the true self of Sophia's offspring belongs to the heavenly church, even though they are still living in the world.

6.2.2. The Creation of the Soul and Its Embodiment

After the creation of the spiritual seed by Sophia in the realm below the Pleroma, the focus is shifted to the creation of the first earthly human being by the Demiurge. This process of creation is described in *Haer.* 1.5.5 and *Exc.* 50.1–51.1:

> "Taking dust from the earth": not of the dry land but a portion of the complex and diverse matter, he made a soul, earthly and material, irrational and of the same essence as the beasts. This is the human "according to the image." But the human who is "according to the likeness" of the Demiurge himself, is the one whom he breathed into and sowed into the former, placing in him through the angels something consubstantial with himself. Because he is invisible and incorporeal, he called his essence "breath of life," and when it had been formed, it became "living soul," and he confesses it himself in the prophetic scriptures.²⁶ (*Exc.* 50 [my trans.])

> After the world had been created, the Demiurge in turn made the human being consisting of dust. He did not make him from this dry earth, but from the invisible essence, from the fusible and fluid matter; then they decree, into this part he breathed the psychic element. This is he who was made "after the image and likeness." The material element is after the image, by which it comes near to God, though it is not of the same

---

25. On the relationship between the heavenly *ecclesia*, the Savior, and the hidden identities of the saved in the soteriology of the Tripartite Tractate, see Thomassen, *Spiritual Seed*, 50–52.

26. "Λαβὼν χοῦν ἀπὸ τῆς γῆς", οὐ τῆς ξηρᾶς, ἀλλὰ τῆς πολυμεροῦς καὶ ποικίλης ὕλης μέρος, ψυχὴν γεώδη καὶ ὑλικὴν ἐτεκτήνατο ἄλογον καὶ τῇ τῶν θηρίων ὁμοούσιον· οὗτος "κατ' εἰκόνα" ἄνθρωπος. Ὁ δὲ "καθ' ὁμοίωσιν" τὴν αὐτοῦ τοῦ Δημιουργοῦ ἐκεῖνός ἐστιν, ὃν εἰς τοῦτον "ἐνεφύσησέν" τε καὶ ἐνέσπειρεν, ὁμοούσιόν τι αὐτῷ δι' Ἀγγέλων ἐνθείς· καθὸ μὲν ἀόρατός ἐστι καὶ ἀσώματος, τὴν οὐσίαν αὐτοῦ "πνοὴν ζωῆς" προσεῖπεν, μορφωθὲν δέ, "ψυχὴ ζῶσα" ἐγένετο, ὅπερ εἶναι, καὶ αὐτὸς ἐν ταῖς προφητικαῖς γραφαῖς ὁμολογεῖ.

essence as he; the psychic element is after the likeness. Hence his essence was also called the Spirit of life, since it came from a spiritual emanation.[27] (Irenaeus, *Haer.* 1.5.5 [Unger, modified])

In both accounts, the creation of Adam's soul is interpreted in light of a combination of Gen 1:26 and 2:7. The human being created "according to the likeness" of the Demiurge is breathed into the material soul, which is depicted as the human being "according to the image." In *Exc.* 50–51, angels are said to be mediators of the psychic element, which may refer to the plurality of the creators in Plato's *Timaeus*, to whom God delegates the creation of the lower parts of Adam's soul.[28] In Irenaeus's version, the collectiveness of the creators is not explicitly mentioned. However, the Demiurge is called Hebdomad, which may represent a personification of the collective planetary powers depicted as angels. It is thus possible that, in Irenaeus's account, too, there is an allusion to the collectiveness of the creators of the lower parts of Adam's soul.[29] It is explicitly remarked that Adam is created in the fourth heaven, where the hylic soul cannot ascend:[30]

---

27. Δημιουργήσαντα δὴ τὸν κόσμον, πεποιηκέναι καὶ τὸν ἄνθρωπον τὸν χοϊκόν· οὐκ ἀπὸ ταύτης δὲ τῆς ξηρᾶς γῆς, ἀλλ' ἀπὸ τῆς ἀοράτου οὐσίας, ἀπὸ τοῦ κεχυμένου καὶ ῥευστοῦ τῆς ὕλης λαβόντα· καὶ εἰς τοῦτον ἐμφυσῆσαι τὸν ψυχικὸν διορίζονται. Καὶ τοῦτον εἶναι τὸν κατ' εἰκόνα καὶ ὁμοίωσιν γεγονότα· κατ' εἰκόνα μὲν τὸν ὑλικὸν ὑπάρχειν, παραπλήσιον μέν, ἀλλ' οὐχ ὁμοούσιον τῷ Θεῷ· καθ' ὁμοίωσιν δὲ τὸν ψυχικόν· ὅθεν καὶ πνεῦμα ζωῆς τὴν οὐσίαν αὐτοῦ εἰρῆσθαι, ἐκ πνευματικῆς ἀπορροίας οὖσαν.

28. In *Exc.* 50.2, the psychic soul was infused into the soul of Adam by the Demiurge with the help of angels. This may refer to the idea of the plurality of the creators in Gen 1:26, going back to the teaching in Valentinus's fragment in Clement, *Strom.* 2.36.2–4. The idea of the plurality of the creators of the human soul is also mentioned in Tri. Trac. 105–106; there, the powers are said to be cocreators of God, having a similar role in the creation of human beings as the younger gods in Plato's *Timaeus*. The powers imitate the creative activity of the Logos. While the powers of the left and right create the hylic and psychic souls, the "living soul" is produced by the Logos. The role of the powers, however, differs in the Tripartite Tractate from Philo's account in *Opif.* 69–70. In the Tripartite Tractate, the powers are archons that lust for power, but, in *Opif.* 69–70, God's assistants are positive cosmic beings. Philo maintains that the moral ambiguity of the earthly soul is the reason that assistants are needed in the creation process, as God alone is the creator of the good. This motif is lacking in the Tripartite Tractate and other Valentinian texts.

29. See Thomassen, *Spiritual Seed*, 432–33.

30. The distinction between the terms χοϊκός and ὑλικός is possibly based on the double-reading of the text, which says: καὶ ἔπλασεν ὁ Θεὸς τὸν ἄνθρωπον χοῦν ἀπο τῆς γῆς καὶ ἐνεφύσησεν εἰς τὸ πρόσωπον αὐτοῦ πνοὴν ζωῆς, καὶ ἐγένετο ὁ ἄνθρωπος

Hence, he was created in paradise, the fourth heaven. For flesh consisted of dust does not ascend there, but it was to the divine (psychic) soul like hylic flesh.³¹ (*Exc.* 51.1 [my trans.])

And paradise is above the third heaven and is virtually the fourth archangel, and that Adam received something from him when he passed time within it.³² (*Haer.* 1.5.2 [Unger, modified])

In *Exc.* 51.1, χοϊκὴ σάρξ and σὰρξ ἡ ὑλική are synonyms denoting the irrational soul-body, which cannot ascend to the fourth heaven, where the psychic Adam is created. The hylic soul, that is, the flesh, serves as the body (σῶμα) for the psychic and divine soul, referred to as the bone. "'This is now bone of my bones' (Gen 2:23)—it hints at the divine soul, which is hidden in the flesh, firm and hard to suffer and very potent—and 'flesh of my flesh'—the material soul which is the body of the divine soul" (*Exc.* 51.2 [my trans.]).³³ In *Haer.* 1.5.5, the irrational soul of Adam is not taken from the "dry earth" (ξηρὰ γῆ) but "from the invisible substance consisting of fusible and fluid matter" (ἀπὸ τῆς ἀοράτου οὐσίας, ἀπὸ τοῦ κεχυμένου καὶ ῥευστοῦ τῆς ὕλης λαβόντα).³⁴ *Excerpta* 50.1 says practically the same thing: the Demiurge does not take matter for the irrational soul from the dry land but from a "portion of matter of varied constitution and color" (τῆς πολυμεροῦς καὶ ποικίλης ὕλης μέρος). The hylic soul is made out of confused matter that must be distinguished from the dry earth, possibly referring to

---

εἰς ψυχὴν ζῶσαν (LXX; Gen 2:7). The Valentinian commentators made a distinction between the earthly human (τὸν ἄνθρωπον χοῦν) and the human being which was made out of earth (ἀπὸ τῆς γῆς). The latter describes the human being consisting of the material body, and the former refers to the material soul.

31. Ὅθεν ἐν τῷ Παραδείσῳ, τῷ τετάρτῳ οὐρανῷ, δημιουργεῖται· ἐκεῖ γὰρ χοϊκὴ σὰρξ οὐκ ἀναβαίνει, ἀλλ᾽ ἦν τῇ ψυχῇ θείᾳ οἷον σὰρξ ἡ ὑλική.

32. Ὡς καὶ τὸν Παράδεισον ὑπὲρ τρίτον οὐρανὸν ὄντα, τέταρτον Ἄγγελον λέγουσι δυνάμει ὑπάρχειν, καὶ ἀπὸ τούτου τι εἰληφέναι τὸν Ἀδὰμ διατετριφότα ἐν αὐτῷ The idea that paradise was in the fourth heaven is also mentioned in the rabbinical haggadah (see Unger, *Against Heresies*, 34 n. 13).

33. "τοῦτο νῦν ὀστοῦν ἐκ τῶν ὀστῶν μου," τὴν θείαν ψυχὴν αἰνίσσεται τὴν ἐγκεκρυμμένην τῇ σαρκὶ καὶ στερεὰν καὶ δυσπαθῆ καὶ δυνατωτέραν, "καὶ σὰρξ ἐκ τῆς σαρκός μου" τὴν ὑλικὴν ψυχὴν σῶμα οὖσαν τῆς θείας ψυχῆς.

34. As I noted in the previous chapter, the term ἀόρατος does not necessarily refer to the invisibility of matter but its unstructured essence. However, in *Exc.* 59, it is explicitly mentioned that the psychic essence of the Savior is invisible, out of which a visible body was spun to be able to function in the visible world.

6. The Creation of the First Human in Allegorical Exegesis

the element of earth out of which Adam's body was created. It is unclear, however, whether the "earthlike" (γεώδης) soul is made out of some kind of proto-material essence or whether this is an allegorical description of the soul's inclination to the earthly and irrational impulses. I suggest that both levels of meaning apply: unlike the psychic soul, the irrational soul is material, which makes it prone to bodily passions. Eventually, the Demiurge breathes the likeness of himself—that is, the invisible psychic soul created in the fourth heaven—into the hylic soul of Adam, but at the same time, he unknowingly mediates the spiritual seed:

> But Adam had the spiritual seed, which had been sown into his soul without his knowledge by Sophia. He (Paul) says: "Established through angels by the hand of a mediator. But the mediator is not one, while God is one" (Gal 3:19–20). Therefore, through male angels the seeds are assisted, those that were emitted into birth by Sophia, insofar as it is possible for them to exist.[35] (*Exc.* 53:2–3)

> Furthermore, they declare that the Demiurge himself was ignorant of the offspring of Achamoth, their Mother, which were conceived by virtue of her contemplation of the angels who surround the Savior and which were spiritual like the Mother. Secretly, without his knowledge, she deposited this (offspring) in him that through him it might be planted as a "seed" in the soul which came from him, and thence in this material body; and having been borne in them as in a womb and grown, it might become fit for the reception of perfect [knowledge].[36] (Irenaeus, *Haer.* 1.5.6 [Unger, modified])

---

35. Trans. Brakke and Layton, *Gnostic Scriptures*, 519; my modifications: Ἔσχεν δὲ ὁ Ἀδὰμ ἀδήλως αὐτῷ ὑπὸ τῆς Σοφίας ἐνσπαρὲν τὸ σπέρμα τὸ πνευματικὸν εἰς τὴν ψυχήν· "διαταγείς," φησί, "δι' Ἀγγέλων, ἐν χειρὶ μεσίτου· ὁ δὲ μεσίτης ἑνὸς οὐκ ἔστιν· ὁ δὲ Θεὸς εἷς ἐστιν." δι' ἀγγέλων οὖν τῶν ἀρρένων τὰ σπέρματα ὑπηρετεῖται τὰ εἰς γένεσιν προβληθέντα ὑπὸ τῆς Σοφίας, καθὸ ἐγχωρεῖ γίνεσθαι.

36. Τὸ δὲ κύημα τῆς μητρὸς αὐτῶν τῆς Ἀχαμώθ, ὃ κατὰ τὴν θεωρίαν τῶν περὶ τὸν Σωτῆρα ἀγγέλων ἀπεκύησεν, ὁμοούσιον ὑπάρχον τῇ μητρί, πνευματικόν, καὶ αὐτὸ ἠγνοηκέναι τὸν Δημιουργὸν λέγουσι· καὶ λεληθότως κατατεθεῖσθαι εἰς αὐτόν, μὴ εἰδότος αὐτοῦ, ἵνα δι' αὐτοῦ εἰς τὴν ἀπ' αὐτοῦ ψυχὴν σπαρέν, καὶ εἰς τὸ ὑλικὸν τοῦτο σῶμα, κυοφορηθὲν ἐν τούτοις καὶ αὐξηθὲν ἕτοιμον γένηται πρὸς ὑποδοχὴν τοῦ τελείου [λόγου]. In Epiphanius's Greek text there is only "for perfect" without mentioning knowledge or teaching. The Latin version has *perfactae rationis*, whereas Tertullian speaks about *sermoni perfecto* (*Val.* 25.2). Both *ratio* and *sermo* suppose *logos*, which can be translated "knowledge" (see Unger, *Against Heresies*, 163).

There are important differences between these accounts. First, in *Haer.* 1.5.6, it is not the "spiritual seed" (σπέρμα τὸ πνευματικόν), as in *Exc.* 53, but "the offspring of the mother" (κύημα τῆς μητρός) that is deposited into the soul of Adam through the instrumentality of the Demiurge. There is no substantial difference between these statements, because it is also stated in Irenaeus that the offspring of Sophia is of the same spiritual substance as the mother. Second, in *Haer.* 1.5.6, the spiritual seed is deposited by Sophia *into the Demiurge,* who is used as an instrument by her. Thus, it is the breath of the Demiurge that mediates the spiritual seed to Adam. In *Exc.* 53.2–3, the seed of Sophia is deposited directly into the psychic soul of Adam, without any mention of the breath of the Demiurge, only the angels. Although the breath of the Demiurge may be the most logical means for the mediation of the seed of Sophia, it cannot be excluded that it might have been inserted into the soul of Adam during his sleep.[37] Be that as it may, in both accounts the soul of Adam consists, at least, of hylic (irrational), psychic (rational), and spiritual (intellectual) elements. In the end, the Demiurge clothes Adam in the "garment of skin" (τὸν δερμάτινον χιτῶνα), which is also described as "the sense-perceptible bit of flesh" (τὸ αἰσθητὸν σαρκίον). It is notable that the fall of Adam is not mentioned. The

---

37. In *Exc.* 2.1–2, the Logos implants the male seed (σπέρμα ἀρρενικόν) into the psychic soul of Adam while he is sleeping. In addition, it is not only the male seed, which was produced by Sophia, but also Adam's soul and flesh. The term "male seed" does not appear anywhere in Clement's account, instead seeming to be a sort of combination of τὸ διαφέρον σπέρμα and τὰ ἀρρενικά, which describe different kinds of seeds by Sophia (see also *Exc.* 21.1–2). Although the name *Logos* may be a variant for *Sophia,* as in the Tripartite Tractate, Logos is not here a synonym for Sophia but represents, besides Sophia, a separate agent in the creation of Adam. Also, the idea of Sophia as an agent in the creation of the material parts of a human being is not mentioned in any other Valentinian sources. It is therefore likely that these discrepancies are an outcome of Clement's careless paraphrasing of the source material. It is possible, however, that the implantation of the spiritual seed when Adam is asleep and the idea of the unifying function of the spiritual seed are authentic descriptions of the Valentinian teaching. A similar view is mentioned in Gos. Phil. 70.22–34, where the soul that was given to Adam through breath is said to be replaced by the spirit of the Mother possibly during his sleep: "Adam's soul came from a breath. The soul's companion is spirit, and the spirit given to him is his mother. His soul was [taken] from him and replaced with [spirit]. When he was united with spirit, [he] uttered words superior to the powers, and the powers envied him. They [separated him from his] spiritual companion … hidden … bridal chamber.…"

embodiment of the soul is thus the outcome of the creation, which is propagated to all humankind without any connection to personal moral flaws.

6.2.3. The Threefold Division of Humankind

The distribution of three essences in Adam forms the basis for the anthropological division of humankind into hylic, psychic, and spiritual human beings. The historical narrative is thus transformed into a universal typology. Irenaeus mentions this division in *Haer.* 1.7.5: the three natures (φύσεις) of Adam are no longer found in one person but are considered as forming three classes of human beings. Irenaeus does not, however, give any explanation as to why the three natures are distributed unequally, causing division among all humanity. The account in *Exc.* 55.1–56.2, on the other hand, gives a more detailed description, stating that the higher essences of the soul—that is, the psychic and spiritual elements—are mediated *through* Adam, not *by* him. This means that Adam was only an instrumental cause (δι' αὐτοῦ) for the psychic and spiritual essences, not an efficient cause (ὑπ' αὐτοῦ).[38] Only the material soul of Adam is capable of mixing with the semen of Adam and will be mediated to the later generations. The psychic and spiritual essences are not mediated by Adam naturally but through him as a result of divine providence.[39]

Valentinian anthropology can be traced back to Middle Platonic views about different kinds of soul-bodies and the role of the intellect as a distinct element of the soul. The irrational soul of Adam (Gen 2:7) serves as an instrumental soul-body for the psychic soul (1:26), which contains the spiritual seed, that is, an image of the angelic *ecclesia* (1:27). The spiritual seed functions in the same way as the "inner man" (ὁ ἐντὸς ἄνθρωπος) in Plato's description of the tripartite soul (see, e.g., *Resp.* 588b–589d).[40] Evidently, the heavenly *ecclesia* referred to the Pauline idea of the church as

---

38. The "metaphysics of the prepositions" goes back to Aristotle's definitions of causes, which were elaborated by Middle Platonic and Stoic teachers. See Heinrich Dörrie, "Präpositionen und Metaphysik: Wechselwirkung zweier Prinzipienreihen," *MH* 26 (1969): 217–28; Wolfson, *Philo*, 1:261–67; Tobin, *Creation of Man*, 67–70; Runia, *Philo of Alexandria*, 171; Sterling, "Platonizing Exegetical Traditions," 127–30.

39. *Exc.* 55–56.2 has a parallel in Philo's *Cher.* 128. The distribution of the essences of Adam to the later generations is investigated in chapter 7 below, in the context of the division of humankind.

40. On the inner person, see Theo K. Heckel, *Der Innere Mensch: die paulinische Verarbeitung eines platonischen Motivs*, WUNT 2/53 (Tübingen: Mohr Siebeck, 1993).

the mystical body revealed by the Savior. Paul may have interpreted Plato's conception of the inner man eschatologically (see 2 Cor 4:10–18), but the Valentinians understood the term *protologically*. That is, the redemptive mission of the Savior was enacted before the creation of humankind, with profound soteriological effects. The mystical body of the Savior and the spiritual identities of the saved were produced even before the foundation of the visible cosmos. Thus, humankind already possesses the potential for redemption because of the precosmic salvation of Sophia by the Savior. In other words: humankind was created for salvation from the beginning.[41]

The distinction between the psychic soul and the spiritual seed recalls the Aristotelian theory about *nous* in potency and *nous* in action. The psychic soul is only potentially spiritual, because it contains the seed of Sophia, which is not yet perfectly integrated into its higher self, that is, the angelic archetype. In *Exc.* 53.4–5, the psychic soul serves as an instrumental body for the spiritual seed: "For just as the Demiurge, moved by Sophia without his knowledge, thinks that he is self-moved [αὐτοκίνητος], so also do humans. At first, Sophia emitted the spiritual seed in Adam, so that the bone (i.e., the rational and heavenly soul) would not be empty but filled with spiritual marrow" (my trans.).[42] The psychic soul is explicitly

---

41. Hippolytus, *Haer.* 6.34.3–4, may represent another Valentinian teaching that differs from Irenaeus, *Haer.* 1.5.5, and *Exc.* 50–51 as well as from Theodotus and the Tripartite Tractate. Hippolytus describes how Sophia and the Savior produce seventy *logoi*, "which are heavenly angels who live in the Jerusalem above, which is in heaven." The angels of heaven are not called images but the offspring of Sophia and the Savior, having been "set right" (διόρθειν) already before their incarnation. In addition, the creation of the first human being is presented solely in light of Gen 2:7. The Demiurge fashions bodies from the *hylic* and "devilish essence" for the souls to be breathed into the *hylic* body by the Demiurge. Dunderberg is of the opinion that the body mentioned in Hippolytus's account denotes the earthly body, drawn together from the material and the diabolic essence, because the garments of skin as a symbol of the earthly body are not mentioned. See Dunderberg, *Beyond Gnosticism*, 141.

42. Ἅτε γὰρ Δημιουργός, ἀδήλως κινούμενος ὑπὸ τῆς Σοφίας, οἴεται αὐτοκίνητος εἶναι, ὁμοίως καὶ οἱ ἄνθρωποι. Πρῶτον οὖν σπέρμα πνευματικὸν τὸ ἐν τῷ Ἀδὰμ προέβαλεν ἡ Σοφία, ἵνα ᾖ «τὸ ὀστοῦν,» ἡ λογικὴ καὶ οὐρανία ψυχή, μὴ κενή, ἀλλὰ μυελοῦ γέμουσα πνευματικοῦ. Casey's translation misleadingly links the spiritual seed to the bone, even though it is explicitly stated earlier in the text that the psychic soul is the bone of Adam, while the *hylic* soul is the flesh. The spiritual element is the marrow of the bone "so that the bone (i.e., the reasonable and divine soul) would not be empty but full of spiritual marrow" (ἵνα ᾖ τὸ ὀστοῦν, ἡ λογικὴ καὶ οὐρανία ψυχή, μὴ κενή ἀλλὰ μυελοῦ γέμουσα πνευματικοῦ). Casey's translation in *Exc.* 62.3 also links the

said not to be self-motioned, resonating with the Aristotelian criticism of the Platonic theory of the self-moving soul. As the cosmic intellect, the Demiurge, is set into motion by Sophia, the spiritual marrow produced by Sophia sets the soul of Adam into motion. Thus, the spiritual seed is not an independent entity because it is breathed into Adam's earthly soul *together* with the psychic soul. The goal of the spiritual seed is not to escape from the psychic soul but to help the psychic soul reach its perfection and salvation from the bondage of the flesh by integrating itself to its angelic counterpart.[43]

Each of the elements of Adam's tripartite soul bears soteriological significance, which can be comprehended in light of the Valentinian protological myth. The fall and salvation of Sophia not only account for the origin of the creation of the cosmos but also serve as the soteriological paradigm for all human beings. The psychic soul-substance has its origin in Sophia's conversion and search for the light. This innate movement must be perfected through the awakening of the spiritual seed hidden in the psychic soul, which actualizes its potential intellect. The material soul, on the other hand, which serves as a body for the psychic soul, has its origin in the passions of Sophia, after she was exiled into the darkness of ignorance. It is irrational and consubstantial with the beasts, while the psychic soul is luminous and similar to the angels, who rule the planetary spheres together with the Demiurge. As noted, the psychic soul is not labeled as a negative entity. Rather, it serves a necessary means by which to receive the seed of Sophia and attain perfection.

There were, however, different opinions among the Valentinian teachers concerning the degree of incarnation of the seed of Sophia. In *Haer.* 1.5.5 and *Exc.* 50–51, the spiritual seed does not actually descend to the

---

bone erroneously to the spiritual nature of Christ, even though it evidently says that the spiritual element is *"inside* the bone" (ἐν τῷ ὀστέῳ).

43. The categories of humankind in the Tripartite Tractate are fixed. The Demiurge and the two ranks of powers create souls of their own, which are incarnated into the world. Therefore, humankind was divided in the beginning into three categories. Some human beings contained the spiritual seed in their soul, while some others possessed only the psychic and hylic or only the hylic soul (see Tri. Trac. 104.18–106.25). Theodotus also says, in *Exc.* 67.1–3 that the seed of Sophia (Gen 1:27) was reckoned before the foundation of the world, with childbirth lasting until all the spiritual seed has been incarnated into the world. These Eastern Valentinian traditions represent more deterministic views than with the Western accounts of Irenaeus, *Haer.* 1.1–7 and *Excerpta* C.

level of flesh but only to the level of Adam's psychic soul. In the Eastern tradition represented by Theodotus and the Tripartite Tractate, the seed is fully incarnated into the flesh of Adam. There is no mediating psychic soul that would serve as the soul-body for the spiritual seed. Rather, in these Eastern accounts, the incarnated seed of Sophia is described as an "abortion" (ἔκτρωμα; *Exc.* 68).

The different opinions concerning the degree of incarnation of the seed of Sophia result in christological differences among these Valentinian teachings. In Theodotus and the Tripartite Tractate, the seed must be saved from fleshly existence, which means that the Savior had to adopt a real body. In Tripartite Tractate 113.31–114.22, the Savior is clothed in flesh and "all the instruments necessary for entering into life and with which he descended."[44] In Irenaeus, *Haer.* 1.1–7, and *Excerpta* C, it is the inner man, that is, the spiritual seed itself, that saves the soul, as it is awakened and becomes conscious of its higher self, meaning that all humans contain within themselves, as copies of Adam's soul, the power to achieve immortality by themselves without material sacraments.

6.3. The Creation of Adam in Philo and Valentinian Sources

Philo's anthropological teachings lean on various philosophical and exegetical traditions, with explicit references to some interpreters and occasionally criticisms of their views.[45] In many cases, Philo also modifies and refines his own interpretations in texts, depending on the audience he was targeting. The anthropology in *De opificio mundi*, for instance, differs from the theories in presented his Allegorical Commentary. As Runia points out, in Philo's writings, "a tension may be observed between a presentation as *history*, that is, an account of the life of early mankind, and a presentation in terms of *actualization* and *idealization*, that is, seeing Adam and Eve as types of human beings." The latter view predominates especially in Philo's Allegorical Commentary.[46] Runia's division of the separate aims of Philo's

---

44. See Thomassen, *Spiritual Seed*, 52–58.

45. For allegorical readers of Alexandria, see David M. Hay, "Philo's References to Other Allegorists," *SPhilo* 6 (1979–1980): 41–75.

46. See Runia, *On the Creation*, 24, 332–34; Runia, *Philo of Alexandria*, 335. In Philo's allegorical view, Adam is more a type than a real person. Sami Yli-Karjanmaa also points out that it is essential to make a distinction between Philo's protological and soteriological allegories. In the Allegorical Commentary, Philo seems to ignore

writings provides a useful analogue in interpreting Valentinian anthropological teachings: the creation of the first human being is not understood as a historical narrative but is also taken to represent a universal truth concerning the fate of humankind in light of the myth of Sophia.

Thomas Tobin has made an attempt at defining the pre-Philonic philosophical and exegetical traditions that Philo adopted and readjusted to develop his allegory of the soul.[47] According to Tobin's analysis, there are two main theories concerning the creation of the first human being in Philo's writings: the *single creation theory* and the *double creation theory*. According to the single creation theory, the biblical narratives Gen 1:26–27 and 2:7 describe the creation of the human being from two different philosophical points of views. Genesis 1:26–27 represents a Platonic view, in which the first human being is created according to the image of God. In *Opif.* 69, Philo stresses, however, that what God creates according to the image of God is not the visible body but the ruling part of the soul—namely, the rational mind. Moreover, the archetype for the human mind is not God but his Logos, which is itself an image of God. Therefore, the human mind is "an image of an image."[48]

Another branch of the single creation theory makes use of Gen 2:7, presenting the creation of Adam in light of Stoic anthropological theories. Philo says that God breathes into the soul the "ethereal spirit" (αἰθέριον πνεῦμα), which he describes as the "ruling part of the soul" (ἡγεμονικόν) and also as a "divine fragment" (ἀπόσπασμα θεῖον).[49] Philo was not, how-

---

the protological context of Gen 2–3 altogether, deriving only ethical and soteriological truths from the text. In the Allegorical Commentary as well as in the *Questiones et Solutiones*, Philo does not discuss Adam as a historical person, whereas, in the Exposition of the Law, Philo mainly retells the biblical narrative, speaking of the first human being as the original ancestor of humankind (see esp. *Opif.* 136). Thus we should not uncritically derive Philo's protological views from his allegorizations of Gen 2–3 in the Allegorical Commentary. See Sami Yli-Karjanmaa, "'Call Him Earth': On Philo's Allegorization of Adam in the *Legum allegoriae*," in *Adam and Eve Story in the Hebrew Bible and in Ancient Jewish Writings Including the New Testament*, ed. Antti Laato and Lotta Valve, SRHB 7 (Winona Lake, IN: Eisenbrauns, 2016), 255–56, 263; Yli-Karjanmaa, *Reincarnation in Philo of Alexandria*, SPhiloM 7 (Atlanta: SBL Press, 2015), 4–5.

47. See Tobin, *Creation of Man*, 20–35, especially a schematic outline on 31.

48. For the Platonic views, see Philo, *Opif.* 24–25; *Leg.* 3.95–96; *Her.* 230–231; *Spec.* 1.80–81; 3.83, 207; *QG* 2.62.

49. For the Stoic theories, see Philo, *Leg.* 1.36–40; 3.161; *Her.* 281–283; *Somn.* 1.33–34; *Spec.* 4.123–124; *QG* 2.59.

ever, pleased with Stoic materialism. For Philo, the human mind is a nonmaterial intellect, because it is an image of the cosmic nonmaterial intellect—that is, the Logos. Therefore, Philo argues in *Spec.* 4.123 that the human mind is not a fragment of ether but something better, a "radiance" (ἀπαύγασμα) of the divinity.[50] There is, however, a unifying currency in Philo's interpretations, in which the biblical narratives in Gen 1:26–27 and 2:7 are seen as complementary descriptions of the creation of the first human being: it is the image of the Logos, or the idea of mind, which is breathed into Adam's soul (see *Det.* 83, *Plant.* 18–22, *Mut.* 223).[51]

The double creation theory, on the other hand, posits that Genesis contains two creation narratives of Adam, which can be integrated into the Platonic two-world model. According to this model, Gen 1:26–27 and 2:7 are no longer compatible descriptions for a single human being, but the former is seen as the archetype for the latter.[52] The opposed characteristics of these two human beings can be summarized as follows:

Gen 1:26–27	Gen 2:7
object of thought	object of sense perception
idea or genus or seal	participating in quality
incorporeal	composed of body and soul
neither male nor female[53]	either man or woman
by nature, immortal	by nature, mortal

The relationship between these two human beings, however, is unclear. Runia is of the opinion that the human being created according to the image can hardly represent an idea of a human being in a strictly Platonic sense, as a model for countless earthly human beings. Philo's expression "a

---

50. Although Philo follows Stoics in describing the various parts of the soul, he does not give up the Platonic framework, which makes a fundamental distinction between the rational and irrational parts of the soul (see *Opif.* 117; *Det.* 167–170).

51. See Tobin, *Creation of Man*, 87–101.

52. For the double creation theory, see Philo, *Opif.* 134–135; *Leg.* 1.31–32; *QG* 1.4; 8a.

53. Baer suggests that the most natural interpretation for the expression οὔτ' ἄρρεν οὔτε θῆλυ in *Opif.* 134 is that the rational soul created after the image of God is asexual and lacks the characteristics of the sexes. See Richard Baer, *Philo's Use of the Categories of Male and Female*, ALGHJ 3 (Leiden: Brill, 1970), 21; Tobin, *Creation of Man*, 109–10; Runia, *On the Creation*, 325.

6. The Creation of the First Human in Allegorical Exegesis

kind of idea" (ἰδέα τις) implies that Philo is hesitant to locate the human being created in Gen 1:26–27 in the realm of Ideas. Moreover, that would contradict Philo's view that the Ideas were created during day one (Gen 1:1–5), whereas the human being is created during the sixth day (Gen 1:26–27). Runia argues that, rather than an idea, the human being created in Gen 1:26–27 is "an idealization, i.e., the true human being such as he should and can be when the cares of the body and earthly life have entirely fallen away."[54]

It is of note that the term *seal* (σφραγίς) is used as a technical term for the relationship between model and copy in the Platonic tradition.[55] In addition, the phrase ἰδέα τις can be interpreted as "one idea among others," not "some kind of idea," as Runia suggests. Evidently, the idea of the spirit (*pneuma*) of God—which, in *De opificio mundi*, is one of the seven ideas created in Gen 1:1–5—includes ideas of all the life forms, both rational (mind) and irrational.[56] Thus, Gen 1:27 illustrates not only the ethical idealization of the human beings or the rational part of the soul of the generic human being, as Baer suggests, but also the idea of human mind, though the sensible copy of that idea is created in Gen 1:26. Winston summarizes Philo's double creation model in the following manner:

> As for man, the crown of all things created on earth, Gen 1:27a speaks of the creation of his Form after the image of the Logos, while verses 26, 27b, and 28–30 refer to the creation of sensible man, *which is described a second time in Gen 2:7*. Philo is happy to exploit this second and more explicit description of sensible man's creation in order to contrast the

---

54. See Runia, *On the Creation*, 322–23; Runia, *Philo of Alexandria*, 336–38. Baer argues that Philo does not regard the human being created in Gen 1:26–27 as referring to the idea of human being in Platonic sense but to the creation of the rational/irrational soul of the generic human being. However, the first empirical human being consisting of body and soul is not created until Gen 2:7. Philo's anthropological interpretations of Gen 1–2 can be summarized as follows: ideal (Gen 1:1–5), general/physical (Gen 1:6–2:3), recapitulation of what has taken place (Gen 2:4–6), and particular/physical (Gen 2:7–25; see Baer, *Philo's Use of the Categories*, 26–29; see also Radice, "Philo's Theology," 132–33).

55. Although Plato does not mention in his dialogues the idea of a human being or the idea of the soul, it was rather common in Middle Platonic tradition to postulate the idea of a human being within the intelligible cosmos (see the fragment of Arius Didymus, *On the Doctrines of Plato*, attested in Eusebius, *Praep. ev.* 11.23). See Tobin, *Creation of Man*, 114–19.

56. See Winston, *Logos*, 24.

earthly man who is sense-perceptible, partaking already of such and such quality, consisting of body and soul, man or woman, by nature mortal, with the heavenly man, who is a Form (*idea*) or Type (*genos*) or Seal (*sphragis*), intelligible, incorporeal, neither male nor female, by nature incorruptible. The heavenly man is thus the generic Form of man, which resembles the Logos only in respect of its rational aspect, and which as the generic Form of man contains both male and female, though *qua* Form it is itself neither male nor female.[57]

The distinction between the idea of mind and the Logos is ambiguous because both are located in the intelligible cosmos, and both serve as an archetype of the human intellect. Daniélou points out, however, that the idea of mind (Gen 1:27) can be seen as an archetypal idea *in* the Logos: the human being created according to the image "is an aspect of the Logos *qua* place of archetypal ideas."[58]

The discussion above illustrates that Philo's anthropological theories cannot be easily harmonized with each other. Philo no longer describes the history of the first human being or teaches ontological definitions but uses biblical narratives to teach universal anthropological and ethical truths. The human being who is made as an image of the Logos (Gen 1:27), the heavenly human being, is not only a heavenly archetype or an idea of the soul but is treated also as an ethical goal for humans or a personification of the virtuous soul. The various anthropological narratives in the Bible should be understood as teaching how one *becomes* a heavenly human being.

Philo's allegorical method is exemplified in *Spec.* 1.53–55, in which the human being who is placed in the garden (Gen 2:8) is distinguished from the human being who is placed in the garden to till it and guard it (Gen 2:15; see also Philo, *Leg.* 1.89–90; *Plant.* 44–46; *QG* 1.8). The former is identified with the human being according to the image and idea (Gen 1:27), who "is in need of nothing, but is self-hearing and self-taught and self-instructed." The latter is identified with the "molded mind" (πλαστὸς νοῦς), the "perishable mind" (φθαρτὸς νοῦς), and the "middle mind" (μέσος νοῦς; see also Philo, *Leg.* 3.246). He is progressing to become the human being according to the image, or the heavenly human, who is the real cultivator of the trees of wisdom in paradise. Sometimes, the "ethical" (ἠθικός)

---

57. See Winston, *Logos*, 25; emphasis added.
58. See Daniélou, *Philo of Alexandria*, 139.

and "physical" (φυσικός) allegories are elaborated side by side, as is the case in *Leg.* 2.11–13. The wild beasts created in Gen 2:19 refer allegorically to the creation of the passions as both helpers and enemies. Philo asks, however, why then the wild beasts were created even before the creation of the human being. Ethically, this denotes an abundance in and growth of the passions in the human life; physically (or protologically), it means that the genera of the passions were created before the species.[59] Thus, the protological views are not absolutely abandoned in the interpretations in the Allegorical Commentary, though they are not in all cases in harmony with the views Philo expresses elsewhere in his writings.

6.3.1. The Creation of the Earthly Mind and the Garments of the Skin

Although Tobin's method helps to form an all-encompassing view of Philo's anthropological teachings, it cannot be used as an absolute guide to his oeuvre. As noted above, Philo was a master of multiple exegesis and may have changed his teaching intentionally, depending on the intellectual level of his target audience. Therefore, the discrepancies in his writings do not necessarily indicate the use of different traditions, as Tobin assumes.[60] The teachings of the higher allegorical level can even conflict with the teachings Philo directs to a more literal-minded audience. For example, the distinction between the rational soul as a fragment or a portion of the deity and as an image of the Logos reflects Philo's creative exegesis, synthesizing rather than depending on distinct Stoic and Platonic sources. Philo's innovativeness is apparent in *Fug.* 71–72, where he distinguishes Gen 1:27 and 1:26 from each other.

---

59. Tobin points out that Philo's protological system in *Leg.* 1–3 differs from that present in *De opificio mundi* and may in fact represent an earlier version of Philo's hermeneutical model. The interpretation of Gen 1:24 and 2:19 in *Leg.* 2.11–13 implies that the demarcation line between the ideal world and the sensible is not in Gen 1:5, as in *De opificio mundi*, but all of the creation of the six days refers to the creation of the generic world, which served as a paradigm for its sensible copies. Thus, the human being created in Gen 1:26–27 can be seen as a generic form of human soul, both rational and irrational (see Tobin, *Creation of Man*, 120–32).

60. Runia is skeptical about Tobin's textual archaeology, especially whether it is possible to locate early antianthropological traditions in Philo's *Opif.* 69–71, 72–75 (*Philo of Alexandria*, 556–59; Runia, *On the Creation*, 19–20).

> Wherefore also, while in the former case the expression used was "let us make human being" (Gen 1:26), as though more than one were to do it, there is used afterwards an expression pointing to One, "God made the human being" (Gen 1:27). For the real human, who is absolutely pure Mind [νοῦς ἐστι καθαρώτατος], One, even the only God, is the Maker; but a plurality of makers produce human so-called, one that has an admixture of sense-perception. That is why he who is the human being in the special sense is mentioned with the article. The words run "God made the human being," that invisible reasoning faculty [λογισμόν] free from admixture. The other has no article added; for the words "let us make human being" point to him in whom an irrational and rational nature are woven together. (*Fug.* 71–72, modified)

Philo remarks that God and human being are, in Gen 1:27, referred to with an article (ἐποίησεν ὁ θεὸς τὸν ἄνθρωπον), whereas the human being in Gen 1:26 is referred to without an article (ποιήσωμεν ἄνθρωπον). This gives room for an allegorical reading that the two accounts do not describe the same beings but two distinct beings. The former is created by God alone and is referred to as reasoning faculty of the soul and "the real human being" (ἀληθινὸς ἄνθρωπος), a Philonic synonym for Plato's inner human being. The latter is the earthly human being, whose soul is a mixture of rational and irrational faculties. Philo's exegesis of these two passages is evidently dependent on Plato's *Republic*, where "the human being within us" (ὁ ἐντὸς ἄνθρωπος) dominates the entire human being.[61] As Winston points out above, it seems that Philo combines Gen 1:26 and 2:7 as parallel descriptions of the creation of the sensible human being, though the plurality of the creators is not mentioned in the latter passage. This suggests that, for Philo, Gen 1:26 and 2:7 depict the formation of Adam's soul, which is a mixture of rational and irrational impulses. However, the mortal and perishable body is not mentioned until Adam is clothed with the garments of skin, in Gen 3:21. Philo's double creation theory is also demonstrated in *Leg.* 1.31–32, where he distinguishes the heavenly human being from the creation of the earthly human being:

---

61. On the history of the concept of the inner man, see van Kooten, *Paul's Anthropology*, 358–70; also Theo K. Heckel, *Der Innere Mensch: Die paulinische Verarbeitung eines platonischen Motivs*, WUNT 2/53 (Tübingen: Mohr Siebeck, 1993); Christoph Markschies, "Innerer Mensch," *RAC* 18:276–78.

> "And God formed the human being by taking clay from the earth, and breathed into his face a breath of life, and the human being became a living soul" (Gen 2:7). There are two classes [γένη] of humans: the one a heavenly human being, the other an earthly. The heavenly human being, being made after the image of God, is altogether without part or lot in corruptible and earthlike essence; but the earthly one was made out of the matter scattered here and there, which Moses calls "clay." For this reason he says that the heavenly human being was not moulded, but was stamped with the image of God; while the earthly is a moulded work of the Artificer, but not His offspring. We must account the human being made out of the earth to be mind mingling with, but not yet blended with, body. But his earthlike mind is in reality also corruptible, were not God to breathe into it a power of real life; when He does so, it does not any more undergo moulding, but becomes a soul, not an inefficient and imperfectly formed soul, but one endowed with mind and actually alive; for he says, "the human being became a living soul." (*Leg.* 1.31–32, modified)

Philo maintains that there are "two classes of humans" (διττὰ ἀνθρώπων γένη). The "heavenly human being" (οὐράνιος ἄνθρωπος) is stamped with the image of God, that is, the Logos, and does not participate in any corruptible and earthlike essence, whereas the human being created in Gen 2:7 is corruptible, unless God breathes into him a power of real life.[62] Philo says, however, that the earthly human in Gen 2:7 denotes not the body of Adam but the "earthlike mind" (νοῦς γεώδης), which is molded "out of dispersed matter" (ἐκ σποράδος ὕλης).[63] It is unlikely, however, that Philo would have meant that the soul of the first human being is made out of the element of earth. However, Philo seems to suggest that the irrational soul

---

62. In *Leg.* 1.90, Philo stresses that while earthly Adam represents earthly and perishable mind, "the one made after the image is not earthly but heavenly" (ὁ γὰρ κατ' εἰκόνα οὐ γήϊνος, ἀλλ' οὐράνιος).

63. Yli-Karjanmaa suggests that the earthly mind refers to the incoherent and matter-oriented soul that is yet untouched by the breath of God. It is linked to incoherent and sporadic "sand," which is the symbol of the wicked mind (*Leg.* 3.37–38). Therefore, when Moses hit the Egyptian, he hid him in the sand, with the allegorical meaning that the dead Egyptian "has hidden himself in himself," a symbol of delusional ignorance (see Yli-Karjanmaa, "'Call Him Earth,'" 274–76). *Leg.* 1.31–32, seems to be in conflict with *Opif.* 136, where Philo interprets Gen 2:7 as denoting the body of Adam, which is "unmixed and undefiled and pure, as well as receptive and easy to work with."

is material.⁶⁴ Thus, without life-giving spirit, the earthly mind would be connected to the disorientation and dominated by the chaotic irrationality of matter.

Philo adds, however, that the human being made out of the earth to be "mind mingling with, but not yet blended with, body" (νοῦν εἰσκρινόμενον σώματι, οὔπω δ' εἰσκεκριμένον), indicating that his intention was not to describe solely the creation of the soul of Adam but also its relationship with the body. It is notable that the verb *blend* (εἰσκρίνειν) is used to describe the incarnation of the soul. In addition to *Leg.* 1.32, it is used in *Plant.* 14 and *Somn.* 1.31. In both of the latter cases, the context of the term is the mixing of the preexistent soul with the body. In *Somn.* 1.31, Philo is describing the cooling process of the soul, when it is mixed with the body. He wonders whether the "dominant mind" (ἡγεμὼν νοῦς) is infused into us at our birth. In *Plant.* 14, Philo is speaking about incorporeal souls in the air that are infused into the mortal bodies and that will come back after some period. Thus, Philo seems to include in *Leg.* 1.31–32 an allusion to the incarnation of the prenatal soul. He is describing not only the creation of Adam's soul and its entombment in the body when it is clothed with leather garments but the incarnation of souls generally. This means that prenatal souls have an orientation to bodily life and irrationality before their incarnation.⁶⁵

It seems that, in *Fug.* 71–72 and *Leg.* 1.31–32, Philo regards Gen 1:26 and 2:7 as complementary descriptions of the creation of Adam's soul, which is a mixture of rational and irrational impulses. Therefore, God could not create Adam's mortal part of the soul directly but only through his assistants.⁶⁶ Evidently, Philo is here following Plato's description in the *Timaeus*, where the creation of the irrational soul and the mortal parts of a human being is left for the younger gods. Philo says in *Opif.* 69–70 that the assistants are needed because it is not suitable for God's goodness to

---

64. See Wolfson, *Philo*, 1:385–89. Philo is undecided whether the irrational soul, which humans have in common with the animals, is made out of air (see *Somn.* 1.136–137), blood (*Det.* 83–84), or originated from the moist seed (see *Opif.* 67–68).

65. Yli-Karjanmaa proposes a new reading of *Leg.* 1.31–32, that Philo is not speaking about the *creation* of the human being at all but of the soteriological condition of the soul in its interincarnational stage ("'Call Him Earth,'" 272). I agree that Philo occasionally introduces nonprotological universal views in his allegories, but I do not regard the reincarnational interpretation of *Leg.* 1.31–32 as necessary.

66. In *Mut.* 31, Philo argues that "he is a human of virtue to whom God says, 'I am thy God,' for he has God alone for his maker without the co-operation of others."

create by himself a human mind, which is prone to morally questionable and irrational impulses.

Philonic innovations investigated above are reflected in Valentinian anthropological accounts, which likewise distinguish the creation of the human being in Gen 1:27 from that in 1:26, with the latter combined with 2:7 to denote the creation of the irrational soul by the Demiurge. In *Exc.* 50, the term "earthly soul" (ψυχὴ γεώδης) parallels Philo's "earthly *nous*" (νοῦς γεώδης), which is created in Gen 2:7 from "dispersed matter" (σπορᾶς ὕλη). The adjective σπορᾶς refers to confusion and disorder, which implies that the earthly mind is in a state of confusion before any contact with the breath of God.[67] According to the conventional Platonic view, matter was in confusion before the cosmic elements were separated out of it by the Demiurge. This parallels the Valentinian accounts, which maintain that the material and irrational soul is not created "out of dry earth" (ἀπὸ τῆς ξηρᾶς γῆς) but from an invisible substance that is in a chaotic state. As in Philo, this does not mean that the earthly mind was made out of the element of earth but from some kind of proto-material substance having an inclination to escape rationality.

In *Leg.* 3.69–77, the physical body of Adam is said not to be made out of pure matter, as Philo writes in *Opif.* 136, but it is referred to as leather mass and is not mentioned until the separation of the sexes and Adam's fall (see Gen 3:21). The garment of skin as an allegory of the body is also mentioned by Philo:

> Accordingly, the tunics of skin, if we judge truly, are to be considered a more precious possession than varicoloured dies and purple stuffs. So much, then, for the literal meaning. But according to the deeper meaning, the tunic of skin is symbolically the natural skin of the body. For when God formed the first mind, He called it Adam; then he formed the sense, which he called Life; in the third place, of necessity He made his body also, calling is symbolically a tunic of skin, for it was proper that the mind and sense should be clothed in the body as in a tunic of skin, in order that His handiwork might first appear worthy of the divine power. (*QG* 1.53)

---

67. Philo uses the term σπορᾶς as denoting the soul without shepherd (*Abr.* 49), a scattered and disoriented mind that escapes order (*Leg.* 3.37–38) and scattering the nations (*Congr.* 58).

The image of the leather garment appears also in *Exc.* 55.1, in the list of categories of humans—that is, the spirituals, the psychics, and the hylics, related to the spiritual, rational, and irrational parts of the soul. In addition to these are the garments of skin, which refer allegorically to the earthly body. In Irenaeus's account, the image of the garment of skin is given at the end of the description of the creation of the first human being and his visible body.

> Upon Adam, in addition to these three incorporeal (parts), the one consisting of dust wears a fourth, the "garments of skin."[68] (*Exc.* 55.1)

> Finally, they say, he was clothed in a garment of skin, and this is the perceptible flesh.[69] (Irenaeus, *Haer.* 1.5.5 [my trans.])

The allegory of the garments of skin as a reference to the physical body is also attested in Hippolytus, *Haer.* 10.13.4 as a saying from Valentinus, though the authenticity of the saying is uncertain: "He [Valentinus] supposes that flesh will not be saved and calls it 'the garment of skin' and 'the corrupt human being.'" Origen was also familiar with the same allegory, likely having learned about it from Philo's writings. There is no reason to think that the Valentinian teachers either would have had any other source for this teaching.[70]

As in *Leg.* 1.31–32, the Valentinian accounts do not see in Gen 2:7 the creation of the physical body of Adam but only Adam's soul, which is prone to irrational impulses. However, the existence of the physical body into which Adam was clothed is simply assumed without any references to his moral degeneration. In *Leg.* 3.69–77, the body, that is, the leather mass, is said to be a "wicked and a plotter against the soul and is even a corpse and a dead thing," which God hates without any reason. Thus, in *Leg.* 1–3, bodily existence is neither a neutral nor even an excellent condition of human beings, as it is seen in *De opificio mundi*, but is seen as a *result* of or punishment for the errors made by Adam, evidently forming the basic condition of all incarnated human souls.

---

68. Trans. Brakke and Layton, *Gnostic Scriptures*, 520. Τοῖς τρισὶν ἀσωμάτοις ἐπὶ τοῦ Ἀδὰμ τέταρτον ἐπενδύεται ὁ χοϊκός, τοὺς "δερματίνους χιτῶνας."

69. "Ὕστερον δὲ περιτεθεῖσθαι λέγουσιν αὐτῷ τὸν δερμάτινον χιτῶνα· τοῦτο δὲ τὸ αἰσθητὸν σαρκίον εἶναι λέγουσι.

70. See Dunderberg, *Beyond Gnosticism*, 66–67 n. 62.

Common to Philo's soteriological framework and Valentinian anthropology is the notion of salvation as a return to the soul's *nonbodily* existence. In *Leg.* 2.49–50, the return to the prelapsarian wholeness of the soul, in which the (female) sense perceptions are ruled by the (male) reason, is the reverse of the embodiment and takes place when the mind stops following the fleshly passions and is released from the dying body. In Valentinian soteriology, the soul is saved when it is integrated with its heavenly counterpart and liberated not only from the physical body but eventually from the psychic soul-body during the heavenly wedding feast.

6.3.2. The Heavenly Human Being and the Allegory of the Soul in Philo

Philo is the first known ancient author to mention the "heavenly human being" (οὐράνιος ἄνθρωπος) explicitly, though it is not always clear whether he represents, in Philo's understanding, an archetypal human being—that is, an idea of human beings—or a symbol of virtuous person. Evidently, Philo did not invent the idea of the heavenly human being, but he came to know of it from the preceding Hellenistic Jewish traditions.[71] Tobin points out that, in prior Jewish interpretations, the heavenly human being was seen as a real heavenly being, a sort of proto-Adam or primal *anthrōpos* in heaven. Philo conceptualizes the figure of this heavenly human, locating it in the intelligible cosmos as a paradigm for humankind. This means that the human being created in Gen 1:27 is both an intelligible archetype and a copy of the original seal—that is, the Logos of God.[72] In some cases, the concept of the heavenly human being is completely assimilated to the figure of the Logos.[73] In *Conf.* 142–149, Philo criticizes those who ascribe to existing things many causal principles, whereas the "sons of God" sees only one causal agent, that is, the

---

71. The Jewish heavenly human being tradition had its basis in the mystical speculations of the throne vision in Ezek 1:26, 28, according to which on the heavenly throne sits a human figure representing the likeness of the glory of the Lord. This led to a speculative belief in an anthropomorphic second power in heaven. See Ian K. Smith, *Heavenly Perspective: A Study of the Apostle Paul's Response to a Jewish Mystical Movement at Colossae* (London: T&T Clark, 2006), 42–47. On the Jewish *merkabah* tradition, see Gershom Scholem, *Major Trends in Jewish Mysticism* (New York: Schocken Books, 1995).

72. Tobin, *Creation of Man*, 106–7. Dillon notes the similarities between Philo's heavenly human being and the "essential human" of the Hermetic tradition in *Poimandres* 12–15 (see Dillon, *Middle Platonists*, 174–76).

73. See Tobin, *Creation of Man*, 102–8, 118–19, 139–42.

Logos. In *Conf.* 146, it is the Logos who is called "firstborn" (πρωτόγονος), the "human being" (ἄνθρωπος) after the image, and Israel:

> But if there be any as yet unfit to be called a Son of God, let him press to take his place under God's First-born, the Logos, who holds the eldership among the angels, their ruler as it were. And many names are his, for he is called, "the Beginning," and "the Name of God," and "His Logos," and "the Human being after His image," and "he that sees," that is, Israel. (*Conf.* 146, modified)

In addition to the passage above, Philo in *Conf.* 41 calls the Logos "God's human being" (ἄνθρωπος θεοῦ), and in *Conf.* 63, the Logos is described as the "eldest son" (πρεσβύτατος υἱός), who shaped the world, including human beings, by looking to the archetypal patterns of the Father. Although Philo conceptualizes the heavenly human being as a paradigm, it seems to retain its earlier anthropomorphic features. This peculiar character is prominent in *Leg.* 2.4, in which the human being made after the image of God (Gen 1:27) is *yearning* for that of which it is a copy, that is, the Logos.

As noted, in Philo's further allegorical development the protological allegory is transformed to soteriology, such that the figure of the heavenly human being becomes an ethical idealization of the earthly humans. The breath of God in Gen 2:7 is taken as mediating the image of the Logos, meaning that human beings have the power to *become* heavenly human being. In *Det.* 83, Philo explains that that the spirit is not "air in motion but a certain impression and character of divine power, which Moses calls by an appropriate name image." However, Philo in *Leg.* 1.42 draws a distinction between the spirit and the breath. While the heavenly human being made in Gen 1:27 participates in the spirit vigorously, Adam participates only in the breath of the spirit and the fragrance of the divinity. This distinction would mean that the image of the Logos, that is, the idea of mind, was not mediated to Adam and his descendants in its entirety but is present in the human souls only sporadically, to be activated through learning and practice.

6.3.3. The Heavenly Human Being and the Free Speech of Adam in Valentinian Sources

The Valentinian accounts investigated above do not explicitly mention the heavenly human being.[74] Instead of the heavenly human, the Valentinian accounts mention the angels of the Savior as archetypes and spiritual identities of the soul, which can be collectively approximate with Philo's heavenly human being. There is, however, one fragment from Valentinus in which the figure of the preexistent human appears in the context of creation of Adam by the angels. Clement of Alexandria preserves this passage in *Strom.* 2.36.2–4.[75]

> And just as in the presence of that modelled figure, fear fell on the angels when it emitted sounds that surpassed its modelling because of the one who had invisibly deposited in it a seed of the substance above and openly spoke, thus also among the generations of cosmic humans the works of humans become objects of fear for those who make them, as in the case of statues, images and everything that have been fashioned in the name of God. For having been modeled in the name of the "Man," Adam caused fear of the pre-existent Man, since he in fact was present in him. So, they were terrified and quickly did away with their work.[76]

The biblical context of Valentinus's fragment is evidently Gen 2:7, which describes the creation of a human being out of earth. However, the plurality of neither the creators nor angels is mentioned in Gen 2:7. This implies that the interpretation of Gen 2:7 is connected to the creation narrative of

---

74. According to Schenke's analysis, the gnostic texts can be divided into two groups in terms of the conception of the primal *anthrōpos*. In some texts, God is regarded as primal *anthrōpos*, and the earthly human beings are fashioned as copies of it. In some other texts, there is, in addition to these figures, the second primal *anthrōpos*, which serves as an archetype for the earthly humans (Schenke, *Der Gott "Mensch" in der Gnosis*, 23). Philo's view seems to represent the latter interpretation (Tobin, *Creation of Man*, 102–8). On the Jewish origin of the notion of the primal *anthrōpos*, see also C. H. Dodd, *The Bible and the Greeks* (London: Hodder & Stoughton, 1934), 146; Robert McL. Wilson, "The Early History of the Exegesis of Gen 1:26," StPatr 1 (1957): 420–37.

75. Clement says that the fragment is a direct quotation from Valentinus's letter. Thomassen suggests that Valentinus might be referring to an existing and well-known narrative or have explained the story earlier in the letter (*Spiritual Seed*, 431).

76. Trans. Thomassen, *Spritual Seed*, 430–31.

Gen 1:26, where the plurality of the creators is attested ("Let us create…"). It seems, then, that Valentinus's teaching parallels that in *Exc.* 50–51 and *Haer.* 1.5.5, where Gen 1:26 and 2:7 are approached as complementary descriptions of the creation of the soul of the first human being. There are, however, some significant elements in Valentinus's fragment that distinguish it from these accounts. First, Valentinus does not mention the Demiurge as the creator of Adam but the angels alone. Second, the generation of the seed of the higher essence is not mentioned, and it is not told how the seed was planted into the soul of Adam and who is in charge of the implantation of the seed. The breath of the Demiurge is also not mentioned, and the seed is inserted into Adam's soul by a male agent, not by Sophia. Thus, it seems that the modeling of the protoplast and the depositing of the seed of the higher essence are actualized simultaneously.[77] Third, in later Valentinian tradition, the motifs of fear, envy, or any hostile reaction toward Adam by the Demiurge or his cocreators are absent, as well as the role of the angels in the formation of Adam's earthly soul-body.

Although Valentinus's fragment presupposes the idea of the preexistent human being as a model for the angel's protoplast, it also differs from Philo's elaborations of the heavenly human being tradition. Valentinus seems to think that the preexistent human is a transcendent real being, not an intelligible paradigm for humankind, as in Philo. In addition, the expression "to model in the name of man" does not refer to creation according to the image of human being but in honor of somebody. Whereas works and statues are made in the honor of God, the angels make the protoplast in honor of the preexistent human being. Although the angels knew of the existence of the preexistent human, they were not aware of his spiritual power as he reveals himself in the angels' creation.[78] It is unclear what Valentinus means that the angels "did away with their work." The most probable interpretation would be that the angels sent their psychic pro-

---

77. Thomassen suggests that Valentinus's fragment parallels *Exc.* 2–3, according to which a male figure—not Sophia—is the one who deposits the seed into Adam's soul (*Spiritual Seed*, 434–35, esp. n. 18).

78. See Dunderberg, *Beyond Gnosticism*, 48; Thomassen, *Spiritual Seed*, 435–36. It is unlikely that Valentinus would have meant that the cult statues contain spiritual power. Valentinus's intention was rather to show that the objects of the statues are higher than those who made them. Therefore, they can inspire awe not because of the statues themselves but because of the gods or rulers they represent.

toplast into the lowest region of matter, meaning that Adam was clothed with a body made out of elements of the world.

It is commonly noted that Valentinus's fragment parallels the creation of Adam in the Sethian Secret Book of John.[79] It is likely that both Valentinus and the author of the Secret Book of John made use of a similar Jewish exegetical tradition that taught how Adam was spiritually superior to the angels that fashioned his body.[80] There are, however, notable differences concerning the reason for the angels' malevolent acts in Valentinus's fragment and the Secret Book of John. In Valentinus's fragment, the angels act in fear of Adam, while in the Sethian narrative they do so out of jealousy. Furthermore, in the Secret Book of John, this jealousy is caused by Adam's better understanding, while Valentinus maintains that it is Adam's free speaking that causes fear among the angels.[81]

Dunderberg points out that the differences between Valentinus and Sethian mythology can be explained as Valentinus's modifications, which go back to the vindication of the righteous in the book of Wisdom (5:1–2). The righteous speak boldly in the presence of those who suppress them,

---

79. A similar account concerning Adam's creation is found in Gos. Phil. 70.22–30. In both the Apocryphon of John and the Gospel of Philip, the creator angels are said to become envious of Adam. In the Apocryphon of John, the reason for this envy is Adam's intelligence, whereas in the Gospel of Philip the reason is the fact that Adam's words are superior to their powers. In both cases, it is not Adam's frank speech as such that creates fear but the intelligence or intellectual nature of his speech that causes envy. It is quite likely that these motifs circulated widely in the Hellenistic Jewish exegetical tradition and were adopted by both gnostic and Valentinian groups without any direct literal dependency. The motif of the fear of the angels in the creation of Adam is also attested in Orig. World 115.11–30. In this text, the reason that the creator angels experience fear is not Adam's intelligence or his speech but his ability to move (see Thomassen, *Spiritual Seed*, 445–47).

80. See Dunderberg, *Beyond Gnosticism*, 51–52; Thomassen, *Spiritual Seed*, 450–51. It is highly unlikely that the Secret Book of John would have been dependent on Valentinus, given strikingly conflicting themes and motifs between Valentinus's fragment and the Secret Book of John (see also Logan, *Gnostic Truth and Christian Heresy*, 55).

81. See Dunderberg, *Beyond Gnosticism*, 49–52. It is unclear who is the agent of free speaking. Two possibilities include the seed and the one charged with the implantation of the seed. Thomassen suggests that the latter option is more probable (*Spiritual Seed*, 443). I, on the other hand, would suggest that the former is more likely: the agent of free speaking is the molded human being, who possesses higher authority as a result of his spiritual essence and can speak freely with God.

paralleling the idea of frank speech in Valentinus's fragment.[82] However, frank speech is there not the response to suppressors, as in the book of Wisdom, but it is frank speech itself that creates fear and subsequently the suppression of Adam.

It is of note that the motif of parrhesia is also mentioned in Philo's writings. In Philo, frank speech is a divine virtue that belongs to God (*Sacr.* 66), whose "words can outstrip and overtake everything," but it also characterizes a virtuous soul, who is "filled with the graces of God" (*Ebr.* 150). For Philo, however, frank speech is not so much about speaking boldly before enemies but speaking freely among friends of God (*Her.* 6, 21, 24). Philo says that it is unwise to speak boldly or arrogantly before suppressors but that one should remain silent (*Somn.* 2.83–85, 92). Philo maintains that it was the lack of fear that made Abraham capable of free speech when he asked boldly of God, "What do you give to me?" (Gen 15:1–2). Noble souls possess something authoritative within them, which is not obscured even before those who are high in rank. In his later philosophical works, Philo mentions Calanus, a gymnosophist, and Choereas, a zealous follower of Diogenes the Cynic, as examples of freedom of speech and human equality (*Prob.* 95, 125–126).

It is possible that Valentinus elaborated Sethian creation narratives in light of the Hellenistic Jewish wisdom theology attested in the book of Wisdom and Philo's writings. Valentinus might, however, have been familiar with a somewhat different myth that had preceded the Sethian version reported in the Secret Book of John and related texts. In particular, Valentinus expounds the motif of the fear of the creator angels, which the free speech of Adam caused. The parrhesia of Adam causes fear among the creator angels because they realize that they are not equal to the preexistent human, who is present in Adam and who can speak freely with God, as if among friends. This would mean that it is the friendliness with which he talks with the highest God that causes fear among the angels. This is because free speech is seen as a mark of divine virtue and cosubstantiality with the supreme God, who is present in Adam's soul. This kind of free speech thus reveals the inferior rank of the angels in relation to Adam, causing fear.

It is rather unlikely that Valentinus knew of the traditions of the heavenly human being in the way that it appears in Philo's writings. Valen-

---

82. Dunderberg, *Beyond Gnosticism*, 50.

tinus's fragment lacks all the essential allegorical motifs that make Philo's use of the heavenly human being tradition unique. However, Valentinus's teachings were elaborated by his disciples in a way that brought their interpretations closer to Philo's view of the heavenly human being as an archetypal model of the intellect. In *Excerpta* C and *Haer.* 1.1–7, the angels of the Savior serve as archetypes for the seed of Sophia. The Pleroma is a multiple entity, which manifests itself simultaneously as one and many, designated, in some Valentinian systems, simply as the Human Being (see *Haer.* 1.4.5; 5.6).[83] The Savior himself is an offspring of the Pleroma, but at the same time he can be considered as an image of the aeon "the Human Being–*ecclesia*" (see *Exc.* 43.2–5; Irenaeus, *Haer.* 1.2.6).[84] Comparing this with Philo, the Savior can be roughly equated with the Logos, and his angels collectively represent the "heavenly human being," who serve as a model for Sophia's spiritual emanation. In *Excerpta* C, the incarnated images of the Savior's angels are described as the spiritual bone marrow of Adam's soul and can be equated with the presence of the seed of the higher essence mentioned in Valentinus's fragment. As noted above, Philo maintains that the breath of God mediates only the fragrance of the spirit—that is, the image of the Logos—meaning that the divine image is only potentially present in Adam's soul. This parallels the Valentinian model, according to which the breath of the Demiurge mediates only an image of the Savior's angels, which must be perfected through knowledge.[85] Both in Philo and the Valentinian sources the archetypal identities—that is, the heavenly human being and the angels of the Savior—do not incarnate but remain in the heavenly realm as higher identities for the earthly minds.

---

83. See Thomassen, *Spiritual Seed*, 437–42.

84. The joint fruit of the Pleroma is Jesus, but he is also called the Savior, the Christ, the Logos, and the All. In Tri. Trac. 66.10–12, the Savior is described as the image of the Father and the whole, i.e., the Pleroma.

85. The metaphor of fragrance as a representation of spiritual presence is also found in Tri. Trac. 71.35–72, where the Spirit of the Father is described being breathed through the members of the Pleroma. The fragrance of the Spirit then gives an innate inclination for seeking out the source of that fragrance. The Father reveals himself through the spirit and presents himself as something to be reflected on and sought after, but he does not want the aeons to know him perfectly. Fragrance as a metaphor for the children of the Father is also attested in Gos. Truth 33.33–34.34 (see Dunderberg, "Stoic Tradition," 224). In 2 Cor 2:14–16 Paul also uses the metaphor of fragrance denoting the spiritual essence of the believers.

6.4. Valentinus's Psalm *Harvest* and Its Intellectual Background

There is still one further fragment from Valentinus of anthropological importance that indicates the use of Hellenistic Jewish exegetical traditions. It is the psalm composed by Valentinus called *Harvest* (Hippolytus, *Haer.* 6.37.7), the entirety of which reads as follows:

Θέρος
πάντα κρεμάμενα πνεύματι βλέπω,
πάντα δ' ὀχούμενα πνεύματι νοῶ·
σάρκα μὲν ἐκ ψυχῆς κρεμαμένην,
ψυχὴν δ' ἀέρος ἐξεχομένην,
ἀέρα δ' ἐξ αἴθρης κρεμάμενον·
ἐκ δὲ βυθοῦ καρποὺς φερομένους,
ἐκ μήτρας δὲ βρέφος φερόμενον

Harvest
All things hanging in Spirit I see,
All things carried in Spirit I know:
Flesh from soul hanging,
Soul from air proceeding,
Air from ether hanging.
Fruit borne from the deep,
Child borne from the womb.[86]

As a literary work, the composition of the psalm reflects artistic skill and excellent knowledge of the conventions of Greek meter.[87] The consensus is that the psalm itself is an authentic literary work of Valentinus. Accord-

---

86. The translation of Valentinus's psalm is taken from Andrew McGowan, "Valentinus Poeta: Notes on ΘΕΡΟΣ," *VC* 51 (1997): 159.

87. McGowan remarks that the "mouse-tailed" verses indicate a somewhat inspired intensity or at least a certain spontaneity. It is possible that the psalm was the outcome of prophetic inspiration experienced within communal service or composed to be used in such a context (McGowan, "Valentinus Poeta," 159). The spirit (πνεῦμα) mentioned in the opening two lines must be interpreted as an instrumental dative, but it is not clear whether it depicts the bond described in lines 3–5 or a mode of seeing and understanding in lines 1–2. I suggest that the former option is more likely. The author of the psalm is thus describing how things are ("I see all things are carried in/through spirit"), not the way he sees them ("I see in spirit"). Layton interprets the sentence according to the latter option: "I see in spirit … I know in spirit" (*Gnostic Scriptures*, 306).

ing to patristic evidence, Valentinus did write his own psalms, with the author of the Canon Muratori mentioning Valentinus's psalm book, which was banned from the list of canonical Scriptures.[88] It is unclear, however, whether the commentary that follows the psalm comes from Valentinus. It may come instead from the followers of Valentinus or from Hippolytus himself.[89] In the commentary, the growing of the fruits and generation of a child describe allegorically generation within the transcendent reality. Valentinus's psalm is paralleled in the Tripartite Tractate, in which the themes of womb, fruits, and child are used as metaphorical descriptions for the generation of the aeons of the Pleroma.[90] I suggest, however, that the main message of the psalm is anthropological. Rather than describing the generation of the aeons within the transcendental level, Valentinus's psalm describes the condition of the human soul, which is equated with

---

88. See Thomassen, "Going to Church with the Valentinians," 185–86.

89. Thomassen suggests that it is difficult to believe that Valentinus or anyone within his school could have confused the immaterial Pleroma with the ether, as is the case with the commentary that follows Valentinus's psalm (*Spiritual Seed*, 480 n. 124). Dunderberg, on the other hand, does not rule out the possibility that someone within the school of Valentinus could have written the commentary that follows the psalm, even though Valentinus's intention was not to describe protological reality (*Beyond Gnosticism*, 62–63, 72–73; see also McGowan, "Valentinus Poeta," 166–67).

90. The expression ἐκ δέ at the beginning of lines 6–7 indicates that they stand in contrast with the preceding text (see Thomassen, *Spiritual Seed*, 484–85). The change in verb from κρεμαννύναι to φέρειν implies that there is an ontological difference in *how* certain elements depend on each other. While the flesh and air are "hanging" from the "higher" elements and the spirit carries all the elements, the fruits from the depth and a child from the womb are "brought forth" as a process of generation. McGowan suggests that the verbs used in lines 1–2 describe the ontological shift in lines 5–6. The participle κρεμάμενα implies suspension from above (lines 3–5), whereas ὀχούμενα describes support from below (lines 6–7). These two modes of dependency necessitate different kinds of intellectual activity: the author of the psalm sees the things that are hanging (βλέπειν), while he knows (νοεῖν) the things carried. The latter phrase refers to the intelligible realm, which can be known, though it is not perceptible. Although this interpretation may seem convincing, it is notable that the verbs κρεμάμενα and ὀχούμενα are closely connected with each other in the account of Philo in *Mos.* 2.121, as Thomassen correctly observes (see also McGowan, "Valentinus Poeta," 161–63). Although these notions indicate that the last two sentences describe something different from the previous lines, this does not necessarily have to be transcendent reality. It is just as possible that the end of the psalm is grammatically distinguished from the other part of the text to separate the ethical cultivation of human soul (lines 6–7) from speculation about the bond between the elements of human beings (lines 3–5).

the structure of the cosmos.⁹¹ The closest parallels with Valentinus's psalm are the Hermetic literature and Philo's allegories of the temple and the high priest, in which the human soul is seen as a microcosm.⁹² As the cosmos is harmoniously bound together through the Logos, at an anthropological level the same function has been reserved for the Spirit. The bearing of fruit and producing of offspring do not denote generation within the transcendent realm, as is suggested in the commentary that follows the psalm, but should be understood in light of Philo's allegories concerning the cultivation of the trees of wisdom within the human soul, which produce fruit and bear children by the Spirit.⁹³

6.4.1. The Cosmic Sympathy of the Soul

Although Valentinus's psalm contains some well-known cosmic elements, it is not likely that he is describing solely the structure of the cosmos. This would have meant that Valentinus had changed the ancient theory of the structure of the cosmos and the elements of the world significantly, with flesh taking the place of water and earth, and the world soul being set below air and ether. It is difficult to find any reason for such a confusion. It is not likely that Valentinus would have mistakenly confused these elements. Instead, the rather odd combination of cosmic elements more likely results from Valentinus's purpose of mixing anthropological and cosmological elements.

The key elements in Valentinus's psalm are the flesh, the soul, ether, and the Spirit. It is notable that the flesh and air both hang (κρεμάννυμι) from the higher elements—the flesh from the soul, air from ether—but

---

91. For an anthropological interpretation, see Ismo Dunderberg, "Stoic Traditions in the School of Valentinus," in *Stoicism in Early Christianity*, ed. Tuomas Rasimus, Troels Engberg-Pedersen, and Ismo Dunderberg (Grand Rapids: Baker Academic, 2010), 223; Jens Holzhausen, "Ein gnostischer Psalm?," *JAC* 30 (1993): 71.

92. Dunderberg detects various similarities between Valentinus's psalm and some Hermetic passages that describe the cosmic bond being carried by the spirit— Corp. herm. 12.14: "the finest matter is air, the finest air is soul, the finest soul is mind, and the finest mind is god." Dunderberg suggests that Valentinus was familiar with Hermetic cosmology, which he used for his poetic vision of the structure of the world and its microcosmic representation (*Beyond Gnosticism*, 66).

93. Markschies suggests that *Harvest* can be interpreted literally: the divine order can be seen in the fruits of matter and equally in pregnancy of mothers and in fertility of the earth (*Valentinus Gnosticus?*, 247).

the soul is not described as hanging but proceeding (ἐξεχομένη) from air.[94] It is unlikely that Valentinus would have thought that the essence of the soul is the air from which it comes. It is more likely that air in Valentinus's psalm refers to the cosmic region of air. Valentinus may thus have been influenced by the theory mentioned by Philo that the location of prenatal souls before their incarnation was not the stars, as in Plato (*Tim.* 41d), but the region of air. The following passage elucidates Philo's views (see also *Somn.* 1.135–136).[95]

> On earth and in the air the maker made two kinds. In the air he made the winged creatures which are sense-perceptible, and also other powers which can in no way be perceived by sense-perception. This is the band of incorporeal souls who have been arrayed in differing ranks. It is reported that some of them enter into mortal bodies and at certain appointed times depart from them again. Others who have obtained a more divine constitution disregard the earthly realm totally and reside in the highest place near the ether itself. These are beings of the greatest purity, whom the philosophers among the Greeks call "heroes," but Moses names them with an accurate term "angels," since they report as envoys the good things that come from the leader to his subjects, as well as reporting to the king what his subjects are in need of. (*Plant.* 14 [Geljion and Runia])

---

94. The term ἐξέχειν in Valentinus's psalm is used commonly for the shining of the sun (see McGowan, "Valentinus Poeta," 175 n. 51). In Philo, the verb is used to describe how the branches of the menorah project out on each side (*Her.* 218) and how Onan's seed spills out on the ground (*Post.* 180).

95. The region of air as an abode of spiritual beings is also attested in some Stoic sources. Sextus Empericus (*Math.* 9.87) reports that the Stoics were of the opinion that, if there are living beings in the air, there must also be living beings in the ethereal realm as well, and it is from the ether that human beings derive their intellectual power (see Winston, *Logos*, 31–36). Yli-Karjanmaa points out that the notion of the air being filled with souls may be originally Pythagorean. This idea was known already during the Old Academy, though it seems not to have attained the position of an essential doctrine (see Yli-Karjanmaa, *Reincarnation in Philo*, 134). It was common in the Platonic tradition to think that the soul adopted different kinds of instrumental bodies during its prenatal descent into the world (see Plotinus, *Enn.* 4.3.15). The body of the soul becomes heavier and visible when it descends from the firmament through the regions of ether and air into the corporeal body. During the incarnation, the soul experiences a cooling process when it mingles with the air. Indeed, the Greek word for the soul (ψυχή) was often explained as deriving from the word *cold* (ψῦχος) or "to make cool" (ψυχεῖν). The theory of the cooling down of the soul is also attested in Philo, *Somn.* 1.31; Origen, *Princ.* 2.8.3 (see Dunderberg, "Stoic Traditions," 223).

In Valentinus's psalm, the Spirit is not described as being dependent on any of the cosmic elements but binds all flesh, soul, air, and ether together. This parallels Philo's anthropology, according to which the intellect of the soul—that is, its "rational Spirit" (λογικὸν πνεῦμα)—is the "ruler" (ἡγεμονικόν), which is made according to the archetypal form of the divine image and binds together the elements of the human being, the body and the soul, into a harmonious whole.[96] For Philo, the Spirit is synonymous with the intellect, because the Spirit is an image of the Logos and able to generate thoughts.[97] That is, the task of the Spirit is to vivify the mind, which in turn vivifies its subordinate parts, that is, the irrational soul and the body (see *Leg.* 1.40). In *Spec.* 4.123, Philo mentions another view, according to which the ruling part of the soul is made of "ether" (αἰθήρ), being a "divine fragment" (ἀπόσπασμα θεῖον), for God breathed into Adam's face a breath of life, and he became a living soul. This reflects the Stoic conception of the world and human beings, which was commonly adopted by Middle Platonic philosophers, though they rejected Stoic materialism. The ether in which the intellect is enveloped is no longer the subtle fire of the Stoics

---

96. For Philo's view about the intellect as a ruler, see *Spec.* 1.171, 276–277; *Leg.* 1.39–40, 60–62.

97. In *Det.* 82–84, Philo divides the soul of human beings into two parts, according to the sacred number two. Human beings possess an irrational soul similar to that of the animals, but they also have a rational soul, which is an image of God's mind. While the irrational part is related to the vivifying (ζωτική) power and has blood for its essence, the rational (λογική) faculty is spiritual and is associated with ether. In *QG* 2.59, Philo divides the soul into three parts. The soul has nutritive, sensitive, and rational parts. The nutritive and sensitive parts of the soul are related to flesh and blood, which contain the senses and passions. These lower elements of the soul lack intellect and thought, which belong to the rational soul alone. The blood of the flesh contains air, which is mingled with blood in different degrees. The vessels that carry a pulse, i.e., the arteries, contain less blood and more pure and unmixed air, whereas the vessels without a pulse, i.e., the veins, contain less breath, i.e., air, and more blood. The differences concerning the amount of air in the blood also carry an ethical dimension. Courage is related to the warm and fiery blood, which contains more air. The soul, which is full of courage, despises all the food and luxuries of life. Whoever has a low amount of spirit in their blood is a wanderer, becoming lazy and indolent because of an interest in leading a luxurious life. A similar teaching is attested in Corp. herm. 10.13, where it is taught that it is erroneous to think of the soul as the blood; rather, the soul is "the breath passing through veins, arteries and blood that sets the living being in motion and in a manner supports it" (see Dunderberg, *Beyond Gnosticism*, 65).

but the fifth substance of Aristotle, out of which the heavenly bodies and stars are also made.[98] Philo seems to sympathize with this view, though he stresses that it is was not only the "ethereal spirit" (αἰθέριον πνεῦμα) that was breathed into Adam's soul but something better: a divine "radiance" (ἀπαύγασμα).[99] In *Det*. 83, Philo says that the breath of God is "not moving air, but, as it were, an impression stamped by the divine power, to which Moses gives the appropriate title of image, thus indicating that God is the Archetype of rational existence, while a human being is a copy and likeness." Although the essence of the human mind may remain vague in Philo, the harmony of the soul has an equivalent in the sympathy of the cosmos. While the cosmos is ruled by the Logos, the soul is ruled by the Spirit, meaning his intellect. These notions can be found in Philo's allegories of the tabernacle and the high priest, which describe the structures of the cosmos and the human soul.

6.4.2. The Soul as a Temple of God

For Philo, the earthly temple is but a copy of the more profound heavenly temple, that is, the cosmos, and the human being as its microcosmic

---

98. See Merlan, "Greek Philosophy," 40–42; Luttikhuizen, *Gnostic Revisions*, 37–39.The identification of the essence of the soul with the *quinta essentia* of the celestial gods is mentioned by Cicero: "If there is a kind of fifth nature, first introduced by Aristotle, this is the nature of gods and souls" (*Tusc.* 1.10.22; 26.65–66; translated in Winston, *Logos*, 65). The old Stoa parted from Aristotle in claiming that ether was not a cosmic element of its own but simply a purer form of fire. It became common, however, among Middle Platonic circles since Antiochus of Ascalon to regard ether as *quinta essentia*, which forms the substratum of the soul (see Winston, *Logos*, 64–65 n. 3; Tobin, *Creation of Man*, 82–84).

99. In *Leg.* 3.161, Philo maintains that the soul is of the upper air, being a portion of an ethereal nature. Therefore, it is fed by divine food, i.e., knowledge, not by meat and drink like the body. In *Somn.* 1.34, the essence of mind is not explicitly mentioned, but it is compared with the heaven, which is contrasted with earth, water, and air. In *Her.* 283, Philo mentions a common view that the soul will return after death of the body to the realm of the fifth substance. Although Philo may have used Stoic vocabulary, he departed from the Stoic materialism. In *Plant.* 18, Philo explicitly writes: "Now while others, by asserting that our human mind is a particle of the ethereal substance, have claimed for man a kinship with the upper air; our great Moses likened the fashion of the reasonable soul to no created thing, but averred it to be a genuine coinage of that dread Spirit, the Divine and Invisible One, signed and impressed by the seal of God, the stamp of which is the Eternal Word" (see Wolfson, *Philo*, 1:394–95).

representation.[100] This would mean that human beings could come into contact with the Creator without entering into the temple of Jerusalem by contemplating directly oneself and the universe. These ideas form the background to Philo's allegories, where the temple, cosmos, and human soul are brought together.

The building of the temple is, according to Philo, a symbolic reenactment of the creation of the world. In *Spec.* 1.66, Philo claims that the highest and truest temple of God is the universe. The sanctuary, that is, the holy of holies, is heaven; the votive offerings, the stars; and the priests, the angels, who are pure intelligences in the likenesses of the Monad. Philo is not consistent in his allegories, however, as, in *QE* 2.68–69, the holy of holies is not said to be heaven, as in *Spec.* 1.66, but stands instead as a symbol for the world of Ideas. The holy place refers to heaven and the outer section the world below the moon. In *Fug.* 108–112, Philo describes the high priest as a representation of the Logos clothed with the elements of the world, being the bond of everything that holds them together, preventing them from becoming loosened.

In *Her.* 112–113, Philo explains that the tabernacle is not only a representation of the cosmos but the soul also: the soul of the properly initiated human being is a living temple of the Father. Philo interprets the phrase "the tabernacle was set up in the midst of our uncleanness" to mean the purification of the soul "after washing off and purging away all that sullies our life." Moreover, in *QE* 2.54 Philo explains that the inner side of the ark of the covenant in the holy of holies refers to the rational mind, which adorns and controls its exterior, that is, the body and sense perceptions. The pure mind can be compared with the high priest, whose physical perfection represents purity of soul. Thus, the high priest is not only a symbol of the Logos but a perfect sage, free from grief and any other passions, who worships God on behalf of the whole world (see Philo, *Spec.* 1.80–82; 4.192; *QG* 3.44; 4.25–27, 76).[101]

Valentinus's psalm can be understood in light of Philo's allegories of the tabernacle and the high priest, in which the sympathy of the soul and the that of the cosmos are intertwined. In *Mos.* 2.121–126, Philo explains

---

100. For the role of the temple in Philo's theology, see Wolfson, *Philo*, 2:237–52; Winston, *Philo of Alexandria*, 279; see also Schwartz, "Philo," 26–27.

101. See Wolfson, *Philo*, 2:340–41; Jean Laporte, "The High Priest in Philo of Alexandria," *SPhiloA* 3 (1991): 78–81. Everyone who obeys right reason has the potential of becoming the high priest of his own soul (see *Fug.* 116–118).

that the vestments of the high priest depict the harmony of the cosmos. The tunic of the high priest symbolizes the element of air, being the color of the hyacinth. To the hem of the tunic is attached a fringe of pomegranates, as well as flowers and bells, which symbolize earth and water. The mantle over the tunic is a representation of heaven, that is, ether, and the "breastplate" (τὸ λογεῖον) is a symbol of the firmament and an emblem of reason, which regulates the whole universe. In Philo's allegory of the vestments of the high priest, the lowest cosmic elements, "earth and water in a sense hang from the air, for air is their chariot" (ἀπ' ἀέρος τρόπον τινὰ γῆ καὶ ὕδωρ ἐκκρέμανται, τὸ γὰρ ὄχημα τούτων ἐστὶν ἀήρ). This description seems to parallel Valentinus's psalm, in which the "flesh hangs from the soul" (σάρκα μὲν ἐκ ψυχῆς κρεμαμένην), the "soul proceeds from air" (ψυχὴν δ' ἀέρος ἐξεχομένην), and "air hangs from ether" (ἀέρα δ' ἐξ αἴθρης κρεμάμενον). Thus, the Spirit is not a separate essence of the soul but carries the flesh and the soul into harmony, just like Philo's high priest is a symbol of the Logos, who clothes the whole cosmos.

Although Valentinus's psalm does not explicitly mention the temple or the high priest, these symbols are used in various Valentinian sources as symbols of the purification of the soul. Origen preserves Heracleon's comment on the purification of the temple by the Savior in John's gospel (see Origen, *Comm. Jo.* 10; frags. 11–16 Völker).[102] For Heracleon, the temple of Jerusalem serves as an image of the human soul seized by the bodily passions. The purification of the temple means the annihilation of the bodily passions through the Spirit and an entering into the holy of holies, where the union with the Pleroma will be actualized. This understanding parallels a passage in the Gospel of Philip where the holy of holies is said to refer to the bridal chamber, where the soul is married to her angelic counterpart (Gos. Phil. 69.14–70.4).[103] Even though Valentinus's anthro-

---

102. According to Heracleon, the resurrection of the Savior is a symbol for the spiritual resurrection of the *ecclesia* replacing the psychic temple in Jerusalem. Thomassen stresses that "it would not be justified to infer that Heracleon attributes to the resurrection of Jesus only a symbolic significance, with no redemptive effect in itself…. In fact, we have already seen how the incarnation, the passion and the death of Jesus possess a salvific effect for Heracleon by virtue of a logic of mutual participation" (*Spiritual Seed*, 103–15).

103. The temple is not divided in this passage into two sections (viz., the holy building and the holy of holies), as would be expected, but into three chambers, referring to baptism (the holy building), ransom (the holy of the holy), and the bridal chamber (the holy of holies). It is likely that the porch is counted here as a separate

pological psalm does not contain symbols related to the worship in the temple, it can be interpreted rather easily on grounds of the archetypes attested in Philo's works.

6.4.3. The Spirit as a Bond of the Human Soul and Cultivator of the Trees of Virtue

In Valentinus's psalm, the spirit not only carries and brings together the faculties of human beings but also makes the soul fertile and fruitful. This idea has a parallel in Philo, who maintains that the Spirit of God is a teacher of wisdom and the source of good works. In *Gig.* 27 (see also 47), Philo calls the Spirit of God "the divine spirit of wisdom" (τὸ σοφίας πνεῦμα θεῖον), characterizing it as "wise, the divine, the indivisible, the good spirit that is diffused to fill all" (πνεῦμά ἐστι τὸ σοφόν, τὸ θεῖον, τὸ ἄτμητον, τὸ ἀδιαίρετον, τὸ ἀστεῖον, τὸ πάντῃ δι' ὅλων ἐκπεπληρωμένον). The Spirit of God breathed by God into the human soul also plays a role as a prophetic Spirit through which the soul frees itself from all bodily influences and becomes filled with the knowledge of God.[104] The rational Spirit thus mediates the presence of the Logos in an earthly mind, making it virtuous and productive. Therefore, Philo uses the metaphors of producing fruit and generating children as descriptions for the cultivation of the human mind through the Spirit of wisdom. In *Plant.* 37, Philo interprets the verse "God planted a paradise in Eden" as referring to the planting of the trees of virtue in the human mind:

> These plants would of necessity not belong to the soil, but to the rational soul, the one path leading to excellence with life and immortality as its end, the other leading to evil, flight from these goals and death. We

---

room. Philo also describes three sections in *Mos.* 2.101 but in reference to the tabernacle, not the temple. On the allegory of the temple in the Gospel of Philip, see Robert McL. Wilson, *The Gospel of Philip: Translated from the Coptic Text, with an Introduction and Commentary* (London: Mowbray, 1962), 139–41. In *Exc.* 38, the allegory of the temple is related to the ascent of the pneumatics to the Pleroma. Jesus is identified with the high priest, who is allowed to enter the holy of holies. Strikingly, the holy of holies is not taken to represent the Pleroma but the throne of the Demiurge, which is covered with a veil so that the spiritual human beings are not destroyed upon sight of it. The task of the Savior is to subdue the flames and to provide an entrance for the pneumatics to the Pleroma.

104. For the role of the Spirit of God in Philo, see Wolfson, *Philo*, 1:24–36.

should, therefore, understand that God in his generosity has planted in the soul a kind of paradise of virtues and their corresponding actions, a paradise that leads it to perfect felicity. (Geljion and Runia; see also *Leg.* 1.43–47; *Opif.* 153–154)[105]

In *QG* 1.6, Philo interprets the trees of paradise as denoting the trees of wisdom, which are planted in the human soul through the breath of God. The bodily influences and irrational impulses should be guarded and cultivated to produce good fruit. Philo maintains that the works of human beings are the offspring of the soul. In *Gig.* 4, he explains that those who have failed to cultivate their souls become parents of female children, whereas the fruits of the tree of virtue are "male beings."[106] Also, in *Mut.* 74–75, Philo compares the study of philosophy to a field; the physical study is likened to plants, the logic to the walls and fences, and ethics to the fruit. As the owner of the field build the wall and fences to guard the trees, "in the same way in philosophy physical and logical research should be brought to bear on ethics by which the character is bettered and yearns to acquire and also to make use of virtue."

In Valentinus's psalm, the metaphors of depths and womb can be seen as referring to the ethical cultivation of the soul.[107] The metaphor of the

---

105. This is one of those biblical passages that according to Philo must be interpreted allegorically. It would be absurd to say that God could have worked as gardener.

106. The allegory of the human intelligence as a plantation in paradise is also attested in the Valentinian Gospel of Truth. The perfect human beings are verbal expressions of the Father's thoughts that are planted in paradise. "He is acquainted with His plants, for it is He who has planted them in His paradise garden. Now His paradise is His realm of repose: it is the perfection within the Father's thought, and they are the verbal expressions of His meditation. Each of His verbal expressions is the product of His will and the manifestation of His speaking" (Gos. Truth [NHC I 36.35–37.2]; trans. Layton, *Gnostic Scriptures*, 324). Sterling points out that both Philo and the author of the Gospel of Truth "associate the notion of planting with divine thinking" ("School of Sacred Laws," 162).

107. The term *depths* is in the plural, and the offspring that is brought forth from the womb is in the singular, making problematic the association with the unitary source of and the connection to the multitude of aeons that are produced from this source. It is more likely that the terms *depths* and *womb* serve as metaphors for the spiritual darkness and lack of understanding, which is contrasted with production of the fruit of the spirit. In Plato, the human soul lost all its cognitive capacities, when it was bound in a mortal body (*Tim.* 43b). It is thus possible that the womb is a metaphor for forgetfulness that is corrected through education as the child grows. Also, the

womb is attested in *Haer.* 1.5.6, where the spiritual seed of Sophia is said to be deposited into the psychic soul of Adam as in a womb to grow and reach perfect rationality. Fruit and children are thus metaphors for ethical cultivation, brought forth when the spirit rules the human soul.

6.5. Conclusions

Comparison of the anthropologies of Philo and the Valentinians reveals some of the closest parallels in these texts. The Valentinians were dependent on Plato's anthropology and on Aristotelian psychology. In the Valentinian accounts the spiritual part of the soul is enclosed in psychic soul-body, which in turn is attached to the irrational soul. The intellect of the soul is not a part of the soul but a distinct genus that is breathed by God into the soul and must be awakened through contemplation of the transcendent reality, which reflect the common Middle Platonic view derived from Aristotle.

Although Philo was influenced by Stoic anthropology, the Platonizing interpretation of the creation narratives dominates his allegorical framework. According to this model, Gen 1:26–27 and 2:7 are no longer descriptions for a creation of the single human being, but the former is seen as the archetype for the latter. In *Fug.* 71–72, however, Philo makes an important distinction between Gen 1:27 and 1:26: the former is taken to describe the creation of the pure mind, while the latter is taken to describe the soul, which is a mixture of rational and irrational impulses, created by the assistants of God. The creation in Gen 1:26 is reiterated in 2:7, where the image of the Logos—that is, the idea of mind—is mediated through the breath of God into Adam's earthly soul.

The Valentinian teachers elaborated these innovations of Philo, combining them with the myth of Sophia. In *Excerpta* C and *Haer.* 1.5.6, Sophia creates the spiritual seed as images of the Savior's angels (Gen 1:27). As in Philo, Gen 1:26 and 2:7 are taken to describe the creation of the soul, which is a mixture of rational and irrational impulses. The seed of Sophia is inserted into Adam's soul-body by the psychic breath of the Demiurge. As the heavenly human being in Philo, the angels of the Savior, which are referred to as the *ecclesia* above, serve as archetypes for the intellect and

---

ground from which the harvest is gathered is dark and deep, and it is light and water as metaphors for wisdom that make the ground fertile.

exemplify collectively the truest identity of the earthly souls. The spiritual seed of Sophia is comparable with the Platonic inner human, or the real human being in Philo's anthropology.

In Philo's *Leg.* 1.31–32, Gen 2:7 (that is, Gen 1:26) does not represent a description of the creation of the *body* of Adam, as in *De opificio mundi*, but the earthly *mind*, which is associated with chaotic matter. The mortal body is not mentioned until Adam is clothed in the garments of skin (Gen 3:21), which is a punishment for Adam's failure to obey God's commandments. In *Excerpta* C, the term "earthly soul" parallels "earthly mind" in Philo, which is created out of sporadic matter. This indicates that the irrational part of the soul is made up of proto-material essence. In the Valentinian accounts, bodily existence is not the outcome of Adam's wrong choice but the result of the precosmic fall of Sophia. This mythological feature is lacking in Philo's allegories.

In this chapter, I also discussed two fragments of Valentinus. The first fragment dealt with the creation of Adam's prematerial soul-body by the angels. Valentinus was evidently dependent on the Hellenistic Jewish heavenly human being tradition and Sethian anthropology, which he reformulated in light of the concept of free speech mentioned in the book of Wisdom as well as in Philo's writings. It is rather unlikely that Valentinus knew of the traditions of the heavenly human in the form that they appear in Philo's writings. Valentinus's fragment lacks all the essential allegorical motifs that make Philo's use of the heavenly human being tradition unique. However, Valentinus's teachings were elaborated by the Valentinians in a such way that brought their interpretations closer to Philo's view of the heavenly human being as a conceptual paradigm and an ethical idealization of the humankind.

The second fragment I discussed was Valentinus's psalm *Harvest*, which describes the structure of the human soul as a microcosm. Valentinus's psalm can be interpreted in light of Philo's allegories of the tabernacle and the high priest, where the sympathy of the soul and that of the cosmos are intertwined. Valentinus may also have been influenced by Philo's theory that the location of prenatal souls is not the firmament, as in Plato, but the region of air. The metaphors of fruit and children can be seen in Valentinus's psalm as allegories for the cultivation of the soul and the producing of good works. It would seem that, if someone tried to compose a psalm on the ground of Philo's anthropological allegories, it would be fairly similar to what we have in Valentinus's *Harvest*.

7
Cain, Abel, Seth, and Israel in Allegorical Exegesis

The influence of Eudorus of Alexandria on the Platonic traditions of Alexandria in the first century BCE was notable. In addition to the theory concerning the derivation of matter from the One, Eudorus brought various writings of Plato together to articulate the goal of ethics as "becoming like God" (ὁμοίωσις θεῷ). Eudorus's transcendental anthropology was based on an innovative reading of Plato's *Theaetetus*. Eudorus explains Plato's view in the following way: "Socrates and Plato agree with Pythagoras that the goal is assimilation to God [ὁμοίωσις θεῷ]. Plato defined this more clearly by adding: 'according as is possible [κατὰ τὸ δυνατόν];' and it is only possible by wisdom [φρόνησις], that is to say, as a result of living in accordance with virtue."[1] Eudorus portrays Pythagoras as the originator of the ethical theory that regards assimilation to God or becoming like God as the fundamental goal of human beings. Although Plato may have meant "insofar as it is possible" (κατὰ τὸ δυνατόν) to refer only to human potential as a mortal being, Eudorus interprets it as a reference to the rational part of the soul, which is only capable of imitating God and living according to virtue. Eudorus claims that becoming like God forms the essential part of Plato's anthropology, explaining that it is exemplified in different ways throughout Plato's writing.[2]

---

1. Eudorus's book *Division of Philosophical Reasoning* is found in Stobaeus, *Flor.* 2.7.3. It was mediated through Arius Didymus, the first-century (BCE) Alexandrian philosopher. The translation is taken from Van Kooten, *Paul's Anthropology*, 142. Plato's original texts is as follows: "Therefore we ought to try to escape from earth to the dwelling of the gods as quickly as we can; and *to escape is to become like God*, so far as this is possible; and to become like God is to become righteous and holy and wise" (*Theaet.* 176b [Fowler], emphasis added).
2. See Van Kooten, *Paul's Anthropology*, 141–48.

Flight from the world and assimilation to the divine realm also form the philosophical background for both Philo and Valentinian theologians. These Platonic views were combined with Aristotelian transcendental psychology, according to which the intellect is present in the human soul only potentially and must awaken and be integrated into the higher self through the contemplation of the transcendent realm. Aristotle declares that the "contemplation" (θεωρία) is characterized by self-sufficiency, which is also the main characteristic of happiness (*Eth. nic.* 1097b.6–20). The contemplative life is the exercise of wisdom, and it fulfills the criterion of self-sufficiency, because the sages could always turn their thoughts to objects of contemplation. Therefore, the sages were not in need of aid from anybody or anything to be perfectly happy (*Eth. nic.* 1177a.27–b.1).[3]

The Aristotelian ideals of the contemplative life and self-sufficiency were taken over by the Stoics and the Middle Platonic teachers. However, it seems that the ideal of the wise man as self-taught and self-sufficient came to Philo from the Stoic teachers. Winston points out that Philo's concept of conscience as God's gift and an aid for the perfection of the natural law parallels the Stoic belief that "no man can be good without the help of God."[4] In Philo's *Deus* 135–138, conscience is said to enter the soul like a pure ray of light, to reveal its hidden sins in order to purify and heal us. Although Philo's portrait of the wise man is identical with the Stoics' description, the all-wise Moses superseded the level of wisdom that any Stoic sages could achieve.[5]

In *Gig.* 60–61, Philo divides humankind into three categories: the earth-born, the heaven-born, and the God-born. Earth-born humans are devoted to the bodily pleasures, and the heaven-born are lovers of learning, but the God-born are "priests and prophets," who have risen above the world and live as free men, "being inscribed in the commonwealth of incorruptible and incorporeal Ideas" (ἐγγραφέντες ἀφθάρτων καὶ ἀσωμάτων ἰδεῶν πολιτείᾳ). Philo affirms that while some perfect human beings are

---

3. For Aristotle, a thing's perfection corresponds to the extent to which it is chosen for its own sake (see *Eth. nic.* 1097a.30–b6). See Anthony Kenny, *Aristotle on the Perfect Life* (Oxford: Clarendon, 1992), 87–102.

4. Winston, "Philo's Ethical Theory," 389; see also Seneca, *Ep.* 41.1–2, 4–5.

5. See David Winston, "Sage and Supersage in Philo of Alexandria," in *Pomegranates and Golden Bells: Studies in Jewish and Near Eastern Ritual, Law and Literature in Honor of Jacob Milgrom*, ed. David P. Wright, David Noel Freedman, and Avi Hurvitz (Winona Lake, IN: Eisenbrauns, 1995), 815–24; Winston, *Philo of Alexandria*, 24–30.

born as sages, such as Isaac, some others are *reborn* as sages, after a long and laborious spiritual journey, as with Abraham and Jacob. This distinction between the perfect and the progressive humans forms the basis for the various allegories concerning biblical names, themes, and stories in Philo and the Valentinian sources, which are explored in this chapter.

7.1. Philo's Platonic Anthropology

According to Philo, the contemplation of the intelligible world is the highest goal of human life. He derives this principle not from the Jewish Scriptures but from Platonism. The object of worship is "the Self-existent who is better than the good, purer than the One and more primordial than the Monad" (*Contempl.* 2).[6] Philo agrees with Eudorus that flight from the realm of matter and becoming like God form the basis for ethics and soteriology. Quoting Plato's *Theaet.* 176a–b, Philo writes in *De fuga et inventione*:

> This truth found noble utterance in the *Theaetetus*, where a man highly esteemed, one of those admired for their wisdom, says: "Evils can never pass away; for there must always remain something which is antagonistic to good. Having no place among the gods in heaven, of necessity they hover around the mortal nature and this earthly sphere. Wherefore we ought to fly away from earth to heaven as quickly as we can; and to fly away is to become like God, as far as this is possible; and to become like Him is to become holy, just, and wise." (*Fug.* 63)

Clearly, Philo adopted Eudorus's theory of godliness as an essential part of his transcendental ethics. In *Fug.* 56, Philo stresses that only those who take refuge in God are really alive, while all others are dead. Niehoff argues that Philo introduces a radically new approach for Jewish ethics that does not make a difference between spiritual and material realms.[7] Philo frequently stresses, however, that the human mind can achieve knowledge only about God's existence, not his essence, which remains unknowable even to the perfect soul (see, e.g., *Praem.* 40–44).[8] The notion of the unknowability

---

6. See Winston, *Logos*, 54.
7. Niehoff, *Philo of Alexandria*, 202–6.
8. The intention to comprehend the essence of God is, according to Philo, absolutely "silly." There is, however, at least something that can be said about God's essence. Philo states that God's essence is single and one. In addition, in *Sacr.* 65–68 Philo

of God goes back to Plato's *Parmenides*, according to which the supreme principle, the One, is unknown.[9]

Despite God's absolute transcendence, Philo suggests in *Leg.* 3.96 that a human mind can achieve a vision of God through the Logos, which is the shadow of God, and the model for both the visible creation and human mind (see also *Cher.* 27–28).[10] Philo represents Middle Platonic epistemological dualism, according to which there are two ways of achieving knowledge of God: discursive reason (philosophy) and wisdom (intuition).[11] The former approach is to gain knowledge of God from the created things through the natural capacities of the human soul, "as one may learn the abiding thing from the shadows [σκιαί]." The approach of wisdom is based on intuition, as the mind perceives itself as an image of the Logos and rises "above and beyond creation and obtains a clear vision" (*Leg.* 3.99–103).[12]

---

reduces God's property to one single property—i.e., acting. Unlike the human being, whose thinking and acting are two distinct things, God's thinking and acting are simultaneous, comprising all creation. God acts through his thoughts and words (see Winston, *Logos*, 18–19).

9. This view was adopted also by Clement of Alexandria, who evidently was dependent on Platonic transcendental monotheism and Philo (*Strom.* 2.6.1; 4.156.1; 5.65.2, 71.5, 81.4, 82.4; see Lilla, *Clement of Alexandria*, 212–26).

10. God's gracious and legislative powers are expressions of the Logos and the manifestations of God's thinking and acting (see Winston, *Logos*, 19).

11. For the epistemological dualism of pre-Plotinian Platonism, see Dörrie, "Logos-Religion," 115–36; Luttikhuizen, *Gnostic Revisions*, 34–35. The distinction between philosophy and wisdom was common among many Stoic teachers (see, e.g., Seneca, *Ep.* 89.4–9). David Winston says that, when Philo defines philosophy as devotion to wisdom, he means that philosophy is identical with the revelation of the Torah, whose laws are in harmony with the natural law. Thus, Philo does not mean that philosophy is inferior to the law; the distinction is made rather between imperfect and perfect (= wisdom) modes of knowledge. As Philo writes in *Leg.* 1.22, "And what is more godlike … than reason, which once it is full grown and brought to perfection is rightly called wisdom."

12. See Wolfson, *Philo*, 2:7–11, 83–84, 92. Philo uses the term *shadow* in two ways. On the one hand, the Logos is God's shadow, but on the other hand the creation is the shadow of the Logos. Wolfson points out that Philo's terms related to the direct and indirect ways of knowing God evoke the vocabulary used by Plato in his "parable of the cave" (*Resp.* 514a–517a, 532b). Plato suggests that indirect knowledge rests on the shadows perceived by the senses. Direct knowledge is based instead on the vision of the Ideas when the mind ascends above the subterranean cave. Philo differs from Plato, however, in that he calls direct knowledge a prophecy, whereas, in Plato, it is ἀνάμνησις. Erwin Goodenough suggests that these two types of knowledge, philoso-

Actually, Philo stresses in *Praem*. 46 that the authentic investigation of the visible creation (Dyad) should be preceded by the vision of God through his Logos (Monad), that is, the intelligible light: "They then do but make a happy guess, who are at pains to discern the Uncreated, and Creator of all from His creation, and are on the same footing as those who try to trace the nature of the monad from the dyad, whereas observation of the dyad should begin with the monad which is the starting point. The seekers for truth are those who envisage God through God, light through light" (*Praem*. 46).[13] Although humans have a natural longing for God, the proactivity of God in gaining knowledge of the divine things is essential. Thus, the intuitive knowledge of God cannot be achieved solely on the grounds of human efforts, as Philo explains in *Abr*. 80: "And that is why it is said, not that the sage saw God, but that God was seen (Gen 12:7) by the sage; for it was impossible for anyone on his own to grasp the One who truly is, unless He revealed and showed Himself" (Birnbaum and Dillon). According to Philo, the fundamental step in the process of salvation is to confess one's nothingness and devote oneself to God. This involves the realization that it is God alone who acts and is the power underlying the mind's mental capacities. In *Somn*. 1.60, Philo presents Abraham as a model for intellectual modesty.

> Among these is Abraham who gained much progress and improvement towards the acquisition of the highest knowledge: for when most

---

phy and wisdom, reflect two kinds of mysteries, the lesser and the higher. The former represents the mystery of Aaron and is connected to the worship of God through the creation, represented in the cult of the temple. The latter represents the mystery of Moses, which was based on direct knowledge of God through God's Logos (see Goodenough, *By Light, Light*, 95–96). In *Congr*. 79–80, Philo's allegorical interpretation of Abraham's wives, Hagar represents knowledge gained through encyclical studies, whereas Sarah signifies knowledge based on wisdom—i.e., genuine philosophy— which gives honor to God. The offspring of Abraham's two unions represent the result of these modes of knowledge: Ishmael is a sophist, whereas Isaac is a God-born man who sees God. Philo explains, however, that Abraham must first be united with Hagar, i.e., encyclical studies, to purify himself from the passions of the flesh and errors of poor philosophy before he can be ready for union with Sarah, i.e., the wisdom of God. Just as encyclical studies are the handmaiden of philosophy, so is philosophy the handmaiden of wisdom.

13. Winston remarks that the phrase seeing "light by light" (φωτὶ φῶς) is the same as that used by Plotinus in *Enn*. 5.3.17.34–37; 5.10. Winston suggests that both Philo and Plotinus were dependent on Plato's sun image in *Resp*. 507c–509b (*Logos*, 43–44 n. 8).

he knew himself, then most did he despair of himself, in order that he might attain to an exact knowledge of Him Who in reality is. And this is nature's law: he who has thoroughly comprehended himself, thoroughly despairs of himself self, having as a step to this ascertained the nothingness in all respects of created being. And the human being who has despaired of himself is beginning to know Him that is. (*Somn.* 1.160)

For Philo, nothing would be more impious than to think that the virtues and the human cognitive capacities are our own achievements and gifts alone (see *Leg.* 1.45–52; *Sacr.* 56–58). Philo criticizes philosophers for regarding human faculties as their own property. Philo says that the ancient saying "Know thyself" refers instead to knowledge that the external senses and the human cognitive dispositions (senses, speech, memory, and reason) are gifts of God and guided by the Logos (see *Somn.* 1.52–60; *Her.* 105–110).

The nothingness of the soul is associated with its passivity and femininity. In *Abr.* 102, Philo regards the soul, which receives the seed of virtue, as feminine, because it is passive and "is put in motion by another and is instructed and benefited, and, in short, is altogether the patient, as its passive state is its own safety" (see also *Leg.* 2.38). Virtue, on the other hand, even though grammatically feminine, is masculine, because "it puts things in motion, and arranges them, and suggests good conceptions of noble actions and speeches." Philo says in *Cher.* 49 that, unlike a man, who makes a virgin a woman, the Father of All makes a woman, which denotes a soul polluted by passions, again a virgin by sowing the seed of wisdom into good soil.

After the confession of one's nothingness, devotion to God, and extirpation of the passions, the human mind can be engaged in intellectual prayer, a sort of analytical meditation on God's presence in the mind and all creation. In *Migr.* 184–195, Abraham's migration from Chaldea to Haran—the latter of which, according to Philo, means "holes"—is seen as an allegory for the soul's migration from the futile thoughts based on sense perceptions to meditation on one's inner self. Instead of meditating on the visible cosmos, one must meditate on one's sense organs and their function to understand that there is a mind within us that is distinct from the sense organs and that this mind rules and controls the sense perceptions, just as the divine Mind controls the whole creation without assimilating to it.[14] In this way, one learns to control the passions and

---

14. The etymological basis for Haran referring to "holes" is surprising. According to Philo, the term *holes* refers to the sense organs, which are in holes (eye sockets,

experience timeless union with the divine mind, which is full of passionless joy.

There are, however, only a few perfect human beings who have succeeded in their path to salvation already in their own lifetimes. Most of those who are striving to God are only making progress, just like Philo himself.[15] Philo thus notes the difference between human beings who are perfect and those still making progress toward perfection. The perfect humans have completely eliminated the fleshly passions, whereas those making progress are merely controlling them (see *Leg.* 3.140; *Somn.* 2.234).[16] In the end, after the soul has departed from the body, the human mind "becomes equal to angels" (ἴσος ἀγγέλοις γεγονώς), even though the perfect ones died spiritually to the body even before their physical deaths.[17] Philo claims, however, that not only the body but also the human soul can die if it loses contact with the Logos. It seems that the death of the soul is reserved, however, only for the most wretched type of soul, referred to as

---

nostrils, ears, mouth). Thus, bad emotions (e.g., fear, distress, desire, and delight) come from these holes, i.e., from the sense perceptions. Therefore, it is important to learn that there is a mind within us, whose task is to control the holes, converting bad emotions to good ones. Michael Cover notices important variations between Philo's Exposition of the Law and the Allegorical Commentary concerning the interpretation of Abraham's migration from Chaldea to Haran. In *Abr.* 72–76, the etymology of Haran signifies Abraham's migration from superstition to accurate sense perception. Philo aims to show that Abraham transforms himself from an astrologer to a self-reflecting sage (*Abr.* 77–84). In the Allegorical Commentary, the etymology of Haran is related to Abraham's departure from the city: "It will stay no longer in Haran, the organs of sense, but withdraw into itself" (*Migr.* 195). Thus, the allegory of Abraham's migration "becomes an allegory of the sage's need to quit the concerns of the body and attend to heavenly things." See Michael Cover, *Lifting the Veil: 2 Corinthians 3:7–18 in Light of Jewish Homiletic and Commentary Traditions*, BZNW 210 (Berlin: de Gruyter, 2015), 121–24.

15. In *Her.* 275, Philo counts himself among those who are imperfect and victims both of war and slavery: "hard-won is our release from the terrors which menace us." For Philo's autobiographical comments, see Michael B. Cover, "Philo's 'Confessions': An Alexandrian Jew between Nothing and Something," *SPhiloA* 32 (2020): 113–36.

16. See Michael L. Satlow, "Philo on Human Perfection," *JTS* 59 (2008): 504–6. On the distinction between perfect and progressive humans in Philo, see Winston, "Philo's Ethical Theory," 405–14.

17. Philo maintains in *Sacr.* 5: "So too, when Abraham left this mortal life, he is added to the people of God (Gen. 25:8), in that he inherited incorruption and became equal to the angels (ἴσος ἀγγέλοις γεγονώς), for angels—those unbodied and blessed souls—are the host and people of God."

the "tyrannical man" in Plato, *Resp.* 571b–d.[18] The all-wise Moses seems to be an exceptional case, whose vision outstripped the visions of all other sages of Israel. Moses is not only unified with the transcendental realm but divinized by ascending to God.[19]

The Christian Platonists of Alexandria continued the traditions of intellectual ethics attested in Philo's writings. For them, *gnosis*—that, is consciousness of one's divine origin—revealed by Christ was a perfect mode of wisdom, purged of errors of philosophers. The Valentinians maintained that the Father of All wanted to be known and loved through the Spirit of knowledge and the Spirit of love, though knowledge of his essence lay beyond all understanding (see *Exc.* 6–7). The Spirit of knowledge not only provides information about the divine realm but also has the power to transform the essence of the soul. Just as Sophia was re-formed through knowledge, consciousness of one's own origin makes the soul active, integrating it into one's higher self, that is, the archetypal angel and the *ecclesia* above. As a result, the soul is liberated from the irrational passions and becomes joyful, which is the greatest spiritual gift and makes the soul productive.

As noted in chapter 6, in Valentinian anthropology the highest part of the human soul is created as an image of the angelic *ecclesia* above. According to the Valentinian *ordo salutis*, salvation is a reunification of the soul with one's angel, which was a distinctively Valentinian idea in early Christian soteriology. Unification with an angel, which may take place already during one's lifetime, prepares the soul for the eschatological wedding feast and assimilation with the aeons of the Pleroma. The spiritual seed is potentially present in the soul, as it exists in the womb, and must be awakened and strengthened to ready it for the final unification with the Pleroma. Therefore, human beings exist in different phases in the process of salvation. As in Philo, there are those who have been perfect since birth,

---

18. See Philo's argumentation in *Leg.* 1.107–108. On Philo's conception of soul death, see Emma Wasserman, *The Death of the Soul in Romans 7*, WUNT 256 (Tübingen: Mohr Siebeck, 2008), 60–67; Wasserman, "The Death of the Soul in Romans 7: Revisiting Paul's Anthropology in Light of Hellenistic Moral Philosophy," *JBL* 126 (2007): 803–4. Wasserman argues that also Paul's reference in Rom 7 to the struggle of the inner man against bodily passions can be interpreted in light of the Platonic divided soul (see also 2 Cor 4:16).

19. See Winston, *Philo of Alexandria*, 34; Michael B. Cover, "The Sun and the Chariot: The *Republic* and the *Phaedrus* as Sources for Rival Platonic Paradigms of Psychic Vision in Philo's Biblical Commentaries," *SPhiloA* 26 (2014): 164–66.

those who have made themselves perfect during their lifetime, and those still making progress and waiting to be made perfect after their death. The material and irrational human beings will be destroyed with their physical death, together with their bodies, as, in the end, will the whole material world: "When these things have taken place in that manner, they teach that the fire which lies hidden in the world blaze forth and be aflame; and having destroyed all matter will itself all be consumed along with matter, and pass into nothingness" (*Haer.* 1.7.1).

7.2. The Embodiment of the Soul and the School for Controlling Passions

The myth of Sophia forms the intellectual basis for Valentinian ethics and soteriology, in which the healing of Sophia's emotion is paradigmatic for all humans. The cross and the resurrection of Jesus were interpreted as models for the separation of the soul from the material existence and its integration into the spiritual realm. The origin of the Valentinian myth of Sophia is uncertain. A similar myth was evidently taught in other gnostic schools. It is assumed that some Platonizing myth of Sophia preceded both the Valentinian myth of Sophia and that attested in, for instance, the Secret Book of John. While the author of the latter work links the four primary emotions (distress, delight, desire, and fear) to four primary demons, the Valentinian teachers mapped these emotions onto the myth of Sophia. Dunderberg points out, "What the Valentinians had to offer in the intellectual marketplace of their time was a distinctly Christian theory of how desire can be cured. For them, Christ was the healer who came to restore the emotions of the soul."[20]

In the Valentinian accounts, the emotions of Sophia prior to her healing of "ignorance" (ἄγνοια) are "distress" (λύπη), "fear" (φόβος), "perplexity" (ἀπορία), and "consternation" (ἔκπληξις/πλῆξις). The counteremotion to these bad emotions is remorse, which is related to Sophia's will to turn back (ἐπιστορφή) to Light (see *Exc.* 48.2–4; Irenaeus, *Haer.* 1.4.1–2, 1.5.4).[21] In addition, Sophia began to experience "joy" (χαρά) when the Savior visited her and healed her emotions through knowledge. As noted in chapter

---

20. Dunderberg, *Beyond Gnosticism*, 95; see also 110–11.
21. Unger translates ἐπιστορφή as "amendment." The term ἐπιστροφή became a key technical term in Neoplatonism, denoting that all things came into being from the One and have a desire to revert to that from which they proceeded (see, e.g., Proclus, *Elem.* 31–32; Simplicius, *In Arist. Phys.* 147.9).

6, the various emotions of Sophia are related to the corresponding parts of the soul of the first human being. Fear, distress, and perplexity belong to the hylic soul (i.e., the irrational soul) and body, and their counteremotion, repentance, to the psychic soul (i.e., the rational soul). Finally, joy is the essence of the spiritual part of the soul.

The Valentinian teachers were evidently influenced by Stoic theories of the emotions. There are, however, some notable differences when comparing with the main categories of emotions between the Stoic and Valentinian sources. Although the emotions of "fear" (φόβος) and "distress" (λύπη) are found in the Stoic fourfold category of emotions, two other main emotions, "desire" (ἐπιθυμία) and "delight" (ἡδονή), are not mentioned in the Valentinian sources. However, "joy" (χαρά), which Sophia felt after her enlightenment, is also one of the good emotions in the Stoic analysis of the emotions (see *Exc.* 45.1–2).[22] Sophia's bad emotions result from the erroneous opinion that the Father of All can be comprehended and that she is able to create like the Father. These bad emotions are corrected by right knowledge concerning the unknowability of the essence of the Father, which make Sophia a spiritual and joyful being. Therefore, the Valentinian theory of emotions comes rather close to Stoic theories and the ideal of apatheia, which is based on correct knowledge.

Philo's soteriology also has influences from the Stoic theories of emotions, though he interpreted them in light of transcendental ethics. Knowledge of the absolutely transcendent God and consciousness of his presence in the human mind through the Logos liberates one from unreliable knowledge and the errors of philosophy, which are based on the senses and discursive reasoning. Thus, the vision of one God and his presence in the world through the Logos and his powers is the true *oikeiosis*, that is, orientation to the external world.[23]

Philo was clearly concerned with anthropomorphic descriptions of God's emotions in the Bible. He argued that the anthropomorphic language was meant for the masses, who could not comprehend God otherwise. However, Philo did not hesitate to apply the emotion of joy to God, though a wise man's joy could never be the equal of God's pure emotion. Philo states that the angels, the stars, and the whole cosmos share a portion

---

22. On the fourfold division of the passions in Valentinian, Stoic, and Sethian sources, see Dunderberg, *Beyond Gnosticism*, 112.

23. For the influence of the Stoic theories on Philo, see Niehoff, *Philo of Alexandria*, 243–46.

of the divine joy, which is not mixed with sorrow or fear, whereas the joy of humans is always mixed with grief (see *Abr.* 200–207).[24]

For Philo, all irrational passions must be converted to "good emotions" (εὐπάθειαι). As noted, there is a difference between the perfect human being and those who are still making progress in controlling their emotions.[25] Those who have not yet reached perfection have not totally eradicated their passions but are merely controlling them. They behave in a moderate manner because of the commandments of the law. The perfect ones have transformed their passion into good states of mind without being prompted by any command to do so (see *Leg.* 3.140–145). Philo also differed from Stoics in that he saw the passions as not merely unhealthy mental states but God's punishments for the mind's idolatry. In *Conf.* 23–25, Philo states that the deluge (Gen 1:6) was a symbol of an outpouring of streams of each passion in order to destroy humankind, which was accustomed to wickedness.[26] However, Philo follows the Stoics in suggesting that the three "good emotions" (εὐπάθειαι) correspond to bad emotions, which are "the will," "caution" and "joy."[27] These notions are developed in *QG* 2.57, where Philo explains Gen 9:3 ("Every reptile that lives shall be to you for food"): "But as for the deeper meaning, the passions resemble unclean reptiles, while rational emotions clean. And answering to the passion of delight [ἡδονή], there is joy [χαρά] and happiness; answering to desire [ἐπιθυμία], there is will [βούλησις] and counsel; answering to distress [λύπη], there is compunction [δηγμός] and irritation; and answering to fear [φόβος], there is caution [εὐλάβεια]."[28] Philo draws

---

24. See Winston, *Philo of Alexandria*, 30; Winston, "Philo's Conception of the Divine Nature," 23–28.

25. According to Dillon, it is unclear whether Philo is teaching the Stoic extirpation of the passions (*apatheia*) or merely Aristotelian control of the passions (*metriopatheia*). Antiochus of Ascalon, for example, interprets the Stoic ideal of ἀπάθεια in light of the Peripatetic ideal of *metriopatheia*. If a certain passion is controlled by moderation, it is no longer an immoderate passion (see Dillon, *Middle Platonists*, 77–78; Baer, *Philo's Use of the Categories*, 89–93).

26. In describing Cain's punishment, Philo remarks that God increases Cain's torment by removing the pleasurable false opinions from the pleasures (see *Praem.* 71–72; Wasserman, *Death of the Soul*, 126–28).

27. For an analysis of the Stoic theory of emotions, see F. Harry Sandbach, *The Stoics* (Bristol: Bristol Press, 1989), 24–27.

28. Trans. Dillon, *Middle Platonists*, 151, with slight modifications from Winston's translation in *Philo of Alexandria*, 252.

a distinction between unclean passions and clean emotions. That is, for every unclean passion, a corresponding clean emotion exists. Philo differs, however, from the conventional Stoic theory in that he also postulates a corresponding emotion for distress. The Stoics were of the opinion that there could not be a reasonable form of distress. Philo maintains, however, that δηγμός—that is, regret—is a positive form of distress, because it bites the soul and presses it to seek a virtuous life. Thus, regret is a necessary emotion for those who are making progress, because it reminds us that the human being is not yet perfect. The perfect ones do not experience sorrow or regret because they are free from any form of distress.

It is noteworthy that the Valentinian teachers also postulated a counteremotion for distress, fear, and perplexity, which is related to Sophia's "conversion" (ἐπιστροφή). In *Haer.* 1.4.1, this counteremotion is depicted not only as a mental "disposition" (διάθεσις) but as a strongly "passionate" (ἐμπαθῆ) state of mind. This good emotion appeared after Christ abandoned Sophia and she was prevented from following him by the Boundary. As noted, the emotion related to conversion is associated with the psychic soul, which is not yet perfect but is praying and seeking out the light.[29] Thus, the emotion caused by Sophia's will to turn back to light is not labeled a negative passion but a necessary condition for the vision of God and the healing of the bad emotions by the Savior. Thus, as in Philo, distress has a positive countermotion, that is, repentance, which is important in one's ethical progress, because it bites the soul and forces it to seek immortality. In *Exc.* 53.1, the fleshly passions are said to be like "tares" (ζιζάνιον) growing together with "the good seed" (τὸ χρηστὸν σπέρμα). One should not only control the passions but annihilate them, because they are the "seed of the Devil" (σπέρμα τοῦ διαβόλου), which should not be nourished but destroyed altogether and put to death.

The theory of the passions forms the background to Philo's allegory of the separation of the sexes in Gen 2:21–23. Philo does not interpret the separation biologically but allegorically, as a description of the division of

---

29. Prayer and repentance are also mentioned as a means to conversion in the Tripartite Tractate. The Logos repents that his presumptuous thought had produced evil powers. The Logos then turns away from evil and toward the good. He prays and remembers his brothers in the Pleroma, and these prayers produce a new order of psychic powers, who realize that something greater than themselves existed before them. The psychic powers and all they produce are made out of the good intention of the Logos, having the ability to seek what is glorious (*Tri. Trac.* 80.11–83.33).

7. Cain, Abel, Seth, and Israel in Allegorical Exegesis

male reason (i.e., the rational part of the soul) and female sense perceptions (i.e., the irrational part of the soul). Philo insists that a literal interpretation would be absurd and therefore that the allegorical interpretation is not only possible but obligatory. In *Leg.* 2.41, Philo interprets the phrase "filling the space with the flesh" in Gen 2:21 as denoting a process in which the soul of Adam becomes passionate. Philo maintains that "bone of my bones" means "power of my powers" (δύναμις ἐκ τῶν ἐμῶν δυνάμεων) because the bone is a symbol of strength and domination, and "flesh of my flesh" means "passions of my passions" (πάθος ἐκ τῶν ἐμῶν παθῶν) because all passions caused by the senses also affect the mind. A strikingly similar allegory is attested in *Exc.* 51.2: "'This is now bone of my bones,'—it hints at the divine soul which is hidden in the flesh, firm and hard to suffer [δυσπαθῆ] and very potent [δυνατωτέραν],—and 'flesh of my flesh'—the material soul which is the body of the divine soul [τὴν ὑλικὴν ψυχὴν σῶμα οὖσαν τῆς θείας ψυχῆς]" (my trans.).[30] In both accounts, bone is a symbol of power. In Philo, the bone is "power and strength" (δύναμις καὶ ἰσχύς), just as the bone is said to be "firm and very potent" (στερεὰν καὶ δυνατωτέραν) in the Valentinian account. Although flesh is not explicitly referred to as a symbol for passions, as in Philo (πάθος ἐκ τῶν ἐμῶν παθῶν), the bone is contrasted with the flesh as an essence that is *not* capable of suffering (δυσπαθῆ). In both accounts, the bone of Adam is understood allegorically, as a symbol for power and domination, as well as the flesh, as a symbol for the passions.

In *Leg.* 2.35–45, Philo makes a distinction between the existence of the irrational faculties of Adam's soul "according to habit" (καθ' ἕξιν) and those "according to actualization" (κατ' ἐνέργειαν). Before the separation of the sexes, the irrational faculty is only habitually part of the mind and is made active as the female part of the soul, that is, the sense perceptions, are separated out of Adam. The senses are not inherently good or bad but may become bad, should the rational mind lose control over them and pleasures become attached to them. In *Leg.* 2.49, Philo interprets God's speech to Adam in Gen 2:24 ("Therefore a man leaves his father and his mother and cleaves to his wife, and they become one flesh") as denoting the negative condition of human existence. When the mind (Adam) leaves

---

30. Brakke translates δυσπαθῆ as "susceptible to suffer." I think that both translations, "hard to suffer" and "susceptible to suffer," are correct. The psychic part of the soul is a mediator between flesh and spirit. However, human beings have capability to resist passions by turning back to the spiritual realm, i.e., light (see Brakke and Layton, *Gnostic Scriptures*, 518).

his father (God) and mother (Wisdom) and cleaves to his wife (sense perceptions), he will be dissolved into fleshly passions: "For the sake of sense-perception the Mind, when it has become her slave, abandons both God the Father of the universe, and God's excellence and wisdom, the Mother of all things, and cleaves to and becomes one with sense-perception and it resolves into sense-perception so that the two become one flesh and one experience" (*Leg.* 2.49). According to Philo, the separation of the mind from its divine origin is the cause of misery and mortality, because it causes the dissolution of the mind into the flesh. Freedom from passion is achieved again, when Eve, that is, sense perception, is brought back to the dominion of Adam, that is, the mind. Then, the mind is no longer divided and corrupted by the passions, but the mind regains control of the senses and will be integrated into its original unity (see *Leg.* 2.50). The themes of separation and unification in Gen 2:21–25 as a soteriological paradigm are attested in the Gospel of Philip.

> When Eve was in Adam, there was no death. When she was separated from him, death came. If <she> enters into him again and he embraces <her>, death will cease to be. [—] If the female had not separated from the male, the female and the male would not have died. The separation of male and female was the beginning of death. Christ came to heal the separation that was from the beginning and reunite the two, in order to give life to those who died through separation and unite them. A woman is united with her husband in the bridal chamber, and those united in the bridal chamber will not be separated again. That is why Eve became separated from Adam, because she had not united with him in the bridal chamber. (Gos. Phil. 68.22–26, 70.9–22)

It is notable, however, that the Gospel of Philip does not mention the allegory of Eve as a symbol for the sense perceptions or passions. In addition, the biblical lemma is Gen 2:22, whereas Philo uses Gen 2:24 in *Leg.* 2.49. Moreover, in Philo it is not the separation itself, as in the Gospel of Philip, but Adam's cleaving to his wife causing fleshly passions. In both cases, however, it is the woman who must be joined to her husband, which challenges God's order for unification in Gen 2:24.

The unification of the sexes is also handled in Gos. Phil. 65.1–26, which describes the activity of the unclean spirits. As long as the human soul is solitary, it can be polluted by the unclean spirits, which are male and female in form. But when they see husband and wife together, the unclean spirits are powerless. In Gos. Phil. 70, the unification is said to take place when the image is united with its angel in the mystical bridal chamber. It is unclear whether the bridal chamber mentioned in the Valentinian sources refers to a specific ritual such as baptism or anointing or a combination of them, or whether it only depicts the inner mental process through which the human being will be unified with his spiritual archetype. It seems, at any rate, that in the Gospel of Philip and related Eastern Valentinian sources, the woman is not a symbol of sense perception and passions, as in Philo and *Excerpta* C, but is taken to stand for the incarnated seed of Sophia, which is depicted as feminine.[31] Thus, the separation of Adam and Eve is understood in the Gospel of Philip protologically as the separation of the spiritual seed from their male counterpart in the intelligible realm before their incarnation. Salvation, then, only happens when the incarnated seed is reunited with her angelic counterpart in the bridal chamber.

7.3. The Division of Humankind in the Valentinian Myth and Philo

The threefold division of humankind into "spiritual" (πνευματικοί), "psychic" (ψυχικοί), and "material" (ὑλικοί) categories is one of the main features of Valentinian anthropology. Dunderberg points out, however, that the Valentinian sources do not present the threefold division of humankind consistently. In some cases, the Valentinian division of humankind is not based on the creation of humankind but ethnic and religious boundaries. According to the Tripartite Tractate, the hylics follow the vain thoughts of Greek and barbarian wisdom, the psychics obey the law of the Hebrews, and the spiritual ones possess perfect knowledge of the Father of All (see

---

31. In *Exc.* 2.1–2, the spiritual seed is described as leaven, which unites what seemed to have been divided, soul and flesh. The seed of Sophia is an effluence of the angelic power (ἀπόρροια τοῦ ἀγγελικοῦ) so that there would be no deficiency (ὑστέρημα) in the soul. In *Exc.* 21–22, the unification of the female seed (Eve) with its male counterpart (Adam) is not actualized in a conventional water baptism but in the proxy baptism for the dead described by Paul in 1 Cor 15:29. For an analysis of the passage in *Exc.* 21–22, see Thomassen, *Spiritual Seed*, 377–83. In the Tripartite Tractate, those who wish to achieve salvation must be trained, as in a school, to experience ignorance and its pains and taste the things that are evil. This would mean that the suffering caused by erroneous opinions is a necessary precondition for the reception of knowledge concerning the Father of All. Hence, the offspring of Sophia has to go through the same suffering as their mother to be saved (see Tri. Trac. 122.3–22; 125.24–127.25). See also 184 n. 37 above.

Tri. Trac. 118–119).³² This model of division is also attested in Heracleon, who says that the hylics denote the gentiles; the psychics, the Jews; and the pneumatics, worshipers of the Father in spirit and truth (Heracleon, frag. 21, on John 4:22). Moreover, Irenaeus maintains in *Haer.* 1.6.2, 4 that the psychic and spiritual categories represent the distinction between ordinary Christians and the Valentinians themselves.

It is commonly noticed that the anthropological division is already attested in Paul's First Letter to the Corinthians, which may have influenced the Valentinian doctrine. In 1 Cor 2:14–15, Paul draws a distinction between two levels of the members of the *ecclesia*. Psychics lack perfect understanding of divine things, whereas spiritual human beings recognize all things. It is notable that Paul does not divide the whole of humankind into the aforesaid soteriological classes. While the Valentinian anthropological division concerns the whole of humankind, including specific ethnic groups, the Pauline division concerns only the members of the *ecclesia*.

Pearson argues that Paul did not invent the names of the aforesaid categories by himself but adopted them from his opponents in Corinth. They, for their part, derived these terms from the Hellenistic Jewish exegesis of Gen 2:7, which distinguishes spirit and soul and consequently those who are living according to spirit, in contrast to those who live according to their lower soul. While these teachers in Corinth claimed that all humans possessed an immortal and spiritual element in them on the grounds of creation, Paul interprets Gen 2:7 eschatologically: Christ is the last Adam, whose resurrection is the only basis for possession of the life-giving spirit (1 Cor 15:44–47).³³

---

32. See Dunderberg, *Beyond Gnosticism*, 174–88.

33. Birger A. Pearson, *The Pneumatikos-Psychikos Terminology in First Corinthians: A Study in the Theology of the Corinthian Opponents of Paul and Its Relation to Gnosticism*, SBLDS 12 (Missoula, MT: Scholars Press, 1973), 10–11. The Teachings of Silvanus also contains a threefold division of humankind and the idea of the natural capability to live according to one's mind-spirit (92.10–94.29; see Pearson, *Gnosticism, Judaism, and Egyptian Christianity*, 165–82). Dunderberg argues that Paul was not necessarily dependent on the anthropological mythology of his opponents in Corinth. The distinction between psychic and spiritual members of *ecclesia* may reflect the common Greco-Roman philosophy that recognized the potential threat of the soul being assimilated with irrationality and the bodily impulses. The psychics are likewise in constant danger of being assimilated into the flesh, whereas the spiritual ones have fortified their psychic essence. They are no longer in need of preliminary teaching but

It seems that the Valentinian anthropology was closer to Paul's opponents in Corinth, having its basis in the Hellenistic Jewish allegorical tradition. In the Valentinian accounts, the division of humankind is developed on the grounds of an allegorical exegesis of Gen 1:26–27 and 2:7, which were linked to the myth of Sophia. The threefold essence of Adam's soul forms a typological model for the categories of humankind, as Irenaeus reports in *Haer.* 1.7.5: "these three natures [of Adam] are no longer found in one person, but constitute various kinds [of human beings]." Moreover, the three sons of Adam—Cain, Abel, and Seth—are taken as allegorical representations of the hylic (Gen 2:7), psychic (Gen 1:26), and spiritual (Gen 1:27) elements of the first human being and accordingly the categories of humankind.

It is noteworthy that Irenaeus does not give any explanation as to how the three aspects of the first human being caused the threefold division of the whole of humanity. Irenaeus's strategy is rather to portray Valentinianism as a deterministic system, according to which the categories of humankind are fixed. However, *Exc.* 55.2–56.2 does offer an explanation to the division of humankind: Adam was not able mediate the spiritual and psychic essences to the following generations, but only the hylic soul and the material body:

> Therefore, Adam neither sows from the Spirit nor, therefore, from that which was breathed into him, for both are divine and both are emitted through him but not by him. But his material essence is active for seed and generation, because it is mixed with seed and unable to stand apart from this linkage during life. It is in this sense that our father Adam is "the first human being of the earth consisting of dust" (1 Cor 15:37). But if he had sown from psychic and spiritual as well as from material essence, then all would have become equal and righteous, and the teaching would have been in everyone. Therefore, many are material but not many are psychic, and few are spiritual. (my trans.)[34]

---

obey the law of Christ in the Spirit (see Dunderberg, "Paul and Valentinian Morality," 158–59).

34. Οὔτ' οὖν ἀπὸ τοῦ Πνεύματος οὔτ' οὖν ἀπὸ τοῦ ἐμφυσήματος σπείρει ὁ Ἀδάμ· θεῖα γὰρ ἄμφω, καὶ δι' αὐτοῦ μέν, οὐχ ὑπ' αὐτοῦ δέ, προβάλλεται ἄμφω· τὸ δὲ ὑλικὸν αὐτοῦ ἐνεργὸν εἰς σπέρμα καὶ γένεσιν, ὡς ἂν τῷ σπέρματι συγκεκραμένου καὶ ταύτης ἐν ζωῇ τῆς ἁρμονίας ἀποστῆναι μὴ δυνάμενος. Κατὰ τοῦτο, πατὴρ ἡμῶν ὁ Ἀδάμ, "ὁ πρῶτος δ' ἄνθρωπος ἐκ γῆς χοϊκός." Εἰ δὲ καὶ ἐκ ψυχικοῦ ἔσπειρεν καὶ ἐκ πνευματικοῦ, καθάπερ ἐξ ὑλικοῦ, πάντες ἂν ἴσοι καὶ δίκαιοι ἐγεγόνεισαν, καὶ ἐν πᾶσιν ἂν ἡ διδαχὴ ἦν. Διὰ τοῦτο πολλοὶ μὲν οἱ ὑλικοί, οὐ πολλοὶ δὲ οἱ ψυχικοί · σπάνιοι δὲ οἱ πνευματικοί.

As the psychic and spiritual essences are said to be mediated through Adam "but not by him" (δι' αὐτοῦ μέν, οὐχ ὑπ' αὐτοῦ), it would seem that beneath these Valentinian speculations lies a similar theory of the metaphysics of prepositions to that attested in Philo's discussion concerning the birth of Cain in Gen 4:1: "I have gotten a man by means of God." Philo argues that Adam is not the effective cause of Cain's birth but an instrumental cause only; God is the effective cause.[35] "Because God is a cause, not an instrument; and that which comes into being is brought into being through an instrument, but by a cause. For to bring anything into being needs all these conjointly, the 'by which,' the 'from which,' the 'through which,' and the 'for which.' Now the 'by which' is the cause, the 'from which,' the matter, the 'through which,' the tool; and the 'for which,' is the object" (*Cher.* 125, modified).[36] In *Cher.* 128, Philo explains that an individual human being consisting of body and soul is collectively a single "tool" (ὄργανον) "through whom" (δι' ὦν) the energies of the soul are developed, in states of both tension and relaxation. It is God, however, who makes the "percussion" (πλῆξις) for the "potentialities of the body and soul" and "by whom" (ὑφ' οὗ) "all is put in motion" (πάντα κινεῖται).

The distribution of the natures of Adam in *Exc.* 55–56 can be comprehended in light of these notions. This would mean that, concerning the psychical and spiritual essences, Adam is only an "instrumental cause" (δι' αὐτοῦ), not an "effective cause" (ὑπ' αὐτοῦ). Only the hylic and irrational soul of Adam is capable of mixing with his semen and proceeding to later generations. Adam can only be an instrumental cause for the two higher parts of the soul, which are caused by God and activated through "teaching" (διδαχή).[37] Indeed, it is stated that, if Adam were sowing both

---

35. On the metaphysics of the prepositions in Middle Platonism, see 115 n. 53 above.

36. ὅτι ὁ θεὸς αἴτιον, οὐκ ὄργανον, τὸ δὲ γινόμενον δι' ὀργάνου μὲν ὑπὸ δὲ αἰτίου πάντως γίνεται. πρὸς γὰρ τὴν τινος γένεσιν πολλὰ δεῖ συνελθεῖν, τὸ ὑφ' οὗ, τὸ ἐξ οὗ, τὸ δι' οὗ, τὸ δι' ὅ· καὶ ἔστι τὸ μὲν ὑφ' οὗ τὸ αἴτιον, ἐξ οὗ δὲ ἡ ὕλη, δι' οὗ δὲ τὸ ἐργαλεῖον, δι' ὃ δὲ ἡ αἰτία.

37. This seems to be derived from Aristotle, who says that "a human begets a human" (ἄνθρωπος γὰρ ἄνθρωπον γεννᾷ), which means that all the mental capacities are mediated to the later generations through natural procreations (*Metaph.* 12.1070a35–1070b30). The form of the body, i.e., the soul, does not exist independently but is mediated through natural generation. In *Gen. an.* 736b27–29, Aristotle says that the mind is present already in the human semen, but only potentially: "For all three kinds of soul, not only the nutritive, must be possessed potentially before they are possessed in actuality" (Barnes). As noted in chapter 6, the higher capacities of the soul (reason

psychic and spiritual elements as he had sown the hylic soul, then "the teaching would be in all" (ἐν πᾶσιν ἂν ἡ διδαχὴ ἦν), which means that there would be no intellectual divisions among humankind and "all would have become equal and righteous."

In Valentinian soteriology, the activation of the spiritual soul parallels the phases of the salvation of Sophia. First, Sophia was given form by Christ, who bestows the promise of light and immortality on Sophia. Second, the Savior forms Sophia according to knowledge, through which she becomes spiritual and begins to procreate. As descendants of Adam, all humans are by nature born in a similar stage to Sophia outside the Pleroma and have the capability of activating their spiritual potentialities through *gnosis*, which contains "the promise of better things." The psychic soul includes the spiritual seed, as in a womb, and it longs for immortality, but it must be formed and activated by "perfect teaching" (*sermone perfecto*). It thus seems that all human beings begin their life in a psychic condition, with their spiritual intellect at a potential stage within their soul.[38] Therefore, the categories of humankind are not fixed according to one's nature but according to one's choices. The flexibility of these soteriological categories of humankind is mentioned in the following accounts:

> Thus, the spiritual kind is saved by nature, but the psychic, because it is self-determined, has an inclination toward faith and incorruptibility, as well as toward unbelief and corruption according to its own choice; but the material kind perishes by nature.[39] (*Exc.* 56.3 [my trans.])

---

and the mind) must be activated through learning (*De an.* 430a). See Luttikhuizen, *Gnostic Revisions*, 40–41; John M. Rist, *The Mind of Aristotle: A Study in Philosophical Growth* (Toronto: University of Toronto Press, 1989), 180–81.

38. Thomassen suggests that, according to Heracleon, all humans were psychics before the advent of the Savior. Thus, human beings fell into three categories (hylic, psychic, and spiritual) since the advent of the Savior depending on how they responded to the gospel. Heracleon seems to reject the idea that those who acted in a material way did so according to their nature (φύσις). One is not material by nature but become so through one's behavior. As in the Tripartite Tractate, unhesitating recognition of the Savior is characteristic of the pneumatics only. The psychics hesitate, while the material ones reject the Savior completely (Tri. Trac. 118–119). Thomassen points out that it is possible that there may have been an inner-Valentinian debate concerning the status of human beings before the advent of the Savior ("Heracleon," 182–83, 190–93).

39. Τὸ μὲν οὖν πνευματικὸν φύσει σῳζόμενον, τὸ δὲ ψυχικόν, αὐτεξούσιον ὄν ἐπιτηδειότητα ἔχει πρός τε πίστιν καὶ ἀφθαρσίαν καὶ πρὸς ἀπιστίαν καὶ φθοράν, κατὰ τὴν

There are, then, three kinds: the material—which they also call "left"—must of necessity, they say, perish, because it cannot receive any breath [πνοή] of incorruptibility. The psychic—which they also term "right"—stands midway between the spiritual and the material, and consequently passes to whichever side it is inclined. The spiritual was sent forth in order that, being linked with the psychic, it might be formed and educated in company with it.[40] (*Haer.* 1.6.1)

There are two opposite categories of human beings, the spiritual and the hylics, whose positions are defined according to their nature. The psychics belong to the middle category, having "self-determination" (αὐτεξούσιον) and "inclination" (ἐπιτηδειότης) for both faith and destruction. It is noteworthy that, although there are three categories of human beings, there are only two options for the choices. The soul can choose either salvation or destruction. There is no option to become a psychic, as the human soul is, at least in most cases, psychic by nature, because it has the capability of making a choice between two options.[41] Irenaeus maintains, however, that not all souls have an equal possibility for choosing and receiving the spiritual seed.[42] "Again, subdividing the souls, they say that some are good

---

οἰκείαν αἵρεσιν· τὸ δὲ ὑλικὸν φύσει ἀπόλλυται. Brakke translates, "Therefore, the spiritual (element) is saved by nature; the animate (element), because it is under its own power, has an inclination toward faith and incorruptibility and toward lack of faith and corruption, according to its own choice; but the material (element) is destroyed by nature" (see Brakke and Layton, *Gnostic Scriptures*, 520). It is not clear whether the text speaks about the essences of Adam or categories of human beings, which are both discussed in *Exc.* 55.1–2.

40. Trans. Thomassen, *Spiritual Seed*, 59; my modifications: Τριῶν οὖν ὄντων, τὸ μὲν ὑλικόν, ὃ καὶ ἀριστερὸν καλοῦσι, κατὰ ἀνάγκην ἀπόλλυσθαι λέγουσιν, ἅτε μηδεμίαν ἐπιδέξασθαι πνοὴν ἀφθαρσίας δυνάμενον· τὸ δὲ ψυχικόν, ὃ καὶ δεξιὸν προσαγορεύουσιν, ἅτε μέσον ὂν τοῦ τε πνευματικοῦ καὶ ὑλικοῦ, ἐκεῖσε χωρεῖν, ὅπου ἂν καὶ τὴν πρόσκλισιν ποιήσηται· τὸ δὲ πνευματικὸν ἐκπεπέμφθαι, ὅπως ἐνθάδε τῷ ψυχικῷ συζυγὲν μορφωθῇ, συμπαιδευθὲν αὐτῷ ἐν τῇ ἀναστροφῇ. Unger translates "elements" instead of "kinds" (*Against Heresies*, 36).

41. This double orientation of the soul is also mentioned in Hippolytus's account, in which the soul is the locus where the choices between demons and *logoi* are made. The *logoi* cannot exist in the soul where demons dwell. Therefore, the soul must make a decision between two options (see Hippolytus, *Haer.* 6.32.9; Dunderberg, "Valentinian Theories," 146–47; Dunderberg, *Beyond Gnosticism*, 140–41).

42. *Gos. Phil.* 64.22–31 also refers to those who have been baptized but have not received anything. It is likely that this refers to the same people mentioned in Irenaeus, *Haer.* 1.7.1, who are never able to receive the seed.

by nature and some evil by nature. The good are those that are capable of receiving the 'seed,' whereas those evil by nature never receive that 'seed'" (*Haer.* 1.7.5 [my trans.]).[43] Irenaeus asserts that good souls can receive the seed within the psychic soul, while the bad ones are never able to receive the seed. Therefore, the hylics, who are doomed according to their nature, consist of two kinds of human beings. This group comprises those who are not able to receive the seed and those who had once received the promise of salvation but lost the battle against their fleshly passions. It seems that the hylic nature has gradually taken a dominant position in humankind because the gift of spirituality was not taken advantage of by many.[44] Therefore, there are only a few spiritual human beings, though many had been called into life and immortality.

Although there are some hylics who are predestined to damnation, in most cases the hylics are simply failed psychics. In the end, they will be annihilated according to their nature because they have not succeeded in activating the spiritual potentialities within their soul. The spiritual ones are good psychics, who have made a choice for the better and succeeded in their process of regenerating of self. It cannot be excluded, however, that there are some exceptional human beings who, without having made any choice, have possessed the spiritual seed perfectly and the knowledge of the divine things since their birth. They parallel the supersages in the writings of Philo, such as Isaac or Moses. They are sent into the world to form a union with those who are making progress toward salvation and to teach them conversion. Paul the apostle may have been the same kind of supersage for the Valentinians as Moses was for Philo.[45]

In the Tripartite Tractate, we can find the same threefold category of humankind. It tells of how the material ("those on the left") and psychical ("those on the right") powers each contributed to the composition of the first human. In addition to a body and a soul, the first human received the spiritual seed from the Logos. Thus, the creation of Adam became a symbol for the three categories of human beings based on their spiritual status. The tripartite division of humankind is described in the Tripartite Tractate as follows:

---

43. Καὶ αὐτὰς μὲν τὰς ψυχικὰς [ψυχὰς] πάλιν ὑπομερίζοντες λέγουσιν, ἃς μὲν φύσει ἀγαθάς, ἃς δὲ φύσει πονηράς. Καὶ τὰς μὲν ἀγαθὰς ταύτας εἶναι τὰς δεκτικὰς τοῦ σπέρματος γινομένας· τὰς δὲ φύσει πονηρὰς μηδέποτε ἂν ἐπιδέξασθαι ἐκεῖνο τὸ σπέρμα.

44. See Dunderberg, *Beyond Gnosticism*, 139.

45. For the legend of Paul in the Valentinian tradition, see page 55.

> Now, humanity came to exist as three kinds with regard to essence—spiritual, psychical, and material—reproducing the pattern of the three kinds of disposition of the Word, from which sprung material, psychical, and spiritual beings. The essences of the three kinds can each be known from its fruit. They were nevertheless not known at first, but only when the Savior came to them, shedding light upon the saints and revealing what each one was. (Tri. Trac. 118.14–28)

In the Tripartite Tractate, the advent of the Savior uncovers the soteriological dispositions of humans, which reflect the precosmic division of the Logos. The material ones are doomed by nature to perdition, while the psychics have some kind of initial understanding and capability for progress. The spiritual humans only possess the spiritual seed and are predetermined to salvation, as "light from light, and spirit from spirit."[46] Although, in the Tripartite Tractate, the names for these categories parallel *Excerpta* C, the soteriological status of these groups differs especially concerning the psychics, who are prone to change not between material or spiritual categories but between good and evil "in accordance with their *determination*" (Tri. Trac. 119.16–24, emphasis added).[47] Thus, in the Tripartite Tractate, the capability of the psychics to change concerns moral progress within one's group, not change from one group to another. The task of the spiritual beings is to unite with psychics to help them grow. While, in *Haer.* 1.1–7 and *Excerpta* C, this union may lead to a change in one's essence (from psychic to pneumatic), this is not a possibility in the Tripartite Tractate, where the categories are said to be fixed.

It seems, then, that the Valentinian theologians did not directly adopt the division of humankind from Paul, who also divided the members of the *ecclesia* into psychic, pneumatic, and material categories. The basis for the anthropological division was not in Christ, as it is in Paul, but in the creation of Adam, whose essences reflect the precosmic fall and salvation of Sophia. This model is closer to the division of humankind and the allegory of the soul in Philo's writings, which may have gained popularity in Corinth through Alexandrian Jewish-Christian missionar-

---

46. See Linjamaa, *Ethics of the Tripartite Tractate* 164–70.

47. Paul Linjamaa points out that the Coptic term used in the Tripartite Tractate for the capacity of the psychics is ⲧⲱϣ, suggesting that the capacity is "determined, fixed, or bound," which is the opposite of "free power" (αὐτεξούσιον), the term used in *Excerpta* C (see Linjamaa, *Ethics of the Tripartite Tractate*, 163).

ies. Presumably, Paul's teaching in 1 Corinthians was a response to these Corinthian Platonists.

As noted earlier, Philo teaches that the creation of the human being in Gen 1:27 depicts the creation of the heavenly human being, who serves as an archetype of the human beings—or, more precisely, of human mind ruled by the Logos. At an individual level, the heavenly human being becomes the model of the perfect human who is not in need of instruction but is self-taught and self-instructed (*Leg.* 1.53–55, 92–95; 3.140–144). In *Her.* 56–57, Philo divides the human beings into the perfect ones and those who live by the pleasures of the flesh.

> For the Maker of all, he says, "breathed into his face the breath of life and he became a living soul"; just as we are also told that he was fashioned after the image of his Maker. So we have two kinds of humans [ὥστε διττὸν εἶδος ἀνθρώπων], one that of those who live by reason, the divine inbreathing, and the other of those who live by blood and the pleasure of the flesh. This last is a moulded clod of earth, the other is the faithful impress of the divine image. (*Her.* 56–57, modified)

In this passage, the two kinds of humans do not refer to the heavenly and earthly humans *but to two categories of earthly human beings*. The Creator's breathing the spirit into Adam's soul forms the basis for the division of humankind into those who live by the Spirit and those who obey the pleasures of the flesh. The former category refers to those whose mind imitates the divine mind—that is, the Logos—while the latter group consists of those who have lost their potentiality for a virtuous life. Philo elaborates on this distinction in *Post.* 78–79 by saying that those who live according to the Logos are divided into two subcategories, the perfect ones and those who are making progress toward perfection. Therefore, there are also in Philo three classes of human beings: material, progressing, and perfect groups of humans.

> Not without purpose have the differences between these cases been recorded in the lawgiver's pages. For to those who welcome training, who make progress, and improve [τοῖς μὲν γὰρ ἀσκηταῖς προκόπτουσι καὶ βελτιουμένοις], witness is borne of their deliberate choice of the good, that their very endeavour may not be left unrewarded. But the fitting lot of those who have been held worthy of a wisdom that needs no other teaching and no other learning [τοῖς δ' αὐτοδιδάκτου καὶ αὐτομαθοῦς σοφίας ἀξιωθεῖσιν] is, apart from any agency of their own, to accept from

God's hands Reason as their plighted spouse, and to receive Knowledge, which is partner in the life of the wise. But he that has been cast away from things human, the low and groveling Lamech, marries as his first wife Ada, which means "Witness." He has arranged the marriage for himself, for he fancies that the prime good for a man is the smooth movement and passage of the mind along the line of well-aimed projects, with nothing to hinder its working toward easy attainment. (*Post.* 78–79, modified)

Philo maintains that humankind is divided not into two but three categories. The first category of humans consists of those progressing toward virtue; the second, those who have reached perfection; and the third, those who have lost their intellectuality absolutely and are devoted to earthly things.

The tripartite division of humankind in the Valentinian accounts thus parallels the division in Philo. Although the idea of progress is not explicitly stated in the Valentinian source material described above, the psychic humans can be equated with this category. *Excerpta et Theodoto* 59.4–61.3 contains a description of the Savior's body, which is spun out of invisible psychic essence in the womb of his mother. The words of the Savior in John 11:25, 14:6, and 10:30, "It is I who am life," "It is I who am truth," "I and the Father are one," are taken to denote Savior's spiritual essence, while the saying in Luke 2:40, "the child grew [ηὔξανεν] and advanced [προέκοπτεν] greatly," is taken to describe the psychic nature, or the psychic Christ, which is supposed to grow and make progress.

In *Excerpta* C and *Haer.* 1.1–7, the psychics, those on the right, are in the middle of the material and the spiritual categories, and their status depends on their choice. The spiritual ones are saved according to their nature, meaning that they have transformed and stabilized their intellect according to the image of the angels. They are not in need of instruction or commandments because they obey the spirit spontaneously. The hylics, those on the left, have lost their capability for progress and salvation.[48] The categories of left and right are also mentioned in Philo's allegory of the visitation of the three men at Abraham's home (see *Abr.* 119–130). The terms *left* and *right* represent three different aspects of God: on the right

---

48. In the Tripartite Tractate, the categories left and right are related to the creation of the first human being, whose material and psychic parts of the soul are fashioned by the two ranks of powers—i.e., those on the left and those on the right (see Tri. Trac. 104.18–106.25).

is God's creative power, on the left his ruling power, and in the middle is God himself, or his Logos. Philo divides the humans according to these attributes of God. Those who see God on the right hope to win blessings, those who see God on the left worship him to obtain remission from punishment, and those who see God in the middle worship God for his own sake.[49] Philo explains that to the heaven-born mind, which has passed on beyond the dyad, that is, the world of sense perceptions, God appears as one in which God's powers are brought together.[50]

There are some striking similarities and differences between Philo and Valentinian accounts concerning the categories of left and right. Those who see God on the right, worshiping God in expectation of a reward, parallel the category of the psychics in the Valentinian anthropology. In Philo, the middle category, those who see God as he is and worship him out of love, parallels the pneumatics, who obey God spontaneously, without any external force or moral reward. However, those who see God on the left, worshiping him out of fear, are not doomed, like the left ones in the Valentinian accounts. It is of note that in Philo lemma in question is the visitation of the three men at Abraham's home in Gen 18. This biblical theme is absent in the Valentinian accounts, which derives these terms instead from the precosmic creative powers, without any biblical references explicitly given.[51] It seems that the categories of left and right do not have in Philo any independent metaphysical or protological connotations, as in the Valentinian accounts, but are derived from the text in question.[52]

Taking into account the similarities and dissimilarities between Philo and the Valentinian accounts handled above, it is plausible to think that

---

49. See Wolfson, *Philo*, 2:296–97.

50. Winston, "Philo's Ethical Theory," 374.

51. Although Philo suggests that God used helpers when creating the human being (*Opif.* 69) or his powers, referred to as ideas, in forming matter (see *Spec.* 1.329), there is no indication of the activity of malevolent or imperfect powers, as in Valentinian or other gnostic texts.

52. Philo also interpreted left and right ethically to be positions on either side of Aristotle's mean. Philo writes: "Courage is the mean between rashness and cowardice, economy between careless extravagance and illiberal parsimony, prudence between knavery and folly, and finally piety between superstition and impiety" (*Deus* 164). Comparing with the Valentinian categories of left and right, both of them are described by Philo negatively, whereas in the Valentinian anthropology the right is described positively. In Valentinian soteriology, there is no golden mean between left and right, but the spiritual option is something above them.

the Valentinian teachers derived the tripartite division of humankind from Hellenistic Jewish allegorical traditions, which they were able to find in Philo's allegorical commentaries. Although the names of the psychic and pneumatic categories of humankind may have been derived from Paul's writings, the allegorical pattern itself comes from an exegetical tradition similar to that of Philo. However, the anthropology of the Tripartite Tractate, with fixed categories of humankind, seems to be a later modification of the Valentinian anthropology, in which free choice is essential. As noted, the division of humankind is also related to the allegory of the descendants of Adam—Cain, Abel, and Seth—which is found both in Philo and in Valentinian sources, in *Haer.* 1.1–7 and *Excerpta C.*

7.4. Seth as a Symbol for the Virtuous Human

In his allegory of Cain, Abel, and Seth, Philo explains in *Sacr.* 1–3 that Cain and Abel represent two opposite attitudes toward God and the virtuous life, seeing them not as two distinct persons but as symbols of "opinions" (δόξαι) of the same soul. Philo might even see Cain and Abel as twins, like Jacob and Esau, whose combat with each other is used as an allegory for the combat between the rational and irrational impulses of the soul (see *Leg.* 3.88–89). In *Sacr.* 2–3, the battle between these qualities is denoted by the conflict between the self-loving Cain and the God-loving Abel. Although they are both brought forth from the same root—that is, as the offspring of Adam—they are enemies of each other and combat each other until one of them finally gains dominance:[53]

> It is a fact that there are two opposite and contending views of life, one which ascribes all things to the mind as our master, whether we are using our reason or our senses, in motion or at rest, and the other which follows God, whose handiwork it believes itself to be. The first of these views is figured by Cain who is called Possession, because he thinks he possesses all things, the other by Abel, whose name is "one who refers (all things) to God." Now both of these views or conceptions lie in the womb of the single soul. But when they are brought to the birth they

---

[53]. In Apoc. Mos. 1.1–3, Cain and Abel are seen as twins. In Gen. Rab. 22.3 it is remarked that Cain and Abel were born simultaneously. The phrase "and she again bore" implies an additional birth, not an additional pregnancy. See Albertus F. J. Klijn, *Seth in Jewish, Christian, and Gnostic Literature*, NovTSup 46 (Leiden: Brill, 1977), 6–7, 18–19.

must needs be separated, for enemies cannot live together for ever. Thus so long as the soul had not brought forth the God-loving principle in Abel, the self-loving principle in Cain made her his dwelling. But when she bore the principle which acknowledges the Cause, she abandoned that which looks to the mind with its fancied wisdom. (*Sacr.* 2–3)

Philo's etymological explanation for the name of Cain as "possession" (κτῆσις) indicates that Cain is a symbol for the self-loving human, being one who takes honor for himself. Abel's name, on the other hand, is taken to mean "referring to God" (ἀναφέρων ἐπὶ θεόν), which means that he gives honor to God for all his works. In *Sacr.* 45, Philo maintains that the professions of Cain and Abel also reflect the basic characteristics of these persons. Abel is a shepherd and Cain a tiller of the ground (see also QG 1.59). Allegorically, this means that Abel is the shepherd of the outward senses, while Cain devotes his attention to earthly and inanimate objects. In *Sacr.* 104, Philo explains that the impulses of irrational sense perceptions are equated with cattle, and it is the task of every wise human being to guide this herd to reach perfection. Thus, the battle between Cain and Abel denotes an ongoing spiritual conflict within the human soul. The murder of Abel by the self-loving Cain represents the demolition of the God-loving principle of the soul. The Abel-principle depicts the rational mind, which loses the battle against the fleshly passions at the moment it fails to recognize its nothingness and total dependence on God.

Whereas the figures of Cain and Abel in Philo's Allegorical Commentary are rather easily comprehended, Seth is a more shadowy figure. Philo explains the verse in Gen 4:25 as follows:

Let us consider what may be called the re-birth [παλιγγενεσίαν] of the murdered Abel. "Adam," it says, "knew Eve his wife, and she conceived and bore a son, and called his name Seth (saying): God hath raised up to me another seed in the place of Abel [σπέρμα ἕτερον ἀντὶ Ἄβελ], whom Cain slew." "Seth" means "watering" [ποτισμός]. As, then, the seeds and plants in the earth, when watered, grow and sprout and are prolific in producing fruit, but, if no water be poured on them, wither away, so the soul, as is evident, when it is fostered with a fresh sweet stream of wisdom shoots up and improves. Watering is either the act of one watering, or the experience of one being watered. Would not everyone say that each of the senses is watered from the mind as from a spring, and that it broadens and extends their powers as water does channels? For instance, nobody of sound sense would say that eyes see, but mind by means of eyes, nor that ears hear, but mind by their agency, nor that noses smell, but the ruling faculty by using them. (*Post.* 124–125; see also Philo, *Post.* 10, 170)[54]

In *Post.* 172–174, Philo ponders what Moses meant by saying that God had raised Eve "another seed" (σπέρμα ἕτερον). Philo defines this seed as one superseding all mortal seed, including the seed of Abel, being a sort of seed above. Abel's seed was connected to the mortal body and, after having quitted the mortal body, departed to the better existence in heaven (see also *Det.* 45–51). The seed of Seth is different, because it is the "seed of human virtue" (σπέρμα ἀνθρωπίνης ἀρετῆς), and "it will never quit the race of humankind" (οὐδέποτε τὸ ἀνθρώπων ἀπολείψει γένος). Thus, Seth represents a germ of virtue, which forms the basis for the growth of the righteous generations of Noah, Abraham, and Moses. There is a sense of progression among these generations: Noah was more virtuous than Seth, and Abraham continued where Noah left off, but Moses, the seventh from Abraham, was the wisest among humans. He does not seek initiation but served "as a hierophant" (ὥσπερ ἱεροφάντης), having his abode in the inner sanctuary, the holy of holies (see *Post.* 173).

Albertus Klijn points out that Philo is probably the first Jewish author to mention Seth as a symbol for human virtue and an idea of the righteous human being.[55] In the Allegorical Commentary, Philo does not connect the figure of Seth with some historically known group or ethnically distinct race but is himself a symbol for all those who are striving for the

---

54. In *QG* 1.78, Philo gives a different explanation, saying that *Seth* means the "one who drinks water." The term παλιγγενεσία refers in Philo's theology to the regeneration or rebirth of the soul after death; carnal resurrection of the body does not play any role in Philo's soteriology. Regeneration is related to the migration of the soul toward immortality and, apart from some exceptional humans, such as Moses or Isaac, is a lifelong process, which will not be made perfect until the final separation of the soul and body in death. In *Cher.* 113–115, Philo maintains that after death the soul will be separated from the body, and we will proceed to our rebirth (παλιγγενεσίαν ὁρμήσομεν) among nonbodily beings. See Fred W. Burnett, "Philo on Immortality: A Thematic Study of Philo's Concept of παλιγγενεσία," *CBQ* 46 (1984): 447–70; also Wolfson, *Philo*, 1:405. Yli-Karjanmaa sees in *Cher.* 114 an explicit reference to the reincarnation of the imperfect soul. Yli-Karjanmaa argues that there is also in *Post.* 124 a metaphorical reference to reincarnation (ὥσπερ παλιγγενεσίαν), though "the possibility of Philo's meaning that Seth's soul had actually been Abel's would be also anomalous given that the later entity is inferior to the earlier one" (*Reincarnation*, 164).

55. Klijn, *Seth in Jewish, Christian, and Gnostic Literature*, 26–27.

7. Cain, Abel, Seth, and Israel in Allegorical Exegesis

virtuous life.[56] A similar kind of allegorical framework concerning Cain, Abel, and Seth is also found in *Exc.* 54.1–3 and *Haer.* 1.7.4.

> From Adam three natures are begotten: first, the irrational, which was Cain's, second, the rational and righteous, which was Abel's, third, the spiritual, which was Seth's. The human being consisting of dust is "according to the image," the psychic according to the "likeness" of god, and the spiritual is after its own. With reference to these three, apart from Adam's other children, it is said, "This is the book of the generation of human beings" (Gen 5:1). Because Seth is spiritual, he neither tends flocks nor tills the soil but produces children as fruit, as spiritual (beings). And him, who "hoped to call upon the name of the Lord" (Gen 4:26) who looked upwards and whose "citizenship is in heaven" (Phil 3:20)—for him the world does have room.[57] (*Exc.* 54.1–3 [my trans.])

---

56. In Sethian Gnosticism, Seth is seen as a historical progenitor of a distinct spiritual race. The Sethians are referred to by Irenaeus (*Haer.* 1.1.30) as Sethian-Ophites, by Pseudo-Tertullian (*Against All Heresies*) and Hippolytus (*Haer.* 6.20) as Sethians, and by Epiphanius (*Pan.* 39–40) as Sethians or Archontics. See Birger Pearson's article "The Figure of Seth in Gnostic Literature," in Pearson, *Gnosticism, Judaism and Egyptian Christianity*, 473–78; see also Klijn, *Seth in Jewish, Christian, and Gnostic Literature*, 90–107. In the gnostic sources, it is usual to think that Cain and Abel were born as the result of the defilement of Eve (see Nat. Rulers 91.11–92.2 and the longer recession of Ap. John 24.15–36). In these texts, Cain or both Cain and Abel are the offspring that results from the union of Eve and the archons. Pearson suggests that these speculations are based on earlier Jewish haggadic traditions, according to which Cain and Abel were the sons of the devil rather than of Adam. Pearson refers to Targum Ps.-Jonathan, which contains a tradition according to which Eve is made pregnant by Sammael, the angel of death ("Seth in Gnostic Literature," 478–79). Klijn refers to the stories in Genesis Rabbah and Pirqe Rabbi Eliezer, according to which Cain was not Adam's son and Adam did not have intercourse with Eve before he begat Seth. The speculation concerning Seth's presence during Adam's burial and his astrological knowledge in Life of Adam and Eve and Josephus (*A.J.* 1.60–65) are, according to Klijn, isolated stories that should be distinguished from aforesaid Jewish haggadic literature (*Seth in Jewish, Christian, and Gnostic Literature*, 6–10, 119).

57. Ἀπὸ δὲ τοῦ Ἀδὰμ τρεῖς φύσεις γεννῶνται, πρώτη μὲν ἡ ἄλογος, ἧς ἦν Κάϊν, δευτέρα δὲ ἡ λογικὴ καὶ ἡ δικαία, ἧς ἦν Ἄβελ· τρίτη δὲ ἡ πνευματική, ἧς ἦν Σήθ. Καὶ ὁ μὲν χοϊκός ἐστι "κατ᾽ εἰκόνα," ὁ δὲ ψυχικὸς "καθ᾽ ὁμοίωσιν" Θεοῦ· ὁ δὲ πνευματικὸς κατ᾽ ἰδίαν, ἐφ᾽ οἷς τρισίν, ἄνευ τῶν ἄλλων παίδων τοῦ Ἀδάμ, εἴρηται· "Αὕτη ἡ βίβλος γενέσεως ἀνθρώπων." Ὅτι δὲ πνευματικὸς ὁ Σήθ, οὔτε ποιμαίνει οὔτε γεωργεῖ, ἀλλὰ παῖδα καρποφορεῖ, ὡς τὰ πνευματικά· Καὶ τοῦτον, ὃς "ἤλπισεν ἐπικαλεῖσθαι τὸ Ὄνομα Κυρίου," ἄνω βλέποντα, οὗ "τὸ πολίτευμα ἐν οὐρανῷ," τοῦτον ὁ κόσμος οὐ χωρεῖ.

> They suppose that there are three classes of people—the spiritual, the psychic, and the earthly (i.e., the one consisting of dust)—as Cain, Abel, and Seth were; and from them derive the three natures [φύσεις] by considering them no longer as individuals [καθ' ἕν] but as a class [γένος]. The earthly goes into corruption; but the psychic, if he chooses the better things, will rest in the intermediate region [ἐν τῷ τῆς μεσότητος τόπῳ]; if, however, he chooses the worse things, he too will go to the realm of those like itself.[58] (Irenaeus, *Haer.* 1.7.5 [my trans.])

The allegory of Cain, Abel, and Seth is connected in these passages to the threefold division of humankind handled in the previous chapter. In *Exc.* 54.1, it is stated that, from Adam, "three natures" (τρεῖς φύσεις) are born, which form the "book of generations of human beings" (ἡ βίβλος γενέσεως ἀνθρώπων). The irrational nature is represented by Cain, the reasonable and just nature by Abel, and the spiritual nature by Seth. It is also stated that the irrational soul is created according to the image, whereas the psychic soul is created according to the likeness of God (Gen 1:26). The spiritual part of the soul represents Adam's true nature, which has been created according to the Savior's angels (1:27) and implanted secretly into Adam's earthly soul (2:7).

As in Philo, the descendants of Adam are also distinguished in *Exc.* 54.1 with regard to their professions: Cain tills the soil, and Abel tends to the flock, which refers to their irrational and rational natures. Notably, the profession of Seth is not mentioned. It is only mentioned that Seth was spiritual and therefore "neither tends the flock nor tills the soil but produces a child, as spiritual beings do" (οὔτε ποιμαίνει, οὔτε γεωργεῖ, ἀλλὰ παῖδα καρποφορεῖ, ὡς τὰ πνευματικά). Thus, Seth represents a perfect human being who does not work, unlike those who are still progressing (Abel) or who are attracted to fleshly things (Cain), but instead produces spiritual offspring.[59] Although Seth in the Valentinian interpretation parallels Philo's view on Seth as a symbol for the perfect

---

58. Ἀνθρώπων δὲ τρία γένη ὑφίστανται, πνευματικόν, χοϊκόν, ψυχικόν, καθὼς ἐγένοντο Κάϊν, Ἄβελ, Σήθ· καὶ ἐκ τούτων τὰς τρεῖς φύσεις, οὐκέτι καθ' ἕν, ἀλλὰ κατὰ γένος. Καὶ τὸ μὲν χοϊκὸν εἰς φθορὰν χωρεῖν· καὶ τὸ ψυχικόν, ἐὰν τὰ βελτίονα ἕληται, ἐν τῷ τῆς μεσότητος τόπῳ ἀναπαύ[σ]εσθαι· ἐὰν δὲ τὰ χείρω, χωρήσειν καὶ αὐτὸ πρὸς τὰ ὅμοια.

59. The verb καρποφορεῖν resembles the expression in Valentinus's psalm *Harvest*, discussed in chapter 6. Valentinus writes that the Spirit produces a harmonious soul, which is described as "begetting children and producing fruit from the depths" (ἐκ δὲ βυθοῦ καρποὺς φερομένους, ἐκ μήτρας δὲ βρέφος φερόμενον).

human being, the metaphor of his role is somewhat different. Seth does not water the lower parts of the soul, but he produces a child, imitating Sophia. In both cases, however, the metaphor for Seth's essence is related to natural growth and producing life. It reflects the ancient ideal of the perfect human being, one who obeys right reason intuitively, by nature, without command or instruction.[60]

While Seth represents perfection, Abel belongs to the middle category in Philo. He is not perfect but is rather struggling against the passions and making progress toward the virtuous life. In the Valentinian account, Abel is referred to as a psychic human who can reach salvation by choice. He is similar to those in Philo's teaching who are making progress by virtue of being on the boundary between two extremes. Philo describes them in *Somn.* 1.151 by saying they frequently go up and down, as on a ladder, whereas the wicked, that is, those who are similar to Cain, are destined for an eternal death, metaphorically referred to as Hades.

The Valentinian allegory of Cain, Abel, and Seth is thus closer to Philo's symbolic view than to the gnostic speculation of Seth's race. In the Valentinian accounts, Cain, Abel, and Seth are allegorical symbols for the categories of humankind, not progenitors of historical races. The seed of Seth in the Valentinian accounts parallels Philo's conception of it as "another seed" (σπέρμα ἕτερον) or the "seed of virtue" (σπέρμα ἀρετῆς), whose presence is expanded from Adam through Seth to the later generations, who have activated their spiritual potentialities.[61]

7.5. The Patriarchs and Israel

Philo maintains that all humans share the same spiritual goal, because "God has created no soul absolutely barren of good, even if the employment of

---

60. See Ismo Dunderberg, *Gnostic Morality Revisited*, WUNT 347 (Tübingen: Mohr Siebeck, 2015), 81–86.

61. It seems that, later on, the symbolic and the mythical merged together in the Valentinian and Sethian gnostic traditions. Hippolytus (*Haer.* 5.20), for instance, describes some gnostic groups developing the role of Seth in a more symbolic direction, functioning as a symbol of Light that is contrasted with Darkness (i.e., Cain) and the Intermediate Spirit (i.e., Abel; see Pearson, "Seth in the Gnostic Literature," 490–91). Although the illicit generation of Cain and Abel is absent in the accounts of Irenaeus and Clement, it is attested in Val. Exp. 38.22, according to which the devil begat Cain and Abel. See Guy G. Stroumsa, *Another Seed: Studies in Gnostic Mythology*, NHS 24 (Leiden: Brill, 1984), 33–34.

that good is beyond the reach of some people" (*Leg.* 1.34). However, only a few persons can reach perfection during their lifetime. It seems that for Philo the majority of people are those who are making laborious progress and will not be able to achieve perfection, until they have left behind their earthly life.[62] In Philo, the triad of the patriarchs, Abraham, Isaac, and Jacob, represents the common ancient pedagogical method through which one can reach the vision of God (see *Abr.* 52–55, *Praem.* 27–51).[63] In this pedagogical triad, Abraham represents "learning" (μάθησις); Isaac, virtue based on "nature" (φύσις); and Jacob, "practice" (ἄσκησις). Learning is related to "faith" (πίστις), because it is necessary that the learner believe the instructions of his teacher. Virtue by nature is followed by "joy" (χαρά), because it is a joyful thing to be dictated by intrinsic will without any command to do so. Practice is rewarded by "vision of God" (ὅρασις θεοῦ), because the active life of the youth is followed by the contemplative life of old age (see *Praem.* 47–51). Philo maintains, however, that these methods—nature, learning, and practice—are not three distinct means to the virtuous life, as some philosophers taught, but form a unified whole:

> However, one should not ignore the fact that, while each of them lays claim to all three capacities, each acquires its title from that capacity which is dominant within it; for it is not possible for instruction to be

---

62. While the patriarchs Abraham, Isaac, and Jacob serve as models for human perfection, the virtues of Moses supersede the capabilities of ordinary humans, going beyond what any Stoic sage could ever possess. See Winston, "Sage and Supersage," 815–24; Ian W. Scott, "Is Philo's Moses a Divine Man?," *SPhiloA* 14 (2002): 87–111. Thus, the difference between Moses and other human beings concerns not only the method through which the perfection was achieved but also its quality.

63. Birnbaum and Dillon, *On the Life of Abraham*, 189–91. The notion that three elements were necessary for the attainment of virtue goes back to Aristotle and was adopted in the Platonic tradition of Alexandria. In the *Pythagorica*, the triad is mentioned in the form *physis*, *ascesis*, and *eidesis* (see Dillon, *Middle Platonists*, 152). Wolfson points out that there was a disagreement between the Peripatetic and Stoic traditions of philosophical *paideia*, and Philo was actually closer to Peripatetic and Platonic tradition (*Philo* 2:196–99). Philo's allegories of the patriarchs parallel the Platonists' interpretation of the adventures of Odysseus as descriptions of the soul's journey to its true homeland in heaven. In *Quaest. conv.* 9.14.6, Plutarch's teacher M. Annius Ammonius interprets the encounter between Odysseus and the sirens, describing the music of the sirens as attracting the soul upward after its death. Tobin points out that this allegory is also attested in Numenius (frag. 33; see Tobin, *Creation of Man*, 150–51; Winston, *Logos*, 36–37).

brought to perfection without natural ability or practice, nor can nature rise to its proper limit without learning or practice, nor yet can practice, if it be not based on the foundations of nature and instruction. (*Abr.* 53 [Birnbaum and Dillon])

Philo seems to think that, unlike the first triad of Enos, Enoch, and Noah, the members of the higher triad, Abraham, Isaac, and Jacob, are on the same level of excellence. They drive toward one and the same goal and form one race of virtuous beings. In the Allegorical Commentary, however, Isaac has a special role in the pedagogical triad, being based on one's innate character and serving as the "root" (ῥίζα) for the other two methods: "There being, then, three methods by which virtue accrues, it is the first and third that are most intimately connected; for what comes by practice is the offspring and product of that which comes by learning; whereas that which comes by nature is, to be sure, of kin with them, being like a root [ῥίζα] at the bottom of all three" (*Somn.* 1.169). Michael Satlow argues that actually Isaac is not imitable, because he possesses perfection from his birth, being a precursor to Moses. Philo maintains that unlike Abraham's and Jacob's polygamous marriages, Isaac had a single wife, and his name was never changed (see *Congr.* 34–38).[64] This means that only the two other methods, the way of Abraham (i.e., learning) and the way of Jacob (i.e., practice), are open to ordinary humans. However, learning is the superior path, because it changes the ontological status of the human soul, whereas the way of Jacob (i.e., ascesis) leads to nonlinear progress. In *Mut.* 83, Philo notes that Jacob is occasionally called by his former name in the Bible, which means that Jacob's perfective character remains vague.

Despite the differences related to the method through which perfection of the soul is attained, all patriarchs represent the spiritual Israel referring to vision of God, though the name Israel is given first to Jacob. In *Abr.* 56–57, Philo says that Israel forms one royal, holy, and priestly nation. "It is called in the Hebrew tongue 'Israel,' which is interpreted 'seeing God'" (προσονομάζεται γὰρ Ἑβραίων γλώττῃ τὸ ἔθνος Ἰσραήλ, ὅπερ ἑρμηνευθέν ἐστιν "ὁρῶν θεόν"; see also Philo, *Migr.* 125).[65]

---

64. See Satlow, "Philo on Human Perfection," 508–11, 515–18. Satlow sees these two paths, philosophy and practice, as being exemplified in two ancient communities described by Philo: the Therapeutae followed Abraham's model in their contemplative life, whereas the Essenes followed that of Jacob.

65. The allegory of Israel is attested *Fug.* 208; *Conf.* 92, 146; *Her.* 78; *Mut.* 82–83;

Philo's allegory of the pedagogical triad is not mentioned in the Valentinian sources, but the allegory of Israel as the one who sees God is, in *Exc.* 56.4–5. The context of the allegory of Israel is the eschatological gathering of the psychics and pneumatics in light of Paul's metaphors of the olive tree in Rom 11:23–26 and the two covenants in Gal 4:21–31:

> Therefore, when the psychic (kinds) "are engrafted onto cultivated olive tree," that is, into faith and incorruptibility, and share in "the fatness of the olive tree," and when "the Gentiles come in," then "all Israel shall be saved in this way." Israel refers allegorically to the spiritual human being, the one who will see God, the lawful son of the faithful Abraham, the one who is "from free woman," not the one "according to the flesh" who is from the Egyptian slave. Therefore, there comes to be from the three classes the formation [μόρφωσις] of the spiritual, on the one hand, and the change [μετάθεσις] of the psychic from slavery into freedom, on the other. (my trans.)[66]

The allegory of Israel also appears in Clement's writings. Clement mentions it in *Paed.* 1.57.2 and *Strom.* 1.31.4.[67] It is noteworthy that the allegory of Israel in *Strom.* 1.31.4 is part of one of the four main passages where Clem-

---

Somn. 1.171; 2.173; *Praem.* 44; *Congr.* 51; *Abr.* 57; *Migr.* 125. It is notable that the faculty of seeing as a characteristic of the perfect human being is not always related to Jacob or the allegory of Israel. Philo compares knowing with seeing: God's voice is not heard but seen, referring to mystical illumination through the Logos. On the etymology of Philo's allegory of Israel, see Birnbaum and Dillon, *On the Life of Abraham*, 197–98.

66. "Ὅταν οὖν τὰ ψυχικὰ "ἐγκεντρισθῇ τῇ καλλιελαίῳ" εἰς πίστιν καὶ ἀφθαρσίαν, καὶ μετάσχῃ "τῆς πιότητος τῆς ἐλαίας," καὶ ὅταν "εἰσέλθῃ τὰ ἔθνη," τότε "οὕτω πᾶς Ἰσραὴλ [σωθήσεται]." Ἰσραὴλ δὲ ἀλληγορεῖται ὁ πνευματικός, ὁ ὀψόμενος τὸν Θεόν, ὁ τοῦ πιστοῦ Ἀβραὰμ υἱὸς γνήσιος ὁ "ἐκ τῆς ἐλευθέρας," οὐχ ὁ "κατὰ σάρκα," ὁ ἐκ τῆς δούλης τῆς Αἰγυπτίας. Γίνεται οὖν ἐκ τῶν γενῶν τῶν τριῶν τοῦ μὲν μόρφωσις τοῦ πνευματικοῦ, τοῦ δὲ μετάθεσις τοῦ ψυχικοῦ ἐκ δουλείας εἰς ἐλευθερίαν.

67. In *Paed.* 1.57.2, the allegory of Israel is drawn from an interpretation of Jacob's wrestling with an angel in the context of the naming of Jacob. It is noteworthy that the angel who wrestles with Jacob is, according to Clement, "God, the Logos, the teacher" (ὁ θεός, ὁ λόγος, ὁ παιδαγωγός). Philo calls the Logos an angel in *Mut.* 87, which is quite likely behind Clement's interpretation. In *Strom.* 1.31.4, the allegory of Israel is related to the discussion of the wives of the patriarchs and the change of Jacob's name. Van den Hoek suggests that the allegory in *Strom.* 1.31.4 is a combination of Philo's *Congr.* 51 and *Her.* 36, where Philo declares that Jacob is finally initiated into the "seeing race" (*Clement of Alexandria*, 181).

ent mentions Philo by name: ἑρμηνεύει δὲ ὁ Φίλων (1.31.1). Therefore, it is rather certain that Clement derives this allegory from Philo.[68] It is thus highly plausible to think that the Valentinian variant of the allegory in *Excerpta* C also goes back to Philo.[69] Notably, in *Exc.* 56.5, the allegory of Israel is related to Isaac, which is based on Paul's comparison of the two covenants in Gal 4:21–31. It is Isaac, not Jacob, who is a spiritual model for pneumatics, and he is contrasted with Ishmael, the son of Egyptian slave. A similar kind of comparison is attested in Philo's *De fuga et inventione*, where Philo compares Ishmael (hearing) and the freeborn and firstborn son, Isaac (sight):

> For so doing you shall give birth with easy travail to a male offspring, Ishmael by name, since thou shalt have been chastened by hearkening to words of God; for "Ishmael" means "hearkening to God." Hearing takes the second place, yielding the first to sight, and sight is the portion of Israel, the lawful son and first-born son [ὁ γνήσιος υἱὸς καὶ πρωτόγονος]; for "seeing God" is the translation of "Israel." It is possible to hear the false and take it for true, because hearing is deceptive, but sight, by which we discern what really is, is devoid of falseness. (*Fug.* 208, modified)[70]

Philo uses the description "a lawful son" or "a son born in wedlock" (γνήσιος υἱός) fourteen times in his corpus. In *Leg.* 2.94, Jacob's sons with

---

68. In addition to *Strom.* 1.31.1, Clement mentions Philo by name in *Strom.* 1.72.4, 153.2; 2.100.3.

69. The allegory of Israel as the firstborn who sees God also appears in the gnostic treatise On the Origin of the World (NHC II, 5). The allegory is linked there to the creation of a congregation of angels, a firstborn called Israel, and Jesus, before the creation of earthly human beings (see Orig. World 105.20–106.19). In this passage, Israel does not refer to the earthly human being, the legitimate son of Sarah and Abraham, but is merely seen as a divine being, together with the angels and Jesus. It is unlikely, then, that the author of On the Origin of the World would have been dependent on Philo, but he may have been familiar with the Valentinian teaching, where the allegory of Israel also appears. In addition, there are some other Valentinian motifs in On the Origin of the World, such as the tripartite division of humankind into spiritual, psychic, and earthly categories (Orig. World 121.27–123.2). See Birger Pearson, *Gnosticism and Christianity in Roman and Coptic Egypt* (New York: T&T Clark, 2004), 69.

70. οὕτως γὰρ πραϋτόκοις ὠδῖσιν ἄρρενα γενεὰν ἀποκυήσεις, ὄνομα Ἰσμαὴλ ἀκοαῖς θείαις σωφρονισθεῖσα· ἑρμηνεύεται γὰρ Ἰσμαὴλ ἀκοὴ θεοῦ. ἀκοὴ δ' ὁράσεως τὰ δευτερεῖα φέρεται, ὅρασιν δὲ ὁ γνήσιος υἱὸς καὶ πρωτόγονος Ἰσραὴλ κεκλήρωται· μεταληφθεὶς γάρ ἐστιν ὁρῶν θεόν. ἀκούειν μὲν γὰρ καὶ ψευδῶν ὡς ἀληθῶν ἔνεστιν, ὅτι ἀπατηλὸν ἀκοή, ἀψευδὲς δ' ὅρασις, ᾗ τὰ ὄντα ὄντως κατανοεῖται.

Leah are also called "lawful sons" and are contrasted with the sons of the concubines (see also *Deus* 121). Although Jacob himself was a lawful son, he was not the firstborn, because Esau, his twin brother, was the first. In most cases, the term "lawful son" refers to offspring born in a legal marriage and does not carry a distinctively spiritual meaning, as may be the case with Isaac, who is designated as a lawful son four times (*Abr.* 110, 132, 168, 254).[71] Namely, Philo writes in *Mut.* 137–140 that it was God who begat Isaac (see also *Leg.* 3.218–219). Philo explains that the name Isaac means "laughter," because God is the creator of joy and is Isaac's real father. "Therefore, O ye initiate, open your ears wide and take in holiest teachings. The 'laughter' is joy, and 'made' is equivalent to 'beget,' so that what is said is of this kind, the Lord begat Isaac; for He is Himself Father of the perfect nature, sowing and begetting happiness in men's souls" (*Leg.* 3.219). Isaac has thus a special status among the sons born in the legal marriages, because his origin goes back to the visitation of the angels to Abraham's home. The comparison to Ishmael in *Fug.* 208 may indicate that it is actually Isaac, Abraham's legal and firstborn son, who is also referred to as Israel. This comparison was also adopted by the Valentinian exegetes in *Exc.* 56.4–5. It is more likely, however, that Philo had Jacob/Israel in mind. Although Jacob was not biologically the firstborn of the twin brothers, Philo interprets Exod 4:22 ("Israel is my firstborn son") as indicating Jacob as a firstborn son: "Accordingly he calls Israel, though younger in age, his 'first-born' son in dignity (Exod 4:22), making it evident that he who sees God, the original Cause of being, is the recipient of honour, as earliest offspring of the Uncreated One, conceived by Virtue the object of the hatred of mortals, and as he to whom there is a law (Deut 21:17) that a double portion, the right of the first-born, should be given as being the eldest" (*Post.* 63).

---

71. The term "lawful son" also carries a spiritual meaning in Corpus Hermeticum. Seeking an explanation for regeneration, Tat says, "Do not refuse me, father; I am your true son [γνήσιος υἱός]; tell me fully the way of rebirth?" Trans. Clement Salaman, Dorine van Oyen, and William D. Wharton, *The Way of Hermes: New Translation of the Corpus Hermeticum* (Rochester: Inner Traditions, 2000), 13. The term γνήσιος υἱός appears once in Clement (*Quis div.* 9) as a designation for Christ. This might have been due to Clement's tendency to equate Isaac and Christ. It is noteworthy that Isaac is not called "lawful son" in the LXX or any other surviving Hellenistic Jewish material except in Philo.

It is possible to suggest, however, that the Valentinian teachers read Philo's allegory in *Fug.* 208 in light of Paul's allegory of two covenants in Galatians, where Isaac and Ishmael are contrasted. It is specifically the category of the psychics that is grafted onto the olive tree of Israel, who represents a spiritual human being who sees God. Therefore, the passage in *Exc.* 56.5 is the clearest evidence of the Valentinian teaching according to which the psychics are explicitly said to be changed into the pneumatics. The psychics, "who are born according to the flesh from the Egyptian slave," experience a "change" (μετάθεσις) from slavery to freedom. Thus, it is possible that the psychics can become the children of the free woman, sharing the same salvation as those who are spiritually lawful sons.

It is unclear, however, whether the Valentinian allegory of Israel speaks about the coming together of the two groups, that is, the psychics and pneumatics, or whether it describes the transformation of in individual soul. Dunderberg argues that the latter is more probable, maintaining that the transformation of the psychics into pneumatics "can be understood as a description of the ideal state of mind in which the soul has made the right choice—it has chosen the spirit instead of matter—and the spirit and the soul now reside together in perfect harmony."[72]

Dunderberg's interpretation means that becoming the children of the free woman represents the transformation of the self, not necessarily the unification of two groups of humans. The other interpretation, however, is also possible. In this case, the salvation of the psychics means grafting oneself onto those who are perfect. The idea of collective salvation is also attested in the Gospel of Philip: "In this world slaves serve the free. In heaven's kingdom the free will serve the slaves and the attendants of the bridal chamber will serve the wedding guests. The attendants of the bridal chamber have only one name, and that is rest. When they are together, they need no other form, [for they are in] contemplation ... perception. They are superior ... among those in ... the glories of glories" (Gos. Phil. 72.17–29). In this passage, the task of those who are free is said to be to serve and unite with those who are slaves. Although the categories of psychics and pneumatics are not explicitly mentioned in this passage, it fits well with the soteriological vision attested in *Exc.* 56.5. The salvation of the psychics is dependent on the union with the perfect ones, and vice versa. In *Haer.* 1.6.1, the pneumatics are the salt and the light of the world and are

---

72. Dunderberg, "Paul and Valentinian Morality," 166.

supposed to unite with the psychics. It seems, however, that the unification of the psychics and the pneumatics in Valentinian soteriology is a process that may already begin during one's earthly life but can only be made perfect in eschatological salvation.

7.6. The Immortality of the Soul and the Practice of Dying

In Valentinian soteriology, the ultimate telos of the immortal soul involves assimilation with the aeons of the Pleroma. Although some souls are not capable of receiving spiritual enlightenment, in most cases transformation of the soul is based on one's choices. There may be some exceptional human beings who are perfect from birth, such as Isaac or Moses in Philo's writings. These are supersages, whose intellectual capability supersedes the level of any other sages. For those who are progressing toward the virtuous life, perfection is related to combating and controlling one's bodily passions, which return the soul to its prenatal unity. In Philo, dying to the world and bodily passions is the sign of the wise human being, because it returns the soul to its original purity. The same idea is also attested in the fragment of Valentinus that is preserved by Clement of Alexandria in *Strom.* 4.89.1–3.

> And Valentinus writes in certain homily, word for word: "From the beginning you are immortal [ἀπ' ἀρχῆς ἀθάνατοί ἐστε], and children of eternal life, and you wished to divide death between you, that you might consume and destroy it, and death might die [ἀποθάνῃ ὁ θάνατος] in you and through you. For when you destroy the world and yourselves are not destroyed, then you will rule over the creation [κυριεύετε τῆς κτίσεως] and over all of corruption."[73]

---

[73]. Trans. Thomassen, *Spiritual Seed*, 460: Οὐαλεντῖνος δὲ ἔν τινι ὁμιλίᾳ κατὰ λέξιν γράφει· ἀπ' ἀρχῆς ἀθάνατοί ἐστε καὶ τέκνα ζωῆς ἐστε αἰωνίας καὶ τὸν θάνατον ἠθέλητε μερίσασθαι εἰς ἑαυτούς, ἵνα δαπανήσητε αὐτὸν καὶ ἀναλώσητε, καὶ ἀποθάνῃ ὁ θάνατος ἐν ὑμῖν καὶ δι' ὑμῶν. ὅταν γὰρ τὸν μὲν κόσμον λύητε, ὑμεῖς δὲ μὴ καταλύησθε, κυριεύετε τῆς κτίσεως καὶ τῆς φθορᾶς ἁπάσης. Clement continues the summary: "Now, like Basilides he supposes that there are people that by its very nature are saved; that this race, indeed, has come down to us for the destruction of death; and that the origination of death is the work of the creator of the world. Accordingly, he understands the scriptural passage (Exod 33:20): 'No one shall see that face of God and live' as though God were the cause of death" (see Brakke and Layton, *Gnostic Scriptures*, 297–98).

There have been attempts to interpret Valentinus's fragment in light of Pauline and Johannine views. The dying of death may refer to baptism.[74] In some cases, it has been seen as a criticism of martyrdom or the Christian Eucharist.[75] It is also possible to interpret Valentinus's fragment in connection with the Valentinian protological systems. Clement's comment, which follows Valentinus's quotation, may support that interpretation. The phrases "from the beginning" and "children" may refer to the beginning of the existence of the seed of Sophia and their descent into the realm of death, that is, the sense-perceptible world.[76]

The phrase "that death might die" (ἀποθάνῃ ὁ θάνατος) in Valentinus's fragment may be also an allusion to Gen 2:17, which contains God's warning to Adam and Eve not to eat from the tree of knowledge because they will "die by death" (θανάτῳ ἀποθανεῖσθε) on that day. It seems, however, that Valentinus introduced a new meaning to Gen 2:17: it is no longer death that will cause dying but death itself that is going to die. This kind of interpretation would parallel the theory of immortality in Philo, where physical death is distinguished from the death of the soul. This distinction is clarified in the following passage:

> And further, he says, "In the day that you eat of it, you shall die the death [θανάτῳ ἀποθανεῖσθε]." And yet after they have eaten, not merely do they not die, but they beget children and become authors of life to others. What, then, is to be said to this? That death is of two kinds, one that of the humans in general, the other that of the soul in particular. The death of the human being is the separation of the soul from the body, but the death of the soul is the decay of virtue and the bringing in of wickedness. (*Leg.* 1.105, modified)

Philo explains that there are two kinds of death: the death of the body and the death of the soul. The phrase θανάτῳ ἀποθανεῖν does not refer to the death of the body, which is natural death, but to the death of the soul, or spiritual death. Natural death waits for everybody, whereas death of the soul is punishment for the wicked only. This means that some humans

---

74. See Markschies, *Valentinus Gnosticus?*, 131–36.
75. On the martyrdom interpretation, see Jens Holzhausen, "Valentinus and Valentinians," in *Dictionary of Gnosis and Western Esotericism*, ed. Wouter J. Hanegraaf (Leiden: Brill, 2005), 2:1144–57. For a summary of different interpretations, see Dunderberg, *Beyond Gnosticism*, 35–37, esp. the notes on 217.
76. For the protological interpretation, see Thomassen, *Spriritual Seed*, 460–65.

may experience soul death even before their physical death (see also *QG* 1.16, 45, 51). According to Philo, natural death, which is the separation of the soul from the body, is ultimately a good thing for the virtuous soul and should be practiced through philosophical study. Those who have died to the life in the body have separated themselves from the body even before their physical death. They are kings and rulers of the bodily passions (see Philo, *Somn.* 2.241–244).[77]

For Philo, the contemplative life is one way of dying to the body and renouncing the bodily passions, which lead to wickedness. Emma Wasserman summarizes Philo's view as follows: "Wickedness is personified as a being that works together with passions to *entomb* the soul, because passions are the root cause of wickedness and vice."[78] Thus, virtuous souls must resist the passions of the body and practice dying to the life of the body through true philosophy to attain immortality. Philo writes in *De gigantibus*: "These last, then, are the souls of those who have given themselves to genuine philosophy, who from first to last study to die to the life in the body [ἐξ ἀρχῆς ἄχρι τέλους μελετῶσαι τὸν μετὰ σωμάτων ἀποθνῄσκειν βίον] that a higher existence immortal and incorporeal, in the presence of Him who is Himself immortal and uncreated, may be their portion" (*Gig.* 14). Philo is clearly dependent on Plato's *Phaedo* (64a; 67d), in which Socrates says, concerning the highest goal of life, that those who truly engage in philosophy "practice nothing but dying and being dead" (οὐδὲν ἄλλο αὐτοὶ ἐπιτηδεύουσιν ἢ ἀποθνῄσκειν τε καὶ τεθνάναι). For Plato, the aim of the "exercise" (μελέτημα) of the philosophers is "the liberation and the separation of the soul from the body" (λύσις καὶ χωρισμὸς ψυχῆς ἀπὸ σώματος). In *Det.* 34, Philo even says that virtuous men are despised and dishonorable and full of diseases, having to undergo these tribulations and even seek them out as a result of their "practicing of dying" (μελετῶντες ἀποθνῄσκειν).[79]

Valentinus's innovative interpretation of Gen 2:17 can be understood in light of Philo's teaching on spiritual death and the practice of dying. Human beings possess immortality by nature but must consume physical death so that "death will die" (ἀποθάνῃ ὁ θάνατος). Valentinus also stresses

---

77. Dunderberg, *Beyond Gnosticism*, 40–41.
78. Wasserman, *Death of the Soul*, 63, emphasis added.
79. Yli-Karjanmaa points out that Philo uses the expression "the practice of dying" both in the Platonic sense (*Gig.* 13–14) and with further developments (e.g., *Det.* 34; see Yli-Karjanmaa, *Reincarnation in Philo*, 122–23).

that his disciples should divide death between themselves to regain their original immortality. This parallels Philo's teaching that misfortune and even deadly diseases belong to the practice of dying.

In Valentinus's homily, gaining rule of one's entire life over corruption depicts the annihilation of the bodily passions.[80] As in Philo, kingship means self-control and ruling over the body and its pleasures as well as the senses and speech. In *Fug.* 113–114, Philo interprets the exhortation of the high priest not to enter a place where there is a dead body (Lev 21:11) as an exhortation to stay away from the passions and wickedness, which can pollute and destroy the soul. The purpose of the philosophical life is then assimilation with the Logos, that is, the cosmic Mind, meaning an "immortal" (ἄφθαρτος) and "bodiless" (ἀσώματος) existence alongside the unbegotten and incorruptible God (see *Gig.* 14). Thus, a wise human being begins the process of dying to bodily life already before his physical death.

According to Valentinus's teaching, attainment of immortality is based on recovering of the fundamental immortality of the human soul. This notion is similar to the teachings attested in the Gospel of Thomas, which supposes that the divine image was not lost in humankind but still persists (see Gos. Thom. 11, 85).[81] The phrase "from the beginning" (ἀπ' ἀρχῆς) may have a double meaning in Valentinus's fragment: it is a temporal expression ("since the beginning") but also refers to immortality as the principal condition of the soul at its present stage ("basically"). Thus, the potentiality

---

80. See Dunderberg, *Beyond Gnosticism*, 42–43.
81. See Dunderberg, *Beyond Gnosticism*, 44–45; Elaine Pagels, "Exegesis of Genesis 1 in the Gospel of Thomas and John," *JBL* 118 (1999): 477–96; Stevan Davies, "The Christology and Protology of *the Gospel of Thomas*," *JBL* 111 (1992): 663–82. The relationship between Philo of Alexandria and the Gospel of Thomas cannot be handled thoroughly in this study. It is rather likely that the Gospel of Thomas was written in the scholarly circles of Alexandria, which owed much to an intellectual heritage of Platonizing Judaism similar to that of Philo. The relationship between Plato and the Gospel of Thomas is discussed in Ivan Miroshnikov's *The Gospel of Thomas and Plato: A Study of the Impact on the "Fifth Gospel*," NHMS 93 (Leiden: Brill, 2018). Miroshnikov summarizes his conclusions as follows: "What seems clear, at any rate, is that the nineteen Platonizing sayings and, consequently, the Gospel of Thomas as a whole bear testimony to the fact that, during the nascent years of Christianity, certain individuals acknowledged *de facto* that the Platonist tradition possessed theoretical principles, concepts, and terminologies that could adequately describe and convincingly explain the nature of ultimate reality. These Christians recognized, though perhaps implicitly, the validity of the claim that Plato, at least to a certain degree, came to know the way things truly are" (259).

of salvation has been present since the creation of the first human being and is also inherited by later generations. This immortality requires, however, external *impetus* to become active, and only a few human beings have been able to acquire such spiritual gifts. Most human beings have lost their spirituality, as well as the battle against fleshly passions, which may have resulted from the degeneration of the essence of the soul, as Philo taught.[82] It is notable that Valentinus does not connect immortality to the crucifixion and resurrection of Jesus or baptism or any ritual practices of early Christianity. Immortality is instead a gift that has been implanted in the soul of Adam and his descendants, though it must be actualized through correct teaching. This view parallels *Haer.* 1.1–7 and *Excerpta* C, which likewise do not contain any etiology of the sacraments, only an etiology of the passions and how they can be healed through knowledge.[83]

7.7. The Eschatological Wedding Feast and Unification with the Angels

The Valentinian allegory of the spiritual Israel contains a vision of the unification of the psychics and pneumatics, which can be seen as a unification of the "perfect ones" (τέλειοι) and those who are "making progress" (προκόπτοντες) in the community of the believers. While the pneumatics have completed the transformation of the soul, the psychics are still making progress in their fight against the bodily passions. In *Haer.* 1.6.4, Irenaeus complains that Valentinians dismissed ordinary Christians as psychics "who possessed the grace on loan only." In reality, Valentinians did not evaluate psychics negatively, because the existence of the different groups was a part of soteriological dynamics. Unlike the psychics, who were still progressing on the spiritual path, the pneumatics possessed grace steadfastly. Thus, some had not yet made their calling firm, some had stagnated in their spiritual development, and some had lost their calling altogether. This division among the believers did not lead, however,

---

82. In *Opif.* 140–141, Philo maintains that the first human being was spiritually superior to the present race of humankind. Just as sculptures are inferior imitations of the original model or the degree of magnetic attraction weakens from iron to iron, so the human soul has lost its original power through the generations. Despite this degeneration, the soul contains a fragment of the divine intellect, which is potentially present and can still be revivified, so long as one begins to live a contemplative life and dies to bodily passions.

83. See Dunderberg, *Beyond Gnosticism*, 96–97.

to two separate communities but a mixed community, where spiritually immature humans could benefit from advanced ones.⁸⁴ As noted earlier, the allegory of Israel can be understood both as a description of individual mental transformation and as a collective event in which the pneumatics are united with the psychics. It is unclear, however, whether this unification takes place already in the present or finally in the eschatological fulfillment of salvation.

Philo discusses the afterlife in his Allegorical Commentary on the death of Abraham in *Her.* 280–283, evaluating popular opinions concerning the destiny of the soul after death. Philo tries to find a proper interpretation for the affirmation that Abraham was taken to his fathers. Philo rejects the literal interpretation of the fathers and enumerates three alternative explanations about the place to which Abraham departed. First, the destiny of Abraham's soul may have been the realm of the sun, the moon, and the stars. Second, the place may be the intelligible cosmos and the "commonwealth of incorporeal ideas" (ἀσωμάτων ἰδεῶν πολιτεία). Third, the fathers may refer to the elements of the world out of which the body and the soul are made (earth, water, air, fire, and ether). Philo concludes this discussion by ruling out the first and the third options, writing that the souls of the sages will be integrated into the intelligible cosmos from which the human intellect is a fragment. Also in *Gig.* 61, Philo writes that those who are born of God are also priests and prophets, and they have quitted the sense-perceptible world, perceiving the world that is perceptible only by the intellect. In the end, they will settle themselves in the intelligible cosmos and are reckoned to be among the ideas.

In *QG* 3.11, Philo gives still another explanation: "the fathers" refers to the incorporeal substances and inhabitants of the divine world, that is, the angels. For Philo, the angels are "incorporeal souls [ἀσώματοι ψυχαί], pure intelligences in the likeness of the Monad" (*Spec.* 1.66; see also *Conf.* 177).⁸⁵ The angels belong to the frontier of the intelligible realm, being mediators of the knowledge of the ideas. In *Somn.* 1.140–141, Philo

---

84. See Dunderberg, *Beyond Gnosticism*, 147–48, 156–58. The relationship between the perfect and the progressive ones in the Valentinian community is described in Interp. Know. 15–19.15: "Rather, by laboring with one another, they will work with one another, and if one of them suffers, they will suffer with him, and when each one is saved, they are saved together."

85. See Winston, *Logos*, 33–34. It is notable that in Philo the angels are not absolutely without bodies even though they are called bodiless souls. Although the angels

writes that the angels are divine intellects and "ministers of the Ruler of all" (ὕπαρχοι τοῦ πανηγεμόνος). Thus, their task is to "communicate" (διαγγέλλειν) the commands of the Father to humankind, from which, according to Philo, their name is derived.

The abode of the angels as the final destiny for the righteous souls is mentioned also in *Sacr.* 5–7, where Philo makes a distinction between λαός (Gen 25:9) and γένος (Gen 35:29). Philo says that Abraham and Jacob were both "added" (προστιθέναι) to the "people" (λαός) of God and "became equal to angels" (ἴσος ἀγγέλοις γεγονώς). Isaac, belonging to the self-taught race, was added to another company, "passing over" (μετανιστάναι) to the "immortal and most perfect *genus* of beings" (τὸ ἄφθαρτον καὶ τελεώτατον γένος).[86] Philo explains that the difference between people and genus represents the distinction between those who have advanced to perfection by learning or practice and those who have received knowledge effortlessly, such as Isaac. While there are many progressing people, striving to their heavenly archetype, there are only a few humans who can participate in the genus of human beings by nature. Although Philo says that that the lot of the latter group is happier, this does not necessarily refer to any difference in the final destiny of the soul, only the method through which the salvation of the soul is accomplished. As noted earlier, Isaac did not experience any transformation during his lifetime, because his soul had already been perfect from his birth.

Although Isaac, and possibly other sages as well, were integrated into the intelligible cosmos, there was still an ontological difference between their souls and the Logos. There was, however, one exception to all human beings able to "advance even above the species and genera" (ἀνωτέρω προαγαγὼν εἴδη καὶ γένη) of the patriarchs (see *Sacr.* 8). That was the all-wise Moses, who differed from every other human being, including the self-taught race of Isaac. The difference between Moses and his predecessors did not concern only the *method* through which he attained perfection but the *quality* of that attainment. While all other human beings are taken from their mortal bodily existence and added to the heavenly abode

---

lack an earthly body similar to that of humans, they have a body made out of the purest form of air, or ether.

86. This is a difficult passage, as Goodenough also notes: "I find it hard to take this passage seriously in its details" ("Philo on Immortality," 104 n. 73).

through physical death, Moses did not experience "subtraction or addition," like the other sages did (see Philo, *Sacr.* 8–10).[87]

For Philo, Moses was an exceptional human being, placed above the highest triad of sages, Abraham, Isaac, and Jacob. In *Gig.* 53–54, Philo argues that Moses was not only an "initiate" (μύστης), as other sages, but "a hierophant of the rituals and a teacher of the divine things" (ἱεροφάντης ὀργίων καὶ διδάσκαλος θείων). In *Mos.* 1.155–158, Philo describes Moses's ascent to Sinai as representing his vocation to become a priest and prophet. Moses was metamorphosed to be "named as god and king of the whole nation" (ὠνομάσθη γὰρ ὅλου τοῦ ἔθνους θεὸς καὶ βασιλεύς). The mind of Moses became like the Monad, and he not only came to rule over his bodily passions but also became coregnant and partner in the governance of God's creation. Thus, Moses can be seen as representing a Pythagorean "third type of being" (τρίτον γένος) between humanity and deity.[88]

Upon his death, Moses's body and soul were resolved, and he was converted into the mind, "pure as sunlight" (see *Mos.* 2.288; *Virt.* 76). Philo suggests that Moses could not die like the other sages because he had already separated from this body, which he left during death as a mere oyster shell. Commenting on Gen 5:24 in *QG* 1.86, Philo follows a widespread Jewish tradition in including Moses (see Deut 34:6) among those who, like Enoch and Elijah, did not die a normal bodily death but were simply "raptured" (ἁρπασθῆναι) to their heavenly abode before their physical death.[89]

Philo does not explicitly describe the destiny of imperfect but repentant souls. There have been some attempts to integrate Philo's soteriology with the Platonic transmigration of the soul. This would mean that imper-

---

87. See Satlow, "Philo on Human Perfection," 506–8. It is noteworthy that, in *Sacr.* 8, Philo speaks in plural of those who have advanced beyond "form and genus" to the same level as Moses. This would mean that Moses was not the only representative of his type of human being.

88. See Litwa, "Deification of Moses," 9–11; Goodenough, *By Light, Light*, 223–29.

89. See Wolfson, *Philo*, 1:403–4; Litwa, "Deification of Moses," 20–22. Philo presents the life and apotheosis of Moses in a way that parallels Alexandrian playwright Ezekiel's Ἐξαγωγή. Gregory Sterling argues that many verbal parallels, exegetical traditions, and thematic similarities demonstrate that it is likely that Philo knew Ezekiel's play or similar stories, which served as literary source material for Philo's own portrayal of the life of Moses. See Sterling, "From the Thick Marshes of the Nile to the Throne of God: Moses in Ezekiel the Tragedian and Philo of Alexandria," *SPhiloA* 26 (2014): 115–33.

fect souls must undergo further transmigrations to become pure before they can be added to the rank of embodied angels.[90] Taking into account the sparse and highly speculative allusions to the idea of reincarnation in Philo's vast corpus of writings, it is unlikely that this was an essential part of his soteriology. It may have been an option for further elaboration, but Philo's relative silence on the idea of metempsychosis in those passage where it could or should have been explicitly developed implies that it played a marginal role in his thinking.[91]

Philo presumes that the basic condition of the soul is one of immortality, though he clearly says that the soul may experience death as a punishment for wickedness, which is to be distinguished from bodily death. It seems, however, that soul death was only reserved for the worst of persons.[92] Commenting on Adam's expulsion from paradise in *Cher.* 2, Philo makes a distinction between "sent forth" and "cast forth." The former expression applied to the imperfect but repentant soul, whereas the latter

---

90. Winston suggests that Philo taught about not only the preexistence of the soul but also the reincarnation of the soul. On the one hand, the reincarnation of the soul is caused by the fact that most of the human souls do not lose their love of the body after their death, which causes their rebirth into a new body. On the other, he taught that the souls are "selected for return according to the numbers and periods determined by nature," an argument that is also found in Middle Platonic literature as a proof of the subsequent reincarnations of the soul (see Winston, *Logos*, 34–35, 41–42). More recently, Yli-Karjanmaa has challenged the scholarly consensus that reincarnation did not play a crucial role in Philo's thinking. Yli-Karjanmaa summarizes his argument as follows: "In my view, although Philo is quite silent, he *did want to communicate* to his audience also the view that souls transmigrate. His vagueness is not impenetrable. This enables us to conclude that while he in his surviving works did not want the references to reincarnation to be immediately understood by *anyone* (*Somn.* 1.139 is an exception) he did not want to hide his position so well that *nobody* can find it. Indeed, the history of Philonic scholarship on this issue bears testimony to precisely this: some scholars have found his references, others have not—or they have considered them isolated or anomalous. The question then becomes, can we better understand Philo's anthropology, ethics, soteriology and individual eschatology with or without reincarnation, and, if without, what is the more probable alternative. The reasons for Philo's reticence about explicitly speaking of reincarnation would merit a study of its own" (*Reincarnation in Philo*, 245–46, emphasis original).

91. For a detailed analysis of Yli-Karjanmaa's argument, see David Runia, "Is Philo Committed to the Doctrine of Reincarnation?," *SPhiloA* 31 (2019): 107–26.

92. See Wasserman, *Death of the Soul*, 65.

applied to the "unmanly soul," meaning that the soul assimilated with the flesh and pleasures.

> He who is sent forth [ὁ μὲν οὖν ἀποστελλόμενος] is not thereby prevented from returning. He who is cast forth by God [ὁ δ' ἐκβληθεὶς ὑπὸ θεοῦ] is subject to eternal banishment. For to him who is not as yet firmly in the grip of wickedness it is open to repent and return to the virtue from which he was driven, as an exile returns to his fatherland. But to him that is weighed down and enslaved by that fierce and incurable malady, the horrors of the future must needs be undying and eternal: he is thrust forth to the place of the impious, there to endure misery continuous and unrelieved. (*Cher.* 2; see also 78)

Although Philo suggests that perfection during one's lifetime is reserved only for some exceptional human beings, he does not claim that God punishes involuntary errors and imperfection, should a human being *be mostly* making progress in a virtuous life (see *Sobr.* 44–50; *Mut.* 181–185). As noted, Jacob's character remains unstable, and it is not clear whether he reached perfection during his lifetime; nevertheless, he was added to the realm of the angels after his death. In the allegory of Cain and Abel, Philo assumes that Abel was shifted into heaven after his death, even though it is clearly assumed that Abel was not a perfect human, because he had lost his innate battle against Cain's useless arguments. Joseph was also a dubious hero, because he lived a luxurious life Egypt, which was the symbol of a body from which the Israelites were liberated. However, the bones of Joseph, which represented his undefiled soul, were carried to the promised land. This means, according to Philo, that Joseph's spiritual mind returned to the divine source, but those parts that were devoted to the slavery of the body were buried in Egypt (*Migr.* 17–24).[93] On kindness even to the unworthy, Philo writes the following:

> And so the psalmist said somewhere "I will sing to you of mercy and judgment" (Ps 100:1). For if God should will to judge the race of mortals without mercy, His sentence will be one of condemnation, since there is no human who self-sustained has run the course of life from birth to death without stumbling, but in every case his footsteps have slipped through errors, some voluntary, some involuntary. So then that the race may subsist, though many of those that go to form it are swallowed up by the deep, He tempers His judgment with the mercy that He shows in doing kindness

---

93. See Goodenough, "Philo on Immortality," 98–100.

even to the unworthy. And not only does this mercy follow His judgment, but it also precedes it. For mercy with Him is older than justice, since He knows who is worthy of punishment, not only after judgment is given, but before it. (Deus. 75–76, modified; see also 104–108)

For Philo, with regard to the imperfect but repentant souls, the most likely explanation is that death was a necessary means to attain freedom from the fleshly impulses for those unable to reach perfection during their lifetime. In *Abr.* 230, Philo suggests that death is the end of everything in life and liberates people from their misfortunes and troubles, which lie in wait for the living. For wicked humans, however, death is only the beginning of suffering—that is, "a deathless and undying death" (see *Praem.* 69–70).[94] Unlike the imperfect humans, the perfect ones do not experience any transformation in their death because their souls have already been transformed during their lifetime. Finally, all these human beings, the perfect ones and those who are making progress, will return to the megalopolis from which they migrated into the body and will be integrated into the realm of ideas. It is not clear, however, whether Philo taught that human souls preserved their personalities after death. The most logical conclusion in light of Philo's discussion in *Sacr.* 1–5 is that the saved were finally made equal with each other and integrated into one "undying genera" (ἀθάνατα γένη).[95]

The aspects of the Valentinian soteriological system become comprehensible when it is compared to Philo's views described above. As in Philo, the fundamental goal of salvation of human beings is to be integrated into the noetic cosmos. In *Exc.* 61.4–8, the crucifixion and resurrection of Jesus describe allegorically the separation of his spiritual and psychic essences (elements of the soul), which forms the basis for the salvation of the pneumatics and the psychics.

---

94. In *Post.* 39, Philo speaks of the eternal death (ὁ ἀίδιος θάνατος) that awaits the wicked. For Philo, to die in wickedness was a horrible fate (see Goodenough, "Philo on Immortality," 87–89).

95. In *Opif.* 134–135, Philo uses the term γένος to refer to the idea of mind, which is "a kind of idea or genus or seal" (ἰδέα τις ἢ γένος ἢ σφραγίς). In *Post.* 43, the lovers of virtue are said to be translated after death into the "undying genera" (ἀθάνατα γένη), which may refer to the heavenly human being in a sense of the collective humankind. See also Samuel Sandmel, *Philo of Alexandria: An Introduction* (New York: Oxford University Press, 1979), 116–17. Sandmel suggests that in Philo, immortality of the soul is "natural destiny" of human beings, not a reward for virtue.

And when he says, "The son of man must be rejected, insulted, crucified," (Matt 8:31) he seems to be speaking of someone else, that is, of him who experiences passion. And he says, "On the third day I will go before you into Galilee" (Matt 26:32). For he goes before all [προάγει πάντα] and indicates that he will raise up the soul that is invisibly saved and will restore it to the place where he is now leading the way. He died at the departure of the Spirit, which had descended upon him at the Jordan, not by existing on its own, but it was withdrawn in order that death might operate, since how could the body have died when the life was present in him? For in that case death would have prevailed over the Savior himself, which is absurd. Instead, the death was outwitted through guile. For when the body died and death seized it, the Savior sent forth the ray of power that had come upon him, and it destroyed death and raised up the mortal body [τὸ θνητὸν σῶμα], having put off passions. In this way, therefore, the psychic kinds [τὰ ψυχικά] are raised and are saved, but the spiritual kinds who believe [πιστεύοντα δὲ τὰ πνευματικά] are saved in a manner surpassing the former [ὑπὲρ ἐκεῖνα σῴζεται], having received their souls as "wedding garments." (my trans.)[96]

The phrase τὰ πνευματικὰ ὑπὲρ ἐκεῖνα σῴζεται in the passage above is commonly interpreted as referring to a *superior* salvation for the pneumatics compared with the psychics. However, the context of the text refers to a chronological difference in the process of salvation between these groups instead of superior type of salvation reserved solely for the

---

96. Καὶ ὅταν λέγῃ «Δεῖ τὸν Υἱὸν τοῦ Ἀνθρώπου ἀποδοκιμασθῆναι, ὑβρισθῆναι, σταυρωθῆναι,» ὡς περὶ ἄλλου φαίνεται λέγων, δηλονότι τοῦ ἐμπαθοῦς. Καὶ· «Προάξω ὑμᾶς,» λέγει, «τῇ τρίτῃ τῶν ἡμερῶν εἰς τὴν Γαλιλαίαν.» αὐτὸς γὰρ προάγει πάντα· καὶ τὴν ἀφανῶς σῳζομένην ψυχὴν ἀναστήσειν ἠνίσσετο, καὶ ἀποκαταστήσειν οὗ νῦν προάγει. Ἀπέθανεν δὲ ἀποστάντος τοῦ καταβάντος ἐπ' αὐτῷ ἐπὶ τῷ Ἰορδάνῃ Πνεύματος, οὐκ ἰδίᾳ γενομένου, ἀλλὰ συσταλέντος, ἵνα καὶ ἐνεργήσῃ ὁ θάνατος, ἐπεὶ πῶς, τῆς Ζωῆς παρούσης ἐν αὐτῷ, ἀπέθανεν τὸ σῶμα; οὕτω γὰρ ἂν καὶ αὐτοῦ τοῦ Σωτῆρος ὁ θάνατος ἐκράτησεν ἄν, ὅπερ ἄτοπον. Δόλῳ δὲ ὁ θάνατος κατεστρατηγήθη· ἀποθανόντος γὰρ τοῦ σώματος καὶ κρατήσαντος αὐτὸ{ν} τοῦ θανάτου, ἀναστείλας τὴν ἐπελθοῦσαν ἀκτῖνα τῆς δυνάμεως, ὁ Σωτὴρ ἀπώλεσε μὲν τὸν θάνατον, τὸ δὲ θνητὸν σῶμα, ἀποβαλὼν πάθη, ἀνέστησεν. Τὰ ψυχικὰ μὲν οὖν οὕτως ἀνίσταται καὶ ἀνασῴζεται, πιστεύσαντα δὲ τὰ πνευματικὰ ὑπὲρ ἐκεῖνα σῴζεται, «ἐνδύματα γάμων» τὰς ψυχὰς λαβόντα. "Mortal body" evidently refers here to the Savior's visible and passionate body, which was spun out of psychic substance. Although the Savior's soul was prone to the passions, the Spirit that came down on him in the Jordan saved him from passions and united to the everlasting life. The effluences that flowed from his side during his crucifixion were mark of the soul that was purified from the passions and capable for salvation (see *Exc.* 61.3, 6).

spiritual humans. The resurrection of the Savior's body in the two phases forms an eschatological archetype for the salvation of the saints. As the spirit departs from the Savior on the cross and his psychic soul-body is resurrected *after* three days, the pneumatics enter into the Ogdoad *before* the psychics. Thus, *Exc.* 61.9 does not depict the supremacy of the pneumatics but describes their temporal priority in reaching the Ogdoad. The psychics, too, will join the common wedding feast in the Ogdoad, during the day of the Lord, before they enter the Pleroma together with the pneumatics. The final union of the psychics and pneumatics appears in the allegory of the wedding feast in *Exc.* 63.1–65.2:

> The repose of the spiritual ones is on the lord's day, that is, in the Ogdoad, which is called the lord's day, with the Mother, while they have their souls, the (wedding) garments, until the final consummation; but the other faithful souls are with the Demiurge, but at the final consummation they also go up in the Ogdoad. Next comes the marriage feast, common to all who are saved, until all become equal and know each other. Henceforth the spiritual (kinds) having put off their souls, together with the Mother who escorts the bridegroom, they also escort bridegrooms, their angels; they enter the bridal chamber through the Boundary and attain the vision of the Father—having become intellectual aeons—in the intellectual and eternal marriages of the syzygy. And the "master" of the feast, who is the "chief steward" of the marriage, "and friend of the bridegroom (John 2:9), standing outside the bridal chamber, hearing the voice of the bridegroom, rejoices greatly." This is the "fullness of his joy" and repose (John 3:29). (my trans.)[97]

It seems that, according to this particular passage, at the end salvation is given equally both to the spirituals and the psychics, that is, the other

---

97. Ἡ μὲν οὖν τῶν πνευματικῶν ἀνάπαυσις ἐν κυριακῇ, ἐν Ὀγδοάδι, ἣ Κυριακὴ ὀνομάζεται, παρὰ τῇ Μητρί, ἐχόντων τὰς ψυχάς, τὰ ἐνδύματα, ἄχρι συντελείας. αἱ δὲ ἄλλαι πισταὶ ψυχαί, παρὰ τῷ Δημιουργῷ περὶ δὲ τὴν συντέλειαν ἀναχωροῦσι καὶ αὗται εἰς Ὀγδόαδα. Εἶτα, τὸ δεῖπνον τῶν γάμων κοινὸν πάντων τῶν σωζομένων, ἄχρις ἂν ἀπισωθῇ πάντα καὶ ἄλληλα γνωρίσῃ. Τὸ δὲ ἐντεῦθεν, ἀποθέμενα τὰ πνευματικὰ τὰς ψυχάς, ἅμα τῇ Μητρὶ κομιζομένῃ τὸν Νυμφίον, κομιζόμενα καὶ αὐτὰ τοὺς νυμφίους, τοὺς Ἀγγέλους ἑαυτῶν, εἰς τὸν Νυμφῶνα ἐντὸς τοῦ Ὅρου εἰσίασι, καὶ πρὸς τὴν τοῦ Πατρὸς ὄψιν ἔρχονται, Αἰῶνες νοεροὶ γενόμενα, εἰς τοὺς νοεροὺς καὶ αἰωνίους γάμους τῆς συζυγίας. Ὁ δὲ τοῦ δείπνου μὲν «ἀρχιτρίκλινος,» τῶν γάμων δὲ παράνυμφος «τοῦ Νυμφίου δὲ Φίλος, ἑστὼς ἔμπροσθεν τοῦ νυμφῶνος, ἀκούων τῆς φωνῆς τοῦ Νυμφίου, χαρᾷ χαίρει.» Τοῦτο αὐτοῦ «τὸ Πλήρωμα τῆς χαρᾶς» καὶ τῆς ἀναπαύσεως.

faithful souls. Those who were progressing are finally perfected, and the distinction between psychic and spiritual humans ultimately disappears. The eschatological wedding feast represents the eschatological fulfillment of the transformation of the soul described in the allegory of Israel.[98] There is, in addition, a parallel version of the description of the eschatology in *Haer.* 1.7.1, which summarizes the account in *Excerpta* C:

> When, however, all the seed have attained perfection, they say that Achamoth, their Mother, will withdraw from the intermediate region and will enter the Pleroma and receive the Savior as her bridegroom, who was made out of all [the aeons], that the conjugal union between Savior and Sophia, that is, Achamoth, may take place. These are the bridegroom and the bride, but the bridal chamber is the entire Pleroma. The spiritual ones, moreover, having put off their souls and having become intellectual spirits, will enter the Pleroma without being seized or seen and will be given as brides to the angels who surrounded the Savior. The Demiurge himself will go into the region of the Mother, Sophia, that is, into the intermediate region. The souls of the righteous will likewise rest in this intermediate region. For nothing of psychic (kind) enters the Pleroma [Μηδὲν γὰρ ψυχικὸν ἐντὸς πληρώματος χωρεῖν]. (Unger, modified)[99]

In the last line, Irenaeus's rhetorical strategy is to prove that Valentinian teaching does not give the hope of an eternal reward for ordinary, psychic Christians. Elaine Pagels argues that Irenaeus intentionally changes the term τὰ πνευματικά, which appears in *Exc.* 63–65, into οἱ πνευματικοί to stress that salvation is for the spiritual persons only. However, it is not the righteous souls, that is, the psychics, as Irenaeus insisted, but the "psychic elements of the soul" (τὰ ψυχικά) that cannot enter the Ple-

---

98. See Dunderberg, *Beyond Gnosticism*, 139–40; Elaine Pagels, "Conflicting Versions of Valentinian Eschatology: Irenaeus' Treatise vs. the Excerpts from Theodotus," *HTR* 67 (1974): 35–53. James F. McCue defends the view that the hylic, psychic, and spiritual categories were fixed and that salvation was for the spiritual ones alone. He argues that the psychics, together with the Demiurge, received an inferior form of salvation than the spiritual ones. See McCue, "Conflicting Versions of Valentinianism? Irenaeus and the *Excerpta ex Theodoto*," in *The School of Valentinus*, vol. 1 of *Rediscovery of Gnosticism: Proceedings of the International Conference on Gnosticism at Yale New Haven, Connecticut, March 28–31, 1978*, ed. Bentley Layton (Leiden: Brill, 1980), 414–16.

99. Unger translates the last line, "For nothing of an ensouled nature enters Fullness."

roma. I do not see the change in terminology as decisive, even though the exclusion of the psychics from the Pleroma was evidently part of Irenaeus's rhetorical depiction.[100]

Although in its basic contours Irenaeus's version is compatible with Clement's longer account, Irenaeus excludes the psychics from the superior salvation. He locates them together with the Demiurge in the intermediate region below the Pleroma into which the spiritual humans only enter together with Sophia. It seems, however, that Clement has preserved a more original and detailed description concerning the Valentinian *ordo salutis*, according to which the final salvation of the psychics and pneumatics is accomplished eschatologically in two phases. In the first phase, the pneumatics, that is, those who have been made perfect already during their earthly life, will find rest in the Ogdoad together with Sophia. They keep their souls as wedding garments, which means that the psychic soul serves as an instrumental soul-body for the spiritual seed. These perfect beings are contrasted with the "other faithful souls," who stay in the realm of the Demiurge together with the psychic Christ until the day of the Lord (see *Exc.* 62.1–3). In the second phase, these psychics also ascend to the Ogdoad, where they are made equal with the pneumatics, who ascended before them. During this equalization of the saved, all are transformed into pneumatics, who will strip off their psychic souls—that is, the instrumental soul-body—and enter the Pleroma. Valentinian eschatology is thus rather optimistic concerning the fate of the psychics and ordinary Christians. The mission of the pneumatics is to form a union with the psychics, which is completed in the common marriage feast (see *Haer.* 1.6.1).[101] The Demiurge, however, is left outside the Pleroma, and his repose is to watch the heavenly marriage common to all who are saved.[102]

---

100. In most translations, the terms τὰ πνευματικά and τὰ ψυχικά are translated as "the spiritual elements" and "psychic elements." The context of these terms indicates that the neuter nominative plural can also be understood as a group designation, meaning in this case the group of spiritual and psychic beings, which is based on the element of the soul (hylic, psychic, or spiritual element), which is dominant in each person (see also McCue, "Conflicting Versions of Valentinianism?," 413). I disagree with McCue in that the dominant part of the soul is fixed in the Valentinian sources used by Clement and Irenaeus. The transformation of one's spiritual condition is possible because the majority of humans contains an innate inclination toward spiritual enlightenment, even though this potentiality is not developed by all of them.

101. See Pagels, "Conflicting Versions of Valentinianism?," 37.

102. Heracleon seems to think that good psychics such as the Demiurge will be

The terms used to describe the equalization of the saved in *Exc.* 63–65 indicate that the unification during the eschatological wedding feast parallels the protological equalization of the aeons after the rupture caused by Sophia's erroneous thought. It is stated in *Exc.* 63.2 that all the psychics and pneumatics "are made equal" (ἀπισωθῇ πάντα) until they come to know each other. Significantly, another verb from the same root is used in the account in *Haer.* 1.2.6, which describes how the Holy Spirit "taught the aeons to give thanks once they have all been made equal with another" (ἐξισωθέντας αὐτοὺς πάντας εὐχαριστεῖν ἐδίδαξεν). The Holy Spirit brings the aeons to "rest" (ἀνάπαυσις), and, after being made equal to each other, there are no more distinct aeons but all are Christs, Truths, Holy Spirits, and so on. In a similar manner, the equalization of the pneumatics and psychics in the eschatological marriage feast represents the process through which the boundaries between the psychic and pneumatic categories are finally removed, and all the saved are made equal with angels as they enter to Pleroma.

As noted above, Philo suggests that the aim of human beings is to become a nonbodily intellect similar to angels and integrated into realm of ideas. A similar kind of soteriological model can be observed in the Valentinian accounts. Thus, both Philo and Valentinians believed that the saved would become similar to angels and be integrated into the intelligible cosmos as some kind of collective personality, both those who made themselves perfect during their lifetime and those who only progressed. Although nuptial imagery was rather common in Christian and Jewish sources as a metaphor for the mystical union with God, *nuptial angelology* does not have an exact parallel in any other early Christian sources and is quite likely a Valentinian innovation.[103]

In Philo, there is no attestation of bridal imagery in the process of integration of the soul to the realm of ideas. Philo did, however, consider the

---

transformed into spiritual beings in the process of salvation (see Thomassen, "Heracleon," 190). In *Exc.* 63–65, the Demiurge is certainly said to be saved, but he is left outside the Pleroma, in the place where Sophia dwelled before entering the Pleroma. Unlike the descendants of Adam, the Demiurge does not possess a spiritual element within himself.

103. See Thomassen, *Spritual Seed*, 377–83, 405. The idea of unification with the angels is also attested in some apocalyptic Jewish literature. In 1 En. 39.4, the heavenly assembly of God is said to consist of a union of the saints with the angels. The idea of communion with the angels is also found in 1QS IX, 7–9 (see Thomassen, *Spiritual Seed*, 325–26).

marriages of the patriarchs as symbols of spiritual enlightenment and unification with the Wisdom of God. The marriage of Isaac with Rebecca was seen by Philo as a mystical marriage with Sophia. Rebecca comes to Isaac, dismounting from a camel, in a manner similar to how Wisdom comes to the mystic, veiled, like the inner secrets of the mystery (QG 4.140–146; see also *Exc.* 44.1–2). Thus, Wisdom is the spiritual wife of the sages. It is rather likely that Valentinian teachers combined the Hellenistic Jewish ideas of the mystical marriage with Wisdom and the union with Sophia's angels in the marriage of the Savior and the church, which is based on Pauline theology (Eph 5:22–33). It is evident, however, that the Valentinian soteriology cannot be understood solely on the basis of Middle Platonic philosophy or Christian tradition. Philo's soteriological speculations concerning the journey of the soul may be the missing link in the Valentinian soteriology investigated in this study.

7.8. Conclusions

The closest parallels between the Valentinian sources and Philo can be found in the anthropological and soteriological allegories, which I discussed in chapters 5–6. Valentinus taught that the gifts of salvation and immortality have been present since the beginning of humankind. However, these gifts must be activated through the practice of dying, meaning the annihilation of the passions through a philosophical way of life. Thus, Valentinus's teaching can be comprehended in light of Philo's interpretation of Gen 2:15–17, in which Philo distinguishes physical death from the death of the soul: for a wise human, physical death is the final liberation of the soul from the bondage of flesh and passions.

Both Philo and the Valentinians were dependent on the Platonic conception of salvation, that the ultimate telos of the human soul is to integrate oneself to the realm of the intelligible cosmos. Although Philo outlines different methods—learning, practice, and nature—to reach salvation, the goal is the same. After death, the righteous soul is integrated into the intelligible realm and becomes equal to the angels, being integrated into the realm of eternal Ideas. Accordingly, Valentinian salvation is depicted as a marriage with one's angelic archetype: after the eschatological wedding feast, the perfected offspring of Sophia enter the Pleroma among the aeons, which parallels Philo's realm of incorporeal Ideas.

In Valentinian soteriology, the precosmic salvation of Sophia and the healing of her emotions through knowledge was paradigmatic for the salvation of all human beings. The role of emotions was also essential in Philo, who was influenced by Stoic theories. Philo interprets the separation of the sexes in Gen 2:21–25 as denoting the conflict between rational mind (referred to as bone) and female passions (referred to as flesh). These bad emotions are healed when the separation is reversed, and mind takes control over the passionate soul. The allegory of Adam's bone and flesh in *Excerpta* C offers a similar understanding: the flesh of Adam is taken to represent the passionate soul, and the bone, the soul, which is free from suffering.

The tripartite division of humankind is one of the main features of Valentinian anthropology and goes back to Hellenistic Jewish models, which can be found in Philo's commentaries. In Philo's Allegorical Commentary, the heavenly human being (Gen 1:27) and the first human being (1:26; 2:7) no longer represent two distinct humans, heavenly and earthly, in a Platonic sense but two categories of earthly humans. The former is seen as a perfect human being, who obeys the law of God spontaneously, by means of the regenerated self, whereas the latter represent those who are making progress toward the virtuous life.

Valentinians integrated the aforesaid soteriological notions into the myth of Sophia's precosmic fall and salvation, which become paradigmatic for all humans. The spiritual (Gen 1:27), psychic (1:26), and hylic essences (2:7) of the first human being have their archetypes in Sophia's emotions: the psychics have their origin in Sophia's conversion and longing for light, whereas the material ones are related to matter and Sophia's irrational emotions. The spiritual humans, finally, have their origin in Sophia's joyful contemplation of the angels of the Savior. The Valentinians differed from Stoics but agreed with Philo that regret was a positive form of distress, because it was a necessary emotion for those who were making spiritual progress.

In *Excerpta* C, the division of humankind is said to result from Adam's incapability to mediate his spiritual essences to his children. This is illustrated through the metaphysics of prepositions, which is also used by Philo in his anthropological allegories. According to Valentinians, Adam could mediate only his irrational soul in an active stage, while the image of the higher self was distributed potentially within the psychic soul, to be activated through right teaching. Both Philo and the Valentinians maintain that, in most cases, salvation is the outcome of the laborious and progressive cultivation of the soul. There may be, however, some exceptional human beings, such as, for Philo, Isaac or Moses, who are perfect from birth and are saved by nature like the pneumatics in the Valentinian teachings.

It is not only the theoretical tripartite division of humankind that connects Valentinians to Philo but also the allegory of Cain, Abel, and Seth and the allegory of Israel, which are based on the division of humankind. In *Excerpta* C, Seth is not regarded as a historical progenitor of a certain race, as in the Sethian gnostic anthropology, but as a metaphor for a seed of virtue, as in Philo. Abel represents the psychics, who are in the middle, capable of making progress according to their free choice. Cain, on the other hand, in both Philo and the Valentinian sources, is the symbol of a delusional human being, whose soul will eventually be annihilated. It seems evident that the Valentinian teachers knew Philo's allegory of Israel in *Fug.* 206, in which Ishmael, the son of Egyptian slave, and the seeing race of Israel, the firstborn son, are compared. The Valentinians incorporated Philo's allegory of Israel into the allegory of the olive tree in Paul's letter to the Romans and the allegory of two covenants in Galatians.

8
The Valentinians and the Survival of Philo's Works: Summary and Conclusions

In this study I have investigated various parallels between the teachings of Philo of Alexandria and the Valentinians. In addition to some fragments of Valentinus, Ptolemy's *Letter to Flora*, passages in the Gospel of Philip, and the Tripartite Tractate, my analysis focused on the Valentinian source included in Clement's *Exc.* 43.2-65 (= *Excerpta* C), which goes back to the Valentinian tradition in Alexandria, elaborated by the disciples of Ptolemy in Rome (Irenaeus, *Haer.* 1.1-7). Taking into account the parallels and differences between these accounts, *Excerpta* C seems to attest an earlier version of the tradition than the one found in *Haer.* 1.1-7. This would make the teaching in *Excerpta* C the oldest-surviving exposition of the Valentinian myth. That the protological model system behind these accounts is based on the Valentinian commentary on the Gospel of John, independently described by Clement (*Exc.* 6-7) and Irenaeus (*Haer.* 1.8.5), confirms that the Valentinian school tradition in question was influential in both Alexandria and Rome.

8.1. Traditions of Exegesis in Philo and Valentinians

Valentinus and his disciples were known for their allegorical interpretation of the Bible, which I have argued they inherited from their Jewish forerunners. Philo and the Valentinians differed from the other Hellenistic philosophers in that the allegorical level of interpretation was not artificially added to the text because they assumed that the biblical texts were intentionally written allegorically in the first place. Therefore, the Scriptures had to be decoded through the allegorical method to gain philosophical information. The texts investigated in this study demonstrate that the Valentinian exegesis is multidimensional. The degree of allegorical symbolism depended on the intellectual level of the audience and the context of the texts, making Valentinian allegorical interpretation similar to Philo, who was also a proponent of multiple exegesis. Although Irenaeus tried to create the impression that the Valentinian teachers were giving arbitrary readings of the Scriptures, Valentinian exegesis in fact contained methodological rules for the use of the allegorical method.

Valentinus's fragments also contain some Philonic themes and ideas. His psalm *Harvest* (Hippolytus, *Haer.* 6.37.7) can be interpreted in light of Philo's allegories of the tabernacle and the high priest, in which the sympathy of the soul and the sympathy of the cosmos are intertwined. Also, Valentinus's theory of immortality (Clement, *Strom.* 4.89.1–3) can be interpreted in light of Philo's theory of immortality, in which a distinction is made between physical death and the death of the soul. Despite these rather general thematic parallels, we do not have evidence that Valentinus adopted these ideas directly from Philo. It is of note that Valentinus's use of the heavenly human being tradition (*Strom.* 2.36.2–4) lacks all the characteristics attested in Philo. In Valentinus's anthropology, the primal *anthrōpos* seems to be a real human being, not a conceptual model for humankind as in Philo.

The closest parallels with Philo's allegorical interpretations are found instead in *Excerpta* C (including *Exc.* 6–7) and related passages in Irenaeus, *Haer.* 1.1–8, which were produced in the circle of Valentinian teachers in Alexandria and the disciples of Ptolemy in Rome. These Valentinians considered John's prologue to be a Platonizing interpretation of Gen 1:1–5, but they modified its semantic and logical structure in a way that indicates that they were also familiar with some of Philo's protological innovations in *Opif.* 25–36, *Conf.* 146, and *Somn.* 1.75. It is also notable that in Philo the intelligible cosmos is already said to contain a conflict, between intelligible light, that is, the Logos, and its rival, the intelligible darkness. Although Philo did not associate the darkness explicitly with matter, as the Valentinians did, he did maintain that intelligible darkness must be controlled by the Boundary to sustain the harmony of the intelligible realm.

In *Excerpta* C, Sophia is associated with the biblical Wisdom, with manifold references to her being the rebellious heavenly being in the Pleroma, the mother of the visible world, and the nurturer of the human soul, which are related to the dyadic and monadic aspects of precosmic Wisdom. These associations are found in a nascent state in Philo's texts, which identify the Platonic Receptacle with the dyadic aspect of Wisdom (see *Ebr.* 31–32, 59–61). The Valentinian teachers and Philo (see *Her.* 133) were dependent on a similar theory concerning the separation of the cosmic matter into four cosmic elements by the Demiurge on the grounds of its physical characteristics, though the essences of the cosmic elements are linked in the Valentinian accounts to the emotions of Sophia. The Valentinians also knew an interpretation of Gen 1:3 as denoting the revelation of the idea of pure light, which parallels Philo's interpretation in *Opif.* 31.

There were, however, significant differences between protological teachings of Philo and Valentinians. In Philo, the creation of the intelligible world serves as an archetype for the creation of the visible cosmos, whereas in the Valentinian accounts the intelligible realm is not taken as an archetype for the visible cosmos; rather, the supreme God creates intelligible beings to be known and loved by them. The visible cosmos subsequently comes into being as a result of an error in the creation of the intelligible cosmos. While Philo regards Gen 1:1–5 in *De opificio mundi* as a description of the creation of the intelligible cosmos, the Valentinian theologians postulated a blatant counterargument, saying that the creation of heaven and earth in Gen 1:1 belonged to the world of becoming. It is not clear, at any rate, whether this criticism of Philo's view was directed at Philo himself or some other Platonic commentators of Genesis whose interpretations the Valentinian teachers explicitly rejected. Taking into account all these protological and cosmological parallels, it is reasonable to think that the interpretations of Valentinian teachers presuppose a framework of allegorical exegesis in which Philo's interpretations were alternately adopted, rejected, and reformed.

The closest parallels with Philo are found in the anthropological interpretations of Genesis, which form the basis for his discussion of soteriology and ethics. Philo and the Valentinians interpreted the creation narratives of Adam in the light of Middle Platonic anthropological theories, which were influenced by Aristotelian psychology. Valentinian teachers maintained that the irrational soul of human beings served as an instrumental soul-body for the rational soul. The intellect was a distinct element of the soul, which must be awakened through knowledge of one's divine origin in order to become active. These views provided an intellectual framework for interpreting Philo's anthropological allegories.

In *Fug.* 71–72, Philo makes an important distinction between Gen 1:27 and 1:26. The former is taken to describe the creation of the pure mind, and the latter to describe the creation of Adam's earthly mind, which was made by the assistants of God. In *Leg.* 1.31–32, Philo maintains that Gen 2:7 does not depict the body of Adam but earthlike mind, which is distinguished from the heavenly human being created as an image of the Logos. Thus, Gen 1:26 and 2:7 can be seen as complementary descriptions of the creation of Adam's soul, into which God breathes the fragment, or an impression, of the heavenly human being created in Gen 1:27 as an image of the Logos (see *Det.* 83).

The Valentinian teachers adopted these hermeneutical patterns and combined them with their own protological myth. As in Philo, Gen 1:26 and 2:7 are a harmonizing description of the creation of Adam's earthly soul by the Demiurge and his assistants, into which the image of the angelic archetype (Gen 1:27)—that is, the spiritual seed of Sophia—was breathed together with the psychic soul. These Valentinians also followed Philo in that Adam's physical and mortal body is not mentioned until he was clothed in the garments of skin. In the Valentinian account, however, Adam's bodily existence was not an outcome of his earthly degeneration, as in Philo, but resulted from the precosmic fall of Sophia. This mythological feature is lacking in Philo's anthropological allegories.

In the Valentinian protological myth, Gen 1:27 is taken to describe the creation of the images of the Savior's angels by Sophia, which is described as the "*ecclesia* above." The Savior's angels can be equated collectively with the heavenly human being in Philo's writings (see *Leg.* 1.31). They are paradigms of the intellect, and they did not incarnate, but their images did when they were breathed into the earthly soul of Adam. Thus, the Valentinians and Philo can be located in the Platonic tradition, according to which the archetypal *nous* is undescended, and it is only the image of *nous* that incarnates into the soul. According to this model, salvation is seen as an awakening of the image of the heavenly *nous*. However, both Philo and the Valentinians thought that the soul could die, which was not only an existential experience but an ontological desolation. This is a deviation from purely Platonic anthropology.

The Valentinian soteriological allegories can be understood in light of Philo's ethical theory, according to which the heavenly human being, or the idea of the intellect, created in Gen 1:27 is an ethical idealization of the earthly soul (Gen 1:26; 2:7). The heavenly and earthly humans no longer represent two distinct humans in a Platonic sense but two categories of earthly souls. The former is seen as the perfect human, who has a clear vision of God and obeys the law of God spontaneously, whereas the latter represents the human being, who is still making progress toward the virtuous life. The Valentinians integrated these views into a myth of Sophia. The psychic essence of Adam (Gen 1:26) is related to those who are making progress, and it has its basis in Sophia's will to turn back to light, whereas Adam's spiritual essence (Gen 1:27) depicts the perfect humans and is based on the healing of Sophia's passions through correct knowledge.

The role of emotions is also essential in Philo, who was evidently influenced by Stoic theories. Philo interprets the separation of the sexes in Gen 2:21–25 as denoting the conflict between the male rational mind and the female passions, referred to allegorically as Adam's bone and flesh (*Leg.* 2.35–45). The same allegory is attested in *Excerpta* C: the flesh of Adam is taken to refer to the passionate soul, whereas the bone represents the soul, which has the capability to escape suffering. Unlike the Stoics, who were of the opinion that there could not be a reasonable form of distress, Philo maintains in *QG* 2.57 that regret or repentance is a positive form of distress, because it is a necessary emotion for those who are making spiritual progress. The Valentinian teachers also postulated a positive counteremotion for distress, which has its basis in Sophia's repentance.

The tripartite division of humankind into material, psychic, and spiritual types is one of the most striking features of the Valentinian anthropology. This division goes back to Hellenistic Jewish models, which can be found in Philo's commentaries (see *Post.* 78–79). In Philo, the tripartite division of the humankind forms the basis for his allegory of Cain, Abel, and Seth (*Sacr.* 2–3, 45, 104; *Post.* 124–125, 173–174). The Valentinian teachers evidently knew a similar kind of allegorical framework. In addition, *Excerpta* C also contains the allegory of Israel attested in Philo's *Fug.* 208, in which Ishmael, the son of an Egyptian slave, and the seeing race of Israel, the firstborn son, are compared. Evidently, the Valentinians revised these allegories in the light of the myth of Sophia and Pauline theology (the allegory of the olive tree in Paul's letter to the Romans and the allegory of two covenants in Galatians).

In *Excerpta* C, the division of humankind results from the fact that Adam could not distribute the essence of his soul equally to his descendants. While the body and the irrational soul are inherited through natural procreation, the image of the higher self is distributed in a potential stage within the psychic soul, to be activated on the grounds of learning and one's choices. This is illustrated on the grounds of prepositional metaphysics, which is also used by Philo in *Cher.* 128.

Although the Valentinians maintain that the cultivation of the soul is an outcome of a laborious process, it cannot be excluded that there are some exceptional human beings, such as Isaac or Moses for Philo, who have been perfect since their birth. In the end, all will be made equal—both the perfect ones and those who are making progress on their path to virtuous life—when the soul is transformed into an angel and enters to the Pleroma together with the Savior and his bride, Sophia. This parallels Philo's eschatological views that the sages are transformed to become equal to angels and integrated into the intelligible cosmos, of which the human intellect is a fragment (see *Her.* 280–283; *Sacr.* 5–7).

8.2. Valentinians as Heirs of Philo

Taking into account the quantity and variety of the parallels discussed in this study, it is reasonable to postulate that there was a historical relationship between Philo and the Valentinians. We can, however, make two important observations concerning the use of Philo's interpretations by the Valentinian theologians. First, the relationship was restricted to one group of Valentinians, whose teachings can be derived from the accounts in *Excerpta* C (including *Exc.* 6–7) and related sections in Irenaeus, *Haer.* 1.1–8. Although the teachings in *Excerpta* C go back to the Valentinian traditions in Alexandria, they were probably used and elaborated in Rome before Irenaeus got to know these teachings through the disciples of Ptolemy at the end of the second century. Second, the Valentinians were interested in different genres of Philo's works. The writings in the Exposition of the Law were written for a wider intellectual audience, whereas the Allegorical Commentary represents Philo's esoteric exegesis addressed to advanced students of the Mosaic law. It is of note that Ptolemy's moderate allegories in the *Letter to Flora* parallel Philo's writings in the Exposition of the Law, while the transcendental allegories of his disciples in *Excerpta* C and related texts in Irenaeus, *Haer.* 1.1–7, can be traced back to Philo's Allegorical Commentary.

It seems that the Valentinian teachers read their source material, both Jewish and Christian, selectively, trying to gather material for their own system of thought from various sources. This would explain the sporadic nature of their borrowings from Philo's corpus, which does not differ much from the borrowing technique of Clement of Alexandria in the *Stromateis*. Although in many cases the original meaning of Philo's text was changed in the light of the Valentinian myth of Sophia, its original biblical context was preserved in Valentinian exegesis, which makes the degree of dependence between Philo and these Valentinians more probable.

8. The Valentinians and the Survival of Philo's Works

It is not clear whether the Valentinian teachers were acquainted with Philo's allegories directly, by reading Philo's works, or indirectly, through notebooks or oral transmission. Although the use of notebooks as a part of intellectual *paideia* was a widely known method for the transmission of literary traditions, I suggest nevertheless that the first option is more probable. Irenaeus would have become acquainted with an elaborated version of *Excerpta* C through Ptolemy's disciples in Rome, which would have been among the source material for *Haer.* 1.1–8. This would mean that the traditions recorded in *Excerpta* C may have been written in Alexandria even before Irenaeus wrote his work (ca. 180 CE or possibly some years earlier). We do not have any information about the sources at that time, including any that might have contained borrowings from Philo's teachings to be used as source material for the Valentinians, except for the extant works of Philo. It was not until the beginning of the third century that Philo's works were deposited in the library of Caesarea, leading to their vast circulation and borrowings through the writings of ecclesiastical authors. Therefore, the most reasonable conclusion is that, during the latter half of the second century in Alexandria, some Valentinians would have participated in intellectual reading clubs, where Philo's works were analyzed, discussed, and copied.

The similarities between Philo and the Valentinian teachers not only raise the question of a historical relationship, but they may also serve as a lens through which the Valentinian tradition can be seen in a new light. This study reveals that the Valentinian teachers not only shared a common Middle Platonic worldview with Philo, but they also adopted some of his allegorical innovations, incorporating them into their own system. Philo's allegories were not chosen accidentally but provided valuable hermeneutical strategies that were useful in Valentinian allegorical exegesis. On the one hand, the Valentinians reshaped the allegories attested in Philo's writings in light of the myth of Sophia. On the other, the Valentinian exegetes reformed the preceding gnostic myth in light of teachings they found in Philo's writings. The Valentinian teachers downplayed the gnostic *mythopoiēsis* and motifs such as the denigration of the creator God and the radical rupture between the Ideal world and the visible world, which were dominant elements in the Sethian gnostic traditions.

8.3. Valentinians and the Survival of Philo's Corpus

Not only are the findings of this study important concerning the development and elaboration of gnostic traditions, but they may shed new light on the question of the preservation and circulation of Philo's writings. Runia proposes that it was Pantaenus, the head of the Catechetical School of Alexandria, who rescued Philo's writings from the ruins of the Jewish community of Alexandria and deposited them in the library of the Catechetical School. Clement of Alexandria would thus have had access to Philo's writings when he started his career as the head of the school.[1] However, this solution does not explain who acquired Philo's works before Pantaenus and how they were preserved for over one hundred years after Philo's death. It is possible that the writings of Philo were already the property of the Catechetical School of Alexandria before Pantaenus, who came to Alexandria in about 180 CE, possibly from Sicily.[2] This would mean that librarians and scribes of the Catechetical School of Alexandria would have saved and preserved the writings of Philo after the Jewish revolt in Egypt. The main problem with this thesis is that we do not have any reliable evidence that the Catechetical School of Alexandria was functioning before the time of Pantaenus. It is more likely that the school was founded at the end of the second century, though Eusebius tries to give the impression that the school of Alexandria had existed "from ancient custom."[3] There was not, therefore, any institutionalized ecclesiastical authority that would have been in charge of the preservation of Philo's library.

Considering the tensions between Jews and Greeks in Alexandria, it is unlikely that the corpus of Philo would have been deposited into the public library of Alexandria either. Rather, Philo would have had a library in his school, probably in his home, in which he kept his own works. After his death, Philo's writings would then have become a part of the private library of some of his students. That Philo's writings survived after the Jewish revolt (115–117 CE) in the hands of Christian teachers indicates

---

1. See Runia, *Philo in Early Christianity*, 22–23.

2. See Annewies van den Hoek, "The 'Catechetical' School of Early Christian Alexandria and Its Philonic Heritage," *HTR* 90 (1997): 79–85.

3. It would seem that the Catechetical School of Alexandria was founded at the same time that Demetrius was nominated bishop of Alexandria (see Griggs, *Early Egyptian Christianity*, 61, 66–67).

that some groups of early Christian intellectuals in Alexandria possessed them already before the revolt.[4]

The main source investigated in this study, *Excerpta* C, goes back to the late second-century Valentinian traditions in Alexandria, which was the most probable time and place for contact with Philo's writings. As noted, the parallels with Philo investigated in this study imply that some Valentinian teachers may have belonged to the circle of Alexandrian Christian Platonists who saw Philo's works as valuable and studied them before they became the property of the Alexandrian Catechetical School—that is, at the end of the second century. That Ptolemy and his disciples can be located in Rome opens up another interesting possibility for the transmission and use of Philo's works by Ptolemy and his disciples.

In *Hist. eccl.* 2.16-17, Eusebius reports that Philo's writings were so well admired that they were thought worthy of storage in the public libraries of Rome during the reign of Claudius. Although Eusebius's information is commonly regarded as uncertain, it is evident that there were some non-Jewish intellectuals in Rome who were interested in Judaism as a philosophical religion. Philo's stay in Rome in 38/39 CE may have provided him an opportunity to present the Jewish biblical tradition to a wider Roman audience. Josephus rather likely knew and used Philo's *De opificio mundi* and *De vita Mosis* and may well have also known *De virtutibus* and other treatises, which he would have obtained when living in Rome after the Jewish revolt at the end of the first century.[5] Thus, it is not unreasonable to think that some copies of Philo's works, especially those belonging to the Exposition of the Law, would have circulated among Roman academics in mid-second-century Rome. These works would have also been available to Ptolemy, whose moderate allegories of the Mosaic law in the *Letter to Flora* indicate a dependence on Philo's *De vita Mosis* but lack the speculative allegorizing of his disciples.

It possible, that Ptolemy could have known Philo's works and moderate allegories even before some Alexandrian Valentinians brought a

---

4. See Sterling, "School of Sacred Laws," 159-61, 163-64.

5. See Gregory Sterling, "'A Man of the Highest Repute': Did Josephus Know the Writings of Philo?," *SPhiloA* 25 (2013): 82-87; Sterling, "Philo of Alexandria," in *A Guide to Early Jewish Texts and Traditions in Christian Transmission*, ed. Alexander Kulik (Oxford: Oxford University Press, 2019), 309–11; see also Enzo Lucchesi, *L'usage de Philon dans l'oeuvre exégétique de Saint Ambroise: une '"Quellenforschung" relative aux commentaires d'Ambroise sur la Genèse*, ALGHJ 9 (Leiden: Brill, 1977), 7-24.

more transcendental system of thought and method of allegorizing, based on Philo's Allegorical Commentary, to their brethren in Rome. It is also possible that the Alexandrian Valentinians brought not only their biblical elaborations of the Valentinian myth to Roman soil but their source material as well—that is, copies of Philo's works—when they arrived in the city. Although these conclusions cannot be but speculative, they are drawn from the observation in this study that Philo's influence on the Valentinian exegesis may have come from various sources and through different groups of Valentinians with different exegetical interests. The focus of Ptolemy was on Philo's moderate interpretations in the Exposition of the Law, whereas some other Valentinians in Alexandria, that is, those who composed the teachings attested in *Excerpta* C, found Philo's transcendental allegories in the Allegorical Commentary more inspiring.

Bibliography

1. Sources, Texts, and Tools

Aristotle. *Aristotelis fragmenta selecta*. Edited by W. David Ross. Repr., Oxford: Clarendon, 1964.
———. *The Complete Works of Aristotle*. Edited by Jonathan Barnes. 2 vols. ROT. Princeton: Princeton University Press, 1984.
———. *On the Soul; Parva Naturalia; On Breath*. Translated by Walter S. Hett. LCL. London: Heinemann, 1957.
Baltussen, Han, Michael Atkinson, Michael Share, and Ian Mueller, trans. *Simplicius: On Aristotle Physics 1.5–9*. London: Bloomsbury Academic, 2012.
Birnbaum, Ellen, and John Dillon. *On the Life of Abraham: Introduction, Translation, and Commentary*. PACS 6. Leiden: Brill, 2021.
Borgen, Peder, Kåre Fuglseth, and Roald Skarsten, eds. *The Works of Philo: Greek Text with Morphology*. Bellingham, WA: Logos Library Systems, 2005.
Butterworth, George W., trans. *Origen: On First Principles*. Notre Dame, IN: Ave Maria, 2013.
Casey, Robert, ed. and trans. *The Excerpta ex Theodoto of Clement of Alexandria*. London: Christophers, 1934.
Colson, Francis H., and George H. Whitaker. *Philo in Ten Volumes (and Two Supplementary Volumes)*. 10 vols. and 2 supplements. LCL. Cambridge: Harvard University Press, 1959–1969.
Cornford, Francis. *Plato's Cosmology: The Timaeus of Plato*. Repr., Cambridge: Hackett, 1997.
Ferguson, John, trans. *Stromateis: Books 1–3*. FC 85. Washington, DC: Catholic University of America Press, 1991.
Geljon, Albert C., and David T. Runia. *On Planting: Introduction, Translation and Commentary*. PACS 5. Leiden: Brill, 2019.

Hippolytus. *Contre les heresies: Livre I*. Edited by Adelin Rousseau and Louis Doutreleau. Vol. 2. SC 264. Paris: Cerf, 1979.
Huby, Pamela, and Christopher C. W. Taylor, trans. *Simplicius: On Aristotle Physics 1.3–4*. London: Bloomsbury, 2011.
Layton, Bentley, and David Brakke, trans. *The Gnostic Scriptures*. 2nd ed. New Haven: Yale University Press, 2021.
Mansfeld, Jaap, and David Runia, eds. *Aëtiana V: An Edition of the Reconstructed Text of the Placita with a Commentary and a Collection of Related Texts*. 4 vols. PhA 153. Leiden: Brill, 2020.
Meyer, Marvin W., ed. *The Nag Hammadi Scriptures*. New York: HarperCollins, 2007.
Philo. *Opera quae supersunt*. Edited by Leopold Cohn and Paul Wendland. 6 vols. Berlin: de Gruyter, 1896–1915.
Plato. *Timaeus; Critias; Cleitophon; Menexenus; Epistles*. Translated by Robert G. Bury. LCL. Cambridge: Harvard University Press, 1929.
———. *Republic*. Edited by Thomas E. Page, Edward Capps, and William H. D. Rouse. Translated by Paul Shorey. Vol. 2. LCL. Cambridge: Harvard University Press, 1937–1942.
Rahlfs, Alfred, ed. *Septuaginta*. Stuttgart: Deutsche Bibelgeschellsaft, 2012.
Runia, David T. *On the Creation of the Cosmos according to Moses: Introduction, Translation and Commentary*. PACS 1. Leiden: Brill, 2001.
Sagnard, Francois, ed. and trans. *Clément d'Alexandrie, Extraits de Théodote, texte grec, introduction, traducion et notes*. Paris: Cerf, 1948.
Salaman, Clement, Dorine van Oyen, William D. Wharton, and Jean-Pierre Mahé. *The Way of Hermes: New Translation of the Corpus Hermeticum and the Definitions of Hermes Trismegistus to Asclepius*. Rochester, VT: Inner Traditions, 2000.
Smith, Geoffrey S., trans. *Valentinian Christianity: Texts and Translations*. Berkeley: University of California Press, 2020.
Tobin, Thomas, ed. *Timaios of Locri, On the Nature of the World and the Soul: Text, Translation and Notes*. SBLTT 26. Chico, CA: Scholars Press, 1985.
Unger, Dominic J., trans. *St. Irenaeus of Lyons Against Heresies, Book One*. Edited by Walter J. Burghardt, Thomas Comerford Lawler, and John J. Dillon. Vol. 1. ACW 55. New York: Newman, 1992.
Winston, David, trans. *Philo of Alexandria: The Contemplative Life, The Giants, and Selections*. New York: Paulist Press, 1981.

2. Literature

Aland, Barbara. "Gnosis und Philosophie." Pages 34–73 in *Proceedings of the International Colloquium on Gnosticism, Stockholm, August 20–25, 1997*. Edited by Geo Widengren. Stockholm: Almqvist & Wiksell, 1977.

Appelbaum, Alan. "A Fresh Look at Philo's Family." *SPhiloA* 30 (2018): 93–113.

Baer, Richard. *Philo's Use of the Categories of Male and Female*. ALGHJ 3. Leiden: Brill, 1970.

Bainbridge, William. *The Sociology of Religious Movements*. New York: Routledge, 1997.

Barnes, Jonathan. "Aristotle's Concept of Mind." Pages 32–41 in *Psychology and Aesthetics*. Vol. 4 of *Articles on Aristotle*. Edited by Jonathan Barnes, Malcolm Schofield, and Richard Sorabji. London: Duckworth, 1979.

Barraclough, Ray. "Philo's Politics." *ANRW* 21.1:417–553.

Bauer, Walter. *Orthodoxy and Heresy in Earliest Christianity*. Translated and edited by Robert A. Kraft and Gerhard Krodel. Philadelphia: Fortress, 1971.

Bianchi, Ugo, ed. *Le origini dello gnosticismo: colloquio di Messina, 13–18 Aprile 1966*. SHR 12. Leiden: Brill, 1967.

Birnbaum, Ellen. "Allegorical Interpretation and Jewish Identity among Alexandrian Jewish Writers." Pages 305–29 n *Neotestamentica et Philonica: Studies in Honor of Peder Borgen*. Edited by David E. Aune, Torrey Seland, and Jarl Henning Ulrichsen. Leiden: Brill, 2003.

Bonazzi, Mauro. "Eudorus of Alexandria and Early Imperial Platonism." Pages 365–77 in *Greek and Roman Philosophy 100 BC–200 AD*. Edited by Robert W. Sharples and Richard Sorabji. BICS 94. London: Institute of Classical Studies, 2007.

———. "Pythagoreanising Aristotle: Eudorus and the Systematization of Platonism." Pages 160–86 in *Aristotle, Plato and Pythagoreanism in the First Century BC*. Edited by Malcolm Schofield. Cambridge: Cambridge University Press, 2013.

Borgen, Peder. "Judaism in Egypt." Pages 71–102 in *Early Christianity and Hellenistic Judaism*. Edited by Peder Borgen Edinburgh: T&T Clark, 1996.

———. "Observations on the Targumic Character of the Prologue of John." *NTS* 16 (1970): 288–95.

Bos, Abraham P. "Aristotelian and Platonic Dualism in Hellenistic and Early Christian Philosophy and Gnosticism." *VC* 56 (2002): 272–91.

———. "Philo of Alexandria: A Platonist in the Likeness of Aristotle." *SPhiloA* 10 (1998): 68–86.

———. *The Soul and Its Instrumental Body: A Reinterpretation of Aristotle's Philosophy of Living Nature.* Leiden: Brill, 2003.

Boyarin, Daniel. "Origen as Theorist of Allegory: Alexandrian Contexts." Pages 39–54 in *The Cambridge Companion to Allegory.* Edited by Rita Copeland and Peter T. Struck. Cambridge: Cambridge University Press, 2010.

Boys-Jones, George R. "The Stoics' Two Types of Allegory." Pages 189–216 in *Metaphor, Allegory, and the Classical Tradition: Ancient Thought and Modern Revisions.* Edited by George R. Boys-Jones. Oxford: Oxford University Press, 2003.

Brakke, David. *The Gnostics: Myth, Ritual and Diversity in Early Christianity.* Cambridge: Harvard University Press, 2010.

———. "Scriptural Practices in Early Christianity: Towards a New History of the New Testament Canon." Pages 263–80 in *Invention, Rewriting, Usurpation: Discursive Fights over Religious Traditions in Antiquity.* Edited by David Brakke, Anders-Christian Jacobsen, and Hans Ulrich. ECCA 11. New York: Lang, 2012.

Brisson, Luc. *How Philosophers Saved Myths: Allegorical Interpretation and Classical Mythology.* Translated by Catherine Tihanyi. Chicago: University of Chicago Press, 2008.

Broek, Roeloef van den. "Juden und Christen in Alexandrien im 2. und 3. Jahrhundert." Pages 101–15 in *Juden und Christen in der Antike.* Edited by Jacobus van Amersfoort and Johannes van Oort. Kampen: Kok, 1990.

Brown, Raymond, E. *The Gospel according to John.* 2 vols. AB 29. Garden City, NY: Doubleday, 1966–1970.

Buell, Denise Kimber. *Making Christians: Clement of Alexandria and the Rhetoric of Legitimacy.* Princeton: Princeton University Press, 1999.

Burnett, Fred. "Philo on Immortality: A Thematic Study of Philo's Concept of παλιγγενεσία." *CBQ* 46 (1984): 447–70.

Burns, Dylan. *Apocalypse of the Alien God: Platonism and the Exile of Sethian Gnosticism.* Philadelphia: University of Pennsylvania Press, 2014.

———. "Is the Apocalypse of Paul a Valentinian Apocalypse? Pseudepigraphy and Group Definition in NHC V, 2." Pages 97–112 in *Die*

Nag-Hammadi-Schriften in der Literatur- und Theologiegeschichte des frühen Christentums. Edited by Jens Schröter and Konrad Schwarz. STAC 106. Tübingen: Mohr Siebeck, 2017.

Camplani, Alberto. "Per la cronologia dei testi valentiniani: il Trattato Tripartito e la crisi Ariana." *Cassiodorus* 1 (1995): 171–95.

Caston, Victor. "Aristotle's Two Intellects: A Modest Proposal." *Phronesis* 44.3 (1999): 199–227.

Chiapparini, Giuliano. "Fragments of An Early 'Lost' Valentinianism." Pages 122–42 in *Valentinianism: New Studies*. Edited by Christoph Markschies and Einar Thomassen. NHMS 96. Leiden: Brill, 2020.

Chiaradonna, Riccardo. "Platonist Approaches to Aristotle: From Antiochus of Ascalon to Eudorus of Alexandria." Pages 28–52 in *Aristotle, Plato and Pythagoreanism in the First Century BC*. Edited by Malcolm Schofield. Cambridge: Cambridge University Press, 2013.

Corrigan, Kevin. "Positive and Negative Matter in Later Platonism: The Uncovering of Plotinus' Dialogue with the Gnostics." Pages 19–56 in *Gnosticism and Later Platonism: Themes, Figures, and Texts*. Edited by John D. Turner and Ruth Majercik. Atlanta: Society of Biblical Literature, 2000.

Cover, Michael B. *Lifting the Veil: 2 Corinthians 3:7–18 in Light of Jewish Homiletic and Commentary Traditions*. BZNW 210. Berlin: de Gruyter, 2015.

———. "Philo's 'Confessions': An Alexandrian Jew between Nothing and Something." *SPhiloA* 32 (2020): 113–35.

———. "The Sun and the Chariot: The *Republic* and the *Phaedrus* as Sources for Rival Platonic Paradigms of Psychic Vision in Philo's Biblical Commentaries." *SPhiloA* 26 (2014): 151–67.

Culpepper, R. Alan. *The Johannine School*. SBLDS 26. Missoula, MT: Scholars Press, 1975.

Cumont, Franz. *Astrology and Religion among the Greeks and Romans*. New York: Putnam, 1912.

Daniélou, Jean. *Philo of Alexandria*. Translated by James G. Colbert. Eugene, OR: Cascade Books, 2014.

Davies, Stevan. "Christology and Protology of the Gospel of Thomas." *JBL* 111 (1992): 663–82.

Dawson, David. *Allegorical Readers and Cultural Revision in Ancient Alexandria*. Berkeley: University of California Press, 1992.

Desjardins, Michel R. *Sin in Valentinianism*. SBLDS 108. Atlanta: Scholars Press, 1990.

Dibelius, Otto. "Studien zur Geschichte der Valentinianer: Die Excerpta ex Theodoto und Irenäus." *ZNW* (1908): 230–47.

Dillon, John. *The Middle Platonists, 80 B.C. to A.D. 220*. New York: Cornell University Press, 1996.

———. "Numenius: Some Ontological Questions." Pages 397–402 in *Greek and Roman Philosophy 100 BC–200 AD*. Edited by Robert W. Sharples and Richard Sorabji. BICS 94. London: Institute of Classical Studies, 2007.

———. "*Pleroma* and Noetic Cosmos: A Comparative Study." Pages 99–110 in *Neoplatonism and Gnosticism*. Edited by Richard T. Wallis and Jay Bregman. ISNS 6. Albany: State University of New York Press, 1992.

Dodd, C. H. *The Bible and the Greeks*. London: Hodder & Stoughton, 1934.

Dörrie, Heinrich. "Präpositionen und Metaphysik: Wechselwirkung zweier Prinzipienreihen." *MH* 26 (1969): 217–28.

Drijvers, Han J. W., ed. "Quq and the Quqites." In *East of Antioch: Studies in Early Syriac Christianity*. London: Variorum Reprints, 1984.

Drummond, James. *Philo Judaeus; or, the Jewish-Alexandrian Philosophy in Its Development and Completion*. 2 vols. London: Williams & Norgate, 1888.

Dubois, Jean-Daniel. "Le Traité Tripartite (Nag Hammadi I, 5) est-il antérieure à Origène?" Pages 303–16 in *Origeniana Octava: Origen and the Alexandrian Tradition; Papers of the Eighth International Origen Congress, Pisa, 27–31 August 2001*. Edited by Lorenzo Perrone. Leuven: Leuven University Press, 2003.

Dunderberg, Ismo. *Beyond Gnosticism*. New York: Columbia University Press, 2008.

———. "Gnostic Interpretations of Genesis." Pages 383–96 in *The Oxford Handbook of the Reception History of the Bible*. Edited by Michael Lieb and Emma Mason. Oxford: Oxford University Press, 2011.

———. *Gnostic Morality Revisited*. WUNT 347. Tübingen: Mohr Siebeck, 2015.

———. "Paul and the Valentinian Morality." Pages 434–56 in *Valentinianism: New Studies*. Edited by Christoph Markschies and Einar Thomassen. NHMS 96. Leiden: Brill, 2020.

———. "Stoic Traditions in the School of Valentinus." Pages 220–38 in *Stoicism in Early Christianity*. Edited by Tuomas Rasimus, Troels Engberg-Pedersen, and Ismo Dunderberg. Grand Rapids: Baker Academic, 2010.

———. "The Valentinian Teachers in Rome." Pages 157–74 in *Christians as a Religious Minority in a Multicultural City*. Edited by Jürgen Zangenberg and Michael Labahn. London: T&T Clark, 2004.

Edwards, Mark. "Pauline Platonism: The Myth of Valentinus." Pages 205–21 in *Christians, Gnostics, and Philosophers in Late Antiquity*. VCS. London: Routledge, 2012.

Engberg-Pedersen, Troels. *John and Philosophy: A New Reading of the Fourth Gospel*. Oxford: Oxford University Press, 2017.

———. "Philo's *De Vita Contemplativa* as a Philosopher's Dream." *JSJ* 30 (1999): 40–64.

Fallon, Francis T. "The Law in Philo and Ptolemy: A Note on the Letter to Flora." *VC* 30 (1976): 45–51.

Ferguson, John. *Clement of Alexandria*. New York: Twayne, 1974.

Foerster, Werner. *Von Valentin zu Heracleon*. Giessen: Töpelmann, 1928.

Fowden, Garth. *The Egyptian Hermes: A Historical Approach to the Late Pagan Mind*. Princeton: Princeton University Press, 1993.

Fredriksen, Paula. *Paul: The Pagan's Apostle*. New Haven: Yale University Press, 2017.

Freidenreich, David M. "Comparisons Compared: A Methodological Survey of Comparisons of Religion from 'A Magic Dwells' to 'A Magic Still Dwells.'" Pages 80–101 in *Method and Theory in the Study of Religion*. Leiden: Brill, 2004.

Friedländer, Moriz. *Der vorchristliche jüdische Gnosticismus*. Göttingen: Vandenhoeck & Ruprecht, 1989.

Fuglseth, Kåre Sigvald. *Johannine Sectarianism in Perspective: A Sociological, Historical and Comparative Analysis of Temple and Social Relationships in the Gospel of John, Philo and Qumran*. NovTSup 119. Leiden: Brill, 2005.

Gedaliah, Alon. *The Jews in Their Land in the Talmudic Age: 70–640 C.E.* Cambridge: Harvard University Press, 1989.

Glucker, John. *Antiochus and the Late Academy*. Göttingen: Vandenhoeck & Ruprecht, 1978.

Goodenough, Erwin. *By Light, Light: The Mystic Gospel of Hellenistic Judaism*. New Haven: Yale University Press, 1935.

Gordley, Matthew E. *The Colossian Hymn in Context*. WUNT 2/228. Tübingen: Mohr Siebeck, 2007.

Grant, Robert. "Theological Education in Alexandria." Pages 178–89 in *The Roots of Egyptian Christianity*. Edited by Birger A. Pearson and James E. Goehring, SAC. Philadelphia: Fortress, 1986.

Griffin, Michael. *Aristotle's "Categories" in the Early Roman Empire*. Oxford: Oxford University Press, 2015.

Griggs, Charles Wilfred. *Early Egyptian Christianity from Its Origins to 451 C.E.* Leiden: Brill, 1990.

Guignard, Christophe. "The Muratorian Fragment as a Late Antique Fake? An Answer to C. K. Rothschild." *RevScRel* 93 (2018): 73–90.

Haas, Christopher. *Alexandria in Late Antiquity: Topography and Social Conflict*. Baltimore: Johns Hopkins University Press, 1997.

Hackforth, Reginald. "Plato's Theism." Pages 439–47 in *Studies in Plato's Metaphysics*. Edited by Reginald E. Allen. London: Routledge & Kegan Paul, 1965.

Hahn, Johannes. *Der Philosoph und die Gesellschatft: Selbstverständis, öffentliches Auftreten und populäre Erwartungen in der hohen Kaiserzeit*. HABES 7. Stuttgart: Steiner, 1987.

Hanson, Richard P. C. *Allegory and Event: A Study of the Sources and Significance of Origen's Interpretation of the Scripture*. Richmond, VA: John Knox, 1959.

Hauser, Alan J., and Duane F. Watson, eds. "Introduction and Overview." Pages 1–54 in *The Ancient Period*. Vol. 1 of *A History of Biblical Interpretation*. Edited by Alan J. Hauser and Duane F. Watson. Grand Rapids: Eerdmans, 2003.

Havrda, Matyáš. *The So-Called Eighth Stromateus by Clement of Alexandria: Early Christian Reception of Greek Scientific Methodology*. PhA 144. Leiden: Brill, 2016.

Hay, David M. "Philo's References to Other Allegorists." *SPhiloA* 6 (1979–1980): 41–75.

Heckel, Theo K. *Der Innere Mensch: Die Paulinische Verarbeitung Eines Platonischen Motivs*. WUNT 2/53. Tübingen: Mohr Siebeck, 1993.

Heijer, Arco den. "Cosmic Mothers in Philo of Alexandria and in Neopythagoreanism." *SPhiloA* 27 (2015): 53–70.

Heimola, Minna. *Christian Identity in the Gospel of Philip*. Helsinki: Finnish Exegetical Society, 2011.

Heinrici, Georg. *Die valentinianische Gnosis und die Heilige Schrift*. Berlin: Wiegandt & Grieben, 1871.

Hoek, Annewies van den. "The 'Catechetical' School of Early Christian Alexandria and Its Philonic Heritage." *HTR* 90 (1997): 59–87.

———. *Clement of Alexandria and His Use of Philo in the "Stromateis": An Early Christian Reshaping of a Jewish Model*. Leiden: Brill, 1988.

———. "Techniques of Quotation in Clement of Alexandria: A View of Ancient Literary Working Methods." *VC* 50 (1996): 223–43.
Holzhausen, Jens. "Ein gnostischer Psalm?" *JAC* 30 (1993): 68–80.
———. "Valentinus and Valentinians." Pages 1144–57 in *Dictionary of Gnosis and Western Esotericism*. Edited by Wouter J. Hanegraaff. Vol. 2. Leiden: Brill, 2005.
Horbury, William. "Jewish Egypt in the Light of the Risings under Trajan." Pages 347–66 in *Israel in Egypt: The Land of Egypt as Concept and Reality for Jews in Antiquity and the Early Medieval Period*. Edited by Alison Salvesen, Sarah Pearce, and Miriam Frenkel. AJEC 110. Leiden: Brill, 2020.
———. *Jewish War under Trajan and Hadrian*. Cambridge: Cambridge University Press, 2014.
Horst, Pieter Willem van der. *Philo's Flaccus: The First Pogrom*. PACS 2. Atlanta: Society of Biblical Literature, 2005.
Huttunen, Niko. *Paul and Epictetus on Law: A Comparison*. London: T&T Clark, 2009.
Jonas, Hans. *The Gnostic Religion: The Message of the Alien God and Beginnings of Christianity*. 3rd ed. Boston: Beacon, 2001.
Jones, Roger. "The Ideas as the Thoughts of God." *CP* 21 (1926): 317–26.
Jorgensen, David W. "Valentinian Influence on Irenaeus: Early Allegorization of the New Testament." Pages 400–413 in *Valentinianism: New Studies*. Edited by Christoph Markschies and Einar Thomassen. NHMS 96. Leiden: Brill, 2020.
Kaler, Michael. *Flora Tells a Story: The Apocalypse of Paul and Its Context*. Waterloo, ON: Wilfrid Laurier University Press, 2008.
Kenney, John Peter. "Ancient Apophatic Theology." Pages 259–75 in *Gnosticism and Later Platonism: Themes, Figures and Texts*. Edited by John D. Turner and Ruth Majercik. Atlanta: Society of Biblical Literature, 2000.
———. *Mystical Monotheism: A Study in Ancient Platonic Theology*. Hanover, NH: Brown University Press, 1991.
———. "The Platonism of the *Tripartite Tractate* (NHC 1,5)." Pages 187–206 in *Neoplatonism and Gnosticism*. Edited by Rich T. Wallis and Jay Bregman. Albany: State University of New York Press, 1992.
Kenny, Anthony. *Aristotle on the Perfect Life*. Oxford: Clarendon, 1992.
King, Karen. *The Secret Revelation*. Cambridge: Harvard University Press, 2006.
———. *What Is Gnosticism?* Cambridge: Harvard University Press, 2003.

Klijn, Albertus F. J. *Seth in Jewish, Christian, and Gnostic Literature*. NovTSup 46. Leiden: Brill, 1977.
Koester, Helmut. *History and Literature of Early Christianity*. Vol. 2 of *Introduction to the New Testament*. New York: de Gruyter, 2000.
Kooten, George H. van. *Paul's Anthropology in Context: The Image of God, Assimilation to God, and Tripartite Man in Ancient Judaism, Ancient Philosophy and Early Christianity*. WUNT 232. Tübingen: Mohr Siebeck, 2008.
Kovacs, Judith L. "Clement of Alexandria and Valentinian Exegesis in the Excerpts from Theodotus." StPatr 43 (2006): 187–200.
⸻. "Echoes of Valentinian Exegesis in Clement of Alexandria and Origen: The Interpretation of 1 Cor 3.1–3." Pages 317–29 in *Origeniana Octava: Origen and the Alexandrian Tradition; Papers of the Eighth International Origen Congress, Pisa 27–31 August 2001*. Vol. 1. Edited by Lorenzo Perrone. Leuven: Leuven University Press, 2003.
Krämer, Hans Joachim. *Der Ursprung der Geistmetaphysik: Untersuchungen zur Geschichte des Platonismus zwischen Platon und Plotin*. 2nd ed. Amsterdam: Grüner, 1967.
Lampe, Peter. *From Paul to Valentinus: Christians in Rome in the First Two Centuries*. Translated by Michael Steinhauser. London: T&T Clark, 2003.
Laporte, Jean. "The High Priest in Philo of Alexandria." SPhiloA 3 (1991): 71–82.
Latyon, Bentley. "Prolegomena to the Study of Ancient Gnosticism." Pages 334–50 in *The Social World of the First Christians: Essays in Honor of Wayne A. Meeks*. Edited by L. Michael White and O. Larry Yarbrough. Minneapolis: Fortress, 1995.
Lee, Richard A., and Christopher P. Long. "Nous and Logos in Aristotle." FZPhTh 54 (2007): 348–67.
Lilla, Salvatore. *Clement of Alexandria: A Study in Christian Platonism and Gnosticism*. Glasgow: Oxford University Press, 1971.
Linjamaa, Paul. *The Ethics of the Tripartite Tractate (NHC I, 5): A Study of Determinism and Early Christian Philosophy of Ethics*. NHMS 95. Leiden: Brill, 2019.
Litwa, David M. "The Deification of Moses in Philo of Alexandria." SPhiloA 26 (2014): 1–27.
Logan, Alastair H. B. *Gnostic Truth and Christian Heresy: A Study in the History of Gnosticism*. Edinburgh: T&T Clark, 1996.

———. "Marcellus of Ancyra (Pseudo-Anthimus), 'On the Holy Church': Text, Translation and Commentary." *JTS* 51 (2000): 81–112.
Long, Anthony A. "Allegory in Philo and Etymology in Stoicism: A Plea for Drawing Distinctions." *SPhiloA* 9 (1997): 198–210.
Lucchesi, Enzo. *L'usage de Philon dans l'oeuvre exégetique de Saint Ambroise: une '"Quellenforschung" relative aux commentaires d'Ambroise sur la Genèse*. ALGHJ 9. Leiden: Brill, 1977.
Lundhaug, Hugo. "Begotten, Not Made, to Arise in This Flesh: The Post-Nicene Soteriology of the Gospel of Philip." Pages 235–71 in *Beyond the Gnostic Gospels: Studies Building on the Work of Elaine Pagels*. Edited by Eduard Iricinschi, Lance Jenott, Nicola Denzey Lewis, and Philippa Townsend. STAC 82. Tübingen: Mohr Siebeck, 2013.
Lundhaug, Hugo, and Lance Jenott. *The Monastic Origins of the Nag Hammadi Codices*. STAC 97. Tübingen: Mohr Siebeck, 2015.
Luttikhuizen, Gerard P. *Gnostic Revisions of Genesis Stories and Early Jesus Traditions*. NHMS 58. Leiden: Brill, 2006.
Mack, Burton L. "Moses on the Mountain Top: A Philonic View." Pages 16–28 in *The School of Moses: Studies in Philo and Hellenistic Religion in Memory of Horst R. Moehring*. Edited by John Peter Kenney. BJS 304. Atlanta: Scholars Press, 1995.
Mackie, Scott D. "Seeing God in Philo of Alexandria: Means, Methods, and Mysticism." *JSJ* 43 (2012): 147–79.
Marjanen, Antti. "Gnosticism." Pages 203–20 in *The Oxford Handbook of Early Christian Studies*. Edited by Susan Ashbrook Harvey and David G. Hunter. Oxford: Oxford University Press, 2008.
———. "The Relationship between the Valentinian and Sethian Sophia Myth Revisited." Pages 109–21 in *Valentinianism: New Studies*. Edited by Christoph Markschies and Einar Thomassen. NHMS 96. Leiden: Brill, 2020.
———. "A Salvific Act of Transformation or a Symbol of Defilement." Pages 245–59 in *Gnosticism, Platonism and the Late Ancient World*. Edited by Kevin Corrigan and Tuomas Rasimus. NHMS 82. Leiden: Brill, 2013.
Markschies, Christoph. "Innerer Mensch." *RAC* 18:266–312.
———. "New Research on Ptolemaeus Gnosticus." *ZAC* 4 (2000): 225–54.
———. "Valentinian Gnosticism: Toward the Anatomy of a School." Pages 401–38 in *The Nag Hammadi Library after Fifty Years*. Edited by John Turner and Anne McGuire. Leiden: Brill, 1997.

———. *Valentinus Gnosticus? Untersuchungen zur valentinianischen Gnosis mit einem Kommentar zu den Fragmenten Valentins.* WUNT 65. Tübingen: Mohr Siebeck, 1992.

Markschies, Christoph, and Einar Thomassen. "Introduction." Pages 1–14 in *Valentinianism: New Studies.* Edited by Christoph Markschies and Einar Thomassen. NHMS 96. Leiden: Brill, 2020.

May, Gerhard. *Creatio ex nihilo: The Doctrine of Creation Out of Nothing in Early Christian Thought.* Translated by A. S. Worral. Edinburgh: T&T Clark, 1994.

McCue, James F. "Conflicting Versions of Valentinianism? Irenaeus and the *Excerpta ex Theodoto.*" Pages 404–16 in *School of Valentinus.* Vol. 1 of *The Rediscovery of Gnosticism: Proceedings of the International Conference on Gnosticism at Yale New Haven, Connecticut, March 28–31, 1978.* Edited by Bentley Layton. Leiden: Brill, 1980.

McGowan, Andrew. "Valentinus Poeta: Notes on ΘΕΡΟΣ." *VC* 51 (1997): 158–78.

Méhat, André. *Études sur les "Stromates" de Clement d'Alexandrie.* Paris: Le Seuil, 1966.

Menn, Stephen. *Plato on God as Nous.* Edited by Richard A. Watson and Charles M. Young. JHPS. Carbondale: Southern Illinois University Press, 1995.

Merlan, Philip. "Greek Philosophy from Plato to Plotinus." Pages 14–83 in *The Cambridge History of Later Greek and Early Medieval Philosophy.* Edited by Arthur H. Armstrong. Cambridge: Cambridge University Press, 1967.

Miroshnikov, Ivan. *The Gospel of Thomas and Plato: A Study of the Impact on the "Fifth Gospel."* NHMS 93. Leiden: Brill, 2018.

Modrzejevski, Josef. *The Jews of Egypt from Rameses II to Emperor Hadrian.* Edinburgh: T&T Clark, 1995.

Narbonne, Jean-Marc. "The Neopythagorean Backdrop to the Fall of the Soul." Pages 411–25 in *Gnosticism, Platonism and the Late Ancient World: Essays in Honour of John D. Turner.* Edited by Kevin Corrigan and Tuomas Rasimus. NHMS 82. Leiden: Brill, 2013.

Nautin, Pierre. "La fin des Stroemates et les Hypotyposes de Clément d'Alexandrie." *VC* 30 (1976): 268–302.

Niehoff, Maren R. "Homeric Scholarship and Bible Exegesis in Ancient Alexandria: Evidence from Philo's 'Quarrelsome' Colleagues." *ClQ* 57 (2007): 166–82.

———. *Philo of Alexandria: An Intellectual Biography*. New Haven: Yale University Press, 2018.
Nock, Arthur D. "Gnosticism." *HTR* 57 (1964): 255–79.
Norman, Richard. "Aristotle's Philosopher-God." Pages 93–102 in *Psychology and Aesthetics*. Vol. 4 of *Articles on Aristotle*. Edited by Jonathan Barnes, Malcolm Schofied, and Richard Sorabji. London: Duckworth, 1979.
Opsomer, Jan. "Plutarch on the One and the Dyad." Pages 379–95 in *Greek and Roman Philosophy 100 BC–200 AD*. Edited by Robert W. Sharples and Richard Sorabji. Vol. 2. BICS 94. London: Institute of Classical Studies, 2007.
Paden, William E. "Elements of New Comparativism." Pages 182–92 in *A Magic Still Dwells: Comparative Religion in the Postmodern Age*. Edited by Kimberley C. Patton and Benjamin C. Ray. Berkeley: University of California Press, 2000.
Pagels, Elaine. "Conflicting Versions of Valentinian Eschatology: Irenaeus' Treatise vs. the Excerpts from Theodotus." *HTR* 67 (1974): 35–53.
———. "Exegesis of Genesis 1 in the Gospel of Thomas and John." *JBL* 118 (1999): 477–96.
———. *The Johannine Gospel in Gnostic Exegesis: Heracleon's Commentary on John*. Nashville: Abingdon, 1973.
———. "A Valentinian Interpretation of Baptism and Eucharist—and Its Critique of 'Orthodox' Sacramental Theology and Practice." *HTR* 65 (1972): 153–69.
Painter, John. "Rereading Genesis in the Prologue of John?" Pages 177–201 in *Neotestamentica et Philonica: Studies in Honor of Peder Borgen*. Edited by David E. Aune, Torrey Seland, and Jarl Henning Ulrichsen. NovTSup 106. Leiden: Brill, 2003.
Pearson, Birger A. *Ancient Gnosticism: Traditions and Literature*. Minneapolis: Fortress, 2007.
———. "Earliest Christianity in Egypt: Further Observations." Pages 97–112 in *The World of Early Egyptian Christianity: Language, Literature, and Social Context; Essays in Honor of David W. Johnson*. Edited by James E. Goehring and Janet A. Timbie. Washington, DC: Catholic University of America Press, 2007.
———. "The Figure of Seth in Gnostic Literature." Pages 473–78 in *Gnosticism, Judaism and Egyptian Christianity*. Minneapolis: Fortress, 1990
———. "Friedländer Revisited: Alexandrian Judaism and Gnostic Origins." *SPhilo* 2 (1973): 23–39.

———. "Gnostic Ritual and Iamblichus' Treatise on the Mysteries of Egypt." Pages 224–48 in *Gnosticism and Christianity in Roman and Coptic Egypt*. New York: T&T Clark, 2004.

———. *Gnosticism and Christianity in Roman and Coptic Egypt*. New York: T&T Clark, 2004.

———. *Gnosticism, Judaism and Egyptian Christianity*. Minneapolis: Fortress, 1990.

———. "Philo and Gnosticism." *ANRW* 21.1:295–341.

———. "Philo, Gnosis, and the New Testament." Pages 165–82 in *The New Testament and Gnosis: Essays in Honor of Robert McL. Wilson*. Edited by Alistair H. B. Logan and Alexander J. M. Wedderburn. Edinburgh: T&T Clark, 1983.

———. *The Pneumatikos-Psychikos Terminology in First Corinthians: A Study in the Theology of the Corinthian Opponents of Paul and Its Relation to Gnosticism*. SBLDS 12. Missoula, MT: Scholars Press, 1973.

———. "The Teachings of Silvanus." Pages 499–522 in *The Nag Hammadi Scriptures*. Edited by Marvin W. Meyer. New York: HarperCollins, 2007.

Perkins, Pheme. "Christologies in the Nag Hammadi Codices." *VC* 35 (1981): 379–96.

———. "Valentinians and the Christian Canon." Pages 371–99 in *Valentinianism: New Studies*, edited by Christoph Markschies and Einar Thomassen,. NHMS 96. Leiden: Brill, 2020.

Pétrement, Simone. *Separate God: The Christian Origin of Gnosticism*. Translated by Carol Harrison. New York: HarperCollins, 1984.

Quispel, Gilles. "The Original Doctrine of Valentinus." *GnosSt* 1 (1974): 27–36.

Radice, Roberto. "Observations on the Theory of the Ideas as Thoughts of God in Philo of Alexandria." *SPhiloA* 3 (1991): 126–34.

———. "Philo's Theology and Theory of Creation." Pages 124–45 in *The Cambridge Companion to Philo*. Edited by Adam Kamesar. Cambridge: Cambridge University Press, 2009.

Rasimus, Tuomas. "Porphyry and the Gnostics: Reassessing Pierre Hadot's Thesis in Light of the Second- and Third-Century Sethian Treatises." Pages 81–110 in *Its Reception in Neoplatonic, Jewish, and Christian Texts*. Vol. 2 of *Plato's Parmenides and Its Heritage*. Edited by John Turner and Kevin Corrigan. WGRWSup 3. Atlanta: Society of Biblical Literature, 2010.

———. "Ptolemaeus and the Valentinian Exegesis of John's Prologue." Pages 145–71 in *The Legacy of John: Second-Century Reception of the Fourth Gospel*. Edited by Tuomas Rasimus. NovTSup 132. Leiden: Brill, 2010.

Rist, John M. "Integration and the Undescended Soul in Plotinus." *AJP* 88 (1967): 410–22.

———. *The Mind of Aristotle: A Study in Philosophical Growth*. Toronto: University of Toronto Press, 1989.

Roberts, Colin H. *Buried Books in Antiquity: Habent sua fata libelli*. AEML 1962. London: Library Association, 1963.

———. "Early Christianity in Egypt: Three Notes." *JEA* 40 (1954): 92–96.

Rothschild, Clare K. "The Muratorian Fragment as Roman Fake." *NovT* 60 (2018): 55–82.

Royse, James R. "The Works of Philo." Pages 32–64 in *The Cambridge Companion to Philo*. Edited by Adam Kamesar. Cambridge: Cambridge University Press, 2009.

Ruben, Paul. *Clementis Alexandrini Excerpta ex Theodoto*. Leipzig: Teubner, 1892.

Runia, David. "The Beginnings of the End: Philo of Alexandria and Hellenistic Theology." Pages 281–316 in *Traditions of Theology: Studies in Hellenistic Theology, Its Background and Aftermath*. Edited by Dorothea Frede and André Laks. PhA 89. Leiden: Brill, 2002.

———. "A Brief History of the Term *Kosmos Noétos* from Plato to Plotinus." Pages 151–71 in *Traditions of Platonism: Essays in Honour of John Dillon*. Edited by John J. Cleary. Aldershot: Ashgate, 1999.

———. "Is Philo Committed to the Doctrine of Reincarnation?" *SPhiloA* 31 (2019): 107–26.

———. "Philo, Alexandrian and Jew." Pages 1–18 in *Exegesis and Philosophy: Studies on Philo of Alexandria*. Aldershot: Variorum, 1990.

———. *Philo in Early Christian Literature: A Survey*. JTECL 3. Leiden: Brill, 1990.

———. "Philo of Alexandria and the Greek *Hairesis*-Model." *VC* 53 (1999): 117–47.

———. *Philo of Alexandria and the Timaeus of Plato*. PhA 44. Leiden: Brill, 1986.

———. "Philo's 'De aeternitate mundi': The Problems of Its Interpretation." *VC* 35 (1981): 105–51.

———. "The Rehabilitation of the Jackdaw: Philo of Alexandria and Ancient Philosophy." Pages 483–500 in *Greek and Roman Philosophy*

100 BC–200 AD. Vol. 2. Edited by Robert W. Sharples and Richard Sorabji. BICS 94. London: Institute of Classical Studies, 2007.

Sandbach, F. Harry. *The Stoics*. Bristol: Bristol Press, 1989.

Sandmel, Samuel "Parallelomania." *JBL* 81 (1962): 1–13.

———. *Philo of Alexandria: An Introduction*. New York: Oxford University Press, 1979.

Satlow, Michael L. "Philo on Human Perfection." *JTS* 59 (2008): 500–519.

Schenke, Hans-Martin. "The Phenomenon and Significance of Gnostic Sethianism." Pages 588–616 in *Sethian Gnosticism*. Vol. 2 of *The Rediscovery of Gnosticism: Proceedings of the International Conference on Gnosticism at Yale New Haven, Connecticut, March 28–31, 1978*. Edited by Bentley Layton. Leiden: Brill, 1981.

Scholem, Gershom. *Major Trends in Jewish Mysticism*. New York: Schocken Books, 1995.

Schwartz, Daniel R. "Philo, His Family, and His Times." Pages 9–32 in *The Cambridge Companion to Philo*. Edited by Adam Kamesar. Cambridge: Cambridge University Press, 2009.

Scott, Ian W. "Is Philo's Moses a Divine Man?" *SPhiloA* 14 (2002): 87–111.

Shaw, Gregory. *The Theurgy of the Soul: The Neoplatonism of Iamblichus*. University Park: Pennsylvania State University Press, 1995.

Shroyer, Montgomery. "Alexandrian Jewish Literalists." *JBL* 55 (1936): 261–84.

Smallwood, E. Mary. *Philonis Alexandrini legatio ad Gaium*. Leiden: Brill, 1961.

Smith, Carl B. *No Longer Jews: The Search for Gnostic Origins*. Peabody, MA: Hendrickson, 2004.

Smith, Ian K. *Heavenly Perspective: A Study of the Apostle Paul's Response to a Jewish Mystical Movement at Colossae*. London: T&T Clark, 2006.

Smith, Jonathan Z. *Drudgery Divine: On the Comparison of Early Christianities and the Religions of Late Antiquity*. JLCRS 14. London: School of Oriental and African Studies, University of London, 1990.

———. "In Comparison a Magic Dwells." Pages in 23–41 in *A Magic Still Dwells: Comparative Religion in the Postmodern Age*. Edited by Kimberley C. Patton and Benjamin C. Ray. Berkeley: University of California Press, 2000.

Smith, Richard. "Sex Education in Gnostic Schools." Pages 345–60 in *Images of the Feminine in Gnosticism*. Edited by Karen L. King. Harrisburg, PA: Trinity Press International, 2000.

Snyder, Gregory H. "The Discovery and Interpretation of the Flavia Sophe Inscription: New Results." *VC* 68 (2014): 1–59.

Sorabji, Richard. *Time, Creation, and the Continuum: Theories in Antiquity and the Early Middle Ages*. Ithaca, NY: Cornell University Press, 1983.

Spoerri, Walter. *Späthellenistische Berichte über Welt, Kultur und Götter*. Basel: Reinhardt, 1959.

Staden, Heinrich von. "Hairesis and Heresy: The Case of the *haireseis iatrikai*." Pages 76–100 in *Self-Definition in the Greco-Roman World*. Vol. 3 of *Jewish and Christian Self-Definition*. Edited by Ben E. Myer and Ed P. Sanders. London: SCM, 1982.

Stark, Rodney, and Bainbridge William. *The Future of Religion: Secularization, Revival and Cult Formation*. Berkeley: University of California Press, 1985.

Stead, George C. "In Search of Valentinus." Pages 73–102 in *The School of Valentinus*. Vol. 1 of *The Rediscovery of Gnosticism: Proceedings of the International Conference on Gnosticism at Yale New Haven, Connecticut, March 28–31, 1978*. Edited by Bentley Layton. Leiden: Brill, 1980.

———. "The Valentinian Myth of Sophia." *JTS* 20 (1969): 75–104.

Sterling, Gregory E. "Creatio temporalis, aeterna, vel continua? An Analysis of the Thought of Philo of Alexandria." *SPhiloA* 4 (1992): 15–41.

———. "Day One: Platonizing Exegetical Traditions of Genesis 1:1–5 in John and Jewish Authors." *SPhiloA* 7 (2005): 118–40.

———. "From the Thick Marshes of the Nile to the Throne of God: Moses in Ezekiel the Tragedian and Philo of Alexandria." *SPhiloA* 26 (2014): 115–33.

———. "'A Man of the Highest Repute': Did Josephus Know the Writings of Philo?" *SPhiloA* 25 (2013): 101–13.

———. "'The Most Perfect Work': The Role of Matter in Philo of Alexandria." Pages 99–118 in *Creation ex nihilo: Origins, Development, Contemporary Challenges*. Edited by Gary A. Anderson and Markus Bockmuehl. Notre Dame, IN: University of Notre Dame Press, 2017.

———. "Philo." Pages 1063–79 in *The Eerdmans Dictionary of Early Judaism*. Edited by John J. Collins and Daniel C. Harlow. Grand Rapids: Eerdmans, 2010.

———. "Philo of Alexandria." Pages 299–316 in *A Guide to Early Jewish Texts and Traditions in Christian Transmission*. Edited by Alexander Kulik. Oxford: Oxford University Press, 2019.

———. "Philo's School: The Social Setting of Ancient Commentaries." Pages 123–42 in *Sophisten in Hellenismus und Kaiserzeit: Orte, Meth-*

oden und Personen der Bildungvermittlung. Edited by Beatrice Wyss, Rainer Hirsch-Luipold, and Solmeng-Jonas Hirschi. STAC 101. Tübingen: Mohr Siebeck, 2017.

———. "Platonizing Moses: Philo and Middle Platonism." *SPhiloA* 5 (1993): 96–111.

———. "Prepositional Metaphysics in Jewish Wisdom Speculations and Early Christian Liturgical Texts." *SPhiloA* 9 (1997): 219–38.

———. "The School of Moses in Alexandria: An Attempt to Reconstruct the School of Philo." Pages 141–66 in *Second Temple Jewish "Paideia" in Context*. Edited by Jason Zurawski and Gabriele Boccaccini. BZNW 228. Berlin: de Gruyter, 2017.

———. "The School of Sacred Laws." *VC* 53 (1999): 148–64.

———. "The Theft of Philosophy: Philo of Alexandria and Numenius of Apamea." *SPhiloA* 27 (2015): 71–85.

Stroumsa, Guy G. *Another Seed: Studies in Gnostic Mythology*. NHS 24. Leiden: Brill, 1984.

Sundberg, Albert C. "Canon Muratori: A Fourth-Century List." *HTR* 66 (1973): 1–41.

Tcherikover, Viktor. "The Decline of the Jewish Diaspora in Egypt in the Roman Period." *JJS* 14 (1963): 1–32.

Tervahauta, Ulla. *A Story of Soul's Journey in the Nag Hammadi Library: A Study of the Authenticos Logos (NHC VI,3)*. NTOA 107. Göttingen: Vandenhoeck & Ruprecht, 2015.

Theiler, Willy. "Philo von Alexandria und der hellenisierte Timaeus." Pages 25–35 in *Philomathes: Studies and Essays in the Humanities in Memory of Philip Merlan*. Edited by Robert B. Palmer and Robert G. Hamerton-Kelly. The Hague: Nijhoff, 1971.

Thomassen, Einar. "The Derivation of Matter in Monistic Gnosticism." Pages 1–17 in *Gnosticism and Later Platonism: Themes, Figures, and Texts*. Edited by John D. Turner and Ruth Majercik. Atlanta: Society of Biblical Literature, 2000.

———. "Going to Church with the Valentinians." Pages 183–97 in *Practicing Gnosis: Ritual, Magic, Theurgy and Liturgy in Nag Hammadi, Manichean and Other Ancient Literature; Essays in Honor of Birger A. Pearson*. Edited by April D. DeConick, Gregory Shaw, and John D. Turner. NHMS 85. Leiden: Brill, 2013.

———. "Heracleon." Pages 173–210 in *Legacy of John: Second-Century Reception of the Fourth Gospel*. NovTSup 132. Leiden, Brill: 2010.

———. *Le Traité Tripartite (NH 5, 1)*. Edited by Louis Painchaus and Einar Thomassen. Québec: Presses de l'Université Laval, 1989.

———. "Orthodoxy and Heresy in Second-Century Rome." *HTR* 97 (2004): 241–56.

———. "The Relative Chronology of the Valentinian System." Pages 17–28 in *Valentinianism: New Studies*. Edited by Christoph Markschies and Einar Thomassen. NHMS 96. Leiden: Brill, 2020.

———. *The Spiritual Seed: The Church of the "Valentinians."* NHMS 60. Leiden: Brill, 2006.

———. "The Tripartite Tractate." Pages 57–102 in *The Nag Hammadi Scriptures*. Edited by Marvin W. Meyer. New York: HarperCollins, 2007.

Tite, Philip L. "An Exploration of Valentinian Paraenesis: Rethinking Gnostic Ethics in the Interpretation of Knowledge (NHC XI, 1)." *HTR* 97 (2004): 275–304.

———. *Valentinian Ethics and Paraenetic Discourse: Determining the Social Function of Moral Exhortation in Valentinian Christianity*. NHMS 67. Leiden: Brill, 2006.

Tobin, Thomas. *The Creation of Man: Philo and the History of Interpretation*. CBQMS 14. Washington, DC: Catholic Biblical Association of America, 1983.

———. "The Prologue of John and Hellenistic Jewish Speculation." *CBQ* 52 (1990): 252–70.

Trapp, Michael. "Neopythagoreans." Pages 347–63 in *Greek and Roman Philosophy 100 BC–200 AD*. Edited by Robert W. Sharples and Richard Sorabji. BICS 94. London: Institute of Classical Studies, 2007.

Turner, John D. "The *Chaldean Oracles* and the Metaphysics of the Sethian Platonizing Treatises." Pages 213–32 in *History and Interpretation from the Old Academy to Later Platonism and Gnosticism*. Vol. 1 of *Plato's Parmenides and Its Heritage*. Edited by John Turner and Kevin Corrigan. WGRWSup 2. Atlanta: Society of Biblical Literature, 2010.

———. "The Curious Philosophical World of Later Religious Gnosticism: The Symbiosis of Late Antique Philosophy and Religion." Pages 151–82 in *Religion and Philosophy in the Platonic and Neoplatonic Traditions: From Antiquity to the Early Medieval Period*. Edited by Kevin Corrigan and John Turner. Sankt Augustin: Academia, 2012.

———. "Ritual in Gnosticism." Pages 83–140 in *Gnosticism and Later Platonism: Themes, Figures, and Texts*. Edited by John D. Turner and Ruth Majercik. Atlanta: Society of Biblical Literature, 2000.

———. *Sethian Gnosticism and the Platonic Tradition.* Quebec: Presses de l'Université Laval, 2001.
Turner, Martha. *The Gospel of Philip: The Sources and Coherence of an Early Christian Collection.* NHMS 38. Leiden: Brill, 1996.
Völker, Walther. *Quellen zur Geschichte der christlichen Gnosis.* Sammlung ausgewählter kirchen- und dogmengeschichtlicher Quellenschriften NS 5. Tübingen: Mohr Siebeck, 1932.
Wasserman, Emma. "The Death of the Soul in Romans 7: Revisiting Paul's Anthropology in Light of Hellenistic Moral Philosophy." *JBL* 126 (2007): 793–816.
———. *The Death of the Soul in Romans 7.* WUNT 256. Tübingen: Mohr Siebeck, 2008.
Weiss, Hans-Friedrich. *Untersuchungen zur Kosmologie des hellenistischen und palästinischen Judentums.* TU 97. Berlin: Akademie, 1966.
Wilson, Robert McL. "The Early History of the Exegesis of Gen 1:26." StPatr 1 (1957): 420–37.
———. *The Gospel of Philip: Translated from the Coptic Text, with an Introduction and Commentary.* London: Mowbray, 1962.
———. "Half a Century of Gnosisforschung—in Retrospect." Pages 95–105 in *Doctrinal Diversity: Varieties of Early Christianity.* Vol. 4 of *Recent Studies in Early Christianity: A Collection of Scholarly Essays.* Edited by Everett Ferguson. New York: Garland, 1999.
———. "Philo of Alexandria and Gnosticism." *Kairos* 14 (1972): 213–19.
Winston, David. "Philo's Conception of the Divine Nature." Pages 21–42 in *Neoplatonism and Jewish Thought.* Edited by Lenn E. Goodman. Albany: State University of New York Press, 1992.
———. "Philo's Ethical Theory." *ANRW* 21.1:372–416.
———. "Sage and Supersage in Philo of Alexandria." Pages 815–24 in *Pomegranates and Golden Bells: Studies in Jewish and Near Eastern Ritual, Law and Literature in of Jacob Milgrom.* Edited by David P. Wright, David Noel Freedman, and Avi Hurvitz. Winona Lake, IN: Eisenbrauns, 1995.
———. *Wisdom of Salomon: A New Translation with Introduction and Commentary.* AB 43. New York: Doubleday, 1979.
Wolfson, Harry. "Extradeical and Intradeical Interpretations of Platonic Ideas." *JHI* 22 (1961): 3–32.
———. *Faith, Trinity, Incarnation.* Vol. 1 of *The Philosophy of the Church Fathers.* Cambridge: Harvard University Press, 1956.

———. *Philo: Foundations of Religious Philosophy of Judaism, Christianity, and Islam.* 2 vols. Cambridge: Harvard University Press, 1948.
Wucherpfennig, Ansgar. *Heracleon Philologus: Gnostische Johannesexegese im zweiten Jahrhundert.* WUNT 142. Tübingen: Mohr Siebeck, 2001.
Yamauchi, Edwin. "The Issue of Pre-Christian Gnosticism Reviewed in the Light of the Nag Hammadi Texts." Pages 72–88 in *The Nag Hammadi Library after Fifty Years.* Edited by John Turner and Anne McGuire. NHMS 44. Leiden: Brill, 1997.
Yli-Karjanmaa, Sami. "'Call Him Earth': On Philo's Allegorization of Adam in the *Legum allegoriae*." Pages 253–93 in *Adam and Eve Story in the Hebrew Bible and in Ancient Jewish Writings Including the New Testament.* Edited by Antti Laato and Lotta Valve. SRHB 7. Winona Lake, IN: Eisenbrauns, 2016.
———. *Reincarnation in Philo of Alexandria.* SPhiloM 7. Atlanta: SBL Press, 2015.
Young, Frances M. "Alexandrian and Antiochene Exegesis." Paes 334–54 in *The Ancient Period.* Vol. 1 of *A History of Biblical Interpretation.* Edited by Alan J. Hauser and Duane F. Watson. Grand Rapids: Eerdmans, 2002.
———. *Biblical Exegesis and the Formation of Christian Culture.* Cambridge: Cambridge University Press, 1997.
Zahn, Theodor von. *Supplementum Clementinum.* FGNK 3. Erlangen: Deichert, 1884.
Zandee, Jan. "Les enseignements de Silvanos et Philon d'Alexandrie." Pages 337–45 in *Mélanges d'histoire des religions offerts á H. C. Puech.* Paris: Presses universitaires de France, 1974.

Ancient Sources Index

Hebrew Bible

Genesis
- 1:1   83, 116–17, 149, 154, 169
- 1:1–2   155
- 1:1–3   41, 150–51
- 1:1–5   113, 125, 127, 155, 167, 191
- 1:2   123–24, 133, 153
- 1:3   35, 119, 122, 160, 167
- 1:4   123
- 1:6   229
- 1:6–8   156
- 1:6–2:4   115, 191
- 1:24   193
- 1:26   13, 169, 176, 185, 248
- 1:26–27   5, 96, 189–90, 216, 235
- 1:27   169, 176, 178, 185, 199, 241, 248
- 2–3   189
- 2:1–41:24   31
- 2:4–6   191
- 2:7   35, 169, 176, 182, 185, 189–90, 234–35, 248
- 2:7–25   191
- 2:8   13
- 2:15   192
- 2:17   257–58
- 2:19   193
- 2:21   231
- 2:21–23   230
- 2:21–25   232
- 2:23   182
- 2:24   97, 231
- 3:21   176, 197
- 4:1   236
- 4:25   245
- 4:26   247
- 5:1   247
- 5:24   263
- 9:3   229
- 11:1–9   72
- 12:7   223
- 15:1–2   204
- 15:7–21   157
- 20:12   144
- 25:8   225
- 25:9   262
- 28:12   163
- 35:29   262

Exodus
- 4:22   254
- 13:1–2   80
- 13:2–12   79
- 33:20   256

Leviticus
- 21:11   259

Deuteronomy
- 21:17   254
- 21:18–21   143
- 32:13   145
- 34:6   263

Psalms
- 100:1   265
- 104:24   141

Proverbs
- 1:22   158

Proverbs (cont.)

2:6	141
3:19	141
8:1	141
8:22–31	141
8:22–36	113
9:1	148, 150, 153
22:20–21	76

Ezekiel

1:26	199
1:28	199

Deuterocanonical Books

Wisdom of Solomon

5:1–2	203
9:9	141
11:17	136

Sirach

22:9	173
24:23	141

Pseudepigrapha

1 Enoch

38.1	14

Apocalypse of Moses

1.1–3	244

Dead Sea Scrolls

1QS

IX, 7–9	14, 271

4Q417	179

Josephus

Antiquitates judaicae

1.60–65	247
13.171–173	59
18.11–22	59

Bellum judaicum

2.119–162	59

Vita

12	59

Philo

De Abrahamo

2–5	85
49	197
52–55	250
53	251
56–57	251
57	252
70	173
72–76	225
80	223
102	224
110	254
119–130	242
132	254
157	161
168	254
200	70
200–207	229
230	266
236	71
254	254

De aeternitate mundi

5	133
8–19	135
12	94, 134
13–14	134
20	134
20–149	134
21–22	134
150	134

De agricultura

96–97	73
130–131	79

Ancient Sources Index

De animalibus
7 — 94

De cherubim
2 — 265
27–28 — 97, 222
30 — 97
43–45 — 146
49 — 224
49–50 — 146
78 — 265
113–115 — 246
124–127 — 115
125 — 35, 236
128 — 185, 236

De confusione linguarum
1–5 — 72
23–25 — 229
41 — 200
63 — 200
92 — 251
142–149 — 199
146 — 80, 118, 126, 140, 200, 251
171–173 — 97
177 — 261
180 — 86
190–193 — 73

De congressu eruditionis gratia
34–38 — 251
51 — 252
58 — 197
79–80 — 223

De decalogo
98 — 87
175–176 — 85

De ebrietate
27 — 143
30–31 — 142
31 — 35
59–61 — 144
61 — 145

101 — 161
150 — 204

De fuga et inventione
56 — 221
63 — 221
66 — 86
71–72 — 35, 193–94, 216
82 — 89
97 — 42
108–112 — 212
109 — 142
113–114 — 259
116–118 — 212
208 — 35, 251–55

De gigantibus
4 — 215
13–14 — 258
14 — 258–59
22 — 157
27 — 120, 214
47 — 120, 214
53–54 — 263
60 — 13
60–61 — 220
61 — 261

De migratione Abrahami
17–24 — 265
47 — 74
89–90 — 51
125 — 251–52
184–195 — 224
195 — 225

De mutatione nominum
6 — 161
11–14 — 93
31 — 196
74–75 — 215
82–83 — 251
83 — 251
87 — 252
137 — 146

De mutatione nominum (*cont.*)

137–140	254	134–135	190, 266
181–185	265	136	189, 195, 197
223	190	140–141	260
		153–154	215

De opificio mundi

1–3	48		
7	135, 150		
7–9	132		
8–9	161		
9–11	135		
10	135		
13	136		
17–19	115		
21–22	132		
25	96, 116, 118, 148		
25–36	125–26		
26–28	121		
26–35	113, 158		
27	163		
29	122, 133, 155, 160		
29–30	121		
29–35	120		
30	121		
31	35, 122, 159, 167		
32	122–23		
33–34	123, 137, 156, 162		
35	117		
36	99		
36–37	162		
36–38	156		
37	125		
45–61	162		
47	164		
55	163–64		
67–68	196		
69	189, 243		
69–70	181, 196		
72	13		
73	162		
89–128	116		
112–117	164		
117	190		
128	48		
134	190		

De plantatione

3	156
3–4	162–63
9	97
14	196
18	211
18–22	190
26	78
36	71
37	214
44–46	192

De posteritate Caini

10	246
39	266
43	266
63	254
78–79	35, 241
124	35
124–125	246
134	161
170	246
171	93
172–174	246
180	209

De praemiis et poenis

1–3	85
27–51	250
40	95, 161
40–44	221
44	252
46	161, 223
47–51	250
69–70	266

De providentia

1.7	135
2.42–44	137
2.52–54	137

De sacrificiis Abeli et Caini
1–3	244
1–5	266
2–3	35
5	225
5–7	262
8	262
8–10	263
45	245
56–58	224
59	177
65–68	135, 221
66	204
104	245

De sobrietate
44–50	265

De somniis
1.14–39	163
1.31	196, 209
1.34	211
1.52–60	224
1.60	223
1.75	119, 120, 122, 125–26, 137, 156
1.76	132
1.115–116	161
1.135–136	209
1.136–137	196
1.139	264
1.140–141	261
1.151	249
1.169	251
1.171	252
1.184	95
2.83–85	204
2.92	204
2.173	252
2.234	225
2.241–244	258
2.242–243	142
2.246	78

De specialibus legibus
1.8–10	86
1.13–20	165
1.39–40	161
1.45–48	97
1.49	49
1.53–55	192
1.59–63	48
1.66	212, 261
1.80–82	212
1.166	163
1.171	210
1.225	132
1.276–277	210
1.328	133
1.329	97, 243
1.345	49
3.1–6	74
4.123	190, 210
4.192	212

De virtutibus
76	263

De vita contemplativa
2	95, 161, 221
28	70
28–30	50
78	74
83–89	69

De vita Mosis
1.21–29	48
1.155–158	263
2.24	87
2.46	85
2.74	74
2.101	214
2.108	86
2.121	14, 207
2.121–126	212
2.194	162
2.211–216	48
2.215	87
2.267	132
2.288	263

In Flaccum

46	2

Legum allegoriae

1.22	222
1.31–32	35, 137, 190, 194–96, 198
1.34	250
1.39–40	210
1.40	210
1.42	200
1.43–47	215
1.45–52	224
1.53–55	241
1.60–62	210
1.65	142
1.88	161
1.89–90	192
1.90	195
1.92–95	241
1.105	257
1.107–108	226
2.4	200
2.11–13	193
2.13–14	70
2.35–45	231
2.38	224
2.41	231
2.49	231–32
2.49–50	199
2.50	232
2.82	146
2.94	253
3.37–38	195, 197
3.69–77	197–98
3.88–89	244
3.96	222
3.99–103	222
3.111	161
3.140	225
3.140–144	241
3.140–145	229
3.161	211
3.218–219	254
3.246	192

Quaestiones et solutiones in Exodum

2.52	74
2.54	212
2.68–69	212

Quaestiones et solutiones in Genesin

1.4	190
1.6	13, 215
1.8	192
1.16	258
1.45	258
1.51	258
1.53	35, 197
1.59	245
1.78	246
1.86	263
2.57	229
3.11	261
3.44	212
4.25–27	212
4.57	162
4.76	212
4.140–146	272

Quod deterius potiori insidiari soleat

15–17	78
34	258
45–51	246
54	142
82–84	210
83	190, 200, 211
83–84	196
86	48
115	145
167–170	190

Quod Deus sit immutabilis

55–56	98
75–76	266
104–108	266
121	254
133	70
135–138	220
164	243

Ancient Sources Index

Quod omnis probus liber sit
2	94
95	204
125–126	204

Quis rerum divinarum heres sit
6	204
21–24	204
36	252
53	145
56–57	35, 241
78	251
98	161
105–110	224
112–113	212
117–119	80
133	35, 159
133–236	156
134–140	133
140	148
187	120
190	120
217	120
218	209
227–236	157, 163
275	225
280–283	261
283	211

New Testament

Matthew
3:12	100
5:16	172
8:31	267
10:34	100
12:25	82
18:12–14	76
20:1–16	75
26:32	267

Mark
5:24b–34	75

Luke
2:23	79
2:25–40	75
2:40	242
2:42	75
6:13	75
8:41	75
15:4–7	120

John
1:1	105
1:1–5	114–17
1:3	83, 107
1:4	107
1:11	83
1:14	107
1:16	69, 120
1:23	75
1:26–27	76
2:9	268
2:12–22	76
3:29	268
10:30	242
11:25	242
14:6	242

Acts
5:17	59
11	53
15:5	59
18:24–27	53
24:5	59
24:14	59
25:5	59
26:5	59
28:22	59

Romans
2:29	86
7	226
11:23–26	252
12:1–2	86
13:11	172

1 Corinthians		Nag Hammadi Writings	
2:14–15	234		
8:6	115	Allogenes the Stranger (NHC XI)	
11:19	59	49.26–38	111
15:29	233	65.32–36	111
15:37	235		
15:44	174	Apocalypse (Revelation) of Paul	
15:44–47	234	(NHC V)	27
2 Corinthians		Berlin Codex	
2:14–16	205	2 24.20–25.1	111
4:10–18	186		
4:16	226	Eugnostos the Blessed (NHC III/V)	
		6.20	111
Galatians		15.21	111
4:21–31	252–53	88.8–9	111
Ephesians		Gospel of Philip (NHC II)	
5:22–33	272	53.23–54.5	75
		64.22–31	238
Philippians		65.1–26	232
3:5–6	59	67.9–27	75
3:20	247	68.22–26	232
		69.14–70.4	213
Colossians		70.9–22	232
1:15	179	70.22–30	203
1:16	115, 118, 120	70.22–34	184
1:24	55	72.17–29	255
2:9–11	69, 179	82.26–29	86
Titus		Gospel of Thomas (NHC II)	
3:10	59	11	259
		85	259
Hebrews			
1:2	115	Gospel of Truth (NHC I)	
		20.6–24	14
2 Peter		28.32–30.23	172
2:1	59	33.33–34.34	205
2:7	216	36.35–37.2	13, 215
Rabbinic Works		Interpretation of Knowledge (NHC XI)	
		15–19.15	261
Genesis Rabbah			
22.3	244	Nature of the Rulers (NHC II)	
		91.11–92.2	247

Ancient Sources Index   315

Origin of the World (NHC II)
  105.20–106.19   253
  115.11–30   203
  121.27–123.2   253

Secret Book of James (NHC I)
  16.8–11   14

Secret Book of John (NHC II/III)
  10.15   111
  24.15–36   247

Teachings of Silvanus (NHC VIII)
  92.10–94.29   234

Tripartite Tractate (NHC I)
  51.8–54.35   98
  54.35–57.23   105
  66.10–12   205
  71.35–72   205
  73.18–74.18   164
  80.11–83.33   230
  86.23–87   177
  92.26   153
  94.10–95.16   178
  104.18–106.25   187, 242
  105–107   33
  113.31–114.22   188
  118–119   234, 237
  118.14–28   14, 240
  119.16–24   240
  122.3–22   233
  125.24–127.25   233

Valentinian Exposition (NHC XI)
  17–24   104
  29–30   104
  35.30–34   148
  38.22   249
  41.21–42.39   67

Wisdom of Jesus Christ (NHC III)
  112.8   111

Zostrianos (NHC VIII)
  64.14–16   111

Other Early Christian Writings

Augustine, *De civitate Dei*
  7.28   95

Augustine, *De utilitate credendi*
  3.5   77

Barnabas   54, 86

Clement of Alexandria, *Excerpta ex Theodoto*
  2–3   202
  2.1–2   184, 233
  3.1–2   172
  6–7   28, 32, 84, 99, 117, 125, 226
  6.1–3   105
  6.1–7.3   105
  7.1–3   106
  7.1–4   99
  7.3–8   107
  8.1   117
  21   177
  21.1   178
  22   118
  22.1   55
  23.3–4   55
  26   118
  26.1–3   179
  31   139
  32   118
  32.3–33.2   41
  34.1–2   178
  38   214
  42.1–3   100
  43.2   99, 118
  43.2–5   205
  44.1   40, 179
  44.1–2   272
  45.1–2   228
  45.3   83
  46.1   140

Clement, Excerpta ex Theodoto (cont.)

46.1–2	42
46.1–47.1	147
47–48	141, 150–51, 167
47.1	42, 153
47.1–4	147
47.1–48.1	41
47.3	41
47.3–48.1	159, 161
47.4	154–55
48.1	153
48.2–4	227
50	197
50–51	176, 202
50.1–51.1	180
50.2	181
50.5	154
51.1	182
51.2	182, 231
53	184
53.1	230
53.2	41
53.2–3	183–84
53.3	41, 179
53.4–5	186
54.1	248
54.1–3	247
55–56	236
55.1	198
55.1–2	238
55.1–56.2	185
55.2–56.2	235
56.3	237
56.4–5	252, 254
56.5	253, 255
59	182
59.4	154
59.4–61.3	242
61.3	267
61.4–8	266
61.6	267
61.9	268
62.1–3	270
62.3	186
63.1	40
63.1–65.2	268
63.2	271
63–65	269, 271
67–68	178
67.1–3	187
68	65, 188

Clement of Alexandria, *Excerpta* C (= *Exc.* 43.2–65) 5, 22, 29, 32, 35, 39–45, 65, 68, 98–99, 104, 108, 113, 116, 118, 125, 137, 140, 147–48, 150, 159–60, 162, 164, 165–67, 177, 179, 187–88, 205, 216–17, 233, 240, 242, 244, 253, 260, 269, 273–76, 279–81, 283–84

Clement of Alexandria, *Paedagogus*

1.57.2	252

Clement of Alexandria, *Quis dives salvetur*

9	254

Clement of Alexandria, *Stromateis*

1.31.4	252
1.72.4	253
1.153.2	253
2.6.1	222
2.36.2–4	181, 201
2.100.3	94, 253
4.71.1	60
4.89.1–3	14, 256
4.89.6–90.1	165
4.156.1	222
5.1.1–5	10
5.65.2	222
5.71.2–3	98
5.71.5	222
5.81.4	222
5.82.4	222
5.93.5–94.5	155
7.106.4	55
8	34–36

Epiphanius, *Panarion*

7.1–2	56

31.2.2–3	55	Irenaeus, *Adversus Haereses*	
39–40	247	1.praef.	40, 68
		1.praef. 1–7	56
Eusebius, *Historia ecclesiastica*		1.praef. 2	60
2.16	53	1.1–2	98
2.16–17	283	1.1–4	99
2.24	53	1.1–7	32, 40
2.18.1–9	30	1.1.1	60, 106
3.14	53	1.1.1–3	32, 84, 99, 125, 138
3.21	53	1.1.3–4.1	124
5.9	53	1.2–4	137
6.30.3	56	1.2.1	105
		1.2.2	41, 106–7, 138
Eusebius, *Praeparatio evangelica*		1.2.2–4	138
1.23	191	1.2.3	41, 124
9.8.1–2	93	1.2.6	118, 205, 271
10a	93	1.3.1–5	75
11.18.13–14	93	1.3.4	79, 179
11.23.6	116	1.3.5	100, 125
11.24.7–12	155	1.3.6	76
		1.4.1	139, 230
Heracleon		1.4.1–2	227
frag. 1	83	1.4.5	41–42, 79, 140, 147, 177
frags. 11–16	213	1.5.1	41, 141, 149–52
frag. 21	234	1.5.2	149, 153–55, 159, 167, 182
frag. 35	153	1.5.3	153
		1.5.4	140, 148, 227
Hippolytus, *Refutatio omnium haeresium*		1.5.5	177, 180–82, 198, 202
(Philosophoumena)		1.5.5–6	176
6.20	247	1.5.6	41, 179, 183–84, 216
6.24.1	60	1.6.1	238, 255, 270
6.25	124	1.6.2	234
6.29.3–4	99	1.6.4	234, 260
6.32.7–9	153	1.7.1	153, 227, 269
6.32.9	238	1.7.4	247
6.34.3–4	186	1.7.5	185, 235, 239, 248
6.35.5–7	60, 65	1.8.5	32, 83, 99, 105, 117, 125
6.35.6	56	1.9.1	76
6.37.7	14, 28, 206	1.9.4	76
6.41	66	1.10.1–3	47
6.41–42	28	1.11.1	4, 41, 47, 57
6.42.2	60	1.12.1	112
10.13.4	198	1.13–21	116
30.6–9	41	1.13–22	66
		1.16.1	120

Irenaeus, Adversus Haereses (cont.)
1.18	112
1.21	67
1.21.1	60
1.21.5	26
1.29–30	5, 12
1.29.1	47
1.30.1	111
2.27.1–4	76
3.4.3	55
3.11.7	117
3.15.2	68
3.18–23	76
4.praef. 3	107
4.33.3	68
5.7.1–2	174
5.9–12	76

Jerome, *Commentariorum in Ezechielem libri XVI*
5.16.30–31	77

Jerome, *Epistulae*
120.12	77

Justin, *Dialogus cum Tryphone*
35.6	56

Letter of Instruction (*Pan.* 31.5–6)
28–29, 102	

Origen, *Commentarii in evangelium Joannis*
1–13	28, 75

Origen, *Contra Celsum*
2.60	174
4.51	93
5.61	60

Origen, *Fragmenta ex commentariis in evangelium Matthaei*
17.30	174

Origen, *De principiis (Peri archōn)*
2.8.3	209
4.11–13	76

Ptolemy, *Epistula ad Floram* (*Pan.* 33.3.1–33.7.10)
33.3.5–6	83
33.5.1–6	85
33.5.12–14	86

Tertullian, *Adversus Valentianos*
4.3	56
9.4	99
11.2	60
25.2	183
33.1	60

Tertullian, *De anima*
22	60

Tertullian, *De carne Christi*
17	3
17.1	61

Tertullian, *De praescriptione haereticorum*
30.2	55

Greco-Roman Literature

Aëtius, *Placita*
1.3.20	95, 129
1.7.22	92

Alcinous, *Epitome doctrinae platonicae* (*Didaskalikos*)
9–10	162
10.164.30	98
14	162, 172

Appian of Alexandria, *Bella civilia*
2.90.380	51

Aristotle, *De anima*
1.4.408b.18	171
2.1.412a23–26	172

Ancient Sources Index

2.1.412b.4–6	170	Aristotle, *On Philosophy*	
2.2.413b.24–27	172	frag. 14	163
3.5	171	frag. 18	163
3.5.430a	237		
3.5.430a.10–25	171	Aristotle, *Physica*	
3.10.433b.19	170	192a.31	129
3.432a.1–2	116	209b.11–17	129
Aristotle, *De caelo*		Aristotle, *Topica*	
1.2.269a.31	171	1.102b	148
1.3.270a.12–b.10	171		
1.10–12	131	Chaldean Oracles	
1.10.279b30	131	frag. 16	110
2.6.289a.15	171	frag. 18	110
		frag. 30	110
Aristotle, *De generatione animalium*		frag. 37	12
736b27–29	236	frag. 81	12
Aristotle, *De generatione et corruptione*		Cicero, *Tusculanae disputationes*	
1.2.317a	131	1.10.22	211
2.3.331a	131	26.65–66	211
2.10.337a	131		
6.2.334–335a	131	Corpus hermeticum	
		1.27	172
Aristotle, *De motu animalium*		10.5	172
10.703a4–b2	170	10.13	210
		10.16–17	174
Aristotle, *Ethica nicomachea*			
1097a.30–b6	220	Dio Cassius, *Historiae romanae*	
1097b.6–20	220	Epitome of 68.32.1–2	51
1177a.27–b	220		
		Numenius	
Aristotle, *Eudemus*		frag. 15	124
frag. 1	174	frag. 16	162
frag. 6	174		
		Plato, *Epistulae*	
Aristotle, *Metaphysica*		7.341c–d	64
12.7–9	171		
12.1025a	147	Plato, *Euthyphro*	
12.1026b	147	11b	165
12.1070a35–1070b30	236	15b	165
12.1072b.1–30	91		
12.1074b.1–14	70	Plato, *Leges*	
12.1074b.15–34	96	819b	64
12.1075a.3–5	96	967b.5–6	130

Plato, *Meno*	
80d	26
97d	165

Plato, *Parmenides*	
141e–142a	90

Plato, *Phaedo*	
64a	258
66a.3	161
67b.1	161
67d	258
95e–100a	97

Plato, *Phaedrus*	
275b	64

Plato, *Philebus*	
18b	64
23c–31a	97
26e–30e	90
29c.6–8	130
30c	141

Plato, *Politicus*	
290c–e	64

Plato, *Protagoras*	
320c	63

Plato, *Respublica*	
507c–509b	223
508b13	116
514–518	139
514a–517a	222
517c	139
532b	222
571b–d	226
588b–589d	185
596a–605c	165

Plato, *Sophista*	
247d–e	97
254–256	123–24

Plato, *Theaetetus*	
174	221
176a–b	221
176b	219

Plato, *Timaios*	
21	64
27d–28b	114
28b	130
29–30	128
29d–47e	128
30b–c	171
35a	170
37c–d	163
39e	116
41a–d	163
41d	209
41d–e	170
43b	215
45b.7	161
47e–48a	139
47e–69a	128
48a	154
49a	143
49a6	145
50	128
50c–d	143
50d3	145
51a	143
51b	139, 141
52d5	145
52d–53c	146
52e	128
69a–92c	128
90a	173
88d6	145

Pseudo-Plato, *Epinomis*	
983e–984b	164

Plotinus, *Enneades*	
1.8.2	163
2.9	60
2.9	175
2.9.7–18	175

2.9.7.9–19	175	Simplicius, *In Aristotelis Physicorum libros quattuor priores commentaria*	
2.9.8.36–29	175		
2.9.18.32–35	175	147.9	101, 227
3.5.6	163	181.10–30	90
4.3.15	209	230.34–231.27	137
5.3.17.34–37	223	231.15–22	125, 138
5.8.3	163		
5.8.5	163	Seneca, *Epistulae morales*	
5.10	223	41.1–2, 4–5	220
		89.4–9	222
Plutarch, *De animae procreatione in Timaeo*		90.28	163–64
1026e–f	172	Sextus Empericus, *Adversus mathematicos*	
Plutarch, *De facie in orbe lunae*		9.87	209
943a	173		
		Stobaeus, *Florilegium*	
Plutarch, *De genio Socratis*		2.7.3	219
591d	173		
		Syrianus, *In Aristotelis Metaphysica commentaria*	
Plutarch, *De Iside et Osiride*			
371e	144	M 4, 1078b12, 106.17	110
374a	144		
		Timaios of Locri	
Plutarch, *Quaestionum convivialum libri IX*		94c	129, 162
9.14.6	70, 250		
Plutarch, *Moralia*			
477C	164		
Porphyry, *De abstinentia*			
2.49.2	64		
Porphyry, *Vita Plotini*			
16	60		
Proclus, *Elementatio theologica*			
31–32	101, 227		
Proclus, *In Platonis Timaeum commentaria*			
209.3–25	131		

Modern Authors Index

Aland, Barbara 60
Appelbaum, Alan 2
Baer, Richard 190–91, 229
Bainbridge, William 61
Barnes, Jonathan 98, 170
Barraclough, Ray 2
Bauer, Walter 54
Bianchi, Ugo 5
Birnbaum, Ellen 71, 97, 173, 223, 250–52
Bonazzi, Mauro 90–91
Borgen, Peder 32, 51, 71, 113
Bos, Abraham P. 170–73, 177
Boyarin, Daniel 72
Boys-Jones, George R. 70
Brakke, David 8, 11, 13, 32, 56, 105–6, 146, 151, 183, 198, 231, 238, 256
Brisson, Luc 69–70
Broek, Roeloef van den 52
Brown, Raymond E. 12, 91, 115
Buell, Denise Kimber; 62
Burnett, Fred W. 246
Burns, Dylan M. 8, 27
Camplani, Alberto 34
Casey, Robert 28, 32, 35, 40, 106, 151, 186
Caston, Victor 171
Chiapparini, Giuliano 28
Chiaradonna, Riccardo 90
Cornford, Francis M. 128–29, 143, 154, 163, 170
Corrigan, Kevin 64, 67, 110, 120, 129
Cover, Michael B. 225–26
Culpepper, R. Alan 49
Daniélou, Jean 3, 192
Davies, Stevan 259
Dawson, David 6, 13, 71–72
Desjardins, Michel R. 26–27, 67
Dibelius, Otto 35
Dillon, John 63, 89, 91–93, 97, 124, 129, 131, 137–38, 143–44, 173–74, 199, 223, 229, 250, 252
Dodd, Charles Harold. 201
Dörrie, Heinrich; 185
Drummond, James 70, 132, 134
Dubois, Jean-Daniel 34
Dunderberg, Ismo 5–7, 14–17, 25–28, 40–41, 55–57, 66–67, 81–84, 86, 124, 147, 157, 186, 198, 202–9, 227–28, 233–35, 238–39, 249, 255, 257–61, 269
Edwards, Mark 63–64
Engberg-Pedersen, Troels 50, 114, 115
Enzo, Lucchesi 283
Fallon, Francis T. 14
Ferguson, John 36
Fredriksen, Paula 2
Freidenreich, David M. 18
Friedländer, Moriz 12
Fuglseth, Kåre Sigvald 32, 49, 62, 72
Glucker, John 57–59
Goodenough, Erwin 49, 222–23, 262–63, 265–66
Gordley, Matthew E. 120
Grant, Robert 53
Griffin, Michael 91
Griggs, Charles Wilfred 53–55
Guignard, Christophe 68
Haas, Christopher 52
Hackforth, Reginald 130

Hahn, Johannes	63	McGowan, Andrew	206–7, 209
Hanson, Richard P. C.	77	Menn, Stephen	130
Hauser, Alan J.	78	Merlan, Philip	95, 138, 172, 211
Havrda, Matyáš	37–38	Miroshnikov, Ivan	259
Hay, David M.	188	Modrzejewski, Josef	51–52
Heckel, Theo K.	185, 194	Narbonne, Jean-Marc	120
Heijer, Arco den	110, 144	Nautin, Pierre	37
Heimola, Minna	16	Niehoff, Maren R.	31–32, 48–49, 69, 71–72, 89–90, 94, 221, 228
Heinrici, Georg	35		
Hoek, Annewies van den	20, 37, 155, 252	Nock, Arthur D	10
		Norman, Richard	98
Holzhausen, Jens	208, 257	Opsomer, Jan	92
Horbury, William	51–52	Paden, William E.	19
Horst, Pieter Willem van der	2	Pagels, Elaine	34, 67, 77, 83, 259, 269, 270
Huttunen, Niko	18		
Jenott, Lance	33	Painter, John	113
Kenney, John Peter	5, 73, 91, 98, 104	Pearson, Birger A.	6–8, 11–12, 15, 17, 47, 53–54, 65, 68, 234, 247, 249, 253
Kenny, Anthony	220		
King, Karen	7, 53, 111, 178	Perkins, Pheme	16, 78, 82, 104
Klijn, Albertus F. J.	244, 246–47	Pétrement, Simone	8
Koester, Helmut	53–54	Quispel, Gilles	35
Kooten, George H. van	95, 179, 194	Radice, Radice	72, 95, 97, 191
Kovacs, Judith L.	17, 18, 37–38	Rasimus, Tuomas	67, 82–84, 110–11, 120
Krämer, Hans Joachim	108		
Lampe, Peter	4, 63	Rist, John M.	175, 237
Laporte, Jean	212	Rist, John M.	175, 237
Layton, Bentley	5–6, 13, 38, 58, 85, 105–6, 146–47, 151, 183, 198, 206, 215, 231, 238, 256	Roberts, Colin H.	11, 30, 54–55, 76, 83
		Rothschild, Clare	68
		Royse, James R.	30, 32
Lee, Richard A.	172	Runia, David	3–4, 15–16, 20, 30–31, 34, 36, 48, 54, 58–59, 71, 89, 92, 96–97, 115–17, 121–23, 129, 133–34, 136, 143, 148, 150, 156, 158, 160, 162–65, 173, 185, 188, 190–91, 193, 209, 215, 264, 282
Lilla, Salvatore	134, 155, 222		
Linjamaa, Paul	34, 240		
Litwa, David M	97, 263		
Logan, Alastair H. B	8–11, 29, 203		
Long, Christopher P.	172		
Lundhaug, Hugo	33–34	Sagnard, Francois	34–35, 40
Luttikhuizen, Gerard P.	169, 174, 211, 222, 237	Sandbach, F. Harry	229
		Sandmel, Samuel	19, 266
Mack, Burton L.	73	Satlow, Michael L.	225, 251, 263
Mackie, Scott D.	74	Schenke, Hans-Martin	6, 201
Marjanen, Antti	6, 10, 67	Scholem, Gershom	199
Markschies, Christoph	4, 7, 14, 28, 36, 60, 63, 81–83, 194, 208, 257	Schwartz, Daniel R.	2
		Shaw, Gregory	64–65, 68, 175
May, Gerhard	133–34	Shroyer, Montgomery J.	72
McCue, James F.	269–70	Smallwood, Mary E.	2

Smith, Carl B. 51, 53
Smith, Geoffrey S. 32, 151
Smith, Ian K. 199
Smith, Ian K. 199
Smith, Jonathan Z. 18
Smith, Jonathan Z. 18
Smith, Richard 178
Snyder, Gregory H. 67
Sorabji, Richard 89, 98, 133, 170
Staden, Heinrich von 58
Stark, Rodney 61
Stead, George C. 8, 12–13, 41, 113
Sterling. Gregory E. 3, 13, 30–31, 49, 89, 93, 113, 115, 131–32, 135–36, 185, 215, 263, 283
Stroumsa, Guy G. 249
Sundberg, Albert 68
Tcherikover, Viktor 51
Tervahauta, Ulla 27
Theiler, Willy 95
Thomassen, Einar 4, 13–14, 26, 29, 34, 40–42, 55–57, 60–62, 65, 67–68, 76, 82–84, 102, 104, 106, 109, 110–11, 138, 148, 153, 157, 165, 178–81, 188, 201–3, 205, 207, 213, 233, 237–38, 256–57, 271
Tite, Philip L. 16
Tobin, Thomas 70, 113, 115, 128–29, 163, 185, 189, 190–93, 199, 201, 211, 250
Trapp, Michael 90, 137, 303
Turner, John D 9, 67, 108, 110
Turner, John 8–9, 64, 110–111
Turner, Martha 38
Unger, Dominic J. 32, 47, 79, 99, 112, 147, 177, 181–83, 227, 238, 269
Wasserman, Emma 226, 229, 258, 264
Watson, Duanne F. 78
Weiss, Hans-Friedrich 134
Wilson, Robert McLean 8, 11, 201, 214
Winston, David 48, 50, 70, 89, 96–97, 131–33, 135–36, 141, 144, 158, 162–64, 191–92, 194, 209, 211–12, 220–23, 225–26, 229, 243, 250, 261, 264

Wolfson, Harry 49, 70–71, 77, 93, 95–98, 116, 121–22, 133, 136, 141–42, 185, 196, 211–12, 214, 222, 243, 246, 263
Wucherpfennig, Ansgar 57
Yamauchi, Edvin 8
Yli-Karjanmaa, Sami 188–89, 195–96, 209, 246, 258, 264
Young, Frances M. 69, 78
Zahn, Theodor von 37

Subject Index

Abraham, 86, 97, 144, 170–73, 204, 221, 242–3, 246, 250–54, 261–63
   allegory of migration, 224–25
   as pedagogical model, 250–51
Abel, 6, 24, 35, 42, 45– 46, 219, 235, 244–49, 265, 274, 279
Adam's body, 35, 183, 195, 197–198
   as garments of skin, 169, 176, 186, 194, 198, 217, 278
Adam's soul, 41, 67, 179, 181, 184, 188, 194, 196, 198, 202, 204–205, 211, 231, 235, 241
   as an image of the Logos, 96, 189–93, 200, 205, 210, 216, 222, 278
Adversus haereses, 28, 32, 40–43, 45, 54–55
aeons, 41, 69, 100–11, 115, 117–20, 127, 138–40, 161, 166, 177, 207, 215, 226, 256, 268–69, 271–72
   as archetypes, 16, 75, 102, 108–9, 112, 127, 149, 151–52, 154, 164, 205
   as intelligent beings, 12, 29, 106
afterlife, 261–64, 266–272
Agrippa I, 2
Alexandria, museum, 48
Alexandrian Christianity, 53–55
allegorical method, 69–72, 78–79
allegorists, extreme, 50–51, 72, 76
allegory of the cave, 139–40
allegory of the soul, 189, 199, 240
ancient *haireseis,* 4, 11, 22, 48, 57–59, 60–62
angels, 10–11, 86, 180–85, 209, 228, 248, 253–54
   as creators of Adam, 202–205

angels (*cont.*)
   as psychic images, 43, 103, 148, 150–54
   as pure intelligences, 163–64, 212
   as spiritual archetypes, 41, 101–102, 169, 176–80, 201, 216, 242, 278
   union with angels, 14, 225, 261–65, 259, 271, 280
another seed, 245–46, 249
apocalyptic tradition, 8, 14, 54, 179, 271
apophatic theology, 98, 111
Ardesianes, 65
Aristotelian anthropology, 169–72, 174, 176, 186–87, 220, 229, 277
arithmology, 116, 120
Axionicus, 65
baptism, 66–67, 118, 213, 233, 257, 260
Bardeanes, 56
Basilides, 56
boundary, 6, 100, 101, 108, 121, 138, 140, 162, 230, 268, 276. See also *horos*
bridal chamber, 27, 67, 184, 213, 232–33, 255, 268–69
bridegroom, 27, 268–69
Caesarea, 30, 36, 38–39, 51, 281
Cain, 24, 35, 42, 45–46, 229, 235–36, 244–45, 247–49, 265, 274, 279
catechetical school, 30, 54, 282–83
Chaldea, 173, 224–25
Chaldean Oracles, 12, 63–64, 77, 110
circumcision, 85–86
Claudius, 283
confusion of language, 73–75
conjugal union. See spiritual marriage
conversion (of Sophia), 41, 101, 140, 148, 187, 230, 239, 273

cosmic bodies, 133, 140–41, 154, 156, 162–63
cosmic elements, 23, 45, 102–3, 121–22, 128–29, 133, 140–41, 148–49, 157, 160, 163, 167, 197, 208, 210, 213, 277
cosmic sympathy, 164–166, 209–211
creatio aeterna, 130, 132–35
creatio ex nihilo, 136–37
crucifixion, 100, 260, 266–67
darkness (intelligible), 107, 118–21, 123–25, 137, 156, 158, 162, 173, 276
  as a symbol of ignorance, 187, 139–40, 215, 249
day one, 115–17, 121–22, 124, 126, 155, 162, 191
death of the soul. *See* soul: death of the
Demiurge, 82–83, 102, 146–49
diakrisis-theory, 157, 159–160
dietary laws, 86
divine triad, 110, 129
double reading, 79–81
double creation theory, 190–192
Dyad, 23, 90–92, 94, 100, 126, 132, 144, 166, 223, 243, 276
earthly *nous*, 35, 193, 195–97, 214, 217, 277
ecclesia, 61–62, 234, 240
Edessa, 56
Eleazer, high priest, 71
emotions/passions, 79, 141, 147–48, 167, 187, 224–25, 230, 272, 279
epistemological dualism, 222–23
ethereal essence, 92, 156, 162, 189, 209, 211
  as psychic essence, 159, 162
Eudorus of Alexandria, 23, 90–91, 93, 95, 127, 130, 134, 166, 219, 221
Excerpta C (*Exc.* 43.2–65), 22, 29, 32, 35, 39–45, 65, 68, 98–99, 104, 108, 113, 116, 118, 125, 137, 140, 147, 148, 150, 159, 160, 162, 164, 165–67, 177, 179, 187–88, 205, 216–17, 233, 240, 242, 244, 253, 260, 269, 273–76, 279–81, 283–84
  and *Haer.* 1.1–7, 40–44, 45–46

Eve, 71, 188–89, 232–33, 245–47, 257
fasting, 87
Father of All, 41, 84, 98, 100, 102, 104, 117, 126, 139, 140, 144–45, 152, 164, 224, 226, 228, 233
fifth element, 163, 171
free speech, 201–204
  as divine virtue, 204
Fullness (*Pleroma*), 27, 40, 69, 99–101, 107, 118–20, 124–25, 149, 164, 179, 268–69
gnosis, 5, 11, 16, 68, 226, 237
Gnosticism, 4–8, 110–13
God, highest, 2, 6, 82, 91, 204
God's voice, 73–74
haireseis, ancient. *See* ancient *haireseis*
Haran, 224–25
Harvest, psalm, 206
heaven, 156–58, 162–66
  creation of, 149–54, 156–60
  as boundary (*horos*), 162–63
heavenly bodies, 122–27, 130, 160–65, 171
  as psychic intellects, 127, 149, 154, 164
heavenly *ecclesia*, 176, 179–80, 213, 217, 226
  as heavenly human, 205, 278
  as mystical body of Christ, 185–86
heavenly human, 192, 194–95, 199–202, 204–205, 216–17, 241, 266, 273, 276, 278
Heracleon, 17, 33, 56–57, 60, 88, 153, 213, 234, 270–71
  commentary on John, 75–76, 83, 108
hermetic tradition, 68, 254
high priest, 208, 211–13, 259, 276
historikon, 77–78
holes, 224–25
horos, 100, 138, 156, 162
humankind, division of, 12, 16, 23–24, 29, 35, 42, 46, 61, 185, 220, 233–35, 237, 239, 242, 244, 248–49, 273–74, 279
humans, perfect, 215, 220, 225, 229, 241, 248, 249, 252, 265, 273, 278
hylic essence, 29, 42–43, 101–2, 139–41, 146–48

hylic essence (cont.)
  forming the irrational soul, 169, 176, 180–85, 228, 235–37, 273
hylics, 39, 198, 233–34, 239, 242
Ideas, 96–97, 121–24, 128–30, 132–33, 140
  as thoughts of God, 91, 94–96, 118, 129
immortality, 2, 14, 101, 140, 144, 188, 214, 230, 237, 239, 246, 257–60, 262, 266, 272
incarnation, 8, 39, 65, 87, 175, 178, 186–88, 196, 209, 233
  of the Savior, 42, 45–46, 65–66, 104, 115, 212
intelligible cosmos, 89, 127, 137
intention (Sophia's), 26, 41, 76–78, 99, 104, 106–7, 112, 120, 125, 129, 138–39, 196, 202, 207, 221, 230
intuition, 222–23, 171
irrational soul, 194–97, 210, 216, 279
Isaac, 31, 253–54, 262–63, 272–73, 279
  as a lawful son, 252–255
  as a pedagogical model, 250–51
  as a perfect human, 146, 221, 223, 239, 246, 250–51, 256, 279
  as a symbol of joy, 254
Israel, 71, 80, 132, 226
  as an allegory, 15, 24, 35, 46, 118, 251–55, 260–61, 269
  as the seeing race, 52, 274, 200, 279
Jacob, 31, 221, 244, 254, 262–63, 265
  as a pedagogical model, 250–53
Jesus, 75–76, 65–66, 179
Jewish *politeuma*, 17, 49
Jewish revolt, 3, 22, 47, 51–54, 56, 87, 282–83
Jews, 2–3, 17, 31, 49–53, 69, 95, 234, 282
Josephus, 2, 59, 247, 283
joy, 13, 102, 177, 225, 227–29, 250, 254, 268
knowing oneself, 224
Lake Mareotis, 3
law of Moses, 13, 17, 22, 48, 50, 82, 85–86
learning (*mathesis*), 200, 237, 241, 250, 251, 262, 272, 279

Letter to Flora, 13–14, 17, 27–8, 44, 63, 78, 81–6, 117, 275, 280, 283
light, 119, 122–25, 160–61
  as image of the Logos, 122
Logos, 94, 96, 115–116
  and Wisdom, 141–142
  as an archetypal light, 122, 124–25
love, 75, 89, 100–101, 106–7, 112, 137, 226, 243
Marcionite schism, 82–84
Marcosians, 66–67, 111–112
matter (*hyle*), 129, 132, 134–36, 139–41, 146–48
methodikon, 77–78
Moderatus of Gades, 137, 166
Monad, 23, 90–92, 94–95, 110, 119, 126, 132, 155, 164, 212, 221, 223, 263, 276
  as a womb, 109–110
  second Monad, 92, 94, 138
Monism, 9, 95, 129
Moses, 55, 72–74, 80, 93, 96, 119, 124, 134, 155, 162, 195, 200, 209, 211, 223, 246
  as a supersage, 220, 226, 239, 250–51, 256
  as founder of nation, 48–49
  divinization, 262–63
myth of Sophia. *See* Sophia, myth of
Nag Hammadi writings, 4–6, 8, 25–27, 32–34, 55, 67–68
Noah, 246, 251
nous, cosmic, 96, 99, 129–30, 132, 138–39, 141, 144
nous, human, 171–73, 186, 192, 194–95, 197, 278
  as a womb, 80, 206–207, 215–16, 226, 237, 244
nothingness, 223–24, 227, 245
numbers, 12, 72, 93, 108, 110, 116, 120, 146, 264
Ogdoad, 40, 79, 100, 103, 108, 112, 116, 149, 153, 179, 268, 270
One (God), 92, 94
ouranos, 156
Paul, the apostle, 55, 61, 252, 255

pedagogical triad, 250–52
peripatetic tradition, 22, 58, 91, 135, 229, 250
Philo, 1–3
  library, 24, 53, 282
  parallels with *Excerpta* C, 35
  Platonic orientation, 89, 93–94
  school, 3, 48–51
  Valentinians, 11–13, 16–18, 280–84
  writings, 30–31
Platonic anthropology, 170–71, 175, 221–22, 278
Plotinus, 60, 104, 110, 163, 175, 209, 223
pneumatics, 9, 214, 234, 237, 243, 252–53, 255–56, 260–61, 268, 270–71, 274
popular philosophers, 47, 63
Porphyry, 60, 64, 81, 110–11, 138
powers, 86, 92, 95–98, 112, 141, 163, 176–78, 181, 184, 187, 209, 222, 228, 230, 239, 242–43
practice (*ascesis*), 24, 37, 67, 200, 250–51, 258–59, 262, 272
practice of dying, 258–59, 272
prepositional metaphysics, 115, 279
Proclus, 12–13, 58, 101, 131, 163, 227
Profundity (*Bythos*), 99, 100, 109
progressive humans, 223, 225, 227, 229–30, 239–42, 249, 251, 260, 265–66, 273–74, 278–80
Prologue of John, 9, 22–23, 83–84, 104–105, 108–109, 112–118, 125–26, 276
protology, 99–102, 104, 106–108, 112, 117–119, 121, 125, 138, 146
psychic Christ, 65, 152
psychic essence, 42–43, 101–102, 146–149, 154–55, 161, 228, 230, 273
  forming the rational soul, 169, 176, 182, 185–86, 216, 235, 237–39
  as luminous, 43, 102, 141, 153, 155, 161–62, 164, 187
psychics, 39, 198, 233–34, 237–40, 242–43, 255–56, 260–61, 266–74
Ptolemy, 81–86, 88, 283–4
Ptolemy's disciples, 43, 56, 99, 112, 126, 275, 281

Pythagorean revival, 90–91
Pythagorean tradition, 9, 14, 22, 61, 63, 89–94, 99–100, 105, 108–10, 120, 125, 127, 131, 136–38, 143–44, 146, 166, 209, 263
Quqites, 56
rational soul, 35, 50, 111, 173, 190–91, 193, 196, 210, 214, 228, 248, 277
rational spirit, 210, 214
Receptacle, 140–141, 143
redemption, 8, 9, 60, 66–67, 87, 186
regeneration, 221, 246, 273
reincarnation, 196, 246, 264
religio mentis, 65
repentance, 230, 273, 279
resurrection, 14, 46, 74, 172, 174, 213, 227, 234, 246, 260, 266, 268
rituals, 6, 37, 263
  as *propaideia,* 64–68
sabbath, 48, 85–86
sacrifices, 86
salvation, 61, 144, 153, 167, 187, 199, 223, 255–56, 266–273
  as awakening, 172–74, 187, 278
  as equalization, 270–71
  as unification, 29, 226, 232–33, 256, 260–61, 271–72
  by *physis*, 190, 192, 237–40, 242, 248–49, 256, 258, 262
  of Sophia, 101, 113, 139–40
sanctifying firstlings, 79
Sarah, 144–46, 223, 253
Savior (see also Jesus)
  as the fruit of Pleroma, 79, 108, 118, 120, 179, 205
  as an angel, 118
  body, 46, 65, 154, 178, 186, 242, 268
seed, another. *See* another seed
seed of Sophia, 29, 65, 176–80, 184, 186–88, 205, 216–17, 233, 257, 278
separation of sexes, 190, 192, 197
  as an allegory, 199, 215, 230–33, 273, 279
  as a protological model, 92, 129, 136, 143

Subject Index 331

separation of sexes (*cont.*)
  as spiritual emanation, 178–79, 184
Seth, 6, 8, 24, 35, 42–46, 110, 219, 235, 244–49, 279
  as a symbol of virtue, 246, 274
  as another seed, 249
Sethian Gnosticism, 5–9, 90, 108, 247
Silence (*Ennoia*), 109–111
  as a cosmic womb, 99
single creation theory, 189–190
Sophia, myth of, 9, 29–30, 40–42, 61, 63, 79, 110–11, 113, 227, 144, 146, 166–7, 227, 235, 273, 278–279
Sophia Achamoth, 40, 41, 45, 75, 101, 103, 140, 149, 177, 183, 269
Sophia's emotions, 42–43, 81, 103, 148, 227–228, 277
soul
  death of the, 225, 264–65
  prenatal, 196, 209, 217, 256
  undescended, 65, 175, 278
soul-body, 162, 170–71, 173–74, 176–77, 182, 185, 188, 199, 202, 216–17, 268, 270, 277
soul's double liberation, 174
spiritual ascent, 74
spiritual essence, 102–3, 185, 203, 205, 236, 242, 273, 279
spiritual marriage, 66, 268, 270–72
spiritual seed, 41, 45–46, 65–66, 81, 176–80, 183–88, 216–17, 233, 237–40, 278
Stoics, 59, 70, 190, 209–210, 220, 229–30, 273, 279
synagogue, 49, 75
temple, 211–213
Tetrad, 99, 107, 108, 110, 112, 116, 119, 144
Theodotus, 118, 139, 178–79, 186–88
Theodotus's fragments, 28, 36, 38
Therapeutae, 50–51, 95, 251
Theudas, 71, 77
theurgy, 67, 87
Tiberius, 2
time, 116, 130–31, 133, 135–36
transcendental ethics, 219–224

transcendental monotheism, 113, 222
transmigration of the soul, 263–64
triad of sages, 250–52, 262
tripartite soul, 169, 176, 185, 187, 235
undescended soul. *See* soul: undescended
Valentinian tradition, 4–10, 12–18, 32–34, 43–45
  myth, 29–30
  Platonic underworld, 63
  two schools, 64–69
  writings, 25–29
Valentinus, 3–4, 55–57
  disciples, 56–57
  founder of the school, 57–64
  fragments, 23, 28, 30, 217, 275
virtues, 15, 142, 146, 196, 214–15, 219, 224, 242, 250–51, 257, 265–66
vision of God, 222–223, 230, 250–1, 278
Wisdom (Sophia) as mother, 142–46
womb of Mary, 242
world soul, 91, 94, 113, 128–29, 170, 172, 174–75, 208

www.ingramcontent.com/pod-product-compliance
Lightning Source LLC
Chambersburg PA
CBHW050856300426
44111CB00010B/1273